*Routledge Revivals*

# Social Geography

The examination of social questions is a relatively new development in geography, but social geography has now blossomed into a fully fledged sub-discipline which has in fact influenced significantly all other areas of geography. This book, first published in 1987, presents an overview of recent developments in all the major branches of social geography. As such it provides a valuable introduction to the subject, a review of the latest state of the art and a pointer to future research directions.

# Social Geography:

## Progress and Prospect

*Edited by*
**Michael Pacione**

Routledge
Taylor & Francis Group

First published in 1987
by Croom Helm

This edition first published in 2011 by Routledge
2 Park Square, Milton Park, Abingdon, Oxon, OX14 4RN

Simultaneously published in the USA and Canada
by Routledge
270 Madison Avenue, New York, NY 10016

*Routledge is an imprint of the Taylor & Francis Group, an informa business*

© 1987 Michael Pacione

**Publisher's Note**
The publisher has gone to great lengths to ensure the quality of this reprint but
points out that some imperfections in the original copies may be apparent.

**Disclaimer**
The publisher has made every effort to trace copyright holders and welcomes
correspondence from those they have been unable to contact.

A Library of Congress record exists under LC Control Number: 87000506

ISBN 13: 978-0-415-61226-5 (hbk)
ISBN 13: 978-0-415-61232-6 (pbk)

# SOCIAL GEOGRAPHY:
## Progress and Prospect

EDITED BY
MICHAEL PACIONE

CROOM HELM
London • New York • Sydney

© 1987 Michael Pacione
Croom Helm Ltd, Provident House, Burrell Row,
Beckenham, Kent, BR3 1AT

Croom Helm Australia, 44-50 Waterloo Road,
North Ryde, 2113, New South Wales

Published in the USA by
Croom Helm
in association with Methuen, Inc.
29 West 35th Street
New York, NY 10001

British Library Cataloguing in Publication Data

Social geography: progress and prospect. —
   (Croom Helm progress in geography series)
   1. Anthropo-geography
   I. Pacione, Michael
   304.2    GF41

   ISBN 0-7099-4026-2


**Library of Congress Cataloging-in-Publication Data**

Social geography.

   (Croom Helm progress in geography series)
   Contents: Theory and methodology in social geography /
R.J. Johnston — Residential mobility in the private
housing sector / M. Munro — Access to public sector
housing / J. English — [etc.]
   1. Anthropo-geography. 2. Anthropo-geography — Great
Britain. 3. Anthropo-geography — United States.
I. Pacione, Michael. II. Series.
GF49.S66  1987    304.2    87-506
ISBN 0-7099-4026-2

CONTENTS

List of Figures
List of Tables
Preface
Introduction

List of Figures

List of Tables

To Christine, Michael John and Emma Victoria

PREFACE

Although the term social geography has a long
history, with roots in social anthropology and
links to cultural geography, definition of the
nature and objectives of the subject has remained
an elusive goal. It can be argued that social
geography is as much "an approach" as an academic
discipline. For some this eclecticism is a
healthy sign which augurs well for the future of
the subject, while others see this as an argument
for a single unified social science. The scope
and content of social geography has altered
significantly in the course of its development,
particularly over the last two decades. During
this period social geography has been at the
centre of the theoretical and methodological
debates which have affected human geography as a
whole. Humanist and structuralist critiques of
positivism have been incorporated and a major
debate has ensued over the relationship between
social structure and human agency. These trends
have been accompanied by a shift of emphasis from
pattern description towards exploration of
underlying causal processes, with the ultimate aim
of some social geographers being to effect radical
social change. Thus, contemporary social
geography is a pluralist subject in which
traditional ecological-based investigations (for
example of patterns of residential segregation)
have been complemented by new research foci
related to questions of social justice, resource
allocation, the formulation and appraisal of
social policy, the social geography of specific
groups (such as the elderly, women and ethnic
minorities), and analysis of institutions and the
role of the state in the distribution and exercise
of power.
    This collection of original essays is designed
to encapsulate the major themes and recent
developments in a number of areas of central
importance in social geography. The volume is a
response to the need for a text which reviews the
progress and current state of the subject and
which provides a reference point for future
developments in social geography.

Michael Pacione
University of Strathclyde
Glasgow

# INTRODUCTION

The great variety of social phenomena studied by geographers both underlines the need for and compounds the difficulty of achieving a definition of social geography. In chapter 1 Ron Johnston commences a discussion of the subject's theory and methodology by critically reviewing attempts to define the scope and content of the field. It is observed that until recently social geography has been characterised by eclecticism in the range of study topics, a focus on the spatial implications of social processes and an empirical-positivist basis, with relatively little debate over alternative theoretical and methodological frameworks. Two broad perspectives are identified, (a) an 'insider's view' based on the study of how social life is constituted, and (b) the more conventional 'outsider's' view which focuses on the observed patterns of social life. The methodological and theoretical components of each approach are considered before a possible synthesis is suggested. The outsider's view of social geography developed during the 1950s and 1960s in concert with the theoretical and quantitative revolution in human geography. The underlying philosophical base was positivism, in which theory is accumulated through the empirical testing of hypotheses. The demands of the 'scientific method' for data of sufficient validity and reliability resulted in the national census becoming the most common source in social geographic research. Such data are not problem-free, however, and a number of fundamental deficiencies are discussed (eg. the lack of information on 'sensitive' issues such as income or race, the spatial basis of the survey, and the infrequency of censuses). Despite such disadvantages social geographers have assumed pre-eminence in the spatial analysis of census data, with two related types of investigation being undertaken. The first, (aspatial social geography), has been concerned with the relative location of different social groups and is seen in the use of segregation indices, social area analysis, and factorial ecology. Work in the second area (spatial social geography) was stimulated by the classical Chicago ecologists' models of urban land

Introduction

use and the subsequent criticisms and refinements
of these. Reaction against the narrow dependency
upon census data led to the introduction of a
broader range of social indicators in studying
social well-being, to the examination of
particular social themes (eg. crime, health,
housing, the elderly), and to the introduction of
behavioural studies of social groups. Criticism
that the traditional outsider's view provides only
a partial picture of social life and treats people
in a mechanistic way led to the adoption of a
humanistic (insider) perspective in which
ethnographic methods (such as participant
observation) are employed to comprehend the
complexity of social life. The relationship
between humanistic methodology and theory is
discussed and the benefits of interpretive depth
to be gained from an insider's view are emphasised.
Neither the positivist (outsider) or humanist
(insider) approach, however, interrogates the
underlying social forces that produce the observed
social groups, patterns and processes. A key issue
is the debate over the relative importance of
social structure and human agency in producing
social geography. It is suggested that the fundamental links between infrastructure (structural
forces) and superstructure (observed patterns) can
be illuminated by a realist theory of society, in
which man is credited with the ability to
influence the ways in which the structural
preconditions are manifested in the environment.
Clearly, the choice of theoretical perspective
will, in turn, influence views on issues such as
how social geographic knowledge should be applied
(eg. in the context of social engineering or in
promoting political change), and on whether there
is a future for a separate sub-discipline of social
geography (as opposed to a multi-disciplinary
social science). In practising social geography
we are exercising choice in these areas and are
thus contributing to a restructuring of the field.
     Housing is a dominant urban land use, with the
tenure balance varying between societies. In
Britain, the post-war decline in availability of
private-rented housing has not been offset by
growth of alternatives, such as Housing
Associations, and the two major tenure types are
now owner-occupied housing and accommodation rented
from local authorities. In chapter 2 Moria Munro
focuses on the question of residential mobility in
the private housing sector. The importance of this

issue is illustrated by the fact that residential mobility is a major determinant of urban land use; by the relationship between lack of mobility, labour market inefficiency and individual welfare; and by the insight such investigations can provide into household decision-making in an imperfect market. The discussion first identifies the nature and scale of residential mobility in the UK and USA to provide a backcloth for detailed examination of mobility and migration behaviour at the intra-urban level. The basic disequilibrium model is described prior to consideration of various refinements such as the use of discrete choice models, life cycle variables and the development of longitudinal housing profiles. Attention is then devoted to other aspects of household decision-making including models of equilibrium decision-making, interactions with labour markets and housing search behaviour; before a number of areas for further research are identified. Work with disequilibrium models (in which the desire to move is a response to dissatisfaction or stress in an existing household situation) dominated research in the 1970s. The concepts of place utility and of forced-, adjustment-, and induced-moves, and the range of factors underlying housing stress are reviewed. The major difficulty of identifying the independent effect of the various factors underlying the decision to move is underlined. Particular attention is then given to the influence of life cycle on residential mobility. The utility of logit and probit analysis in partialling out the effect of particular variables (such as age of household head) is illustrated. Longitudinal studies add a dynamic element to the concept of life cycle and introduce the notion of 'housing career'. To date, however, empirical work has focused on only part of these temporal profiles (eg. moves at specific times in the life cycle) and, despite data limitations, there is considerable potential for further developments in this field. The key importance of income in determining housing opportunities emphasises the fact that examination of the relationship between a person's labour market and house market careers is essential for a full understanding of residential mobility, and recent research on this theme is discussed. Models of equilibrium decision making (in which, for example, lower wages or higher housing costs in an area can be traded-off against better access to

amenities or climate to maintain a general
equilibrium) are then examined. A major factor
not incorporated in these models is the actual
process of moving. Particular attention has been
devoted to the modelling of housing search
procedures, and the problems and potential of such
approaches are considered. It is suggested that a
hierarchical model may be appropriate to
distinguish between difference stages in housing
search. The role of information sources and the
influence of estate agents and building societies
have also been the subject of investigation.
While many models of residential mobility are
aspatial formulations, others have acknowledged
the causal importance of space and have sought to
simulate spatial patterns of housing search.
Further empirical work, for example into space
preferences and perceptions, is required to
corroborate previous findings. Several areas
worthy of further research attention are
identified. The first refers to the possibility
of incorporating consideration of specific labour
market characteristics into analyses of
residential mobility. Secondly, while the main
factors underlying the decision to move are known,
their relative importance remains uncertain. It
is suggested that longitudinal research strategies
are of particular potential here. Thirdly,
further investigation into the actual search
process and difficulties of moving is required.
Finally, it is emphasised that study of the
motives, processes and outcomes in intra-urban
mobility is of particular importance for
policy-makers seeking to evaluate the effects of
initiatives, (such as renovation schemes, council
house sales, or low-cost ownership strategies),
both in terms of the residents of affected areas
and of the wider urban housing system.

For a large proportion of the British
population, particularly in Scotland, acquiring a
house depends on gaining access to local authority
accommodation. Study of the bureaucratic
processes which allocate this resource is
essential both to advance academic understanding
and to assess the equity of existing practices for
matching housing supply and demand. In chapter 3
John English discusses local authority allocation
procedures and their effect on the housing
opportunities of different groups. A basic
distinction is first drawn between primary
rationing, which determines access to the council

sector in general; and secondary allocation which refers to the distribution of specific units (of differing quality and popularity) to particular people. Within very general legal requirements, (such as a responsibility to house homeless persons), individual local authorities have considerable discretion in determining the criteria for and operating the system of council house allocation. Each of the two related systems is examined. In terms of primary allocation procedures the range of possible eligibility criteria is reviewed (eg. age, marital status, length of residence, existing tenure) and the notions of waiting- and transfer-lists described. It is pointed out that the need for a primary allocation system depends on the relationship between supply and demand. Thus during the inter-war period relatively high rents and the availability of private-rented accommodation produced a near equilibrium position, whereas after the war housing shortages and higher wages resulted in an excess of demand and the consequent introduction of rationing systems. Since the 1970s a reduction in demand has exposed the heterogeneity of the council stock, manifested in the appearance of difficult-to-let estates. This net surplus of housing in many authorities has accordingly lessened the importance of the primary allocation machinery and switched the focus of attention to the secondary procedures which determine 'who gets what' within the council stock. Research into these procedures is hampered, however, by the lack of documentary evidence on decision-making processes within local authority housing departments. A particular outcome which is apparent is the concentration of socio-economic and ethnic population into particular areas; and a key research question is to explain the mechanisms underlying such patterns and, in particular, to identify the role of housing allocation procedures in producing socio-spatial segregation. To date, research into differential allocation has concentrated on the experience of ethnic minorities, and has focused on the outcome (the allocation of 'disadvantaged' groups to poorer housing) rather than on exploration of underlying processes. A number of possible explanatory factors are considered. These include eligibility rules, grading of applicants, and constrained choice (ie. a situation in which applicants tend

# Introduction

to express a preference for a realistic housing
location, and not their ideal choice). It is
suggested that together with the informal and
semi-formal procedures of housing departments this
latter factor offers the greatest explanatory
potential. With reference to the internal
operation of housing authorities, available
evidence indicates that differential allocation
may be accentuated by the requirement of personnel
to achieve certain objectives, (such as minimising
vacancies and avoiding management problems), which
can influence their decisions on which housing to
offer to certain groups. More work which focuses
on the interaction between applicants and housing
departments is required. Attention should also be
given to the policy implications of differential
allocation. While, in theory, the problem
(manifested in stigmatised, run-down estates)
could be reduced, in practice, strategies such as
reducing the heterogeneity of the housing stock
through improvement, or allocating housing
entirely on the basis of need (instead of
incorporating a waiting time component) are
financially and politically problematic. Although
continued residualisation of council housing may
reduce the differential allocation problem by
confining the tenure to a narrower socio-economic
group living on more homogeneous housing estates,
it is unlikely to disappear in the foreseeable
future. For both academic and practical social
reasons further research is required into the
dynamics of the council housing allocation process.
Segregation of land use and of land users is a
ubiquitous feature of urban society. In chapter 4
Fred Boal examines the major themes in the
geographical analysis of segregation, (defined as
the spatial separation of definable groups either
residentially or in terms of the activity networks
of members). Since segregation is a group
phenomenon the important difference between a
group (a collection of people who feel they have
something in common) and a category (a set of
people defined by some externally improved
criteria) is underlined and the research
implications of this distinction discussed.
Several problems in measuring levels of
segregation are then identified. Of particular
significance is the effect of scale of measurement
on the results (briefly, indices of segregation
tend to increase as the population size of the
spatial units decreases). It is suggested that to

aid comparative analysis measures of segregation should be accompanied by specific information on the scale employed. Other problems discussed include the merits of census-based or subject-defined spatial units, and the effect of city size on choice of appropriate areal unit. The utility of the standard measures of segregation, (the Index of Dissimilarity and the Index of Isolation), is assessed, with the choice dependent on whether the researcher is interested in gauging spatial dissimilarity (ID) or the probability of interaction between groups (P*). The difficulties of monitoring segregation over time are then considered. These centre upon the infrequency of census surveys and the problem of interpreting a snapshot pattern which may be either stable or in transition between extremes. The value of a simulation approach for understanding the dynamics of residential segregation is questioned. The interplay of class and ethnicity is one of the most complex questions confronting urban social science. The basic issues are whether the social class characteristics of ethnic groups contribute to ethnic segregation and whether the ethnic composition of different social classes contributes to class segregation. Resolution of this dilemma clearly has practical as well as academic utility. Clearly, if segregation is a product of socio-economic differences, it can be reduced by narrowing the income gap between ethnic groups, but if it is related to non-socio-economic factors, reducing the income differentials will do little to decrease segregation. A variety of empirical evidence which sheds light on the complex relationship between ethnicity and social class is examined. The positive (eg. preservation of cultural heritage) and negative (eg. discriminatory practices) aspects of segregation and the ways in which residential segregation is functional for the reproduction of ethnic groups and social classes are illustrated with reference to a range of international studies. The applicability of the Weberian concept of social closure (the process by which social collectivities seek to maximise rewards by restricting access to resources to a limited circle of eligibles) to the analysis of segregation is also demonstrated. Attention then turns to efforts to classify segregated residential areas and a three-fold scheme, based

on the concepts of colony, enclave and ghetto, is
proposed. The consequences of spatial segregation
for inter-group relations and the implications for
cultural, socio-economic and structural
assimilation are addressed. Geographers have
afforded particular attention to the concept of
territoriality and to the constraining influence
defined territories have on the spatial extent of
social networks. Work in this field, including
the related ideas of 'dominance behaviour' and
'exit, voice and loyalty' is reviewed, before the
concept of critical mass (the size at which a
group becomes an active subculture) is discussed.
Finally, a number of future research questions are
identified. These include the derivation of more
appropriate non-census spatial units; study of
segregation in terms of activity networks as
opposed to residential patterns; and integrated
analyses which consider the patterns, networks and
functional characteristics of segregation in
combination rather than as independent topics.
This latter objective may be best approached using
ethnographic methodology. Above all, the aim is
to develop a sound theoretical framework informed
by appropriate empirical evidence.

Despite some evidence of spatial analyses of
social deviance patterns in the nineteenth century,
only recently have geographers devoted significant
research attention to the field. In chapter 5
David Herbert first defines social deviance and
considers the question of the appropriate level of
analysis. It is argued that despite the
importance of macro-scale processes smaller-scale
empirical studies are essential to illustrate the
local effect of national structural forces. A
major problem encountered in operationalising this
objective is the collection of suitable data,
since deviance is often covert. Various methods
of overcoming these limitations (eg. participant
observation, and newspaper reports) are examined,
as are the deficiencies arising from definitional
diversity and bias in recording. Since official
statistics are the most widely used sources the
potential problems of using such data sets are
examined in depth, with reference to statistics on
crime and mental illness. Attention then turns to
specific geographical contributions to the study
of social deviance. Work in the ecological
tradition dates from the nineteenth-century
cartographic school of criminology which
identified both regional and seasonal variations

in crime rates as well as crime areas or rookeries within cities. Efforts to relate such empirical descriptions to concepts relevant to contemporary society were advanced during the inter-war period, particularly in N. America where the ethnographic approach was exploited to illuminate the socio-spatial mosaic of the city. This ecological tradition continued into the 1970s. Of the various types of social deviance, crime developed into a focus for study, and a range of illustrative examples is considered. In addition, inferential analyses sought explanations for the observed patterns, postulating a range of hypotheses (eg. poor environment, housing class, social disorganisation, differential association, retreatism) with varying degrees of success. Similar work has been undertaken in relation to other kinds of deviance, eg. mental illness, but in most cases the best that has been achieved is the identification of risk factors, with causal explanations dependent upon longitudinal life history studies. Alcoholism, drug abuse, and prostitution represent obvious forms of social deviance to which only limited geographical attention has been given to date. In addition several new perspectives have emerged as areas of geographical research potential. Four particular examples are provided, with reference to the study of deviant areas, environmental criminology, care facilities, and rule makers. In the first, the ecological tradition of identifying problem zones (eg. gang areas, skid-rows, difficult-to-let estates) is complemented by attempts at explanation based on both objective (eg. housing) and subjective (eg. parental attitudes) evidence. The emergence and persistence of deviant areas remains an important research question. A major assumption underlying studies in environmental criminology is that crime events are reactions to environmental opportunities (cf. vulnerable areas and defensible spaces). Geographical research into vulnerable areas is illustrated with reference to residential burglary. The substantial costs inherent in the provision of care facilities have stimulated moves towards deinstitutionalisation of certain types of criminal and mental patients. There is considerable scope for research into the effects of such policies, for example, on the location of patients and the effectiveness of care programmes, and on host communities (house values, migration intentions, crime rates). A fourth area for research concerns the role of rule-makers in influencing revealed patterns. This includes, for example, questions relating to the use of police discretion and the effect of policing strategies upon visible crime rates. The geography of prostitution is provided as an example of how changes in legal policies affect the spatial incidence of social deviance. It is concluded that in seeking to contribute to the study of social deviance geographers should concentrate on their expertise in spatial analysis. While this is unlikely to produce significant new conceptual insights such techniques are of considerable practical utility (eg. the relationship between crime areas and policing strategies, and optimum location models for mental health facilities), and represent a major opportunity in applied social geography.

The profound influence of the public sector on the social geography of post-industrial capitalist states is the subject of chapter 6 in which Paul Knox examines the particular relationship between collective consumption and socio-spatial change. Collective consumption is defined as all collectively organised and managed services that are consumed via non-market mechanisms and at least partly financed through public funds, and includes both 'pure' public goods (such as libraries) and 'impure' public goods (such as education). Several general trends may be identified in the evolution of welfare systems and spending on collective consumption in advanced capitalist societies, including (a) collective consumption's increasing share of GNP, (b) a failure to target effort onto the most disadvantaged in society, (c) the disruptive effects of some programmes, such as urban redevelopment, (d) a reduced emphasis on welfare programmes in states with 'new conservative' governments, and (e) the impact of the new international division of labour and of decentralisation within core economies. The concept of territorial justice is central to the geography of collective consumption and several key questions relating to the definition and measurement of this notion are addressed. Whether such inequalities exhibit systematic spatial patterning is a question of particular interest to social geographers, and the evidence for a number of explanatory hypotheses, (including the under-

Introduction

class hypothesis incorporating the ideas of a power
elite, race preference and class preference; the
inverse care law; and the concept of unpatterned
inequality) is reviewed. The framework of public
choice theory, the dominant paradigm underlying
such hypotheses, is outlined, and recent
investigations of the links between socio-economic
factors (eg. needs and pressure group demands),
political variables and expenditure outputs, and
service provision are considered. The
inconclusive findings to emerge from such work have
stimulated research into aspects of the
institutional settings of public bureaucracies
(eg. gatekeepers and machine politics) and in
particular into decision rules, service delivery
rules, and the influence of citizens on policy
making. Another major research area has examined
the effect of urban structure and ecology on
patterns of collective consumption. Attention then
turns to a consideration of research into
collective consumption and socio-spatial change at
four geographical scales, (a) rural (b)
inter-urban (c) metropolitan and (d) intra-urban.
In rural areas particular problems stem from the
limited fiscal resources and increasing
sensitivity of rural services to economies of
scale. The socio-spatial outcome is a loss of
services in areas suffering selective out
migration, and excessive demand in areas of
population growth, leading to conflict between
locals and incomers (eg. in housing). The utility
of the concept of centrality to explain variations
in levels of collective consumption at the
inter-urban scale is assessed and the implications
of changes in centrality (cf. rustbelt - sunbelt
cities) considered. At the metropolitan scale
decentralisation of jobs and homes has been the
dominant socio-spatial trend in the post war era.
Where this has operated across jurisdictional
boundaries, as in much of the USA, centre-periphery
conflict has arisen over differences in service
commitments and capabilities. Several explanations
for these trends are discussed before attention is
focused on the intra-urban level where additional
factors (such as urban politics, managerial
influences, and community activism) operate.
Particular consideration is given to the local
resources squeeze arising from the conflict
between factors contributing to rising municipal
expenditure (eg. the demand for more and better
services, replacement of social capital, inflation)

and factors which have restricted municipal
incomes (eg. declining tax base). These problems
increase pressures for the kind of retrenchment of
welfare services seen in Britain and the USA since
the early 1970s, (ranging from California's
Proposition 13 to load-shedding through various
forms of privatisation). Such policies produce
new socio-geographic patterns and pose new
research questions (eg. which areas, what types of
household and which aspects of collective
consumption are most affected?). Issues arising
from trends such as the residualisation of council
housing, school closures, and health service
rationalisation represent a research agenda of
particular importance for social geography.

In chapter 7 John Eyles examines the nature
and extent of poverty and deprivation at a variety
of geographic scales and assesses the planning
response to revealed patterns. The complex
concept of poverty is first defined. Reliance
upon an absolutist view of poverty is criticised
on several grounds including the fact that it
abstracts the definition of the necessities of
life from their societal context and assumes
rational spending of resources by the poor. The
alternative relativist conception regards poverty
as an inability to enjoy the living standards
common to a society. Key elements in this
definition are styles of living and resources, and
the possible responses of the poor to their
diminished situation on both dimensions are
considered (including, for example, spending more
time in the home, and dependence upon family and
community support mechanisms). Despite the
definitional difficulties surrounding the concepts
of need, poverty and deprivation, government
policy requires a measure of the poverty level
(eg. based on supplementary benefit rates as in
the UK). A number of possible measures are
reviewed. The definition of poverty and
deprivation forms a central part of the broader
field of research into social well-being or
quality of life. The development of the social
indicators movement is traced and three main types
of indicator identified. These referred to direct
measures of deprivation such as unemployment;
indirect measures which infer the existence of
deprivation, for example, large households; and
interpretative indicators which aid the analysis
of the distribution of direct and indirect
measures, for example, the proportion of council

houses in an area. Following consideration of the
difficulties encountered in the selection of
variables and their measurement, a variety of
examples of single indicator investigations are
presented. Attention then turns to consider the
use of multiple indicators of deprivation with
most studies being criticised as being
data-dependent and consequently having only a
minimal link with theory and policy. An
international selection of illustrative studies at
scales ranging from the regional to the
intra-urban is provided. An inherent problem in
all such spatial investigations of quality of life
is the ecological fallacy, ie. of attributing
average conditions to all residents in an area.
This would suggest the merits of working at the
smallest possible geographical scale. The local
scale is also the level at which the application
of subjective social indicators is most
appropriate to complement the more commonly
employed objective statistics, and the utility of
such measures is emphasised. Three possible types
of policy response to revealed deprivation are
identified - (1) conditional welfare for the few,
which considers poverty as both necessary for the
operation of the economic system and the result of
inadequacy on the part of the deprived; (2)
minimum rights for the many, the basis of the UK
welfare state for most of the post-war period; and
(3) distributional justice for all, which
represents a goal yet to be attained. The
discussion then focuses on socio-spatial planning,
with two forms identified. Social remedial
planning is primarily reactive and is seen in
comprehensive redevelopment programmes, general
improvement areas, housing action areas, the urban
aid programme, community development projects,
inner city partnerships and enterprise zones in
the UK and initiatives such as the Model Cities
programme in the USA. The operation and
achievements of such policies are critically
assessed. Social development planning is an
attempt to engineer social conditions through the
physical planning process and is best seen in the
new town programmes and in the development
corporations established to aid regeneration of
docklands in London and on Merseyside. In
conclusion, it is observed that since the early
1970s social geography has advanced from a
pre-occupation with pattern identification towards
explanation of deprivation and evaluation of

policy responses. However, it is of fundamental importance to recognise that competing policy options reflect not only local material conditions but different political philosophies. This underlines the view that no single policy is naturally correct and that politics, planning and social geography are inextricably linked.

The geography of the elderly represents a growing area of concern in social geography, reflecting the general ageing of population in western society. In chapter 8 Tony Warnes focuses on two aspects of the social geography of the elderly which have received relatively little attention to date. The first refers to the impact of the ageing of the population in many developing countries, while the second concerns the fact that most academic studies have concentrated on the disadvantaged elderly and have effectively ignored the great majority of people in the 'third-age' of life. It is argued that greater attention to the situation in the Third World and to the effects of normal ageing is required. Consideration of the diffusion of demographic ageing suggests that by the end of the century a majority of the world's elderly will live in less developed regions, yet little geographical research has been undertaken on the implications of these trends. The major themes examined to date have been related to the impact of rural-urban migration on the elderly population left in the countryside; the attitudes of young people towards the elderly; and urban-rural and social class differences in the provision of welfare services. Some of these issues are illustrated with reference to recent work in central America and Nigeria. These studies indicate the varying situation of the aged which ranges from those integrated in traditional family units to those isolated in villages (by outmigration) or towns (due to ineligibility for social services). International comparisions serve to underline the great diversity of living conditions experienced by the elderly both between and within countries of the contemporary world. Attention is then focused on the situations in North West Europe, North America and Australia. A brief review of recent demographic developments traces the effects of earlier fertility and mortality trends on the future elderly population. Evidence of declining mortality at later ages in Britain and the USA is open to two possible interpretations. The first postulates

# Introduction

that human life expectancy is reaching its upper limit and that further progress in combating ill-health will mean more people surviving into their eighties. The alternative suggests that further increases in longevity may be anticipated. Clearly, each model has implications for social policy and for the social geography of the elderly. The first implies a healthier, more independent elderly population while the latter projects an increased proportion of disabled elderly with attendant consequences for welfare service provision. The life situation of the elderly is conditioned not only by personal factors but by structural forces which affect the distribution of income, housing and other opportunities. Further structural analyses are required. Generally, however, relatively few geographers have undertaken research into the spatial aspects of ageing and the circumstances of the elderly. Topics which have been dealt with include the distribution and migration behaviour of the elderly, housing conditions and satisfactions, accessibility to services, and spatial aspects of family and social relationships. Opportunities exist for further research in these areas, and specific examples are given with reference to the social situation of the elderly (eg. household arrangements, loneliness, activity patterns, social networks, mental health, and the effect of location and distance on behaviour). It is suggested that given the trend in affluent nations towards smaller households, extra-domiciliary relationships will assume increasing importance in life-satisfaction and that, consequently, the spatial attributes of social networks will attain even greater importance for the elderly. Several broad areas are recommended for future research attention. The first calls for geographical study of the social relationships and dominant activities of people in different age groups and particularly in their later years. Secondly, while most attention will continue to be given to the most disadvantaged elderly, greater effort must be directed to understanding geographical aspects of normal ageing. Finally, the problems posed by a rapidly ageing population in some less developed countries, characterised by insufficient facilities to meet this new demand, represent a research theme of considerable importance, both for improving academic understanding and to inform

Introduction

government decision-makers.

The seeds of the feminist perspective, sown during the intellectual debates of the late 1960s and early 1970s, have grown to provide a distinctive critique of much research in contemporary social geography. In chapter 9 Sophie Bowlby and Linda McDowell examine the impact of feminist concepts and approaches. They first trace the development of the Women's Movement, identifying as a major stimulus the increasing number of women in the labour force and the consequent pressure for equal pay and opportunities. The feminist view emphasises the linkages between social relations in the home and in the workplace and stresses that (a) equal social importance be attached to women's conceptions of the world; (b) differences between men and women are socially constructed rather than biologically determined; (c) male domination within the family is central to understanding women's unequal position; and (d) women's inferior position in the labour market is causally related to their dependent position within the family and lack of social power. A review of recent developments in social geography identifies 'inequality of opportunity' and 'power relations within society' as major issues, both of which are also of central concern to the Women's Movement. The discussion then moves to consider the extent to which work in social geography has been influenced by or contributed to an understanding of women's inequality. Initial studies mainly carried out in the USA, sought to complement traditional geographical analyses with investigations of women in a variety of situations (eg. shopping behaviour, access to facilities, single women, black women, women at home, at work, and in different residential locations). The implicit assumption was that for most women activities are home-based. Only later was such work on gender roles replaced by study of how these are produced by gender relations. It is argued that the substitution of the idea of 'roles' by 'relations' has produced a clearer understanding of women's position in society and has stimulated a shift towards theorization in research. Several examples of how the feminist perspective has been incorporated into social geography are provided but criticism is directed at the continued artificial distinction between home and workplace (as the locus for women and men

respectively), and the descriptive, atheoretical
nature of most studies. It is pointed out that
most recent work on collective consumption ignores
the role of domestic work in providing essential
social services and support. Feminist analysis
recognises these activities as essential to the
operation of the capitalist economy. Such a
perspective affords a more realistic interpretation
of women's role in the labour market, and
underlines the significance of the interrelation-
ship between home, community and workplace in
creating and maintaining gender roles. The
discussion then turns to examine the potential
contribution of feminism to research in social
geography, the basic argument being that gender is
as important a social dimension as class or race
and that by neglecting this dimension a key
structuring element of the division of space is
effectively defined out of the analysis, thus
restricting the power of the explanatory
framework. The particular way in which a feminist
perspective can inform traditional areas of
research in social geography is then demonstrated
with reference to work on gender relations in the
home and in the community. A variety of research
questions are identified, for example, on how the
built environment affects women's lives (in terms
of isolation, journey to work, problem estates,
waged home work); on the relationship between
gender identities and ethnic and class status, and
how these create residential differentiation; and
on locally-based political groups and urban social
movements. In conclusion it is emphasised that
feminist analysis of gender and gender relations
does not advocate study of women alone but rather
seeks a more evenly balanced interpretation of
male and female views of the world.

Chapter One

THEORY AND METHODOLOGY IN SOCIAL GEOGRAPHY

R.J. JOHNSTON

A major problem for anybody setting out to review some aspect of social geography is that it lacks a clear definition. Though the term has been used throughout the present century, social geography has only a short history in the English-speaking world; in North America, for example, it was virtually ignored both in Hartshorne's (1939, 1959) classic statements and in the major review (James and Jones, 1954) of the entire discipline (see Johnston, 1986a). In order to discuss theory and methodology in social geography, therefore, it is necessary first to identify what the subdiscipline is and what its aims are. Within that context, the remainder of the chapter will review two major types of contribution to social geography, and point to a third which supersedes it.

## What is Social Geography?
Geographers are frequently chided - notably by other geographers; perhaps nobody else is very interested! - for providing such naive definitions as 'geography is what geographers do'. The same criticism applies to their subdisciplines. Eyles (1981, p. 309), for example, defines social geography rather baldly as 'The analysis of social phenomena in space' a statement which is not intended to be trite and which faithfully reflects the variety and eclecticism of studies categorised as social geography.

This variety and eclecticism is readily illustrated with reference to a (non-random) selection of recent books on the subject and what they consider 'social phenomena' worthy of consideration. Emrys Jones, the doyen of British social geographers and author of a classic piece

1

Theory and Methodology in Social Geography

of social geographical research (A social geography
of Belfast, 1960), for example, introduced a book
of readings by noting (1975) that 'A subject
dealing with so wide a topic as the spatial
component of human behaviour is not easy to define
(p. 1)'. A brief review, however, leads him to
the statement that

> The social geographer is more concerned with
> describing and explaining spatial elements of
> the society in terms of the structure of that
> society. Holistic and regional, or
> fragmentary and systematic, all approaches
> have this in common; that they begin with
> social groups (p. 3)

and the definition that 'social geography involves
the understanding of the patterns which arise from
the use social groups make of space as they see
it, and of the processes involved in making and
changing such patterns (p. 7)'. He recognises the
difficulties that this introduces, especially with
regard to the definition of social groups:

> The place one should give society itself in
> social geographical studies is difficult to
> assess. In one sense it is central, and in
> another so implicit that to isolate it is to
> talk in purely sociological terms. Most
> courses in social geography will devote some
> time to the study of social groups which may
> be defined in many ways, from statistical
> differentiation to vague notions of community,
> with its countless definitions, and to culture
> groups (pp. 8-9).

This eclecticism was to be welcomed, it seems, and
the book of readings was structured into three
parts, dealing with: (a) patterns of distribution
of social groups and their behaviour; (b) concepts
of space; and (c) the processes which operate in
society and the environment (p. 7) illustrated by
available case studies that lack any cohesion - in
either philosophy or methodology.
    Two years later, in a book co-authored by
John Eyles (Jones and Eyles, 1977) such
eclecticism was both acknowledged and promoted.

> The approach is not a theoretical one, but
> leans heavily on sociological theory. At so

> preliminary a stage, it is difficult to see
> what satisfactory theory may emerge which
> is not subsumed under current sociological
> theory. Rather, we have emphasized an
> empirical approach, drawing on as wide a range
> as possible of studies which fall within our
> framework. The emphasis on patterns is an
> indication of the descriptive and explanatory
> nature of much of the work being done in
> social geography, but the patterns also imply
> much that is discussed under processes (p. 1).

The focus, once again, is 'space, pattern, and
process.' But it is central to ask: patterns of
what and what kinds of processes? (p. 12).
They argue that social geography is not
concerned simply with people, but with people as
members of groups. So their focus is on spatial
patterns of groups and group behaviour, and the
processes involved in creating those patterns,
which involves the threefold study of: what binds
individuals together in groups; how groups
interact; and how groups interact with a changing
society. These are topics of study rather than
parts of an overall subdisciplinary framework,
however, and empirical material is brought
together to illustrate the topics and indicate how
such a framework might be built. The development
of social geography is presented as an inductive
procedure. Jones (1980) is convinced that

> What will bind the studies we call social
> geography together are their focus on the
> social group as a unit of study, and their
> common concern with the spatial implications
> of social processes (p. 260)

but little more:

> There is a very good reason why this essay did
> not begin with a definition of social
> geography: it is because only most diffidently
> can we begin to express a certain agreement on
> topics and aims, and even more hesitantly on
> methodology (p. 258).

The impression we get, therefore, is of a
subdiscipline that focuses on spatial patterns of
social life, individuals as members of groups.
People are categorised, and the where of their
existence as group members - where they live, where

they travel to, where and who they interact with - is to be mapped and accounted for. Much of this mapping focuses on urban environments, as Jones and Eyles recognise, and it has led to the separate identification of an urban social geography. (Not surprisingly, that has stimulated the case for a 'rural social geography', justified by Phillips and Williams (1984, p. 3) because social groups in rural areas experience different 'distance-accessibility' and political contexts from their contemporaries in urban places.) In general, works in this field follow the lead provided by Jones and Eyles, in the pattern-process empirical focus, the eclectic collection of case studies, and the avoidance of any argument for a particular theoretical-cum-methodological framework. Knox (1982), for example, introduces a book that

> is mainly thematic, with an emphasis on pattern and empirical analysis which directly reflects the nature of the work done in urban social geography. Background theory is introduced where relevant but no particular theoretical perspective or academic approach is given special emphasis because the belief which underlies the book is that no single body of theory and no one approach to knowledge can be expected to provide all the answers to the questions currently of concern to urban geographers (p. 4).

One feature of nearly all of the work done in this mould is that it rarely provides much insight into what it is like to be a member of a social group in a particular place. White (1984) expressed this in the Preface to his The West European city: a social geography:

> It is my great regret that, in a book of this scope, it is not possible to convey the real flavour or sense of place of the cities mentioned and discussed ... To convey the real atmosphere of urban living in different Western European city neighbourhoods would, however, require the evocative prose of a Richard Cobb or a Georges Simenon and these are descriptive skills and powers of detailed observation that few geographers possess (p. xiv).

4

Theory and Methodology in Social Geography

This is a call for an insiders' view, for a social
geography of the city written from a study of 'how
social life is constituted' (Jackson and Smith,
1984, p. vii), rather than the conventional
outsiders' view which focuses on the outcomes and
artifacts of social life only. Ley (1977) has
argued for the former, for the study of 'not the
geography that we learn but the geography we come
home to ... the world of everyday experience that
is the ground for decision-making and action in
all realms of behaviour' (p. 12) and his A social
geography of the city (1983) brings the study of
the insider's view to the fore by including 'a
treatment of the geography of everyday life in the
city and the role of culture and values, not only
in defining our experience of the urban environment
but also in moulding the pattern of land use'
(p. xi).
    As currently constituted, therefore, social
geography involves analysis of the spatial
patterns of social life, of the activities of
individuals - as members of social groups - that
have spatial components and connotations. Two
major types of analysis have been practised. The
first involves the analyst as outsider, portraying
social geography from the point of view of the
distant observer. The other involves the analyst
as insider, portraying social geography from the
point of view of the people involved. Each has
its own methodology set in a theoretical frame of
reference, and each will be discussed in turn. A
final section looks at work that might remove the
outsider: insider dualism, and identifies attempts
to replace the separate frames of reference by a
single over-arching structure.


The Outsiders' View
Social geography as defined by Jones and Eyles
emerged during the 1950s and 1960s, as part of
what became widely known as the 'theoretical and
quantitative revolution'. The philosophical base
was that of positivism, involving a belief that
the methods of the experimental natural sciences
could be used not only to provide precise (i.e.
quantitative) descriptions of spatial patterns and
processes but also to develop general laws of such
patterns and the behaviour that produced them. (The
concept of spatial process is one that is rarely
clarified by human geographers: see Johnston and
Hay, 1983. It is usually employed either as a

synonym for mechanism or as a collective term for behaviour, which to a geographer implies behaviour in, or movement across, space.)

Thus, for example, Eyles and Jones (1977):

> begin on the assumption that there are identifiable spatial patterns of behaviour, of group interaction, of response to stimuli ... However unique an individual may feel his own behaviour to be, in most circumstances he will find himself conforming to a recognized scheme of things ... (p. 67).

In the positivist approach to science, generalisations are derived inductively, not through the quasi-random accumulation of findings (what Harvey, 1969, calls the 'Baconian' route) from which inferences are drawn about all cases, but by the structured testing (validation) of hypotheses derived from some general theory - a theory which may be stimulated by quasi-random observations but is only considered valid when it passes stringent empirical tests. The construction of a general theory is a slow process, therefore, involving many rounds of observation, speculation and testing. For social geographers, this has posed particular problems.

The spatial focus of most work in social geography has been in urban areas, large agglomerations of people organised into complex and overlapping sets of social groups and producing an intricate mosaic of residential and other milieux. Analysis of these agglomerations depended almost entirely on data provided by others. The main source of this dependence has been the census-taking agency, which provides a wealth of data on people, households and dwellings from its regular surveys. In the 1930s, the United States Bureau of the Census began reporting these data not only for the urban agglomerations as a whole but also for relatively small subdivisions - termed census tracts: some attempt was made in defining these tracts (areas with average populations of several thousand people only) to relate them to 'natural areas', but they were really only administrative units. Other census agencies followed their lead; for example, the British census began reporting data for enumeration districts (the ad hoc small areas - with less than 1000 residents on average - used in the data collection) with the 1951 census, (Dewdney and Rhind 1986).

There are several problems associated with using these data. The first is that the analyst must accept the census authority's categorisations, so that the social groups studied are those for which information is given: many censuses do not collect data on income and religion, for example, and others are very wary of asking for information on race. The analyst is an outsider, dependent on other outsiders so that, as Timms (1971) showed, it is usually necessary to accept census indicators that are but loosely related to the concepts being studied. (One of the most commonly-studied social groupings is that known generally as class. The indicators available from the census usually relate to socio-economic status, which is not necessarily the same thing, depending - as Dunleavy and Husbands, (1985), argue - on the theory of society which informs one's definition of class.) The second problem is that the data are almost invariably made available for the spatial units only; they can be aggregated up into larger units, but not disaggregated, and there is no access to the original data on the individual respondents.

The spatial patterns that can be described in this sort of work are thus data dependent. Censuses are taken infrequently, if regularly, and provide cross-sectional snapshots only, of where people are at a particular date, usually where they are resident during a particular night; this leads Claval (1985) to the conclusion that 'social geo-graphy is too often the geography of societies at the time when everybody sleeps' (p. 470). Diurnal and seasonal variations cannot be explored, except with simulated data (see Parkes and Taylor, 1975).

In their use of these data, social geographers followed the pioneering work of sociologists. Indeed, they virtually took over the analysis of spatial patterns in census data, continuing to refine the methods and present new descriptive findings long after most sociologists lost interest. Two separate types of work were adopted, and linked.

The first type of work can be described as aspatial social geography, for it was concerned with where different social groups lived in a relative but not an absolute sense. Thus, for example, Duncan and Duncan (1955) used indices of dissimilarity and segregation to explore the degree

to which the members of different social groups
lived apart from each other, the indices measuring
the degree to which they occupied separate census
tracts, irrespective of where those tracts were
relative to each other (Taeuber and Taeuber,
1965). There has been some sophistication of those
indices (Lieberson, 1981; Morgan, 1980, 1982) but,
with few exceptions (e.g. Peach, 1975; Peach,
Robinson and Smith, 1981), geographers have made
relatively little use of them. Instead, they have
been much more attracted to the use of multivariate
statistical procedures to identify the major
components of residential differentiation of social
groups as revealed by census data.

The original stimulus for this work, also
aspatial in the sense defined above, was the
pioneering analysis of Los Angeles and San
Francisco by Eshref Shevky and Wendell Bell
(1955). They presented a model of the changing
structure of urban society along three dimensions
- the changing distribution of occupational
skills; the changing social organisation of
productive activity; and the changing composition
of the population - which they linked to three
dimensions of residential differentiation - termed
economic status, family status, and ethnic status
respectively. Criticisms showed that the link
between the macro-changes (termed increasing scale
by Shevky and Bell) and residential differentiation
was never identified (Timms, 1971) and that the
three dimensions were empirically identified from
their analysis of census data rather than
theoretically derived (Johnston, 1971).

Despite these criticisms, social area analysis
attracted attention because it showed how census
small-area data could be used to characterise the
various parts of a city. Its relatively crude
methods were made obsolete by developments in
computer technology, however, and the ability to
use multivariate statistical procedures for
inductive explorations of census data. These
explorations became known as factorial ecologies;
the procedures of factor and principal components
analysis were used to identify the major
dimensions of residential differentiation and to
classify areas according to their population's
characteristics (Berry, 1971; Johnston, 1976;
Davies, 1984). These were geographical, since
they identified the major groupings of variables
that differentiated areas (although, unlike the
earlier index-based studies, they ignore the degree

of differentiation; Johnston, 1973; Johnston and Newton, 1976), but aspatial in that they were not concerned with the absolute location of the social groups so defined within the urban complex. Most followed Shevky and Bell in the dimensions of differentiation that they found - areas could be characterised by the socio-economic (occupation, income etc.) status of their residents, the tenure and condition of housing, the age of the population, the type of household, and the racial characteristics of the residents - although this may have been as much an artifact of the data as a representation of the social geography of the cities. Few attempts were made to use the inductive findings to structure more explicit tests of the emerging theory, however, and even recent reviews (e.g. Davies, 1984) display a greater concern with the statistical procedures than with integrating the substantive findings into a general understanding of residential differentiation, although the findings have stimulated the search for such an understanding (e.g. Johnston, 1984b).

The second type of work is <u>spatial social geography</u>, displaying a concern not only with the differing social character of areas but also with where within the urban complex areas of particular character are found. The stimulus for this also came from the publications of North American sociologists, especially Ernest Burgess, whose detailed investigation of Chicago led to an inductive model of the spatial organisation of the American city (into a series of concentric zones) based on underlying processes that he assumed were general. The model was, not surprisingly, criticised and refined (see Johnston, 1971), and extended to cover other places and other times (Johnston, 1972). Its particular attraction to social geographers was its provision of a spatial framework for the study of 'who lives where' (Murdie, 1976), and Berry and Rees (1969) used it to provide the spatial matrix for analysing the findings of factorial ecologies.

Both types of work emphasised the quantitative manipulation of data to provide relatively sophisticated descriptions of the residential patterns of cities. It was a crude form of positivism, dominated by an attention to method, and unsurprisingly many geographers soon reacted against it, while accepting the value of the descriptions for particular purposes. Some of the

9

reactions were to the total reliance on the data provided by census agencies, so that the content of social geography was being defined by those data collectors. Smith (1973), for example, argued that censuses provided few insights into the geography of social well-being, of spatial variations in the quality of life, and used a variety of sources in order to map the geography of 'who gets what, where' - of the provision of health care and educational services, for example. Others not only saw the census data as too coarse and narrow in coverage but argued for more detailed study of particular aspects of social well-being and behaviour - such as the geography of crime and deviance (as reviewed in the chapter by David Herbert in this book).

These were further developments of the social area approach only, however. Work on social processes, in what became known as behavioural geography, introduced a new perspective. This, too, was positivistic in its general orientation and inductive in its application. It focused in particular on movement within cities, especially migration and the choice of where to live, but there were also studies of a variety of kinds of social interaction. The data were not readily at hand, already collected by a census or other agency, so social geographers had to develop skills of data collection as well as analysis. The questionnaire became a basic tool and much effort was spent on designing, administering, coding and analysing such instruments.

As already indicated, in 'behavioural social geography' (as in 'spatial pattern social geography') the goal was positivist, for the underlying belief was that it was possible to develop generalisations about how different social groups behave. Some of the work was relatively sophisticated. Rushton (1969), for example, recognised that analyses of what he termed 'behaviour in space' - the actual movement decisions made by people - would not necessarily lead to generalisations about 'spatial behaviour' - 'the rules by which alternative locations are evaluated and choices consequently made' (p. 392) - because of the different contexts within which decisions were being taken. Uncovering those 'rules' needed careful experimental and analytical designs, of the sort reviewed by Golledge and Rushton (1984). But much of the work was relatively cavalier, involving individual case studies - of, for example, distance and directional biases in intra-urban migration in city X - providing a wealth of empirical information that could not readily be incorporated into general theories.

A major stimulus to behavioural geography was a realisation that behaviour is based on information and how it is evaluated (Golledge, Brown and Williamson, 1972). In other areas of geography, theories which assumed perfect decision-making by omniscient humans were being found wanting (Pred, 1967) and it was argued that understanding of how people behave (social processes) required appreciation of how they obtained and used information. Environmental learning became a research focus, therefore (Golledge and Rushton, 1984), as did the impact of the local milieu on socialisation - as in the context of voting behaviour (Taylor and Johnston, 1979). This widened the scope of the data collection exercises, most of which again were case studies of particular people in certain places and provided extra empirical material to be summarised in textbooks rather than explicit tests of general theories of behaviour.

There are two basic characteristics of works presenting the outsiders' views on (mainly urban) social geography, therefore:

1. A reliance on data collected for other purposes, which means that many studies are not only data-led but are constrained by the views of others (also outsiders) on what information should be collected and how it should be released.
2. A general acceptance of the positivist approach to knowledge, but a widespread absence of full application of that approach. It is accepted that general rules of spatial patterns and spatial behaviour are being operated, but most investigations are individual case studies rather than tests specifically designed to evaluate theories with respect to a clearly designated population.

As a consequence the substantial output (Knox's, 1982, bibliography contains some 1100 items) can best be summarised as rampant empiricism. Textbooks have been produced that synthesise this material, but often only either by forcing it into a straitjacket (another outsider's view) or by assuming that a particular place (frequently, though not invariably, in North America) is representative of all places. We have a great deal of information about social patterns and social processes, but much less knowledge about the social worlds which that information purports to describe and explain.

## The Insiders' View

Two major sets of criticism have been levelled at the outsiders' views of social geography. One is that they present a very partial picture of social life, a consequence of the reliance on particular data sets which are derived from questionnaires asking 'objective' questions (how old are you? where were you born? etc.) which give no insight into the individuals themselves, especially since they are aggregated with many others. Thus the descriptions provided by factorial ecologies tell us nothing about the places and the ways in which people react to them; the details of daily life are absent, and instead we get a sanitised, numerical description only. The second is that their acceptance of the positivist approach treats people in a mechanistic way, as programmed responders to stimuli, thereby denying them their individuality and freedom to choose. People are forced into categories defined by the outsiders - class, stage in the family cycle etc. - and treated as exemplars of those categories irrespective of whether they accept such a characterisation. Thus the descriptions, however sophisticated, use the outsiders' terms not the insiders'; they portray social patterns and processes as the outsiders see them, not as the insiders live them. As Ley (1983) expresses it, they lack animation (p. 92): social areas (the outsiders' classifications) are not necessarily the same as neighbourhoods (the districts with which the insiders identify); the city of mind and action, the image that guides the insiders' behaviour, need 'bear little necessary relationship to the comprehensive accomplishments of the cartographer' (p. 130); and the place in which a person lives:

> is not only a phenomenon but also an idea, an object always invested with meaning ... [which] defines what a place is and what it can become ... The settings frequented by social groups begin to take on the group's own

character, so that place is a reinforcing prop in developing distinctive identities. The places we frequent provide a summary of the people we see ourselves to be, for they prescribe the ongoing transactions that characterize a lifestyle (p. 165).

The goal of the social geographer seeking to appreciate neighbourhoods, images and places is to know how people live in their local milieux, milieux which they are involved in creating and sustaining. To Ley (1983) 'if we are serious in developing a truly _social_ geography, then an understanding of the _social_ processes implicit in the construction, maintenance and functioning of informal groups and formal associations is a necessary step' (p.12) since these provide the framework for daily life, not the categories imposed by outside observers - positivist or otherwise. But the reality that these groups and associations provide is not the sole context for urban life. There are other groups and associations - often termed institutions - in which only a small proportion of the population are involved but whose actions are crucial in providing the resources - jobs, housing, transport etc. - essential to daily life. Each, as Ley (1983) recognises, is also 'a cultural entity, a social world, with its own capacity to construct realities' (p. 234). They, too, are outsiders, whose categorisation of the insiders constrains the latter's behaviour. Thus a full social geography is one that studies an area's insiders and outsiders and how they interact.

The approach to understanding that can give us these desired insights into the insiders' views is usually known - to geographers at least - as humanistic. Within this approach there is a number of variants, whose relevance to social geography has been explored by Jackson and Smith (1986). They share the method of '_verstehen_, a form of empathetic understanding gained from the adoption of the subject's own perspective ... [in] a process involving the contextual interpretation of subjectively meaningful social action' (p. 9). This cannot be achieved by the analysis of data about the subjects. It requires prolonged contact within them, appreciating how they learn, act and react, how they obtain, process and transmit information, how they assign meanings to people and places, and how they link their local, intimate

world to the forces of 'the world outside' - all
without influencing them at all, without changing
their behaviour through the act of being studied.

Interestingly, Jackson and Smith (1984)
identify one of the main sources for such an
approach in the same Chicago School of Sociology
that also produced the Burgess model of the city,
so beloved of the outsiders. They show that the
main goal of this school was to understand the
complexity of social milieux and behaviour in the
burgeoning city of Chicago, especially the deviant
behaviour that was rife and which they wanted to
eliminate by removing its causes not by treating
its symptoms (Jackson, 1984). Burgess's model was
a by-product of this work. As he describes it (in
Burgess and Bogue, 1967), an entire programme of
research into natural areas (or neighbourhoods)
was undertaken, having two components: 1) study of
their spatial pattern; and 2) study of their
cultural life. The former was used to identify
the areas and groups to be studied; it was one in
which 'The students made maps of any data we could
find in the city that could be plotted' (p. 6).

But:

> Statistical data and map-plotting tells us
> much, but they don't tell us all ... [they]
> raise questions. Many of these ... can be
> further studied by statistical investigation;
> others, to be understood, require us to get
> below the surface of observable behaviour.
> Cooley thought that these could be studied by
> what he called sympathetic introspection ...
> but it is quite apparent that sympathetic
> introspection has many fallacies. If you and
> I try to imagine how a hobo feels - we have
> not been a homeless man, we have not ridden
> the rails - our mental picture is quite likely
> to be different from what goes on in the mind
> of a hobo. So the superior method is that of
> communication, of scouring personal documents,
> and the life history ... by the use of a
> personal document we are able to get at the
> subjective aspects of life in the city
> (pp. 8-9).

The studies based on these personal documents
are known as <u>urban ethnographies</u> (Jackson,
1985), detailed presentations of the way of
life of particular social groups, almost invariably

spatially defined and based on fieldwork with
those groups combined with other forms of
documentation: as Jackson puts it:

> Ethnographers have shown themselves to be
> willing to employ practically every technique
> available to the social scientist: sample
> surveys, informants, censuses, historical
> documents, direct participation, firsthand
> observations, descriptive linguistics,
> correlational techniques, psychological tests
> and so forth: 'shameless eclecticism' and
> 'methodological opportunism' are defining
> features of the ethnographer (p. 169).

In Chicago, this eclecticism and opportunism led
to the production of a series of classic
monographs, including Zorbaugh's The gold coast
and the slum, Wirth's The ghetto, and Thrasher's
The gang: Thrasher's work documented 1313
separate gangs, and took seven years.
    To obtain the insiders' view, the dominant
research procedure in ethnography is participant
observation (Jackson, 1983), which has no
protocols, only guidelines. The goal is to become
part of the population being studied, so that
one's presence is unobtrusive and it is possible
to observe without in any way influencing
behaviour through awareness that it is being
studied. (The recording of the observations is
then done unobtrusively too.) It may be difficult
to negotiate an entree, however. Ley (1974)
achieved this in the Monroe district of
Philadelphia through initial contacts with a local
Community Association, which agreed to employ him
(unpaid) and to sanction his research, and he also
became a class leader at a local church. In this
way, his presence was accepted and:

> During the six months of residence I walked the
> streets, attended meetings, belonged to a
> church, and spoke informally with neighbourhood
> people. The nature of my work ... brought
> contact with most community 'leaders', and the
> daily round enabled meetings with Monroe
> dwellers in many contexts: in their homes, at
> work, in shops, on the street, at play ...
> Joint activities [with the church class] ranged
> from helping with homework and a bake sale, to
> social evenings at the bowling alley, to
> informal 'raps', and two out-of-town summer
> excursions (pp. 18-19).

The material gained from participant observation provides insights and understanding that cannot be achieved in any other way; full appreciation of how people live can only be obtained empathetically, by sharing their living with them. This can lead to problems of reporting, of conveying to others what it is one has experienced. Positivist research is conducted and reported in a standardised format - review of literature; derivation of hypothesis; construction of 'experiments'; test of hypothesis; evaluation of findings - but this straitjacket is clearly not applicable to accounts of participant observation studies. But straight reporting alone may animate our appreciation of a place and its people, to use Ley's term, but without some imposed structure the result may be little more than random academic voyeurism. Thus, Jackson and Smith (1984) advance:

> the need to treat participant observation as an approach which should not be employed in isolation from or to the exclusion of a range of more quantitative techniques, such as informant interviewing and structured questionnaires. A common inference is that informal methods, such as participant observation, make up, in the potential depth of understanding and interpretation, what they sacrifice in terms of range and representativeness (p. 94).

This is shown in Ley's study. In seeking to appreciate the extent of insecurity felt by Monroe residents he conducted a questionnaire study, designed 'to be experiential, asking interviewees to draw upon _their_ daily experience, to relate questions to people _they_ knew, and events occurring on _their_ block and locality' (p. 136). In this way, his appreciation of the residents' feelings gained by living among them was bolstered by 'hard data'; his interpretation of events that he witnessed and heard of was extended by his more systematic exploration of the elements of life that they appeared to reveal, and he was able to present a more convincing report as a consequence (see also Eyles, 1985).

Research that seeks the insiders' view does not begin with prior categorisations and data collection techniques that structure the analysis; the goal is to understand the people studied, on their own terms. But this does not mean simply that the researcher suddenly decides 'I will investigate the people of neighbourhood A'. The decision to undertake the study is taken in the context of a general academic orientation; it plays a part in a larger plan. And the interpretation of its materials is similarly set in that academic context. The researcher is necessarily to some extent blinkered when setting out on the research, and the nature of the blinkers (put in place by a period of academic socialisation through contact with teachers, other researchers, and the written reports of other studies) directs the choices made with regard to the conduct of the work. Those blinkers similarly direct the presentation of the output, for the research has been conducted in order to add to knowledge in a particular way. (There is always the possibility of a re-evaluation, of course, with the fieldwork leading the researcher to reject the particular blinkers - and to replace them by others!) Thus, for example, Oscar Lewis presented <u>La vida</u> (1957) as an attempt 'to give a voice to people who are rarely heard, and to provide the reader with an inside view of a style of life which is common in many of the deprived and marginal groups in our society' (p. 14). But it was more than that: 'It is my hope that a better understanding of the nature of the culture of poverty will eventually lead to a more sympathetic view of the poor and their problems and will provide a more rational basis for constructive social action' (p. 14). As made clear later on, Lewis was 'concerned with testing the concept of a culture of poverty' (p. 47), characterised by

> both an adaptation and a reaction of the poor to their marginal position in a class-strati-fied, highly individuated, capitalistic society It represents an effort to cope with feelings of hopelessness and despair which develop from the realization of the improbability of achieving success in terms of the values and goals of the larger society (p. 49).

Lewis did not undertake his study in a situation of theoretical agnosticism, therefore. He had his own theory about the pattern of life in particular circumstances - circumstances that could only be detailed through the use of census and other quantitative data - and he was setting out to 'test' that theory. It wasn't a test in the positivist sense; for he didn't predict any particular outcomes, or particular behaviour (as made clear in the unexpected importance of prostitution in the coping strategy of the Rios family). It was a test that involved building up a coherent representation of the reality that he studied, and then transmitting that representation to the reader. The case study is being used not as a representative sample from which generalisations of wide applicability can be drawn but as material to illustrate the researcher's appreciation of the situation. Others may, of course, interpret the material differently, feeding it into a separate appreciation, and debates about the relative coherence and logic of different appreciations - both internally and with respect to the 'evidence' - are possible; in that the 'evidence' on the insider's view is obtained by non-replicable means. However, there can be no final 'test' of which is right, it is simply a question of deciding which interpretation you find more convincing.

Those seeking to elucidate the insiders' view are not random explorers, therefore, but travellers on structured journeys. The Chicago School ethnographers, for example, believed that social life was organised and sustained through communication. Theirs was an interactionist tradition, based on the belief that, 'It is by virtue of an ability to communicate that individuals can share a common experience and maintain a common life. Literally, the history of communication is the history of civilisation' (Jackson and Smith, 1984, p. 79) so that under-standing how society operates involves appreciating how and what people communicate, which is the purpose of the fieldwork. In addition, researchers have their own, outsiders', views of those communications, as with Weber's theories of power and bureaucracy, and they devise research in order to evaluate those views. The image that they are evaluating may be a 'popular' one, a vernacular rather than an academic representation. This was the case with Ley's (1974) Monroe study, which evaluated both the general white image of black America, based on ignorance and fear, and an academic image which promoted the view of increased black consciousness and cohesion. Both were efforts to do the same thing in the face of uncertainty 'to impose an

order upon an elusive world, to establish firm
ground' (p. 265). Both were found wanting once
the insiders' view had been explored. (Ley's monograph on Monroe is one of the few full studies of
the insiders' view undertaken by a geographer -
though see Jackson and Smith, 1984, p. 44. The
essays edited by Buttimer and Seamon, 1980, provide
another major set, as does Western's, 1981, work
in Outcast Cape Town.)

In the contemporary world, some form of
participant observation is clearly the best route
of obtaining the insiders' view; any other source
is second-hand. For historical studies, of
course, it is necessary to rely on second-hand
materials, the texts left by the participants;
historical research involves creating and filling
out coherent interpretations using those texts.
The range of such texts is large, however. Many
interpreters rely on contemporary outsiders' views
- such as the Domesday book. Others employ a range
of personal papers. Literature, too, can provide
insights (as in Pocock, 1981), and not only for
the past, as demonstrated by Alan Paton's superb
novels - Cry the beloved country, Too late the
phalarope and My but your country's beautiful - on
South African apartheid. And the landscape is a
text, an information source that can tell us much
about the society that created it (Lowenthal 1968,
1975, 1985; Lowenthal and Prince, 1965).

Research into the insiders' view is not
presented as an alternative to the outsiders',
therefore, but as an improvement on it. The
researchers accept that they are neither voyeurs
nor academic agnostics; their goal is to provide a
coherent picture of the selected population
because, as Pickles (1985) argues, 'The interpreter
of an event, piecing together the picture of what
happened, may well come to know that event better
than those involved (but in a special way only)'
(p. 173). They provide the interpretative depth
that an outsiders' view alone cannot give. They
also share some of the methodologies employed by
the outsiders, but use them (as with Ley's
questionnaire) in the context of their
appreciation of the local milieu rather than some
externally-defined model whose categories may be
entirely invalid in the particular circumstance.
Their goal is to illuminate social patterns and
processes and to convey the characteristics of
life in places, not as examples of general rules
of behaviour but as illustrations of how people

perceive and respond to particular situations.
They may, on occasions, make inductive generalisations, as a way of synthesising material, but do
not use those to predict behaviour. They have
been criticised for their unwillingness to
generalise, to use the accounts of individual
places to throw light on general social
processes. Jackson (1985), for example, quotes
Steinberg (1981) that

> The ethnic literature abounds with community
> studies that explore the uniqueness and
> complexities of ethnic life. As a rule,
> however, these studies go too far in treating
> ethnic communities as 'worlds unto
> themselves', and tend to gloss over the extent
> to which these communities are integrated into
> and dependent upon the institutions of the
> surrounding society (p. 53).

Like much regional geography - modern as well as
ancient - the place is isolated and studied as if
the only influences on its character are internal
(Johnston, 1984a). Hence the desire of some to
proceed further, to study what it is one group of
social geographers tried to get inside while
another stays outside.

### Inside or Outside - What?

A simple categorisation of these two types of
social geography may be that whereas those
committed to presenting the outsiders' view are
working on society those who seek to appreciate
and convey the insiders' view are working in
society. As suggested above, some social
geographers promote the necessity for both, for
what Buttimer (1974) termed 'an interplay of
"inside" and "outside" views on situations:
sensitivity to the native experience, and yet a
grasp of the dynamics of situations from the
external point of view' (p. 24). But is this
sufficient?

Both of the approaches as presented here have
been criticised as superficial in their treatment
of individuals, groups and societies, since they
do not inquire into the underlying social forces
that lead to the observed social groups, patterns
and processes. The 'outsiders' take certain
categories as given, and not needing explanation.
Students of residential segregation, for example,

accept a) the existence of socio-economic groups and racial groups and b) the desire of members of these groups to congregate together and segregate themselves from members of other groups. They map the results; they may suggest reasons for the congregation-segregation (as in Boal, 1976) but subject neither the existence of the groups nor their apparent 'need' for residential separation to critical scrutiny. The 'insiders' do not apply externally-defined categories but by accepting those used by the people they study again do not question why they act in that way; nor, in seeking to appreciate how choices are made, do they consider why the available choice set presents certain options and not others. Neither group, it is claimed, has a full theory of society.

The sort of theory needed, it is claimed, is realist, which links the worlds of events (the making of decisions) and experiences (the perceived empirical world) to a world of mechanisms. The most frequently advanced theory of that type is Marxism - of which there are many varieties. This contends that all societies are responses to the need to ensure human survival and reproduction, and comprise mechanisms put in place in order to sustain human life. Under capitalism, for example, the people-nature nexus necessary for survival has been commodified. Nature has become a factor of production - land; people another - labour. Production is organised through the buying and selling of these two factors in order to create more of another - capital - and the entire dynamic of the capitalist mode of production is geared to continued accumulation of capital. This is achieved through the relations of production. Land and labour are only put to work if a) owners of capital are prepared to invest in them and b) they perceive a potential return (profit) from the sale of the output. Thus society is divided into two major classes - the owners of capital and the owners of labour - who are in continuous conflict, because accumulation can only be achieved through exploitation of labour; large profits imply low (relative) wages, so the relative size of profits and wages is the focus of contestation.

These fundamental elements of the capitalist mode of production are what Sayer (1984) calls transhistorical claims, and a theory of the capitalist mode of production is built on these necessities (as in Harvey, 1982). But such necessities are not associated with particular empirical outcomes; they are rules that are interpreted by human actors, and there are many ways in which they can be put into operation. The theory of the necessary mechanisms does not predict the events and the outcomes. People activate the mechanisms according to how they interpret them. And they learn how to do that in their local context. They create a superstructure, a set of economic, social, political and cultural institutions within which production, exchange and distribution are organised. Different groups, in different places, may create different sorts of institution. It seems, for example, that a state is a necessity for capitalism, but there is great variety in the nature of the state within capitalism at the present time - centralised (France), partly decentralised (Britain), federal (USA), or highly decentralised (Switzerland); democratic or totalitarian; political parties related to economic class (Britain), to religion and language (Switzerland, Belgium, Holland) or to some historical event (Ireland); and so on. Once created, these institutions structure decision-making - but they don't determine it, since instead of reproducing it (continuing to vote for a class-based party in Britain, say) people could change it (vote for the Alliance), without, of course, altering the mechanisms, only how they are operated.

Positivist theories of society focus only on the empirical, whereas humanistic theories combine empirical and actual, studying the events, as perceived by the insider, as well as the outcomes, perceived by both insider and outsider. Realist theories put these in context, by relating them to the driving forces, or mechanisms, within society (as initially essayed by Eyles, 1974). They are not predictive. Like the humanistic studies, they provide analytical depth, aiding the appreciation not only of how decisions were taken, but also why such decisions were necessary. They cannot be tested in the positivist sense, but only in terms of the coherence of the account that they provide. With them, one can appreciate, for example, not only the existence of residential segregation (as portrayed by the outsider) and the experiences it produces (as illuminated by the insider) but also why there are forces within society that lead to that particular way of organising social life (Harvey, 1975; Johnston, 1984b).

Closely linked to this approach is one that has gained considerable currency among geographers recently - structuration. The core of this (as presented by Giddens, 1984, for example) is that one cannot separate individuals from society: society is individuals, and individuals are society, because society is a set of institutions and rules created by individuals and individuals are enacting those rules as they go about their daily lives (at all 'levels' of society; see Pred, 1984). Such a presentation avoids both the determinist thinking of some social theories (those which claim to predict action) and the voluntarist thinking of others (those which assert that individuals have complete freedom of action). Its implications for the conduct of empirical enquiry are unclear, however (Gregson, 1986), and without clearly linking it to an understanding of the economic mechanisms it is uncertain what it tells us about the relative autonomy of individuals and groups - those elements of culture not closely linked to economic activity. We can only discover what institutions and actions are 'acceptable' empirically, after the event, because the past is never repeated and the conditions within which action occurs are never the same twice. But this approach ensures that human agency is not subjected, theoretically, to deterministic influences - whether cultural (Duncan, 1980) or economic (Duncan and Ley, 1982); it ensures an appreciation of the central role of individuals in the making and remaking of the societal superstructure (Duncan, 1985).


In Summary
Social geography, according to those who seek to define it, is the study of the spatial patterns and processes that can be identified with particular social groups. As this introductory chapter has indicated, three ways of approaching such study have been promoted, each with a particular theoretical stance and associated methodological position. The first we might term naive, sophisticated description: description because its goal is to portray; sophisticated because it uses analytical procedures aimed at explanation via prediction; and naive because it considers the definition of social groups, indeed

their existence, unproblematic. The second we might term <u>innocent appreciation</u>: appreciation because its goal is to understand how processes operate and patterns are created; and innocent because although it accepts popularly-defined social groups rather than imposes them, it too does not inquire into their origins. The third is <u>realistic explanation</u>: explanation because it is concerned to account for the worlds that people experience and act in; and realistic because it accepts that people only produce those worlds in conditions that are not of their own choosing.

Choice of which approach to follow - or whether to fashion another - is clearly an individual decision (perhaps itself an argument for the third: Johnston, 1986b). Which is chosen has implications for two important issues, however.

1. Is there a viable separate sub-discipline of social geography? Realists argue that society is a complex whole and that any academic division of labour within the social sciences is counterproductive. Some divisions are better than others, however, since they are based on 'rational abstractions' (sensibly-selected parts of the whole) rather than 'chaotic conceptions'. Is social geography, as defined here, a chaotic conception? Is it valid to abstract social groups for separate study? (Note Dunleavy's, 1982, argument against a separate study of urban phenomena.)

2. How should the knowledge achieved by social geographers be applied? Each of the approaches outlined here is associated with a particular applied programme (Johnston, 1986b): the first facilitates social control, by providing empirical models from which it is possible either to predict the consequences of certain actions or to indicate what actions are necessary to achieve desired ends; the second advances mutual awareness, removing the ignorance of how other people in other places live (as the quotation from Lewis above indicates); and the third promotes emancipation, the awareness of the mechanisms that direct society.

## Theory and Methodology in Social Geography

As we practise social geography - if we accept that such a subdiscipline should exist - so we make choices that restructure it in particular ways.

REFERENCES

Berry, B.J.L. ed. (1971) Comparative Factorial
    Ecology. Special issue of Economic Geography,
    47, 209-367
Berry, B.J.L. and Rees, P.H. (1969) 'The factorial
    ecology of Calcutta'. Am. J. Sociol, 74,
    445-491
Boal, F.W. (1976) 'Ethnic residential segregation'.
    In D.T. Herbert and R.J. Johnston, eds., Social
    Areas in Cities. Volume I: Spatial Processes
    and Form, John Wiley, Chichester, 41-80
Burgess, E.W. and Bogue, D.J. (1967) 'Research in
    urban society: a long view'. In E.W. Burgess
    and D.J. Bogue, eds., Urban Sociology, Phoenix
    Books, Chicago, 1-14
Buttimer, A. (1974) Values in Geography. Commission
    on College Geography, Association of American
    Geographers, Washington DC
Buttimer, A. and Seaman, D. eds. (1980) The Human
    Experience of Space and Place, Croom Helm,
    London
Davies, W.K.D. (1984) Factorial Ecology, Gower
    Press, Aldershot
Dewdney, J. and Rhind, D. (1986) 'The British and
    United States' Censuses of Population', in M.
    Pacione, Population Geography: Progress and
    Prospect, Croom Helm, London, 35-57
Duncan, J.S. (1980) 'The superorganic in cultural
    geography'. Ann. Ass. Amer. Geog. 70, 181-198
Duncan, J. S. (1985) 'Individual action and
    political power: a structuration perspective'.
    In R.J. Johnston, ed., The Future of Geography.
    Methuen, London, 174-189
Duncan, J.S. and Ley, D. (1982) 'Structural marxism
    and human geography: a critical assessment'.
    Ann. Assoc. Amer. Geog. 72, 30-59
Duncan, O.D. and Duncan, B. (1955) 'Residential
    distribution and occupational stratification'.
    Am. J. Sociol. 60, 493-503
Dunleavy, P. (1982) The Urban Perspective. Course
    D202, Block 1, Unit 3/4 The Open University
    Press, Milton Keynes
Dunleavy, P. and Husbands, C.T. (1985) British
    Democracy at the Crossroads, George Allen and
    Unwin, London
Eyles, J. (1974) 'Social theory and social
    geography'. Prof. Geog. 6, 27-88

Theory and Methodology in Social Geography


Eyles, J. (1981) 'Social geography'. In R.J. Johnston et al., eds., The Dictionary of Human Geography, Basil Blackwell, Oxford, 309-312

Eyles, J. (1985) Sense of Place, Silverwood Press, Warrington

Giddens, A. (1984) The Constitution of Society, Polity Press, Oxford

Golledge, R.G. and Rushton, G. (1984) 'A review of analytic behavioural research in geography'. In D.T. Herbert and R.J. Johnston, eds., Geography and the Urban Environment, Volume 6. John Wiley, Chichester, 1-44

Golledge, R.G., Brown, L.A. and Williamson, F. (1972) 'Behavioural approaches in geography: an overview'. Aust. Geog. 12, 59-79

Gregson, N. (1986) 'On duality and dualism: the case of structuration and time geography'. Prog. Human Geog. 10, 184-205

Hartshorne, R. (1939) The Nature of Geography, The Association of American Geographers, Lancaster Pa.

Hartshorne, R. (1959) Perspective on the Nature of Geography, Rand McNally, Chicago

Harvey, D. (1969) Explanation in Geography, Edward Arnold, London

Harvey, D. (1975) 'Class structure in a capitalist society and the theory of residential differentiation'. In R. Peel, M. Chisholm, and P. Haggett, eds., Processes in Physical and Human Geography, Heinemann, London, 354-369

Harvey, D. (1982) The Limits to Capital, Basil Blackwell, Oxford

Jackson, P. (1983) 'Principles and problems of participant observation'. Geog. Ann. B, 65, 39-46

Jackson, P. (1984) 'Social disorganization and moral order in the city'. Trans. Inst. Brit. Geog. NS9, 168-180

Jackson, P. (1985) 'Urban ethnography'. Prog. Human Geog. 9, 157-176

Jackson, P. and Smith, S.J. (1984) Exploring Social Geography, George Allen and Unwin, London

James, P.E. and Jones, C.E. eds. (1954) American Geography: Inventory and Prospect, Syracuse University Press, Syracuse

Johnston, R.J. (1970) Urban Residential Patterns, G. Bell, London

Johnston, R.J. (1972) 'Towards a general model of intra-urban residential patterns: some cross-cultural observations'. Prog. Geog. 4, 83-124

Johnston, R.J. (1973) 'Possible extensions to the factorial ecology method: a note'. Environ. Plann. A 5, 719-734

Johnston, R.J. (1976) 'Residential area characteristics: research methods for identifying urban sub-areas - social area analysis and factorial ecology'. In D.T. Herbert and R.J. Johnston, eds., Social Areas in Cities: Volume I Social Processes and Forms, John Wiley, Chichester, 193-236

Johnston, R.J. (1984a) 'The world is our oyster'. Trans Inst. Brit. Geog. NS9, 443-459

Johnston, R.J. (1984b) City and Society, Hutchinson London

Johnston, R.J. (1986a) North America. In J. Eyles, ed., Social Geography in Comparative Perspective, Croom Helm, London

Johnston, R.J. (1986b) On Human Geography, Basil Blackwell, Oxford

Johnston, R.J. and Hay, A.M. (1983) 'The study of process in quantitative human geography'. L'Espace Geographique, 12, 69-76

Johnston, R.J. and Newton, P.W. (1976) 'Residential area characteristics and residential area homogeneity'. Environ. Plann. A. 8, 543-552

Jones, E. (1960) A Social Geography of Belfast, Oxford University Press, Oxford

Jones, E. ed. (1975) Readings in Social Geography Oxford University Press, Oxford

Jones, E. (1980) 'Social geography'. In E.H. Brown, ed., Geography: Yesterday and Tomorrow, Oxford University Press, Oxford, 251-262

Jones, E. and Eyles, J. (1977) An Introduction to Social Geography, Oxford University Press, Oxford

Knox, P.L. (1982) Urban Social Geography, Longman, London

Lewis, O. (1957) La Vida, Panther Books, London

Ley, D. (1974) The Black Inner City as Frontier Outpost, Association of American Geographers, Washington DC

Ley, D. (1977) 'The personality of a geographical fact'. Prof. Geog. 29, 8-13

Ley, D. (1983) A Social Geography of the City, Harper and Row, New York

28

Lieberson, S. (1981) 'An asymmetrical approach to segregation'. In C. Peach et al., eds., Ethnic Segregation in cities, Croom Helm, London, 61-82

Lowenthal, D. (1968) 'The American scene'. Geog. Rev. 48, 61-88

Lowenthal, D. (1975) 'Past time, present place: landscape and memory'. Geog. Reg. 65, 1-36

Lowenthal, D. (1985) The Past is a Foreign Country, Cambridge University Press, Cambridge

Lowenthal, D. and Prince, H.C. (1965) English land-scape tastes. Geog. Rev. 55, 186-222

Morgan, B.S. (1980) 'Metropolitan area character-istics and occupational segregation'. Trans. Inst. Brit. Geog. NS5, 174-184

Morgan, B. S. (1982) 'An assessment of some technical problems in the comparative study of residential segregation'. Trans. Inst. Brit. Geog. NS7, 227-233

Murdie, R. A. (1976) 'Spatial form in the residen-tial mosaic'. In D.T. Herbert and R.J. Johnston, eds., Social Areas in Cities: Volume I Spatial Processes and Forms, John Wiley, Chichester, 237-272

Parkes, D. N. and Taylor, P. J. (1975) 'A Kantian view of the city: a factor ecological approach in space and time'. Environ. Plann. A. 7, 671-688

Peach, C. ed. (1975) Urban Social Segregation, Longman, London

Peach, C., Robinson, V. and Smith S.J. eds. (1981) Ethnic Segregation in Cities, Croom Helm, London

Phillips, D. and Williams, A. (1984) Rural Britain: A Social Geography, Basil Blackwell, Oxford

Pickles, J. (1985) Phenomenology, Science and Geography, Cambridge University Press, Cambridge

Pocock, D.C.D. ed. (1981) Humanistic Geography and Literature, Croom Helm, London

Pred, A. (1967) Behaviour and Location I, C.W.K. Gleerup, Lund.

Pred, A. (1984) Place as historically contingent process: Structuration and the time - geography of becoming places. Annals of the Assoc. American Geographers, 74, 279-297

Rushton, G. (1969) Analysis of spatial behaviour by revealed space preferences. Ann. Assoc. Amer. Geog. 59, 391-400

Sayer, A. (1984) Method in Social Science: A Realist Approach, Hutchinson, London

Shevky, E. and Bell, W. (1955) Social Area Analysis, Stanford University Press, Stanford

Smith, D.M. (1973) The Geography of Social Well-Being in the United States, McGraw Hill, New York

Steinberg, S. (1981) The Ethnic Myth, Beacon Press, Boston

Taeuber, K.E. and Taeuber, A.F. (1965) Negroes in Cities, Aldine Press, Chicago

Taylor, P.J. and Johnston, R.J. (1979) Geography of Elections, Penguin Books, London

Timms, D.W.G. (1971) The Urban Mosaic, Cambridge University Press, Cambridge

Western, J.S. (1981) Outcast Cape Town, George Allen and Unwin, London

White, P.E. (1984) The West European City: A Social Geography, Longman, London

Chapter Two

RESIDENTIAL MOBILITY IN THE PRIVATE HOUSING SECTOR

M. MUNRO

## Introduction

In this chapter recent developments in the study of mobility in the housing market will be examined. The focus of this chapter is on the private sector, with the public sector, which is governed by administered rules and contraints, considered separately in chapter 3. It should be emphasised that there are also constraints on mobility in the private sector, although they are different from those in the public sector. Constraints in the private sector are generally considered to be related to income, either in the affordability of the desired alternative or in the expense of the actual moving process. It has also become clear that there is much potential for other sorts of barriers to be put in the way of those wishing to move within the private sector, for instance discrimination by estate agents or financial institutions. These factors will be considered in more detail later. Mobility in the housing market has been the subject of extensive research effort, as will be demonstrated, and it is useful first to consider why the topic has attracted so much attention.

First, lack of mobility is believed to be associated with a general stagnation or a lack of dynamism in the economy. There are likely to be labour market inefficiencies in a situation where labour cannot move into an area where demand is more buoyant. This concern is apparent even in times of economic recession when it may still be difficult for people to move into more prosperous regions which have greater opportunities for employment (SHAC, 1986). Lack of mobility will decrease welfare for the individuals who are unable to meet their housing needs or fulfil their labour market aspirations.

Second, mobility has been seen as a major determinant of the structure of land uses in cities from early work in the urban sphere. This is demonstrated by the importance of population movements in early explanations of city structure such as the filtering model or the access-space trade-off model (for a review of these models see Bassett and Short, 1980). It is vital to the understanding of the evolution of urban areas over time and the interaction between city structures and the population to know why people move within urban areas and the process by which they achieve a desired move.

Third, residential mobility has been examined as an example of household decision making processes in an imperfect market. Urban housing markets are imperfect and for most households the process of searching for and choosing a house entails many practical difficulties that make moving very stressful. Both the direct costs of the transaction and also the associated cost of the time spent in the moving process are considerable. However, most households manage to surmount these many difficulties from time to time and it has been seen as very important to explain when they do so, in order to understand better the dynamics of the urban system as well as yielding general insight into decision-making processes in a complicated market.

The spatial scale at which mobility patterns are studied determines the issues which can be tackled. In most cases moves take place over relatively short distances so that the most appropriate scale of analysis is at the urban/intra-urban level. The focus of intra-urban work is typically the individual household and there is little consideration of local labour market impacts or impact on the whole urban system. The discussion on this chapter will concentrate mainly on intra-urban moves to reflect its relative importance in the work done so far.

At the inter-regional level the main focus is still on the individual household but there is usually at least a tacit assumption that at this level labour markets play a much more important role in motivating the moves that are undertaken. This level of analysis is important because net mobility may influence the demand for many different types of local service and the ability of the local economy to attract industry or maintain economic activity.

## Residential Mobility in the Private Housing Sector

   At the international level there is yet
another distinct set of issues that can be
addressed. These are the least often explored,
which is understandable in light of the relative
rarity of these moves and the difficulty of
getting data. The issues at this level relate to
the international movement of labour and the
balance of human capital, as represented by such
problems as the 'brain drain' (Salt, 1986). There
are also important questions about the movement of
money between rich and poorer countries through
the actions of migrant workers, which in turn may
have important housing market implications if the
money sent back to the home country is used for
housing investment. These issues are, however,
beyond the scope of this chapter.
   This chapter will first consider briefly the
evidence on the scale and direction of mobility in
the U.K. and the U.S.A. to put what follows into
the context of the overall picture of mobility and
migration behaviour in these countries. This will
be followed by a discussion of aspects of the
recent advances in modelling or explaining
mobility behaviour. This will start with the
basic disequilibrium model and then discuss
subsequent refinements, particularly the use of
discrete choice models, lifecycle variables and
the development of longitudinal views of housing
careers. Attention will then be given to other
aspects of household decision making, including
models of equilibrium decision making,
interactions with labour markets and search
behaviour. The literature on mobility behaviour
is quite vast (see also Cadwallader, 1986 and
Greenwood, 1985) and the review of topics is thus
necessarily fairly brief. The chapter will
conclude with some comments as to where
understanding is still partial and where further
research effort might usefully be directed.


### Recent Evidence on Mobility

It is perhaps somewhat surprising to find that
there is relatively little known about rates of
mobility in Britain. By the very nature of the
topic, data on migration are difficult and
expensive to collect. Regular statistics are
collected by the OPCS using new registrations of
people with general practitioners as they move
between Health Board areas, but these data are
clearly not complete as they may miscount those

33

who move but who do not register with a doctor and will include those who register for the first time without a move. They will only take account of moves between districts and thus miss the large numbers of local moves that commonly occur.

The census of 1981 thus provides the most recent, complete record of moves made within the year prior to the census. A total of 8.74 per cent of the population moved within G.B. with about 54 per cent of these moves being made within the same local authority district. The rate of mobility for 'completely moving' households, i.e. households where all members move, is somewhat less at 6.99 per cent of all households. A broad tenure breakdown of these households which moved shows that 46 per cent of them were owner-occupiers at the census, although they may have been in another tenure before their move, 30 per cent were local authority tenants and 24 per cent were in other tenures, chiefly private renting. This last group were the most over-represented compared to their relative importance in the population as a whole, with owner-occupiers being severely under-represented. Local authority tenants have a roughly equal representation in the population of movers as they do in the population as a whole.

It is important to remember that although the majority of the theoretical work that is discussed in this chapter takes moving as a choice, the estimates of the number of people who have been forced from their previous accommodation, by eviction or disputes within the household for example, have frequently been quite high. Rossi (1955), in his seminal work expressed surprise at having 39 per cent of his sample forced to move from their previous house and this has been confirmed as an important reason for move in much subsequent work (see Short, 1978, Kintrea and Clapham, 1986). There is, therefore, a substantial proportion of mobility that lies outside the usual modelling exercise.

There have been some data presented recently on inter-regional mobility using the Health data described above. Ogilvey (1980) presents data on inter-regional migration for 1971 to 1979 and his analysis of the patterns is also indicative of the changes that have probably occurred since that time. In particular he shows that there was a great reduction in the amount of inter-regional mobility that coincided with the recession that

Residential Mobility in the Private Housing Sector

commenced in 1974. He argues that this reduction
in mobility can be linked to the changes in
unemployment, income and the changes in housing
costs. Scotland, the North West, the West
Midlands, the North, and Yorkshire and Humberside
continued to lose population throughout the
period, but after onset of the recession the loss
accelerated, especially in the West Midlands and
the North West. In fact the major change was seen
in the South East, which was a net loser of
population in the earlier part of the period, but
after 1974 showed a dramatic turnaround and
towards the end of the period began to gain in
population. In this and an earlier paper (1979),
Ogilvey associates the change in migration
patterns with economic change. If his line of
argument is correct then it seems likely that
similar trends will be found in the post 1980
recession. In fact the recent OPCS bulletins
confirm that the reduction in the number of moves
in the early 1980s has reversed in recent years
and that the more depressed regions were net
population losers (OPCS, 1984).
    In the U.S.A. the evidence is more generally
available and the changing pattern of migration
has been the subject of much comment over the last
10-15 years (Beale, 1977, Sternlieb and Hughes,
1977, Greenwood, 1985). In particular the South
has superseded the West as the biggest growth
region, although gains in both regions remain very
high. It should be noted that these regions are,
of course, very large and the patterns described
will certainly conceal a great deal of
sub-regional variation. An interesting strand of
the literature has examined these changes in
relation to different environmental amenities of
the various regions. This idea is probably not
easily transferable to the U.K. as there is not
such a great variety of conditions, life-styles or
climates in different regions. In the U.S. there
has been particular emphasis placed on the impact
of different climatic conditions on the quality of
life in the different regions using variables such
as the average temperature, rainfall, range of
temperature and the average number of days that
fall above or below certain levels (Graves, 1979,
Liu, 1975).

## Residential Mobility in the Private Housing Sector

### The Determinants of the Decision to Migrate

In this section some of the studies of the
determinants of the migration decision will be
reviewed. As was described briefly above, this
problem is non-trivial for many reasons. The
housing market is very imperfect and movers find
accurate information costly and probably difficult
to collect and the expense of the move in time and
direct expenditure is such that more households
only undertake a move relatively infrequently.
The durable nature of housing, the importance of
housing to the welfare of households and the
necessary financial burden of the purchase of the
house make it extremely important to households to
make a carefully considered decision. However,
the complexity of the market and the problems of
getting perfect information mean that the ideal of
perfectly rational decision making is bound to be
hampered in practice.

The models that are described in this section
have been dubbed 'disequilibrium' models because
the desire to alter housing consumption through
moving is seen as a response to dissatisfaction
with current housing circumstance. The strategies
that are generally assumed to be available to the
household consist of the simple dichotomy: to move
or to stay. It should, however, be noted that the
mover/stayer dichotomy does no justice to the
potential complexity of responses to
dissatisfaction with housing circumstances, which
ought to include the possibility of making changes
in situ to the existing house. This might range
in practice from relatively simple changes in
decor to more major internal work or building
extensions.

At the heart of these models is the notion
that households move in response to stress in
their housing situation which results from
disequilibrium between the desired and the actual
consumption of housing. This stress may be due to
a gradual evolution of the household so that its
housing needs become increasingly divorced from
its actual housing circumstances or it may be due
to a sudden change in family circumstances such as
that following bereavement or household splitting.
Many studies try to differentiate the source of
disequilibrium by evaluating the housing
consumption before the move in relation either to
the characteristics of the households or to
preceding changes in these characteristics. The
difference between examining levels and changes in

characteristics may be assumed to approximate the difference between gradual and more sudden increases in dissatisfaction. The measurement and evaluation of consumption disequilibrium has been perhaps the most thoroughly investigated ofthe approaches to the question of why people move. It also forms the starting point for many of the more recent developments and so we discuss this in some detail.

Some writers have attempted to categorise moves depending on the source or 'type' of the disequilibrium in a more detailed way than the two-fold classification sketched above. Clark and Onaka (1985) for instance, characterise moves as 'forced', 'adjustment' and 'induced' moves. They try to give mutually exclusive definitions to these moves so that 'forced moves' are "necessitated by events totally beyond the control of the household" (p.5) "adjustment moves" are "those intended to alter the type and quantity of housing consumption" (p.5) and 'induced moves' are 'associated with multiple or ambiguous housing adjustment necessitated by changes in life cycle or other housing characteristics' (p. 6). Whilst it is clearly possible to think of some events that would cause a move and fall neatly into just one category, it seems that many plausible circumstances surrounding a household's decision to move would straddle two or even all of these categories. Indeed we would argue that such a categorisation is impossible to draw in practice so that all such ambiguity is eliminated. A circumstance described by Clark and Onaka as an induced move - that following a sudden drop in income, could easily be the result of some factor outside the control of the household. The distinction between induced and forced moves may have to depend on whether the household had any choice about whether to move, but this is not precise as there are no commonly accepted criteria for deciding what house is 'too big' or 'too expensive' for any particular household. It is not clear in any case what difference might be expected in outcomes from moves of different origins although it may make a good deal of difference to the process of moving.

Among the earliest contributions to the analysis of residential mobility was that of Wolpert (1965) whose concept of place utility has been widely used in subsequent work. He described the decision to migrate as resulting from an explicit comparison of the place utility of the current location with the expected place utilities from all other potential locations. (It should be noted that most work has taken the range of potential locations to be geographically close, whereas the framework is equally applicable to the migration between regions described above.) When the difference between the actual level of utility and the utility to be gained in the best available alternative surpassed a certain 'stress threshold' he predicted that households would move. Brown and Longbrake (1970) in trying to test this concept empirically took an ecological approach, focusing on small areas and finding aggregate place utility functions for each area. They found that the resulting factors were able to distinguish to some degree between rates of mobility but it is clear that this methodology, which looks at overall movement and takes average utilities, displaces the individual household from the central place that was occupied in Wolpert's theoretical model. It is, however, interesting to note that at this early stage there is explicit consideration of the destination as well as the origin of the household.

The notion that individuals moved as a response to disequilibrium in housing consumption dominated work on mobility behaviour throughout the 1970s. This resulted in a weight of evidence as to which factors would be expected to cause disequilibrium and thus prompt mobility. Evidence also accumulated as to which characteristics of the household or dwelling would be the best predictors of the propensity to move.

Goodman (1976) provides an early example of the type of work that formalised the disequilibrium model of mobility. He used a longitudinal data set, the Panel Study of Income Dynamics which was an annual sample of 5000 households interviewed in 1969, 1970 and 1971. He was able to study over 1200 moves that took place between these dates throughout the U.S.A. Although it is a good data set for this sort of work, he faces the general problem that the available data do not allow the calculation of an exact utility function for each household, so he estimates disequilibrium by comparing the housing circumstance of each household with the expected level of housing consumption derived from the average for households sharing similar characteristics, taking income and family size to be the most important dimensions for housing consumption. Using the average in the whole population as the comparitor clearly relies on disequilibrium in over-consumption and under-consumption in the population at large cancelling each other out to give a true estimate of the equilibrium level. The validity of this assumption is questionable in light of his own finding that households are more likely to adjust their housing consumption upwards than downwards, i.e. over-consumption generally engenders less 'housing stress' than under-consumption. Goodman tests and compares two models: the first estimating the disequilibrium resulting from the initial circumstance of the household and the second looking at changes in household circumstances as the cause of disequilibrium. He argues that this second model is the better specification as he believed that the importance of changes in circumstances had been largely under-estimated in previous work. Empirically, however, the two models show very much the same sorts of factors as important. In his results the dwelling characteristic variables add little explanatory power to the household variables such as age of household head, income, tenure, overcrowding and length of time in the house. He also looks at the importance of lifecycle variables, which we will consider in more detail below.

The effect of these various characteristics on the observed propensity to move is largely as expected. Greater propensity to move is found amongst those who are relatively young, those in the private rented sector, the relatively affluent, those who have stayed a shorter time at their current address or those who are overcrowded. Some changes in characteristics are also commonly associated with moving, for instance marriage. Evidence remains unclear as to the influence of some other household characteristics, for instance household size and composition (Long, 1972, Speare, 1970). Accurate identification of the effect of various characteristics is made difficult by the multi-collinearity that exists between some of the potentially important variables, such as age, household size and composition of the household. This identification problem is central to the attempts to assess the influence of lifecycle stage on household mobility.

In the following sections the major refinements to the basic disequilibrium approach outlined above will be identified and then other important developments in the study of residential mobility will be reviewed. First the treatment of the life-cycle stage will be examined. This leads naturally on to a review of some of the work on housing careers and longitudinal views of behaviour in the housing market. Then some different approaches to the problem will be considered, in particular the equilibrium decision making framework, and models that take the disequilibrium in the housing market and the consequent impacts on the actual process of moving as the central concern. A final important area that will be covered is the interactions between mobility in the housing market and the rest of the economy.

## Housing Careers and the Influence of Life-cycles

Initial interest in the influence of life-cycles apparently stemmed from the observation that mobility rates generally decline as age of household head increases. Explanations for this tended not to be made explicit - assuming that there is some naturally increasing 'cumulative inertia' or increasingly conservative behaviour amongst older individuals, or perhaps speculating on increasing psychological costs for the elderly when they suffer the disruption of moving. However, this implicit assumption was soon challenged on the grounds that not only age per se affects mobility but also the impact of changing family situation and these are changes which do not occur at the same age for all individuals. An obvious example is marriage, which can occur at a wide variety of ages, but which very commonly is found to prompt a move. Speare (1970) was an early advocate of the view that life-cycle would be an important influence in mobility behaviour arguing that a 'normal' life-cycle might be characterised by the following stages:

1.  Younger unmarried, age under 45
2.  Just married, the year of marriage
3.  Young married, childless or no school-age children
4.  Married with school aged children
5.  Older married, eldest child 18+
6.  Older retired couples or single people

Speare tried to identify the effects of age and life-cycle independently and found that they both exert an important and separate influence. The use of this sort of scheme of housing career implies that most people follow a predictable progression through these life-cycle stages, but it should be recognised that not everyone will follow through all the stages, as there is likely to be a great diversity with some people marrying several times and some who never marry or never have children. Speare gathered housing career information through a retrospective questionnaire administered to over 2000 residents of Rhode Island. The analytical techniques in Speare's study were relatively crude as they relied basically on a count of different types of move for different groups within the time period.

Subsequent work in this area has been able to make use of more sophisticated techniques; with logit and probit analysis proving especially appropriate to this work. These techniques take a discrete choice framework so that account can be taken in the modelling process of the fact that generally the options facing individuals are not continuous in all characteristics, so that some decisions are 'all or nothing' such as whether or not to move or which residential area to choose. Goodman (1976) was among the first to demonstrate the usefulness of probit analysis for estimating the dichotomous choice of whether to move or to stay. Using a similar definition of life-cycle stage as Speare he sought to isolate the effects of the life-cycle variables from the other determinant variables. He argued that "The net effect of the age of the head of the house is more than twice as great as that of life-cycle stage." (p. 846). He agreed with Speare that life-cycle did indeed have an independent effect separate from age, but showed that some of the effects were rather counter-intuitive, for example "... the net effect of being young and single on the propensity to move is actually negative." (p. 864)

There remains some disagreement about the relative importance of life-cycle factors. Coupe and Morgan (1981) for instance argue that the concentration on age and life-cycle stage has tended to overstate the importance of these factors compared to others that are equally important and argue that the "... the desire for more space for its own sake or for prestige reasons seems to be far more important than has generally been recognised. Nonetheless, changing space needs associated with family life-cycle changes are the most important single stimulus for intra-urban mobility." (p. 213) Their sample was 300 movers in Northampton who answered a questionnaire between putting their current house on the market and moving. This methodology is likely to minimise any distortion arising from post-justification of a decision or from inaccurate recall.

The natural extension of work that looks at life-cycle as a cross-sectional "stage" is to try to take a longitudinal view of the progress from one life-cycle stage to another. This progression is clearly continuous throughout the life-cycle but the changes in housing circumstances must occur in discrete 'jumps'. Thus, changes in housing circumstances may anticipate or lag behind the changes in household accommodation needs, even if the changing need was long anticipated. This view leads naturally to the concept of a 'housing career' which encompasses changes of both dwelling and tenure throughout an individual's lifetime and relates these to changes in life-cycle, including any formation or dissolution of households.

This rather grand concept has generally been drastically curtailed in empirical work to look only at a small subset of all the decisions over the lifetime. Kendig (1984) for instance, is interested in the progress of households into and out of owner occupation and so concentrates only on the moves which include a change of tenure arguing that "... the most important aspect of a housing career is the ability to attain, retain or regain home ownership." (p. 277). He argues, like Coupe and Morgan (1981) that many moves within the owner-occupied sector are mainly prompted by capital gains motives rather than any change in objective circumstances. He gathers, from 700 movers in Adelaide, information on the longitudinal perspective of moves through a questionnaire that incorporates some retrospective questions about the circumstances surrounding the decision to move. As was mentioned above however, people may not be able to recall accurately events that took place some time in the past, so this is probably not a wholly satisfactory basis for drawing inferences relating to very fine distinctions between different motivations.

An alternative methodology was presented by Payne and Payne (1977) in an attempt to approximate the continuous process of life-cycle change by examining simultaneously three cross-sectional samples at subsequent life-cycle stages. For their study they took samples of about 850 married women in Aberdeen at the birth of the first, the second and the third or subsequent child to assess how housing situation changed over this time. They argued that this stage of the life-cycle represents a crucial point which has a profound influence on the subsequent career and probable outcomes in the housing market. The work by Kendig (1984) above confirmed the sharp polarisation in housing careers between those who became owners and those who always rented could be distinguished by whether the household owned or rented at the birth of the first child. Payne and Payne showed that there was some sort of progress to better housing between the birth of the first and the second child, but this improvement seemed to have stopped by the next birth. Clearly the accuracy of their findings in relation to a housing career relies on the validity of the assumption that there is no difference between the cross-sectional samples except their life-cycle stage. Whilst this may not be completely satisfactory it provides a realistic alternative to a full longitudinal study.

Pickles and Davies (1985) examine points in the life-cycle at which households show an increased risk of moving. They use a competing risk model taken from the biological sciences which assumes that a household in a particular dwelling type is continually exposed to the risk of moving to one of a set of competing alternative dwellings. They are able to derive a likelihood function which describes the conditional probabilities of moving contingent on the length of residence in the previous dwelling, which is maximised using a numerical algorithm. They use the same longitudinal data set as Goodman (1976), although they take moves from the longer time-span of 1968-1977. They also exclude from the analysis inter-regional moves. They are able to identify the points on the age scale at which owners and renters face increased risk of undertaking a move and show that the two tenure groups generally have different probabilities of responding to changes in household circumstances. It is also possible to identify responsiveness to such changes for households of different types, for instance different socio-economic status, income group or educational attainment.

Longitudinal work generally has been hampered by the lack of suitable data especially in the U.K. There is a little more data available in the U.S. not only the panel data used by Goodman (1976) and Pickles and Davies (1985). There is also a data set of the migration histories of a sample of 850 white men, aged between 35 and 39 throughout the U.S.A. collected in 1969 by the National Opinion Research Center which has been used in a longitudinal study by Sandefur and Scott (1981). They examined housing and labour market careers (which were constructed from a retrospective questionnaire) and argued that work careers and life-cycle variables were much more important than age in prompting mobility. Other studies have investigated particular parts of the life-cycle (Sandell, 1977, Graves and Linneman, 1979, Murphy, 1984). An alternative approach was taken by Forrest and Kemeny (1982), who look at a particular tenure, that of renting in the private sector and describe how households might use this sector at various points in a housing career. They argue that in a life-cycle there may be several points at which an individual has recourse to the private rented sector, for instance as a young single household, as a landlord in the early stages of repaying a mortgage and then possibly again as a tenant following household splitting or divorce. These interesting ideas on the potential variety of progress through a housing career were not tested with any empirical evidence and there remains scope for investigating the diversity of housing careers.

The concept of a housing career is crucial if we are trying to assess which households "do best" overall and which points are decisive, if any, in determining the overall experience in the housing market. An obvious example where equity between different housing careers is of great concern relates to the widely different access to capital gains apparently afforded to owners rather than tenants and to some owners more than others (Murie and Forrest, 1980, Karn et al., 1984). In this case the size of total relative gains will not be clear until the very end of the housing career. To address issues like this properly we need to examine the life-cycle as a whole and the rough approximations afforded by the methods discussed above can be no more than suggestive of the wealth of results from such an examination.

44

Residential Mobility in the Private Housing Sector

## The interactions Between Housing and Labour Markets

It will have become clear in the discussion, that when taking such a broad view of life-cycle and housing market career, understanding of residential mobility is hampered by the fact that there is no consideration of labour market career. It is vital to link progress in the two markets because of the central role played by earned income in determining housing chances for most people.

Some of these links have been made from the labour market side of the question. For instance, residential location has long been regarded as important in the study of labour markets, especially when trying to explain the likelihood of different people becoming unemployed. There has been a lengthy debate about whether the unusually high rates of unemployment found in some areas, such as the inner-city, were explained more by the characteristics of the population or whether some areas were discriminated against or conferred disadvantage in the labour market (Metcalf and Richardson, 1980). The solution to this question was seen as being related to differential rates of mobility amongst some groups so that the most employable people were also the most likely to leave a very depressed area (Macgregor, 1979).

Johnson et al. (1974) carried out one of the first pieces of work that looked at the specific interaction between housing and labour migration and demonstrated the significant extent to which behaviour in the two markets is related. They found that a major source of difficulty in making longer distance labour market moves was related to the difficulties of finding acceptable housing. They also showed, perhaps more surprisingly, that only about half of these longer distance moves were primarily because of job factors, with the remainder being because of a wide range of social factors, such as wanting to return to a previous area of residence or wanting to move closer to family and friends as well as the straightforward desire to improve housing situation. That is, they found that nearly as many people were willing to change jobs to reach a desirable housing situation as vice versa.

The continuing debate as to whether housing is helping or hindering the mobility of labour and thus the efficient working of the economy is focusing increasingly on the role of council housing and the administrative procedures for allocation of council housing that may play a part in making mobility more difficult (see Chapter 3). This work is dogged by identification problems in that the populations in the two tenures are quite different and many of the distinguishing socio-economic features suffer from multicollinearity with tenure. Any observed difference in mobility may therefore be as much due to the characteristics of the people, which will also have been influential in determining tenure situation, as due to the actual administrative rules, costs or other constraints surrounding the desire to move. (Hughes and McCormick, 1981, 1985, Palmer and Gleave, 1981).

Household Decision Making
There is a theoretically distinct approach to the question of why people move house that relates to two areas discussed above; the influence of household life-cycles and the role of the labour market. This model was developed by Mincer (1978) from the work on household decision making of Becker (1974). This implicitly looks at why life-cycle stage might be important, by explicitly examining the effects on migration of having more than one person in the household who must participate in the decision to move and be affected by it. Mincer takes the particular case of there being a two person household in which both partners work. In this case a long distance move would have labour market consequences for both partners as well as the usual associated social costs of moving. Mincer assumes that the household utility function takes into equal account the gains and losses of both individuals and investigates the mobility outcomes in cases where there are different gains or losses for the two household members from a move. He shows that in this case, which is likely to be the most common in households with more than one person in work, individuals may not always fulfil their own migration plans but be effectively outweighed by their partners to become tied stayers or movers, acting for the overall gain of the household. Mincer is able to derive some intuitively plausible results using this framework. For instance, if both people in a house are earning a relatively high wage in the current location then it requires a higher offer from another region to

one partner to make a move worthwhile than if only one person of the two were working. The exact relationships depend on the wages that can be expected in the new region for both partners and the wages they are each earning in their present location.

Although Mincer uses this theoretical basis only for the two working adults in a house it would be straightforward to extend this model to include other non-working adults or, indeed, any children in the house. An obvious example of the usefulness of such extension might be in the case where there are older children in a household. The presence of older children in a household sometimes inhibits mobility, which has been explained by the losses suffered in their education if they are moved between schools at important stages of their schooling and also perhaps by their own resistance to a move. This factor is often included in the analysis of life-cycle influences on mobility but it is not explicitly stated as an outcome of the process of decision making or balancing of gains and losses to individuals within the household unit.

Models of Equilibrium Decision Making
A logical extension of considering the household as reacting to the anticipated changes in household circumstances, (such as is described in life-cycle models), is to view the household as a decision taking unit sufficiently rational and well informed to be usually at an equilibrium in consumption. Graves and Linneman (1979) develop a model where moving house is seen as a way of adjusting the consumption of non-traded goods which are associated with the actual location of the house and may include a range of facilities such as access to amenities, climate and neighbourhood quality, racial discrimination or crime rates. Lower wages or higher housing costs in a region may thus be compensated by a better climate and a better lifestyle. In this model external changes such as an adjustment in relative wage rates, will be balanced by households moving between regions in such a way as to maintain an equilibrium in household consumption patterns between traded (i.e, normal consumption goods) and non-traded goods.

It can be seen that this equilibrium model is in marked contrast to the disequilibrium models discussed above (such as those of Goodman, 1976, Speare, 1970 or Coupe and Morgan, 1981) in that they reject the assumption that disequilibrium accumulates or increases as the situation of the household gradually changes. Graves and Linneman, rather, categorise the naturally changing life-cycle as perfectly anticipated and thus leading to planned moves at points of expected disequilibrium in consumption. They argue that apart from these well anticipated occasions, moves occur as the household responds to changes in circumstance that are entirely unanticipated such as a divorce, or as households, demands for goods that cannot be traded between areas change. In equilibrium they assume that the utility enjoyed by identical households in different locations is identical so that those areas in which the value of the non-traded goods is low (for instance if there is a bad climate) will have 'compensating differentials' in the form of lower housing costs or higher wages. They test the model using a probit analysis of the propensity to move using the panel income data also used by Goodman (1976) and Pickles and Davies (1985). They find that the model reacts in the expected way to changes in circumstances so that households move in response to changes in life-cycle variables but also in response to relative changes in income between regions.

The view of the importance of the differences in non-traded goods between areas is supported by a closely related piece of work by Graves (1979) which concentrates specifically on the role of climate. If there is a discrete change in the balance of advantages between areas due to changes in living conditions or relative wages, equilibrium in the economic system will be restored by a process of 'arbitrage' in which not all households sharing similar characteristics move, but just a sufficient number to restore the equilibrium position. He is able to show, relating census data of SMSAs to local climatic variables, how the trade-off between income and climate alters through the life-cycle. Income is the more important determinant of moving for individuals between 25 and 35 years of age, then the effect of climate becomes gradually more important in each age cohort until it clearly dominates income for the retired groups. Despite the 'rational expectations' type of framework that they develop, these authors argue that there are problems in viewing the mobility process only as a response to discrete changes in conditions because of the imperfections in the housing market. They argue that these imperfections will make it very difficult for households to act as perfectly informed and perfectly rational agents.


## Incorporating Search into Mobility

This last point, relates to an argument expressed earlier about the nature of the housing market. The housing market is unlikely to move quickly to an equilibrium price due to the difficulties of making decisions within the housing market, but these complexities are not addressed in models reviewed so far. For the most part the very real problems in the actual process of moving are ignored, although for most people it is extremely stressful and difficult. There is a separate literature that looks specifically at the uncertainties and complex choices that are involved in moving, but it is poorly integrated with other modelling approaches. We feel that an understanding of the process of moving has an extremely valuable contribution to make to overall understanding of residential mobility and we turn now to a review of some of the issues raised by this work. There has been a great growth in the literature that looks at the process of housing search (see Clark and Flowerdew, 1982 for a review). The basic model comes from a framework that was developed in economics and modelled consumer behaviour under uncertainty in what became known as 'shopping problems'. These microeconomic models of search can be fairly directly applied to the discussion of housing markets as a particular variant of the problem of a shopper looking for a good buy. However, the basic model has spawned a wide variety of applications by writers from a range of disciplines, that range from the extremely abstract to readily comprehensible studies of observed phenomena.

The starting point for these models is to model the behaviour of a consumer who is searching for some specific commodity, for which there is a variety of price and qualities on offer and for which search is costly. The cost of search is generally supposed to be very high in the housing market as this offers an explanation as to why search for a new house is frequently so short (Clark and Flowerdew, 1982). By making assumptions about the parameters of the decision making process, usually assuming the maximisation of expected utility, it is possible to derive rules which describe when the consumer will stop searching and accept one of the offers that has been made (Hey, 1979, 1981). Flowerdew (1976) presented a straightforward application of these models to the housing market and derived stopping rules for this circumstance. The consumer should stop searching when the first option which gives utility level greater than some critical value is encountered. This critical 'reservation' value depends on the parameters of the distribution of offers, the cost of search and the shape of the expected utility function.

Hey and MacKenna (1979) develop an interesting extension of this idea to long distance moves. They consider the case where the search for a new job is relatively costless, as is the case for professionals who find jobs advertised in the quality press, but for whom the actual process of moving is costly and disruptive, although some of the direct cost may be reimbursed by the new employer. They show some very interesting results that have parallels in observed behaviour. Generally people require a wage offer in a new region which has a present value considerably greater than that of their current wage plus the actual cost of moving to induce a move, but this gap between the cost of moving and the extra wage required is shown to decline as income increases. This implies that lower income people need a greater inducement to move than do high income individuals. This result accords with the findings of Johnson et al. (1974) for instance, that the lower paid are generally less likely to move than the higher paid. Of course, this does not prove that the reason for lower mobility amongst the lower paid is indeed caused by the process described by Hey and MacKenna, as there may be many other factors that influence the likelihood of someone moving long distance for a job, such as the relative expense of the move or the rewards in terms of increased job satisfaction. However, it does suggest a new line of enquiry.

This type of modelling is rather abstract and is generally hard to test explicitly except in a laboratory situation. Although it is sometimes possible to say whether the predictions are in line with the observed behaviour, as in the example above, it is impossible to be sure that the model has isolated the cause of the observed behaviour. Smith and Clark (1982a,b) set up an experimental situation to test an expected utility maximising model by using volunteers' valuations of particular pictures of houses to estimate their own utility functions. They then relate this estimated utility function to the individual's observed search behaviour. Even in this tightly controlled situation they could not test the full model (described in Smith et al., 1979) because of the complexity of the estimation required and so tested a simplified version. They could even then only test the simplest of the implications of the model. For instance, they wanted to see if stress was non-negative at the beginning of search, but although there was a dominance of positive values even this simple proposition could not be entirely supported. The results were, perhaps, rather disappointing in light of the careful following of the samples and the extensive testing in the laboratory.

The experimental method did reveal other findings of interest, however, for instance they showed that a considerable number of people who started looking for a new house were discouraged in some way during the initial search so that they did not ultimately buy a house. This might imply that hierarchical search models may be appropriate to distinguish between the preliminary stage of looking for a house, in which a general assessment of whether the household should move at all is made and the later stage when the household begins to assess the value of particular vacancies. This two stage process would allow for people dropping out at the end of the first stage and would be in accord with some observed patterns of use of information sources, where newspapers and 'driving around' are used in the early stages with more use of formal agencies being observed in later stages (Courant, 1978). This pattern is not always observed, however, and a review of the literature on the use of information sources by Clark and Smith (1979) concluded that there was no commonly observed pattern of use of different information channels or the sequencing of use.

The examination of sources of information has become a valuable part of explanations of outcomes of search in the housing market for different groups. Wood and Maclennan (1982) show that student renters in Glasgow generally did better in their search for a house when they were returning to the privately rented market in their second or subsequent year's study, when they were more able to make use of informal sources of information than students entering the privately rented market for the first time. Courant was also able to show differences in the use of information sources by ethnic minorities (Courant, 1978) and others have shown differences in the use of information by different income groups (Brown and Holmes, 1971). It could be seen in these cases that the information gathered had a profound impact on the eventual residential location of individuals.

The 'shopper's problem' in the housing market is modified by the existence of agencies, such as estate agents, who are able to provide information about vacancies. The range of options available to people may also be constrained by the rules of building societies, who not only restrict the amount of money they will lend to different groups of people, but may also refuse to lend on particular types of properties or in particular areas (Boddy, 1980). The examination of the role of agents in the housing market in guiding and influencing residential mobility, by manipulating information in advertisements and by encouraging people to look at certain properties, has been the focus of much research. In particular this has examined the explicit and implicit discrimination that may be operating against minority racial groups when they are looking for a dwelling (Courant, 1978, Cronin, 1982, Smith and Mertz, 1980). It is generally seen that estate agents can exert a significant influence on the outcomes of search by steering prospective customers towards areas that they know well themselves. This may also act to maintain segregation where estate agents generally steer black customers towards areas where there is already a significant black community, rather than face opposition by trying to introduce blacks into predominantly white neighbourhoods (Palm, 1982).

These models are generally aspatial, in that desired location may act as one of many dimensions of desirable housing quality and may even feature as an important independent factor in household choices, but the actual physical configuration of space is assumed to have no direct influence on search behaviour or preferences. In the discussions of discrimination described above for instance, it was not necessary to the argument to know anything about the exact location or size of segregated minority areas or their geographical relationship to one another or the white areas.

Huff (1982) provides an exception, as in his model the actual space over which search is carried out is central to his modelling exercise. He simulates spatial patterns of search basing his assumptions of the decision making process of individuals on the 'elimination by aspects' theory of Tversky (1972). This basically says that people choose among a large number of items by ranking the attributes that they want by importance to them and then progressively eliminating all options that do not have the most important features. In this model the household cannot be compensated for the absence of some important features by 'extra' amounts of other features. Huff generates search models that are basically a first order Markov chain.

Huff's model reinstates spatial dimensions in the search process and thus to the outcomes in the urban area. The importance of space accords well with much geographical evidence about the well defined patterns of search and the common paths taken (Forbes et al., 1979). It is also supported by the fact that most people have already existing knowledge of the places in which they would like to live before they undertake search for a house (Munro and Lamont, 1985). However, Huff's model remains a theoretical exercise that is not corroborated by any empirical work and there remains more scope for spatial modelling of this kind. Work also remains to be done to connect the spatial patterns of search with preferences for and perceptions of neighbourhoods. The evolution and strength of preferences for different neighbourhoods is certainly an important element in the mobility process, as previous work has shown that people generally have very clear perceptions, or 'mental maps' of the character and extent of different neighbourhoods in cities (Hourihan, 1976a,b, Pacione, 1983, Cadwallader, 1986).

Clark and Onaka (1985) evaluate the importance of neighbourhoods in structuring choice by using a discrete choice framework in which the objects of choice are different housing types and different neighbourhood qualities. They estimated multinomial logit models for each case and found that neighbourhood characteristics were important in the choices of most households, although not generally as important as dwelling type. They used

53

a large data set derived from the Housing Assistance Supply Experiment, testing their model on the subsample of households who were voluntary movers, who moved entirely within the rented sector and who undertook only local moves. They note that their sample of about 300 similar households was just adequate for testing the model, as in allowing discrete choices account has to be taken of the many different combinations of origin and destination. So, although this approach provides an intuitively appealing description of the way that choices are made in the housing market, very substantial data sets are required to make use of these models.

## Summary

This chapter has briefly reviewed some of the major developments in the literature on residential mobility. There is clear agreement among the majority of authors in this field as to the factors that are important in the decision to move, although there is still disagreement as to the relative importance of some of these factors. At the individual level there is a whole range of personal factors such as earnings, employment status, education and age that all have an impact. There is some discussion as to the extent to which the actual levels rather than changes in these levels are the more important determinants of migration. Also of importance, and apparently acting independently, are the influences from the life-cycle stage, such as marriage, the birth of children, or divorce. Extensions of this work have started to take a more holistic view of housing careers, where mobility is the most important adjustment to continuing change in the household's needs and aspirations. This potentially profitable line of enquiry remains relatively under-researched although many of the difficulties are due to the problem of finding adequate data for this purpose.

There has been less consideration of the labour market status of the individual, except as an impact on the personal characteristics of the individual such as income or socio-economic group. It would seem that there is clearly scope for trying to incorporate into the analysis of residential mobility, more explicitly, the relevant labour market characteristics that affect the speed or ease with which an individual may be able to get a job in another region, (which of course is likely to be a pre-condition to the sort of move described by Graves and Linneman (1979)). Labour market factors may not only act as a constraint to residential mobility but may also be the chief reason in prompting mobility. The inclusion of labour market variables into mobility models would need to take account of the particular skills of the individual and the extent of accumulated skills in the job as well as prospects for career progression through mobility.

Another important advance has been made in the incorporation of the process of search into the models. This has allowed a much greater exploration of the difficulties involved in the actual process of moving. Clearly it is necessary to understand the process if we are ever to understand or predict the outcomes of the migration decisions within a city or between regions.

The major lack of understanding that remains, centres on the outcomes that result from the individual decisions and the process of search and this represents the final area that we feel deserves much more attention. As has been described, mobility is generally seen as being an individual problem and of concern to the individual household. This contrasts quite sharply with the broader issues that were raised at the beginning of this chapter, where much of the concern with mobility was justified in relation to the adjustment of the wider system to changing aspirations, job opportunities, or general changes in the local or national economic climate. The models that we have discussed do very little to shed light on issues at the urban or regional scale of analysis.

Mobility is now being looked at in abstract from the overall changes in the structure of the city. Questions that were central to early analysis of the urban system, such as whether the relationship of housing types to the characteristics of their residents could be explained through mobility in a 'filtering' process, have received very little attention. However, study of mobility at the urban system scale would provide insight into the processes and movement that now surround many important policy issues in our cities, such as the impacts of decline and of any subsequent renovation in our

55

inner cities. It is clearly very important in evaluating the success of many of the policy initiatives in the housing field to know whether improved environments are enjoyed by the original residents, or whether they are replaced by higher income 'gentrifiers' for instance. A similar question should be addressed with relation to the new buyers of low-cost home-ownership initiatives. It is important to know not only about the buyers themselves, but also about the changes that the availability of the low cost houses has made to the demand for other areas and other types of houses. Similar questions should be addressed from the decline of the public sector housing stock in many places, and the sale of council houses encouraged under the right to buy.

Why people move and where they move to, remain important elements in assessing policies in the urban system and in identifying causes of inter-regional change. The concentration of much recent work on the determinants of individual behaviour, has tended to lose sight of the more policy oriented questions. It is perhaps this direction that offers the greatest scope for future work.

Acknowledgement:
The author wishes to thank Keith Kintrea of the Centre for Housing Research at Glasgow University for helpful comments on an earlier draft of this paper.

Residential Mobility in the Private Housing Sector

REFERENCES
Bassett, K.A. and J.R. Short (1980) Housing and
    Residential Structure London: Routledge and
    Kegan Paul
Beale, C. L. (1977) 'The recent shift of United
    States population to non-metropolitan areas,
    1970-75', International Regional Science Review
    2, 113-122
Becker, G.S. (1974) A Theory of Marriage in The
    Economics of the Family: Marriage, Children
    and Human Capital, ed. T. Schultz: Univ.
    Chicago Press, pp 299-344
Boddy, M.J. (1980) The Building Societies London:
    Macmillan
Brown, L. and J. Holmes (1971) 'Search behaviour
    in an intra-urban migration context' Environ-
    ment & Planning A 3, 307-326
Brown, L.A. and D.B. Longbrake (1970) 'Migration
    flows in intra-urban space: Place utility
    considerations' Annals of the Association of
    American Geographers 60, 368-384
Cadwallader, M. (1986) 'Migration and intra-urban
    mobility' in M. Pacione (ed) Population
    Geography: Progress and Prospect London: Croom
    Helm, pp 257-283
Clark, W.A.V. and R. Flowerdew (1982) 'A Review of
    Search Models and their Application to Search
    in the Housing Market' in W.A.V. Clark (ed)
    Modelling Housing Market Search London: Croom
    Helm, pp 4-29
Clark, W.A.V. and J.L. Onaka (1985) 'An empirical
    test of a joint model of residential mobility
    and housing choice', Environment and Planning
    A 17, 915-930
Clark, W.A.V. and T.R. Smith (1979) 'Modelling
    information use in a spatial context' Annals
    of the Association of American Geographers 69,
    575-588
Courant, P.N. (1978) 'Racial Prejudice in a search
    model of the urban housing market' Journal of
    Urban Economics 5, 329-345
Coupe, R. T. and B. S. Morgan (1981) 'Towards a
    fuller understanding of residential mobility:
    a case study of Northampton England',
    Environment and Planning A 13, 201-215
Cronin, F.J. (1982) 'Racial Differences in the
    Search for Housing' in Clark, W.A.V. (ed)
    Modelling Housing Market Search London: Croom
    Helm, 81-105
Forbes, J., D. Lamont and I. Robertson (1978)
    Intra-urban Migration in Greater Glasgow
    Scottish Office: Edinburgh

Forrest, R. and J. Kemeny (1983) 'Middle-class housing careers: The relationship between furnished renting and home ownership' Sociological Review 30, 208-222

Flowerdew, R. (1976) 'Search strategies and stopping rules in residential mobility' Transactions of the Institute of British Geographers N.S. 1, 47-57

Goodman, J.L. (1976) 'Housing consumption disequilibrium and local residential mobility' Environment & Planning A 8, 855-874

Graves, P.E. (1979) 'A life-cycle analysis of migration and climate by race', Journal of Urban Economics 6, 135-147

Graves, P.E. and P.D. Linneman (1979) 'Household migration: theoretical and empirical results', Journal of Urban Economics 6, 397-433

Greenwood, M.J. (1985) 'Human migration: Theory models and empirical studies', Journal of Regional Science 25, 521-544

Hey, J.D. (1979) Uncertainty in Microeconomics Martin Robertson: Oxford

Hey, J.D. (1981) Economics in Disequilibrium Martin Robertson; London

Hey, J.D. and C. McKenna (1979) 'To move or not to move?', Economica 46, 175-185

Hourihan, K. (1979a) 'The evaluation of urban neighbourhoods 1: perception', Environment and Planning A pp 1337-1353

Hourihan, K. (1976b) 'The evaluation of urban neighbourhoods 2: preference' Environment and Planning A 11, 1355-1366

Huff, J.O. (1982) 'Spatial aspects of residential search' W.A.V. Clark ed. in Modelling Housing Market Search London: Croom Helm, pp 106-133

Hughes, G. and B. McCormick (1981) 'Do council house policies reduce migration between regions?' Economic Journal 91, 919-937

Hughes, G.A. and B. McCormick (1985) Migration intentions in the UK. Which households want to migrate and which succeed? Supplement to the Economic Journal Vol. 95, pp 113-123 Conference papers

Johnson, J.H., J. Salt and P.A. Wood (1974) Housing and the Migration of Labour in England and Wales, Farnborough, Saxon House

Karn, V., J. Kemeny and P. Williams (1985) Home Ownership in the Inner City Aldershot: Gower

Kendig, H.L. (1984) 'Housing Careers, life cycle and residential mobility; Implications for the Housing Market' Urban Studies 21, 271-283

Residential Mobility in the Private Housing Sector

Residential Mobility in the Private Housing Sector

Kintrea, K. and Clapham, D. (1986) 'Housing choice and search strategies within an administered housing system' Environment and Planning A 18, forthcoming

Liu, B-C. (1975) 'Differential net migration rates and the quality of life' Review of Economics and Statistics 52, 329-337

Long, L. (1972) 'The Influence of Number and Ages of Children on Residential Mobility' Demography 9, 371-382

McGregor, A. (1979) 'Area Externalities and Urban Unemployment' in C. Jones (ed.) Urban Deprivation and the Inner City London: Croom Helm, pp 92-111

Metcalf, D. and R. Richardson (1980) 'Unemployment in London' in Evans, A. and D. Eversley (eds.) The Inner City London: Heinemann

Mincer, J. (1978) 'Family migration decisions', Journal of Political Economy 86, 749-773

Munro, M. and D. Lamont (1985) 'Neighbourhood perception, preference and household mobility in the Glasgow private housing market' Environment and Planning A 17, 1331-1350

Murie, A. and Forrest, R. (1980) 'Wealth, Inheritance and Housing Policy', Policy & Politics 8, 1-19

Murphy, M.J. (1984) 'The influence of fertility, early housing career and socio economic factors on tenure determination in contemporary Britain' Environment and Planning A 16, 1301-1318

Ogilvey, A.A. (1979) 'Migration - the influence of economic change' Futures 11, 383-394

Ogilvey, A.A. (1980) 'Population migration between the regions of Great Britain, 1971-9' Regional Studies 16, 65-73

OPCS (1984) 'Bulletin on Migration' various issues

Pacione, M. (1983) 'Neighbourhood communities in the modern city: some evidence from Glasgow' Scottish Geographical Magazine 99, 169-181

Palm, R. (1982) 'Homebuyer Response to Information Content' in Clark, W.A.V. (ed) Modelling Housing Market Search London: Croom Helm, pp 187-208

Palmer, D. and D. Gleave (1981) 'Employment, housing and mobility in London' London Journal 7, 177-193

Payne, J. and G. Payne (1977) 'Housing pathways and Stratification: a study of life chances in the housing market' Journal of Social Policy 6, 129-156

Pickles, A. and R. Davies (1985) 'The longitudinal analysis of housing careers' Journal of Regional Science 25, 85-101

Quigley, J.M. (1976) 'Housing demand in the short run: An analysis of Polytomous choice' Explorations in Economic Research 3, 76-102

Rossi, P.H. (1955) Why families move: a study in the social psychology of residential mobility Glencoe: Free Press

SHAC (1986) A Job to Move SHAC; London

Salt, J. (1986) 'International Migration: a spatial theoretical approach' in M. Pacione (ed) Population Geography: Progress and Prospect London: Croom Helm, pp 164-193

Sandefur, G.D. and W.J. Scott (1981) 'A dynamic analysis of migration: An assessment of the effects of age, family and career variables' Demography 18, 355-368

Sandell, S.H., 'Women and the economics of family migration' Review of Economics and Statistics 59, 173-178

Short, J. R. (1978) 'Residential Mobility' Progress in Human Geography 2, 419-448

Smith, T.R. and W.A.V. Clark (1982a) 'Housing market search behaviour and expected utility theory: 1. Measuring preferences for housing' Environment and Planning A 14, 681-698

Smith, T.R. and W.A.V. Clark (1982b) 'Housing market search behaviour and expected utility theory: 2. The process of search' Environment and Planning A 14, 717-737

Smith, T.R., W.A.V. Clark, J.O. Huff and P. Shapiro (1979) 'A decision-making and search model for intra-urban migration' Geographical Analysis 11, 1-22

Smith, T.R. and F. Mertz (1980) 'An analysis of the effects of information revision on the outcome of housing market search, with special reference to the influence of realty agents' Environment and Planning A 12, 155-174

Speare, A. (1970) 'Home ownership, Life-cycle stage and residential mobility' Demography 7, 449-58

Sternlier, G. and J.W. Hughes (1977) 'New regional and metropolitan realties of America' Journal of the American Institute of Planners 43, 227-241

Tversky, A. (1972) 'Elimination by aspects: A theory of choice' Psychological Review 79, 281-299

Wolpert, J. (1965) 'Behavioural aspects of the

decision to migrate' Papers of the Regional
Science Association 15, 159-169

Wood, G.A. and D. Maclennan (1982) 'Search adjust-
ments in local housing markets' in Clark,
W.A.V. (ed) Modelling Housing Market Search,
Croom Helm, pp 54-80

Chapter Three

ACCESS TO PUBLIC SECTOR HOUSING

J. ENGLISH

In Britain there are two main housing tenures, the
public sector and owner occupation, and two
fundamentally different ways in which individuals
and families gain access to accommodation. Public
sector rents are set administratively, at a level
which in the past has generally been no more than
sufficient, together with subsidies, to cover
costs. The fact that rents for most public
housing, leaving aside some difficult-to-let
accommodation, are below market clearing levels
means that demand tends to exceed supply. Thus
public landlords, for the most part local
authorities, have developed a plethora of
rationing devices to determine priorities as
between applicants. These allocation procedures,
and particularly their effects on the housing
opportunities of different groups, are the subject
of this chapter. Access to owner-occupied housing
by contrast, although it raises important issues
about, for example, the policies of mortgage
lending institutions, is essentially a matter of
ability to pay market prices which equilibrate
supply and demand. It should be added that
housing associations are also part of the public
sector, and their accommodation is allocated
administratively rather than by price, but
unfortunately little research has yet been done on
how they approach this task.
    Public sector allocation procedures are not,
however, only concerned with access to any council
house; increasingly their function is also to
determine who obtains particular dwellings which
are of widely differing standards. This
distinction has been usefully encapsulated in the
concepts of 'primary' and 'secondary' allocation
(or rationing) (Henderson and Karn, 1986), and the

main concern of this chapter, like that of most recent research, is on the latter aspect of the process, on who gets what. Access to public sector housing has always been determined on the basis of a somewhat uneasy combination of needs and deserts; although the former have tended to be more openly acknowledged, the latter remain important but increasingly at the secondary stage. What constitutes housing need beyond very general propositions is not unproblematic or merely a matter of common sense. The main emphasis in the present discussion, however, is not on concepts of need per se but on the relationship between needs and deserts, and between formal rules and informal practices, chiefly in secondary allocation.

Both the methods and criteria for determining priority adopted in housing allocation are very largely at the discretion of individual local authorities. The legal framework is, with limited exceptions, very loose and is in any case wholly confined to primary allocation. Until fairly recently the only provisions were generalised and exhortatory requirements in the principal Housing Acts (now the 1985 act in England and Wales and the 1966 act in Scotland) to give a 'reasonable preference' in the selection of tenants to groups such as the overcrowded, large families and those living under 'unsatisfactory conditions'. The Land Compensation Act, 1973 introduced a general requirement to rehouse where dwellings are demolished through official action. The Housing (Homeless Persons) Act, 1977 laid down a relatively clear-cut duty to provide for certain categories of the homeless, and in some areas such households constitute a substantial proportion of total allocations. Then the Tenants' Rights, Etc. (Scotland) Act 1980 made residential qualifications and age-bars for registration on waiting lists generally illegal north of the border. Nevertheless, local authorities still possess a high degree of autonomy in allocation, each system is in one way or another unique, and research on the topic is necessarily dependent on a case study approach.

PRIMARY ALLOCATION PROCEDURES

The distinction between primary and secondary allocation is in the final analysis conceptual rather

than administrative, although to some extent it is
reflected in separate procedures. Some aspects of
the allocation process are unambiguously a matter
of primary or secondary allocation respectively.
Rules about who is entitled even to be considered
and to have their priority assessed by registering
on a waiting list are clearly entirely a matter of
primary allocation. Such rules about eligibility
may relate to residence or employment in an area,
age, marital status and existing tenure. But the
subsequent stage of primary allocation,
determining priority between applicants on the
waiting list for access to council housing, is
often inseparable in administrative terms from
decisions about which particular vacant dwelling
should be allocated that is from secondary
allocation (Henderson and Karn, 1986). Only in
some local authorities, and probably increasingly
rarely with the growth of modern 'points' schemes,
are decisions that an applicant should be housed
at a particular time and what offer should be made
discrete even in principle. Indeed, in many areas
the notion that applicants come to the top of a
single waiting list (albeit sub-divided by
dwelling size) is now essentially meaningless; in
practice they are on one or more separate lists
which relate to particular estates or types of
dwelling. There are, however, certain procedures
or informal practices which are largely or wholly
confined to secondary allocation and are concerned
with matching an applicant with an 'appropriate'
vacant dwelling. One thinks of the 'grading' of
applicants according to housekeeping standards or
assumptions by staff about what are suitable
offers for particular households. But even here
the distinction between primary and secondary
allocation may not be complete if decisions about
what constitutes an appropriate offer may, other
things being equal, accelerate or delay access to
the public sector. Finally, there are transfers
within the public sector; in a sense these involve
only secondary allocation as transfer applicants
have already gained access to the sector, although
it is perhaps more useful to see them as passing
through a primary stage which may lay down
requirements for consideration (such as length of
residence in an existing house). At the secondary
stage transfer applicants are often considered
separately from the waiting list, but there is an
increasing tendency to deal with transfers within
a single scheme for determining priority.

## Access to Public Sector Housing

Before discussing the main topic of secondary allocation it is useful to touch on primary allocation systems in so far as a distinction may be made. During the inter-war period, in the early years of council housing on a significant scale, there does not appear to have been much need for elaborate rationing mechanisms. In the 1920s rents (with no rebates) were relatively high relative to working class wages and seem to have come near to equilibrating supply and demand. Deserts, in the sense of 'respectability' or local residence, are also likely to have been of some importance. Then in the 1930s new council accommodation was largely restricted to slum clearance rehousing and the relief of overcrowding. But after 1945 a combination of high rates of household formation, shortages resulting from the wartime cessation of building and bomb damage, and higher wages unleashed a flood of demand on local authorities. Approaches to allocation which were developed at that time – though no doubt often relying a good deal on existing practices – virtually always took into account length of residence in an area ('residential qualifications'), time on the waiting list and severity of need. It is hardly surprising that, in a world of fragmented departmental responsibility for housing at the local level, a low level of professionalism among even senior staff, and perfunctory support and guidance from central government, allocation schemes were almost infinitely varied and generally unsophisticated. But schemes, essentially dealing only with primary allocation, have almost always been formalised and published; some smaller authorities, however, adopted (and a few still use) 'merit' schemes where councillors make allocations within more or less vague guidelines, and there were at least a handful of councils which refused to make their schemes public on the grounds that this would encourage 'abuse', presumably through people 'working the system'.

In the 1940s, 50s and 60s allocation policies and procedures were discussed to some extent in the publications of the then Institute of Housing and Society of Housing Managers and in reports from the housing management sub-committee of the Central Housing Advisory Committee (see, for example, CHAC, 1949, 1953, 1955, 1969), but the concern was practically entirely with primary allocation. Apart from a few allusions to 'difficult tenants', 'grading' and 'suitable' accommodation, the issue was seen as who should have priority for a palpably inadequate supply of council housing. A relatively small council stock and high rate of building meant that available lets were dominated by new units. More or less any dwelling was lettable and difficult-to-let areas were virtually unknown. Among contemporary concerns was the view that councils tended to give undue weight to residential qualifications (either for registration on the waiting list or before an allocation could be made) which led to a failure to take proper account of housing need or to assist labour mobility. Some attention was also given to allocation procedures, where formalised schemes to determine priorities, possibly using 'points', were advocated on grounds of efficient administration and visible fairness. Even as late as 1969 the Cullingworth Committee (CHAC, 1969), which was concerned with the allocation of council housing, dealt almost entirely with primary allocation. Issues of who gets what within a varied public sector stock received little or no attention except for a short discussion of 'grading' and the 'suitability' of applicants.

More recently, however, the focus of attention of those who are concerned with access to council housing has changed dramatically. Above all, this shift was linked with the emergence into prominence during the 1970s of difficult-to-let housing or, more euphemistically, 'less desired' property. It would be unrealistic to suppose that a hierarchy of popularity or acceptability has not existed since the early days of council housing (see, for example, Tucker, 1966; Damer, 1974) and that some estates did not generate severe management problems, but the situation was largely hidden while it was possible without much difficulty to find applicants who were willing to accept, even if reluctantly, any empty house. But the arrival on the scene of council housing which could no longer be readily let, or in extreme cases let at all, brought out into the open the reality that the public sector is extremely heterogeneous, and includes property ranging from the very good to the appalling. And increasingly the question of who gets the better and who gets the worse housing has been asked.

It would, of course, be an overstatement to claim that primary allocation has become unimportant (particularly from point of view of the problems faced by the homeless), but there is at least a grain of truth in this view: in many local authority areas difficult-to-let housing, which is more or less readily available to applicants, co-exists with lengthy waiting (and transfer) lists for more desirable areas. Secondary allocation - the quality of accommodation which is allocated rather than whether any at all is available - is now, it can be argued, the more significant aspect of the housing allocation process.

## SECONDARY ALLOCATION PROCEDURES

The essence of secondary allocation is the decision as to which of a number of dwellings, all of which are in principle appropriate to the (officially-recognised) requirements of an applicant, should be allocated in a particular case. One could say allocated to applicants who have reached the point on the housing register at which allocations are made - have passed through the primary allocation filter - although under many systems there is no single list but rather a large number of separate lists formed on the basis of preferences. In other words, as was pointed out above, primary and secondary allocation are often not discrete processes in administrative terms.

Only a proportion of dwellings which become available for letting could, of course, conceivably be regarded as suitable for a particular applicant. Perhaps the most obvious criterion is appropriate size (particularly in terms of the number of bedrooms) in relation to household composition: local authorities rarely make an allocation which would result in the overcrowding of a dwelling according to their own criteria (which generally approximate to the OPCS bedroom standard), and are unwilling to create substantial under-occupation unless this is unavoidable to overcome a shortage of smaller units. Location is another criterion, though the weight placed on it varies a good deal depending on the geographical size of a local authority and policy on meeting preferences. Whereas before local government reorganisation in the 1970s it may have been realistic for a small urban authority to take the view that, as far as travel to work or nearness to relatives were concerned, any location was satisfactory, such a policy could scarcely be applied today by any council. Then in a limited proportion of cases the particular characteristics of the applicant or dwelling narrow the field of suitability. Applicants with certain health problems for example, may require to be allocated ground floor accommodation whilst, conversely, ground floor units might if they are in short supply be reserved for such applicants. Considerations of this kind apply a fortiori to sheltered and amenity housing.

But when all the officially recognised criteria for appropriate allocations have been taken into account, more than one allocation of a particular vacancy is likely to be possible - in urban areas with large public sector stocks perhaps many possible allocations. This is the dilemma of secondary allocation: how to decide who gets what when criteria of need for a particular dwelling provide no real guidance. In simple terms, there might be two similarly sized dwellings available for letting, one a house with a garden in a pleasant and sought-after area and the other a flat in a run-down block, and two applicant households. Unless there are special reasons why one of the households actually prefers the flat, it can be expected that both applicants would like to be allocated the house, although there is no basis for saying that one 'needs' it more than the other. The problem for the local authority is to decide how the allocations should be made. In practice a whole range of other factors are likely to come into play which are at the core of secondary allocation (Henderson and Karn, 1986). Some of these are matters of institutional policy or informal practice (for example grading or officer discretion), and some relate to the housing and other circumstances of applicants (which affect the urgency of their need and therefore their ability to express preferences, reject offers and to wait). As far as the institutional aspects are concerned, secondary allocation is often far more a matter of informal practice than formalised official policies.

In other words, local authorities have to find ways of coping with a situation of differential demand for council housing: it virtually always seems to be the case that at the extremes some areas and types of dwelling are very popular and

some are difficult to let. Given the existence
of, on the one hand, great variations in standards
of accommodation and environment within the
public sector and, on the other, a relatively
flat structure of rents together with means-tested
assistance for those with low incomes, there is
obviously little incentive for households
voluntarily to choose anything but the best.
There are all kinds of factors which make some
council accommodation less desirable and possibly
difficult to let: that it is in the form of flats
(rather than houses with gardens) especially if
located in large blocks, poor insulation and
expensive heating systems resulting in dampness, a
run-down environment, location away from amenities
or employment opportunities, the poor reputation
of an area and so on.

Finding out how primary allocation operates is
difficult enough: since the 1980 Housing Act and
the Scottish Tenants' Rights Act local authorities
have been obliged to publish their allocation
schemes, but it is still necessary to obtain these
individually and then to analyse not always very
comprehensible documentation. Research into
secondary allocation, however, is much more
difficult as little is published or, indeed,
perhaps even known by the local authority itself.
The results of secondary allocation, in terms of
the characteristics of households which live in
different council estates, have been known at the
level of common observation for long enough.
House administrators, social workers, doctors and
other professionals, as well as in a rough and
ready way the general public, have been aware of
the existence of 'difficult estates' with
concentrations of 'problem families' since the
Second World War if not before. Indeed, something
of a literature on this subject has built up,
which is reviewed by Reynolds (1986). Leaving
aside some isolated local studies, however, the
extent of spatial socio-economic variations within
public sector housing was not coherently
documented until special analyses of small area
statistics from the 1971 Census became available
(see, for example, Twine and Williams, 1983),
exercises which have since been repeated with the
1981 Census. This work, together with the
approximately contemporary emergence of the
problem of difficult-to-let estates, provided a
major impetus to the interest of policy makers and
academics in secondary allocation: they wished to

know how allocation processes operated to create
the socio-economic differentiation of council
estates. The policy interest was not only that
concentrations of poorer households might be
thought undesirable per se, in terms, for
example, of the difficulties generated for schools
and social services and perhaps delinquent
sub-cultures; there was also a remarkable
coincidence between such concentration and the
characteristics and popularity of the housing
itself.

While poorer households are found often to be
concentrated in poorer quality housing, segregation
is far from complete. Substantial numbers of the
relatively deprived live in better quality council
housing, though it is rarer for more affluent
households to be found in the least popular
estates. In other words, administered allocation
procedures for public housing to some extent do
break down the nexus between socio-economic status
and standard of accommodation. The interesting
question is why, being ostensibly needs based,
they fail to do so more completely.

A limitation of census data is the lack of any
direct information on incomes; nevertheless a
range of indicators derived from this source have
effectively demonstrated and quantified the extent
of socio-economic differentiation. A particularly
striking indicator of deprivation is (male)
unemployment levels, which frequently exhibit wide
variations between small areas and cannot be
explained in terms of physical access to jobs.
Other commonly used indicators include
socio-economic group of head of household,
proportion of lone parent households, overcrowding
and car ownership (Twine and Williams, 1983).

A separate but related issue, which also
emerged first at the intuitive level and was later
confirmed by analysis of census data and other
research, is a somewhat similar spatial
concentration of ethnic minority populations in
those towns and cities where substantial numbers
of black and Asian households are found. Such
households are not spread evenly throughout the
public sector but located predominantly in certain
areas. Although generally not areas of high
quality council housing, they are not necessarily
the same estates as those with concentrations
of white households of low socio-economic
status. Ethnic minorities are, for example, not

infrequently found particularly in inner ring housing, in some cases older property which has entered the public sector through municipalisation.

The question which arose, of course, was to explain the mechanisms whereby these concentrations - of both deprived and ethnic minority households - came about and the part played by housing allocation procedures. What came to be referred to as secondary allocation, or differential allocation (Parker and Dugmore, 1976), were placed on the research agenda. Whether differential allocation should be regarded as surprising or merely to be expected is perhaps a matter for debate; but certainly allocation procedures ought not to be the cause, given that council housing is supposed to be allocated on the basis of need, while race should not enter into the process at all. There may be exogenous factors arising from socio-economic position or race (see, for example, Peach, 1983) which tend to produce a pattern of differential allocation. As well as the identification of such factors, a crucial issue is whether allocation procedures on balance reinforce or counteract them. On the face of it, while need may be an important or even predominant factor in determining priority at the primary stage, as far as secondary allocation is concerned it seems to have a very limited or even perverse influence.

EXPLANATIONS OF DIFFERENTIAL ALLOCATION: RESEARCH FINDINGS

Until the mid-1970s there had been little or no substantial research on housing allocation. From time to time, surveys of allocation policies were undertaken, for example for the Central Housing Advisory Committee, but these amounted to little more than the collection of outline information from local authorities and were very largely confined to the primary stage. During the last ten years, however, there has been an increasing volume of research, much of which has been concerned with secondary allocation and with examining differential allocation. Two generalisations can perhaps be made about this research. First, the majority of the studies have been (mainly if not exclusively) focused on the experience of ethnic minorities, and on the quality and location of housing obtained by different racial groups. Second, most of the studies have concentrated on charting the outcomes of the allocation process, and have been comparatively weak (for understandable reasons of the difficulty of the research involved) in disentangling why those outcomes occurred. It has been very fully demonstrated, using census data and special surveys, that Asians and West Indians, as well as households of lower socio-economic status (within a broadly defined working class), tend to receive less good accommodation in the public sector, and this finding must now be regarded beyond any reasonable doubt (see, for example, Runnymede Trust, 1975; Parker and Dugmore, 1976; Flett, Henderson and Brown, 1979; Simpson 1981; Commission for Racial Equality, 1984 a,b; Phillips, 1986). It is the causes which are the interesting issue, about which there is a measure of, but not yet complete, understanding, and on which the remainder of this chapter will concentrate.

There have been two studies of housing allocation which stand out from the rest on account of their sophistication and thoroughness, although they take rather different approaches. The studies are those of Birmingham, carried out at the Centre for Urban and Regional Studies (Karn and Henderson, 1983; Henderson and Karn, 1984, 1986); and of Glasgow, carried out at the Centre for Housing Research (Clapham and Kintrea, 1986, Kintrea and Clapham, 1986). The Birmingham research combined surveys of tenants and applicants, and analysis of housing department records, with a detailed study of informal or semi-formal decision making processes within the housing department which involved time-consuming observations of staff at work. As far as is known, nothing comparable has been attempted elsewhere, so that other studies have had to rely on information about formal policies and procedures, and beyond that assumptions about the behaviour of staff, in order to account for differential allocation. The Glasgow study was chiefly based on a survey of recent allocations (including transfers) within a segment of the city. Other surveys have been undertaken (for example, Commission for Racial Equality, 1984 a,b), but that in Glasgow was notable for the comprehensiveness of the information collected (including direct data about incomes, rarely if ever obtained in other studies) and of the analysis. The Birmingham research was, like many other studies, focused on race and public housing, although it provided an unusually large amount of information o the experience of other households which may be disadvantaged in the allocation process. In Glasgow, by contrast, race was not identified as a cause of differential allocation.

In reviewing research findings on differential allocation, from the Birmingham, Glasgow and other studies, a range of explanations will be examined, some of these will merit fairly extensive discussion, while others are notions which may have had considerable currency in the past but are now generally agreed to be of lesser importance. A difficulty with research on housing allocation is that a combination of variations in the allocation systems being investigated and in the focus of the projects means that conclusions about any particular factor - such as grading, expressed preferences, waiting time or refusal of offers - are fairly limited. If one moves from the level of the specific authority to generalise about allocation, it is necessary to build up a broad picture on the basis of partial information. Nevertheless, it is possible to give examples of the factors which tend to shape the dynamics of housing allocation and to arrive at valid general conclusions.

## Restrictions on Eligibility

Formal rules which debar some households from eligibility to have their need assessed (particularly restrictions on registration on a waiting list) can be an important aspect of primary allocation, and a good deal of attention used to be given to them. But for the reasons outlined earlier in the chapter - the widespread abandonment of such restrictions and that in any case it is often no longer necessary to ration less popular council housing - they have become less significant and none of the more recent studies identifies them as being of major importance. Indeed, in many areas restrictions on eligibility scarcely now exist. The Birmingham research (Henderson and Karn, 1986) did find that eligibility rules were of some significance, especially in the early 1970s before many of them were modified or abandoned. For example, the (continuing) restriction on owner occupiers

adversely affected Asian households both because
of the greater likelihood of their being home
owners and because the rule was applied more
rigidly to them than to whites; residential
qualifications could disadvantage recent
immigrants; and a lower age limit for single
persons indirectly affected West Indians who were
more likely than average to be single parents or
cohabitees. The significance of such restrictions
for the present discussion is not so much that
some households are excluded as that they may
impinge on the secondary stage; for instance,
cohabitees were obliged to register as single
persons in Birmingham.


Grading of Applicants
The concern here is with formal procedures whereby
the housekeeping standards, 'suitability' or,
implicitly, 'respectability' of applicants are
assessed. The categorisation of households is, at
least in theory, made use of in deciding the
quality of accommodation to be allocated. The
rationale for the practice tends to be in terms of
preserving the fabric of good quality property or
(less explicitly) as a criterion for rationing the
most sought-after housing by allocating it to the
most 'deserving'. There has been a long tradition
of grading in British housing management (see, for
example, CHAC, 1938), reflecting an approach which
can perhaps be seen as going back to the era of
Octavia Hill (Brion and Tinker, 1980). While
grading is a matter of secondary allocation
(leaving aside those authorities, including
Glasgow, which once had an 'unsuitable' category),
it was a major concern of some of the earlier
writing about allocation (for example, Burney,
1967; CHAC, 1969; Damer and Madigan, 1974). It is
probably true to say that grading was the first
explanation to be taken up when attention began to
be turned to the issue of differential
allocation. The concern was mainly with the
formal policies of housing departments, which was
perhaps unsurprising at a time when the notion of
'urban gatekeepers' had a considerable vogue.
There was a tendency to see the applicant as
essentially passive in the face of decisions made
by the housing department bureaucracy.
     The significance of formal grading in housing
allocation today is difficult to assess, but
the broad impression from research and other

information about local policies is that it is of
limited and diminishing importance. There is
considerable evidence that many authorities have
abandoned grading as an official policy, although
(as will be explained shortly) this does not mean
that its substance has been wholly eliminated. It
is plausible to conclude that grading has ceased
to be widespread and may have become somewhat
rare. A second reason why grading has become less
significant as an explanation of differential
allocation is that, even where the practice
persists, doubts have been cast on its importance;
for example in Hackney it was found that the
relationship between grades and property allocated
was not strong (Commission for Racial Equality,
1984a). But to anticipate the argument a little,
an important conclusion about grading is that its
abolition may make little or no difference; a form
of de facto grading may continue unofficially
(Henderson and Karn, 1986), and in any case the
circumstances of applicants force them into a
process of 'constrained choice', both of which
tend to produce differential allocations. In
other words, grading, even where it exists,
tends now not to be seen as a strong independent
factor in the pattern of allocations, but as
simply reinforcing other causal factors
(English, 1979).


## Area Preferences
A view that has been put forward to account
for the concentration of, particularly, ethnic
minority households in certain areas is that the
pattern of allocations reflects real preferences
(because, for example, of a desire to live near
other members of a minority group). This
explanation was apparently prevalent in Birmingham
housing department (Henderson and Karn, 1986).
One has even heard housing officials comment that
households with lower standards prefer the more
free and easy, less 'respectable', lifestyle and
expectations of certain estates. There is
certainly evidence from Henderson and Karn's study
that the area preferences recorded for Asian, West
Indian and white applicants were very different,
but these preferences can be a product of negative
as well as positive factors (see also Phillips,
1986). Furthermore, in London it does seem from
press reports that Bengali families wish to be
housed in certain estates in order to avoid racial

attacks. But negative 'preferences' of this kind are probably better seen as an aspect of 'constrained choice': this very important phenomenon, whereby households may 'choose' less popular housing because of the pressures upon them to be housed quickly, is conceptually distinct and is discussed below. An explanation which is closely related to that of area preferences is rent paying capacity. This explanation may have had some validity in the past, in the days of wider differentials in rent levels and before the introduction of a uniform scheme of rent rebates (now housing benefit), but it seems an implausible explanation in present conditions. No research has suggested that inability and unwillingness to afford the rents of better quality accommodation, in so far as they are higher, is of significance in determining preferences.

## Knowledge of the Allocations System

Knowledge of how allocations work is another 'common sense' explanation of why certain groups, particularly ethnic minorities, may do relatively badly. Although the Birmingham study (Henderson and Karn, 1986) found that minority households were less well informed about the allocation system, and it is reasonable to assume that this may generally be the case, none of the research has suggested that this is an important explanation of differential allocation. The findings of the Glasgow research (Kintrea and Clapham, 1986) on the role of information were somewhat inconclusive. Although there were differences between households in the uptake of information and their subsequent search behaviour, the significance of information was hard to interpret; surprisingly, for example, both those who had had an interview at the housing department and those who had seen official booklets on the allocation system were less realistic in their aspirations than other applicants. In so far as the knowledge factor exists, and if it does tend to disadvantage some households, its significance is probably overwhelmed by other factors.

## Constrained Choice

Attention is now turned to the explanation of differential allocation which, together with the informal and semi-formal procedures of housing departments, has been seen in recent years as having the greatest validity. The essence of constrained choice, as was pointed out above, is that households tend to express a preference, particularly on application forms, not for their ideal choice within the public sector but for what in all the circumstances seems to be a realistic one. The chief of these circumstances is that the highest quality and most popular housing can generally only be obtained after a lengthy wait whilst the least popular is likely to be available relatively quickly, in extreme cases almost instantly. Constrained choice is not, however, only a matter of preferences expressed at the time of application; refusal of offers which are seen as unsatisfactory is also usually important.

The significance of constrained choice is that the ability of households to express a preference for high quality housing (which tends to be in short supply) or to refuse offers and wait for something better varies widely. This ability depends on a combination of personal circumstances and the policies of the local authority. One policy variable is the extent to which length of wait determines priority. Traditionally, waiting time has been of considerable importance; indeed in many allocation systems, at least in the past, it has been more significant than housing need. But even where, as in most large authorities, a points scheme now exists, points are generally given for waiting time. Unless, therefore, a local authority operates a points scheme which gives relatively little weight to factors other than housing need, ability to wait is likely to be a crucial factor in obtaining popular council housing. Applicants differ widely, however, in their ability to wait; the most obvious factor is existing housing circumstances. People who are already tolerably well housed (which may apply particularly to transfer applicants) may be ready to wait literally years until accommodation of the type and in the location they prefer becomes available. But those who are living in appalling conditions or are threatened with homelessness are constrained to accept whatever accommodation is offered to them. They cannot afford to be 'choosey', either in the preferences they express on the application form or in turning down offers. One cannot, of course, be certain of the socio-economic circumstances of such households, but there is a high degree of probability that they will be relatively deprived or disadvantaged in other ways apart from their housing conditions. They may have a low income because of unemployment, chronic sickness or unskilled work; or a single parent may never have had a secure home or may have been left without one following a domestic crisis.

The position of households in the competition for good quality public sector housing does not depend, however, only on their ability to wait and the significance of this factor in determining priority. Another important policy variable relates to the way in which applicants are usually placed in a number of broad categories (referred to by terms such as 'quotas' or, in some research reports, as 'channels') which are accorded different degrees of priority by the local authority. These vary between areas, but the basis of most (although there are often further refinements) is a classification of applicants into clearance rehousing, medical priorities, transfers, ordinary waiting list and the homeless cases, generally on a descending scale of priority from the first to the last. The basis of differing priority is some combination of the interests of the authority itself and the extent to which households are seen as 'deserving'. Households whose dwellings the local authority intends to demolish under a slum clearance scheme (a much diminished category in the last decade) or for some other reason may or may not be badly housed. In the past some people living in clearance areas clearly were and ordinarily could not have afforded to be choosey. But because the local authority requires to empty the property by a certain date (and is normally very reluctant to invite the opprobrium of using its powers of eviction) the resident is in fact in a strong bargaining position. Such households tend to be given priority in allocations, though there is evidence that this is more likely to be manifested in area preferences being met than in high quality accommodation (Tucker, 1966; Henderson and Karn, 1986). At the other extreme, the homeless or potentially homeless combine desperation arising from their own circumstances with a low priority because they tend to be seen as undeserving. Typically, the homeless are permitted only limited choice of area and (at least in theory) only a single offer. Not surprisingly they tend to receive lower quality and less popular accommodation.

Expressed Preferences:  Research in Paisley in the
mid-1970s (English, 1979) reported that many
applicants were unwilling to consider moving to
certain unpopular areas, so that only a small
minority of applicants were even considered for
vacancies there.  The bulk of the waiting list
applicants who were willing to do so (that is
excluding transfer applicants, most of whom wished
to move within the areas concerned) were sharing
accommodation with other households, and were
likely to be anxious to obtain accommodation of
their own as rapidly as possible.  A substantial
minority of the applicants did not live in the
local authority district which meant that they
were ineligible for other estates (and they were
only eligible at all because in practice
residential qualifications were not applied to
difficult-to-let areas).  The Birmingham research
(Henderson and Karn, 1986) found that expressed
preferences (in terms of area and willingness to
accept a flat), which incidentally tended to be
subject to 'guidance' at the point of collection
by housing visitors, had a clear relationship with
allocations.  In Glasgow (Clapham and Kintrea,
1986) there was a relationship between applicants
in the lowest income group and preferences.

Waiting time:  This factor is not examined in the
published research to the extent which perhaps
might have been expected.  In Paisley, English
(1979) found that, in an allocation system that in
practice operated essentially on the basis of
simple queuing, length of wait was very strongly
related to allocations of unpopular housing
compared with the remainder of the stock.
Statistics on length of wait from the Glasgow
research have not been published but the make-up
of points totals was investigated (Clapham and
Kintrea, 1986).  It was found that those achieving
the most popular areas tended to have relatively
few points for housing need, and that the bulk
came from waiting time and 'local connection' with
the particular locality.  The opposite tended to
be the case with those moving to the least popular
areas.

Refusal of Offers:  Current practice in many local
authorities, whatever may have happened in the
past or may still be the formal position, is to

permit, within reason, an unlimited number of
offers to be refused (although this liberality is
rarely if ever extended to homeless applicants).
The position may not, however, be made clear in
published information. At any rate, applicants
seem often to believe that there is a limit on the
number of offers (commonly three) after which an
application will be cancelled or suspended. The
significance of such misconceptions, or course, is
that if some groups tend to have less accurate
knowledge than others, differential allocation
could be increased through their being more likely
to accept early and less good offers. It does
seem to be the case that later offers tend to be
higher quality than earlier ones. It was found in
Glasgow that the likelihood of refusal was related
to income, with low income households being more
likely to accept first offers (Clapham and
Kintrea, 1986). There was an increased tendency
for offers to be refused as incomes rose, and for
the quality of subsequent offers to be higher.
Differences in the likelihood of offers being
refused are likely to compound differences in
their quality; in other words, not only do
households of lower socio-economic status tend to
receive lower quality offers, but they are also
more likely to accept them.

## Informal Allocation Procedures

With the notable exception of the Birmingham
study, scarcely any research has been done to
observe the day-to-day work of staff responsible
for allocations. This section is therefore
heavily dependent on that research, although its
findings do fit in with whatever else is known
about the allocation process. Much other research
has identified the existence of differential
allocation and to some extent has been able to
explain it in terms of the factors reviewed
above. But an unexplained residual has generally
remained, which has sometimes been labelled as
'prejudice' or 'discrimination' on the part of
housing department staff. The major contribution
of the work in Birmingham has been to explore
in detail the dynamics of the allocation process,
and to identify the informal and semi-formal
procedures which are of very considerable
importance. The authors emphasise the inter-action
of formal policies and structures, which can do
more than define the parameters within which staff

operate, with less formal practices which have developed as part of day-to-day work. And they are sceptical of the notion of individual and idiosyncratic prejudice; rather, while staff may be influenced by certain commonly held judgemental attitudes about who is and is not deserving, the procedures followed reflect above all the constraints of their work situation and the need to perform their jobs effectively. Many of these constraints reinforce the tendency towards differential allocation.

The research focused on two key groups of staff: allocation control who were responsible for the initial matching of applicants with vacancies, and staff in area offices who screened potential offers and could veto those which were seen as unsuitable. To some extent each group of staff had different objectives and were subject to different constraints, although the contribution of both to the allocation process was to promote differential allocation.

The basic task in housing allocation in any authority is to find people to fill vacant properties, although exceptionally the process is reversed and suitable vacancies are sought for particular applicants (Henderson and Karn, 1986). As was pointed out earlier, within constraints such as appropriate dwelling size and broad location, at least in a major authority a fairly large number of applicants could usually reasonably be offered a particular vacant dwelling from an 'official' point of view. Although in Birmingham offers were supposed to be made to applicants with the highest points level, this criterion was in practice inadequate. The system was computerised but the significance of this was really that information was more readily available so that searching for suitable households was facilitated; the actual allocation process was scarcely less 'manual' in an important sense than if old-fashioned card indexes had been used.

The staff responsible for allocations had a number of objectives, but in essence the most significant of them amounted to making the maximum number of 'successful' matches, so as to minimise vacancies and to satisfy as many applicants as possible. It was thus rational, as far as possible, to make offers which were likely to be accepted; refused offers led to loss of rent income and, in some areas, the danger of vandalism to empty properties. Although formal grading had been abolished in Birmingham, there were enough items of information available to allocation staff, for example on household structure and refusal of previous offers, to enable them to have a very good idea how 'choosey' an applicant was likely to be. In brief, better quality offers were made to choosey applicants and lower quality ones to those who were likely to be more or less desperate. Not only did it not make sense to offer less popular vacancies to applicants who would probably refuse them; neither was it sensible to use up a lot of good offers on the desperate because they were required to satisfy the choosey. The effect of these pressures was reinforced by certain commonly held stereotypes and assumptions relating to what might be called 'atypical' households, such as members of racial minorities and single parent families; it was, for example, believed that the latter often could not cope with gardens and should therefore be allocated flats. Thus the abolition of formal grading appeared to have had little effect, not only because of constrained choices, expressed preferences and so on, but because allocation staff acted in much the same way as they probably had done before, distinguishing between 'respectable' and 'disreputable' households. This was particularly striking in relation to large families (Henderson and Karn, 1986).

In Birmingham, proposed allocations were then screened by staff in area offices, who appear to have blocked a fifth or more. Sometimes this was because a dwelling was not in fact available for letting, but in many cases it was because the offer would not have been 'suitable' in their view. These officers had access to files on applicants (or tenants in the case of transfers) which contained much more detailed information than was available to allocation control, and from which a more complete picture of the household and its 'respectability' could be obtained. While sharing with allocation control the objective of minimising the number of empty dwellings, area officers gave even greater weight to the desirability of avoiding management and neighbour problems. These, it was believed, were liable to arise if 'disreputable' households were placed in 'respectable' areas. Thus the screening of proposed allocations at area offices reinforced tendencies toward differential allocation which already existed.

# Access to Public Sector Housing

There is much more fascinating material in the Birmingham research, for example on the important role of 'advocacy' of particular applicants by staff in the housing department that also tended to produce differential allocation, which it is not possible even to summarise here. The project provided valuable insight into the working of the allocation process in one authority and it has advanced understanding of that process. The need is, of course, to repeat the exercise elsewhere, and to examine allocation systems in other authorities which are formally different but may produce similar outcomes.

## CONCLUSIONS

Allocation procedures are concerned with rationing public housing, in part by determining who should have access to it at all (primary allocation) and, more important in present-day conditions, who should have access to specific properties which are of widely differing quality and popularity (secondary allocation). It is quite clear, particularly from special analyses of census data, that households of varying socio-economic status, composition and race are not distributed randomly over the public sector but are spatially concentrated. There is a strong tendency (though the segregation is far from complete) for the lowest income groups, atypical families (notably single parents) and ethnic minorities to be found in less acceptable housing, either in terms of dwelling types (flats rather than houses) or location or both. These results of the secondary allocation process have been referred to as differential allocation.

The way in which each local authority allocates its housing is, at least in detail, unique, so that researching the allocation process requires a case study approach. There has been a substantial amount of research, much of it focused on the experience of ethnic minorities, but few of the projects have gone very far beyond demonstrating the fact of differential allocation towards explaining precisely how it arises. Nevertheless, enough has been done to make it feasible to draw some tentative general conclusions about causal factors. The fact that differential allocation seems to arise everywhere (although it is possible that there are unresearched exceptions) despite the great variety of formal allocation schemes, reinforces the validity of this exercise as well as suggesting the difficulty of attempting radically to alter the situation.

Some commentators on the allocation process have focused on the local authority bureaucracy, to which applicants for housing are seen as being passively subject (for example through grading) while others have emphasised the role of preferences. Although both these approaches no doubt have some validity, neither provides a satisfactory explanatory framework for differential allocation. The most useful approach is one which emphasises the interaction of applicant households and the housing department; the former seek to obtain the best accommodation which they can achieve within a heterogeneous stock of widely differing acceptability, and the latter endeavour to let vacancies without undue delay and to minimise the likelihood of subsequent management problems. Housing need may or may not be the main 'official' criterion for determining priority, though waiting time appears always to be a factor and in some authorities is a major one, but it is rarely an adequate basis for deciding precisely which vacant dwelling should be offered to a particular applicant. Thus criteria apart from housing need are often crucial in secondary allocation, it is argued, in creating differential allocation.

In broad terms, the main causes of differential allocation appear to centre, first on what can be called the desperation factor - the ability of households to wait for good quality accommodation - and, second, on the strategies followed by allocation staff in attempting to fill vacancies and to house as many applicants as possible. The desperation factor is likely to be manifested (although there may be variations depending on the characteristics of particular allocation systems) in expressed preferences for area or dwelling type, constrained by the probable length of wait implied, and in the refusal of offers in the expectation of getting something better. Allocation staff, basing their working practices on maximising the likelihood of offers being accepted, tend to match popular vacancies with choosey applicants and less popular areas with the more desperate. This approach may often be reinforced by judgemental views about the deserts of 'respectable' and 'disreputable' households. Both the policy of adjusting the quality of offers to choosiness (indicated by previous refusals) or expected choosiness and judgemental attitudes may be facilitated and legitimised by a formal grading system. The absence of grading is, however, unlikely to be decisive, in that allocation staff generally have a good deal of information available about factors such as household composition which is necessarily collected on application forms. There may also be comments by housing visitors which amount to a form of quasi-grading.

Finally, it is useful to move from discussing the existence and causes of differential allocation briefly to comment on the policy implications. A demand for reform so as to eliminate or at least diminish differential allocation has been implicit if not explicit in much of what has been written about housing allocation, particularly where there has been a concern with the experience of ethnic minorities and the possibility of racial discrimination. On the whole, however, specific recommendations for changed policies and procedures have been somewhat limited in scope, perhaps in part because a good deal of weight has tended to be placed on individual prejudice. Before looking at ways in which the outcomes of secondary allocation might be altered, however, it should at least be questioned how far differential allocation is in fact seen as a problem.

The way in which public housing is allocated certainly leads to the creation and perpetuation of deprived areas, and, with the removal of so much pre-1914 slum housing which was used predominantly to accommodate the lowest income groups, some council estates have come to bulk very large among such areas. It is widely accepted that the existence of stigmatised and run-down estates reinforces the individual deprivation suffered by families living in them; more controversially they may be believed to create social costs in terms, for example, of higher crime rates, drug abuse and low educational achievement. In addition, and particularly in relation to ethnic minorities, many would object to the sheer inequity of what they regard as discrimination in the allocation of public housing. Nevertheless it is difficult to escape the conclusion that much of the population at large, as well as many councillors and housing staff, believe that allocation as it operates today is making the best of a bad job. It may be regrettable that there are poor people and poor housing, and that the two often go together, but this is not seen as a justification for cutting across the interests of respectable, moderate income citizens by making it more difficult for them to obtain reasonably good quality accommodation in the public sector. Improving the housing opportunities of groups which currently tend to do badly in the allocation process would undoubtedly be at the expense of other groups, and it is unclear how far a political will exists to do much about differential allocation.

Looking at ways in which differential allocation could be diminished, it is possible to put forward proposals but none of them would provide an easily achievable solution. The most fundamental, but in practical terms a not very feasible solution would be to overcome the heterogeneity in the public housing stock to such an extent that differential allocation becomes a non-issue. Even leaving aside the difficulty of finding the massive resources which would be needed physically to improve the unpopular stock (and in extreme cases to replace it), differences in location, building type and other factors which determine acceptability would to some extent inevitably remain. This is not to say that a strong case does not exist for improving and replacing the worst council housing, but it is unrealistic to believe that such measures could do more than reduce the significance of differential allocation. To the extent that this conclusion is correct, strengthening the position of disadvantaged applicants would, as was pointed out above, necessarily be at the cost of other households.

Another approach is to change allocation systems: in principle priority could be based entirely on housing need, the discretion of allocation staff tightly circumscribed, and steps taken to ensure that expressed preferences or refusals did not affect the quality of offers. Even so, one suspects that it would be extremely difficult entirely to eliminate differential allocation, so ingrained is it in different types of allocation system. And, as for example Glasgow District Council found in the early 1980s (when it introduced a points based allocation scheme that gave far less weight to waiting time than had been traditional in the city and was forced to retreat), the political feasibility in such measures is to say the least uncertain. In any case, an increased emphasis on housing need might be thought to have costs for public housing in that its residualisation might well be accelerated. The not so poor who are economically on the margins of owner occupation, faced with worsened housing opportunities in the public sector, would be likely to strive all the harder to enter home ownership.

The residualisation of council housing - the trend whereby it is increasingly confined to lower socio-economic groups as a result of the little new building, sales and the continued growth of owner occupation - may in fact cause differential allocation slowly to become less significant. It seems reasonable to expect that the public sector will grow more homogeneous, both in terms of residents, as middling income working class households are lost to it, and of dwelling quality as sales continue, so that, although differential allocation will no doubt persist, it will operate within narrower confines on both counts. Until fairly recently, secondary allocation was not properly identified or explored, basically because all council houses could be let easily and to obtain one at all was an achievement which was likely to represent a major improvement in housing conditions. In the future, because council housing will probably represent little more than a level of minimum adequacy for those who cannot gain access to owner occupation, secondary allocation may once again seem less significant. If the public housing stock continues to be diminished in size through sales and a very low rate of building, at least in areas which have never had large stocks, it may once again become an achievement to obtain a council tenancy, but for the poor rather than the mainstream of the working class. Although the primary stage may eventually regain some of its former importance, at present and in the immediate future it is the secondary stage which is the more crucial and interesting aspect of the allocation process. A reasonable though still incomplete understanding of its dynamics has now been developed, and this is a field where further research could usefully be undertaken.

Access to Public Sector Housing

REFERENCES

Brion, M. and Tinker, A. (1980) Women in Housing:
    Access and Influence, Housing Centre Trust,
    London
Burney, E. (1967) Housing on Trial, Oxford Univer-
    sity Press, Oxford
Central Housing Advisory Committee (1938) Manage-
    ment of Municipal Estates, HMSO, London
(1949) Selection of Tenants and Transfers and
    Exchanges, HMSO, London
(1953) Transfers, Exchanges and Rents, HMSO London
(1955) Residential Qualifications, HMSO, London
(1969) Council Housing: Purposes, Procedures and
    Priorities, HMSO, London
Clapham, D. and Kintrea, K. (1986) 'Rationing,
    Choice and Constraint: The Allocation of
    Public Housing in Glasgow', Journal of Social
    Policy, 15, 51-67
Commission for Racial Equality (1984a) Race and
    Council Housing in Hackney, CRE, London
(1984b) Race and Housing in Liverpool. CRE, London
Damer, S. (1974) 'Wine Alley: The Sociology of a
    Dreadful Enclosure', Sociological Review, 22,
    221-248
Damer, S. and Madigan, R. (1974) 'The Housing
    Investigator', New Society, 29, 226-227
English, J. (1979) 'Access and Deprivation in Local
    Authority Housing' in C. Jones (ed.) Urban
    Deprivation and the Inner City, Croom Helm,
    London
Flett, H., Henderson, J. and Brown, B. (1979) 'The
    Practice of Racial Dispersal in Birmingham',
    Journal of Social Policy, 8, 289-309
Henderson, J. and Karn, V. (1984) 'Race, Class and
    the Allocation of Public Housing' Urban
    Studies, 21, 115-128
(1986) Race, Class and State Housing, Gower,
    Aldershot
Karn, V. and Henderson, J. (1983) 'Housing Atypical
    Households' in A. Franklin White (ed.) Family
    Matters, Pergamon, Oxford
Kintrea, K. and Clapham, D. (1986) 'Housing Choice
    and Search Strategies within an Administered
    Housing System', Environment and Planning A, 18
Parker, J. and Dugmore, K. (1976) Colour and the
    Allocation of GLC Housing, Greater London
    Council, London
Peach, G. (1983) 'Ethnicity' in M. Pacione (ed.)
    Progress in Urban Geography, Croom Helm, London

Access to Public Sector Housing

Phillips, D. (1986) 'What Price Equality?' Greater
London Council, London
Reynolds, F. (1986) The Problem Estate, Gower,
Aldershot
Runnymede Trust (1975) Race and Council Housing in
London, Runnymede Trust, London
Simpson, A. (1981) Stacking The Decks, Nottingham
and District Community Relations Council,
Nottingham
Tucker, J. (1966) Honourable Estates, Gollancz,
London
Twine, F. and Williams, N. (1983) 'Social Segrega-
tion in Public Sector Housing: A Case Study',
Transactions of the Institute of British
Geographers, New Series, 8, 253-266

Chapter Four

SEGREGATION

F.W. BOAL

The reader should be made aware at the outset that
this chapter will, to some degree, reflect the
perspectives of the author and the topics of
greatest interest to him. Secondly it should be
noted that a report that referred to all the
writings on segregation during (say) the past
decade would not necessarily be a <u>progress</u> report,
where progress is defined as 'advances or
development especially to better state' (<u>Concise
Oxford Dictionary</u>, 1976). More is not necessarily
better. Equally, the omission of reference to a
paper or book is not to be taken to mean that I
question its value - only that it does not serve
the immediate purposes I have in mind here.

The definition of segregation provides the
first topic for discussion. This is followed by
an examination of a number of aspects of
segregation measurement - the delineation of
appropriate population groups, the spatial scale
of analysis, the possible range of indices to be
employed and the need to give a temporal dimension
to the analysis. The relationship of class and
ethnicity is next reviewed, with particular focus
on the extent to which they separately or jointly
contribute to segregation. The functions performed
by class and ethnic segregation are then discussed,
and, in this functional context, the possibility
for the recognition of a range of types of
segregated area is presented. The impact of
segregation on inter-group relations, a topic of
considerable practical importance, is then
assessed. This is followed by an examination of
two concepts - 'territory' and 'critical mass'
both of which hold considerable promise for the
study of segregation. In conclusion a number
of suggestions are made for further research,

including the study of networks and interaction and the holistic examination of segregated 'communities'.

## Definition of Segregation

The term segregation requires definition. The Concise Oxford Dictionary gives 'segregating or being segregated; enforced separation of different racial groups in a community etc.', with the verb segregate meaning 'put apart from the rest, isolate'. Here we will take segregation as being a state of separation between groups of people, that separation having both social and spatial dimensions. The notion, given by the Concise Oxford, that segregation is an enforced condition is unnecessarily restrictive. Rather we will consider that segregation is a condition that a group finds itself in, possibly because of external force or internal choice, or some combination of the two.

Our perspective is to be geographic - so we will emphasise the spatial dimension of separation, where a definable group residentially occupies a space to some degree separate from the rest of the population, or where the activity networks of the members of the group define spaces distinctive from those that are the product of the activity networks of other groups. Thus we have both residential segregation and activity segregation. Given that the main sources of data on residential segregation are censuses, most analyses are consequentially of 'sleeping' (night-time) populations. The degree to which daytime population distributions display segregation is, in any precise manner, quite unknown.

## Measurement of Segregation

To start, let us consider the measurement of segregation. We have stated that segregation is a group phenomenon - therefore the definition of group membership becomes crucial. A distinction needs to be made between 'group' and 'category'. In this context a category is a set of people defined in terms of some externally imposed criteria, while a group is a collection of people who feel they have something in common with each

other. Two types of segregation have received the
bulk of analytic attention - that based on social
class criteria and that based on ethnicity. In
both instances there has been a great deal of
confusion between groups and categories. Cannadine
(1982) makes this distinction when he writes that
class 'can be used simply as a descriptive term,
denoting the statistical category of people united
by having certain objective criteria of
stratification, not conscious of itself as such'.
Alternatively, class may be defined as class
consciousness; here actors must be aware of their
class identity and act upon that basis (Cannadine,
1982, p. 241). In the first case a series of
categories are defined (usually on the bases of
occupational criteria) and the degree of spatial
segregation between them measured. In the second
case the degree of separation between self-defined
groups is identified. Likewise with ethnic
definition - is 'Asian' in Britain an externally
imposed category that clusters together a series
of groups such as those studied by Robinson in
Blackburn, where the Asian category may be
differentiated in terms of birth-place, language
and religion (Robinson, 1979). Again, Peach has
noted that in Britain distinctive island
identities are frequently subsumed under the 'West
Indian' rubric, the latter being a category in
process of becoming a group, due, as Peach would
insist, to sustained categorization by non-West
Indians - "the very British insensitivity that
failed to notice the heterogeneity of West Indians
has finished by producing the homogeneity that it
perceived" (Peach, 1984, p. 229). In consequence
of the category/group problem, we may put much
energy into the measurement and analysis of
population categories that have little meaning
beyond their imposed criteria of categorization.
This is probably particularly true with the study
of class segregation, where so-called social class
groups are formed by clustering people together in
terms of occupational criteria (Office of
Population Censuses and Surveys, 1980), where such
criteria may not provide meaningful group
boundaries. This problem exists, of course,
because most data are census derived - and I am
not aware of any census that requires respondents
to self-identify themselves in terms of class.

A second problem arises from the fact that
class and ethnicity are continuous variables,

rather than inherent attributes of persons (Yancey et al., 1976). Thus the intensity of identification, both by the persons concerned and by outsiders, varies between individuals and over time - for instance a particular ethnicity may be fiercely felt by one 'Italian' in New York, but only feebly recalled by another. Or, again, intensity of identification may be highly situational in that group membership may be instrumental for individuals at one time, and of minor practical value at another. As Darroch and Marston (1984) have written '... urban ethnicity not only varies from one situational context to another, but ebbs and flows in individual experience, through the phases of individual life-cycles, and in the collective realities of social and economic relations'. Measurement of the intensity of group 'belongingness' is very difficult, but at least we should be aware that our categorizations create discontinuities where none may exist and, furthermore, that they do not allow for change in identificational intensity.

When it comes to actually measuring segregation, two problems have been evident - the first is the spatial scale dependency of segregation measures, and the second is the choice of an appropriate index. The scale dependency issue got its most public airing in the pages of the journal <u>Area</u> (Jones and McEvoy, 1978; Lee, 1978; Peach, 1979), though the point had been made five years earlier (Poole and Boal, 1973). The argument that was aired grew from the fact that indices of segregation increase with decreasing population size of the spatial units being employed. Thus Jones and McEvoy noted that some researchers were concluding that levels of racial segregation in England were much lower than those observed in the United States, despite the fact that many of the areal units used for the measurement in England were much larger than those employed across the Atlantic. Hopefully the issues raised in this 'debate' have now led to a conventional wisdom wherein all researchers take care, when comparing segregation levels, to only make comparisons at compatible scale levels - though as late as 1982 the old error has still been perpetrated (Lambert and Lambert, 1982, p. 83). I would suggest that all tables containing measures of segregation should state specifically at what scale the measures apply - for instance: 'Scale Level Census Tract, with average Tract size 2010 households'.

Another aspect of the debate has involved decisions as to what scale measurement should be made at - using large areal units to catch the broad context of segregation or small units to tap segregation in the immediate street or block context. The answer here lies in appropriateness to the particular study being carried out. In many cases this will mean measurement both at the broad frame level (census tracts, wards etc.) and at the micro-scale of the street. Appropriateness also becomes an issue in another context - should segregation be measured for areal units that are meaningful to the residents rather than for statistical spatial frameworks imposed by the researcher? This, of course, would be a very difficult, time consuming exercise but it would nonetheless be very desirable given the emphasis now on phenomenological approaches in human geography (Wolpert et al., 1972). Finally another unexplored issue needs mention - should segregation be measured for the same sizes of area unit in very large cities as in smaller ones? The problem here is that a large city is likely to have residential areas, homogeneous in class or ethnic terms, that are much larger than similarly homogeneous areas in a small town. In this case the application of a standard size of areal unit for purposes of measuring segregation will produce higher indices for the large city than for the small one (Poole 1982, pp. 293-4). Thus the appropriate scale of unit should perhaps be varied with size of urban area. The form of available data may, unfortunately, preclude such an exercise.

The importance of spatial scale in the measurement of segregation has by now hopefully been firmly established. How segregation is to be measured has also moved to a position of considerable agreement amongst researchers, following what Peach refers to as the 'Index War' of the period between 1947 and 1955 (Peach, 1975, p. 3). Now the Index of Dissimilarity (ID) has become the standard, not only because of its computational simplicity but because it is independent of the relative sizes of the groups being compared (Taeuber and Taeuber, 1965). Of equal importance is the fact that the index can be interpreted in a straightforward manner as the percentage of a population group which would have to shift its residence in order to reproduce a spatial distribution identical with that of the

## Segregation

group with which it is being compared (Peach,
1975, p. 3). The fact that the Index of
Dissimilarity has been widely adopted is not only
an indication of its acceptability but also
because of the value, in comparative research, of
the use of a common measure. As Lieberson (1981,
p. 79) puts it 'the existence of a large body of
existing (sic) data with ID values is not a
trivial matter, if only because standard data are
not that common in the social sciences ...'. If
description and analysis of segregation are to
advance we must be able to build upon a common
base. However it has also recently been pointed
out by Lieberson that the immunity of the Index of
Dissimilarity from compositional influences is not
always a desirable factor, particularly when we
are interested not so much in spatial dissimilarity
as interactional probability. Thus, if a city is
composed of two groups, one of which is much larger
than the other, there will be a greater probability
of a member of the smaller group coming in contact
with a member of the larger group than vice versa.
A measure that allows for this effect will
consequentially be very useful when we are
concerned with activity rather than residential
segregation. Such a measure is P*, the Index of
Isolation, given a new prominence by Lieberson
(1981). P* describes the actual isolation of a
group either from all others or from a specific
group, in a manner which takes into account the
joint influence of population composition and
spatial distribution. A good illustration of the
different insights provided by ID and P* is
provided by Keane (1985) when she measured
Catholic-Protestant segregation in public sector
housing in the Belfast Urban Area (Table 4.1).
There was a massive increase in segregation
between the two years 1969 and 1977 from an ID of
64 to one of almost 92. Since there are many more
Protestant households than Catholic, Protestants
are likely to have a greater opportunity for
contact with Protestants (pP*p) than Catholics have
with Catholics (cP*c). Equally, Catholics are more
likely to have contact with Protestants (cP*p) than
vice versa (pP*c). However the fact that there is
an increasing proportion of public sector households that are Catholic has decreased the probability of Catholic contact with Protestants but has
increased the probability of Protestant contact
with Catholic, despite the very large increase in
spatial segregation indicated by the Indices of
Dissimilarity.

Segregation

| YEAR | ID | cP*c | pP*p | cP*p | pP*c | percent of public sector households that is Catholic |
|------|-----|------|------|------|------|------|
| 1969 | 64.26 | 0.64 | 0.88 | 0.35 | 0.13 | 26.17 |
| 1977 | 91.75 | 0.69 | 0.84 | 0.31 | 0.17 | 34.80 |

Table 4.1: ID and P* measures, public
sector housing, Belfast Urban
Area 1969 and 1977.
(Source: Keane 1985).

[Scale Level: Zone, with average zone
size in 1969 433 households and in
1977 413 households]

One may conclude that widespread use of ID
provides a major boost to comparative studies of
segregation and is to be greatly encouraged.
Equally the use of P* provides additional insight,
particularly where concern is for the impact of
degrees of and changes in degree of spatial
dissimilarity on particular groups of the
population. ID and P* prove themselves to be
highly complementary measures in many contexts,
and, as Lieberson (1981, p. 80) suggests 'it is
reasonable in many research projects to expect
researchers to compute both the index of
dissimilarity and P*-type measures - particularly
since the same data inputs are necessary'.

Most measured segregation records intensity at
a given moment - 'segregation as snapshot'. Change
can be examined by comparison of sequential
snapshots, usually corresponding with census
years. There are two problems here - the first
being the relative infrequency of census based
snapshots, with attempts being made to fill gaps
by use of sample survey, by use of lists
maintained by some groups, usually religious, for
example Jews in London (Waterman and Kosmin, 1986)
or Catholics in Northern Ireland (Poole 1982;
Keane 1985) or by name recognition on Electoral
Registers (Jones and McEvoy, 1974). The second
problem relates to the interpretation of snapshot
patterns. Thus an area may, at a given moment,
display a certain degree of social class or ethnic
residential mixing. However the significance
of such a pattern will depend on whether it is

temporally stable or merely transitional. For instance this author (Boal, 1982) established that many ethnically mixed areas in Belfast were not stable, being cases of transition where the mixing was a passing phase between two segregated and polar opposite conditions. Thus advancement in our understanding of segregation pattern and process depends, at least in part, on the availability of data at frequent time intervals.

A temporal dynamism to the study of residential segregation and desegregation was provided by the simulation studies of the 1960s and the 1970s (Morrill, 1965; Rose, 1970; Woods, 1975) generating spatial distributions of various racial and ethnic groups, both as means of testing understanding of process and of predicting future pattern, the latter hopefully having useful policy implications. However as Robinson (1981, p. 143) has concluded '... simulation to date reveals that neither the theoretical nor practical contribution of the approach has been great. Despite the early enthusiasm generated by the technique, an understanding of the exact causes of residential segregation is little nearer, whilst policies directed at the problem have benefited slightly, if at all, from such an approach.' Nonetheless Robinson feels that simulation does have utility when used as a simple monitoring system, as demonstrated for Chicago (Berry, 1971) and more recently for Blackburn (Robinson, 1981). In both cases simulation is used as a benchmark against which to compare reality and to subsequently judge the efficacy of desegregation policies. Despite Robinson's optimism, it is difficult to see how simulated patterns, with all their methodological shortcomings, can provide a useful benchmark - deviation between benchmark and actuality may be in part a function of the weaknesses of the simulation itself.

Indices of Dissimilarity give measures of the degree of spatial difference between the groups being examined. Where such indices are high there is a tendency to assume that certain areas of a particular city will be overwhelmingly numerically dominated by one particular group.

This may well be so in certain circumstances, particularly where the population is perceived as being composed of only two groups (white-black, Catholic-Protestant etc.). An examination of Belfast in 1977 shows that 79 percent of Protestant households were residing in streets that were entirely or almost entirely Protestant, while 69 percent of Catholic households were residing in streets that were almost entirely Catholic (Keane, 1985, p. 172). On the other hand, particularly in multi-ethnic cities, it has been demonstrated that areas labelled as occupied predominantly by one group ('the Italian area', 'the Greek area', 'the Jewish area' and so on) are in many instances much less homogeneous than their 'image' suggests. Thus Chudacoff, in an analysis of late nineteenth century Omaha, Nebraska, notes that ethnic groups were much more geographically dispersed than 'intuition might suggest'. This intuitive sense of concentration was, he claims, derived from

> a more durable factor [than residential percentages]. Here is where a notion of visibility becomes important. Although the proportion of an ethnic group living in a particular area was significant, the location of that group's business, social and religious institutions was even more conspicuous to those who both lived nearby and further away. That is, the churches and clubs, plus the bakeries, groceries, butchers' shops, shoemakers, tailors, saloons and restaurants which directed their services to a special clientele and were operated by a specific ethnic group, helped markedly to define a neighbourhood's character. (Chudacoff, 1973, p. 88).

Undoubtedly ethnic and racial group visibility does cause observers to exaggerate the degree of spatial dominance of such groups in particular locations, creating what might be called 'Image Areas' (Boal, 1986). Such perceived concentrations can have both positive and negative functional outcomes - positive for attracting tourists in certain instances and for the sense of identity transmitted to members of the 'dominant' neighbourhood group, negative where visual dominance causes reactions from others who feel that the visually obvious group is 'taking over'. Further study of the imagery of residential concentration is clearly called for.

Many segregation studies examine the experience of one particular group, sometimes where only two categories are used, for example, black segregation in a white context or Catholic segregation in a Protestant, and sometimes where

the group is compared to the rest of the
population, the 'rest' being a number of social
class categories or a multitude of ethnic groups.
The two category situation provides the basis for
a relatively straightforward analysis, but we must
be sure that one or both of our categories are not
highly heterogeneous in composition leading to
what might be a fairly meaningless comparison. We
have already touched on the categorization problem
earlier in the chapter.

## Class, Ethnicity and Society

The segregation of class and ethnic groups is a
dimension of the spatial structure of society. In
turn it may be argued that spatial structure is a
product of social structure, the latter being
defined as a set of persistent, patterned social
relationships between groups of people in
different social positions (Morgan, 1984, p. 302).
In a review of the relationships between spatial
structure and social structure, Morgan (1984) has
pointed out that many geographers have viewed
spatial structure as largely a reflection of
aspects of social structure, but he goes on to
indicate that spatial structure also acts to
reinforce and to influence the evolution of social
structure itself. Thus segregation is a product of
the social structuring of groups, while
simultaneously influencing those very relationships.
    Although factor ecological studies have
demonstrated the statistical independence of the
socio-economic (class) and ethnic dimensions of
urban socio-spatial structure (Knox, 1982) it is
clear that class and ethnicity do interact with
each other. As van den Berghe (1981, p. 244) has
written '... the interplay of class and ethnicity
is probably the most difficult problem facing the
analysis of complex societies'. Nevertheless we
must attempt to confront this problem in so far as
it bears on the question of segregation. Here the
basic issue is whether the social class
characteristics of ethnic groups contributes to
ethnic segregation and whether the ethnic
composition of the various social class strata
contributes to class segregation.
    A number of statistical analyses have been
carried out in an attempt to isolate the degree to
which social class characteristics of ethnic groups

## Segregation

(income, occupation etc.) contribute to ethnic segregation. Darroch and Marston (1972) suggest two alternative explanatory models for ethnic segregation. The first, called by them the social class model, claims that differences in socio-economic status largely determine the dissimilarities in residential distributions that do exist. The second, referred to as the ethnic model, indicates that residential segregation is accounted for by more direct references to non socio-economic differences between groups. If segregation is a product of socio-economic differences, then such segregation can be reduced by narrowing the income/occupational differences between ethnic groups. If, on the other hand, segregation is related to non socio-economic characteristics, narrowing of income differentials will not decrease segregation, a point made by Taeuber and Taeuber (1965) in their work on black ('negro') segregation in the United States.

Two statistical techniques have been employed in the exploration of the extent to which class position contributes to ethnic segregation. The first of these, known as direct standardization, measures the degree of interethnic segregation <u>within</u> different socio-economic classes and then compares these segregation levels between classes. For instance Massey (1981) found that Hispanic-white segregation in the South-western United States fell as one moved from the lowest to the highest social class groupings, while Boal et al. (1976) recorded a fall in the dissimilarity index between Protestants and Catholics in Belfast from 0.73 for the 'working class' to 0.57 for the 'middle-class'. On the other hand Massey found that black-white segregation did not decline upwards through the various social-class strata.

The second statistical technique, known as indirect standardization, estimates the degree of ethnic segregation that would be expected if two groups were segregated along class, but not ethnic lines, and then compares this value to the amount of ethnic segregation actually observed. Massey found that the relative share of Hispanic-white segregation that could be attributed to social class (measured by educational attainment) was very low, as was the case with black-white segregation (dissimilarity indices averaging 8.7 for Hispanic-white segregation and 6.4 for black-white). Similarly in Belfast, indirect standardization produced an index of dissimilarity

100

Segregation

of 6 (Boal et al., 1976). Massey concludes that
while indirect standardization does measure the
relative contribution of social class to ethnic
segregation, it does not address the issue of
whether ethnic segregation is inversely related to
socio-economic status. Thus he recommends that
direct standardization be the preferred method for
assessing the effect of social class on ethnic
segregation. Where this method (as with
Hispanic-white segregation in the US or
Catholic-Protestant segregation in Belfast) shows
an inverse relationship between social class level
and degree of ethnic segregation, then the removal
of inter-ethnic income/occupational inequalities
can produce decreased segregation. Where, on the
other hand, there is no clear relationship between
social class level and degree of ethnic
segregation (as with black-white segregation in
the US) then it appears that income-occupational
equalization will, by itself, make little
contribution to desegregation.

The basic assumption that lies behind the
standardization approach is that social class
segregation is 'a fact of life' in cities within
the capitalist economic orbit. It follows from
this that if a particular ethnic group is
disproportionately located in, say, the 'lower'
class stratum, that fact alone will make a
contribution to the segregation observed - that is
ethnic segregation is, at least in part, social
class segregation. To my knowledge no one has
attempted to explore the opposite possibility -
that is that a component of social class
segregation is ethnic segregation. Here the
argument would run something like this - if
members of a particular ethnic group are highly
segregated from the rest of society and if members
of that ethnic group are disproportionately
focused in a specific social class stratum, then
the ethnically based segregation will sharpen the
social class segregation. Perhaps studies that
would examine this possibility have not been done
because of the taken-for-granted nature of social
class segregation in western societies, where it
is ethnic segregation that is viewed as
problematic rather than normal.

The implication of the discussion is that
class and ethnicity are linked - that the process
of class segregation may contribute to ethnic
segregation and vice versa. However it may be
asked whether class and ethnicity are separate

101

societal dimensions? One's answer to this question will depend on one's ideological stance. For instance van den Berghe (1981) sees ethnicity and class as the two principal modes of collective organization in complex societies and goes on to claim that 'the analytic distinction between these two types of social formation is crucial; both are, in principle, equally important, and neither is reducible to the other' (1981, p. 242). Marger (1985, p. 39) also allows that ethnicity and class are distinct dimensions of stratification, but he notes their close relationship - 'in almost all multiethnic societies, people's ethnic classification becomes an important factor in the distribution of social rewards, and, hence, in their economic and political class position'. Finally, and of great importance for certain societies, Lieberson (1972) differentiates between ethnic and other forms of stratification on the grounds that the former is nearly always the basis for the internal disintegration of the existing boundaries of the state where an ethnic group wishes to create an autonomous nation-state as a means of eliminating its subordination in an ethnic hierarchy. Thus, unlike class, ethnicity can become the basis for nationalism, such an outcome giving ethnic segregation in cities as disparate as Nicosia, Belfast, Jerusalem and Montreal a special intensity.

Approaches that treat ethnicity as separate from and as strong or stronger than class as a societal differentiator are seen by Marxists as attempts to mystify rather than clarify the structure of society (Peach, 1981, p. 30). Bourne and Sivanandan (1980) consider that policies encouraging ethnic pluralism are attempts by the state to divert 'black' energies in Britain into 'harmless ethnic channels'. Thus it is claimed that the most significant feature of ethnic minority experience is not ethnicity but place in the class structure. Doherty (1973, p. 50) identifies 'New Commonwealth' immigrants in Britain as having a role as 'labor reserve and scapegoat, acting as a divisive element in the working class creating false consciousness among the indigenous proletariat ...' Robert Miles in his book on Racism and Migrant Labour claims that it is necessary to reject the notion of racial/ethnic conflict as being equivalent to class conflict/division (Miles, 1982, p. 156). He states that '... Migrants occupy a structurally

distinct position in the economic, political and
ideological relations of British capitalism, but
within the boundary of the working class. They
therefore constitute a fraction of the working
class, one that can be identified as a racialized
fraction' (Miles, 1982, p. 165). While Miles
limits his discussion to phenotypically distin-
guishable immigrants (and their descendants), his
analysis could be generalized to include many
immigrant ethnic groups that find themselves
concentrated in the lower layers of the class
hierarchy. From this perspective one could
envisage maps of residential segregation that
would show areas defined by social class criteria,
with the areas occupied by specific classes
spatially 'fractionalized' on the basis of ethnic
characteristics. Thus ethnic segregation can be
subsumed as a dimension of a much more important
class segregation where cultural and/or
phenotypical differences are given a social
significance that places those thus differentiated
into specific positions in the class structure,
and consequentially into specific (segregated)
locations on the ground.

We will return to the class-ethnicity
interweave later when we discuss the functions of
residential segregation. Sufficient for now to
note that a Marxist approach that requires the
reduction of ethnicity to a dimension of class
severely limits understanding of ethnic groups and
ethnic segregation. Equally, an approach that
separates the consideration of ethnicity from that
of class provides an excessively narrow and
unsatisfactory interpretation.


The Functions of Segregation

I have previously reviewed the functions performed
by ethnic spatial segregation (Boal, 1972; 1978b).
In that review I emphasised the conflict context
within which ethnic segregation had its <u>raison
d'etre</u>. Thus ethnic groups developed and
maintained segregation as a response to the
environment they found themselves in - a context
where there were concerns for physical defence and
for avoidance of culturally threatening situations.
I also suggested that segregation had a number of
more positive aspects, creating contexts for
preservation of particular ways of life and bases
for action in the wider society, in an attempt to
improve the material position of the segregated

group. These functional interpretations have been adopted by a number of subsequent authors (e.g. Knox, 1982; Shilhav, 1984).

Perhaps it is now possible to view the functions of ethnic segregation as contributory to the reproduction of ethnic groups. Such reproduction may meet the expressive objectives of ethnic group members, in that they wish to preserve aspects of their cultural heritage and transmit this heritage to subsequent generations - here the role of the family in the context of an ethnic neighbourhood supported by ethnic institutions is crucial (Breton, 1964). There may well also be an instrumental dimension to ethnic group reproduction, in that a strong territorially grounded cluster can provide the base for struggle in the wider society - to rephrase Marx, we have an 'ethnic group for itself'.

Ethnic segregation may be highly functional for the group so segregated, though if the segregation is basically involuntary, then the segregated space may be less of an expressive or instrumental resource and more of a trap. Indeed ethnic segregation may be highly functional not so much for the specific ethnic group or groups but more for the wider society. Thus the defensive function may be seen as one of containment, avoidance may meet the prejudicial needs of the majority community enabling them to avoid sustained contact with 'strange' ways of life, preservation may mean conservation of majority culture from dilution (pollution) due to 'ethnic' influences, while external action may mean the manipulation of electoral geography to prevent the election of ethnic minority candidates or may even mean the availability of clearly defined target population concentrations.

From the functional perspective ethnic segregation may therefore perform roles both for the segregated ethnic groups and for the wider society, though for different reasons. Indeed at times an attribute such as 'containment' that is functional for, say, the wider society may be dysfunctional for the contained group, if such containment is a trap.

A further set of functional interpretations comes from a Marxist perspective, where the ethnic group is viewed as a 'class fraction'. Class fractionalization serves, according to Hall et al., to reproduce the working class in a racially stratified and internally antagonistic form (Hall et al., 1978, p. 346). Miles (1982) claims that a process of 'racialization' operates in Britain in regard to West Indian and Asian immigrants and their offspring to assist both the reproduction of fractions of the working class and the structuring of the formation of a new reserve army of labour. Thus, insofar as ethnic segregation contributes, via the means adumbrated above, to the reproduction of class fractions, so it is functional for the maintenance of the capitalist system.

The ethnic group viewed merely as class fraction brings us back to the question of the relationship between class and ethnicity. Also, if we substitute 'class fraction' for 'ethnic group', we find that we can begin to apply the functional interpretation of ethnic segregation, as outlined above, to the issue of class segregation directly. However, before doing so, it is useful to return to Hall's discussion of the West Indian community in Britain. Although he treats this community as a class fraction, he does suggest a functional role for the segregation of the group that is remarkably close to the present author's indications for the functions of ethnic segregation. Hall claims that the West Indian community faced the likelihood of differential incorporation as a subordinate class. Alternatively they could stress separateness, but to do so:

> required a solid framework and a material base: the construction of the West Indian enclave community - the birth of colony society. At one level the formation of the ghetto 'colony' was a defensive and corporate response. It involves the black community turning in on itself ... In another sense the foundation of Colony Society meant the growth of internal cultural cohesiveness and solidarity within the ranks of the black population inside the corporate boundaries of the ghetto: the winning away of cultural space in which an alternative black social life could flourish .. the 'colony', initially a defensive reaction to the threatening universe of blanket white hostility, has become a defensive base for new strategies of survival amongst the black community as a whole (Hall et al., 1978, pp. 351, 353).

## Segregation

If we accept that residential segregation is functional for the reproduction of ethnic groups, so it follows that such segregation will also be functional for the reproduction of social classes. Morgan (1984) strongly indicates such a link, drawing attention to the interpretations of David Harvey (1975), where segregation brings about differential access to the scarce resources required to acquire 'market capacity':

> Market capacity from this viewpoint comprises a whole set of attitudes, values and aspirations as well as distinctive skills. Socialization, early images and internalized values and norms are deeply embedded in neighbourhood experiences, settings and social class, so that local channels of communication support intergenerational communication of common values, beliefs and aspirations. Working class communities, therefore 'produce' individuals with values conducive to being in the working class ... (Morgan, 1984, p. 307).

He also notes that the school attended by a person is greatly influenced by neighbourhood and, additionally, that selection of marriage partners is circumscribed by residential location - ensuring maintenance of the various class strata. Johnston (1980) makes the same point when the suggests that an aspect of neighbourhood social interaction and the role of 'externalities' concerns the continuation of the class system: 'this is in part guaranteed, as far as possible, by manipulation of the educational system. It may be furthered by marriage' (Johnston, 1980, p. 168).

Residential segregation as a mechanism for class maintenance is clearly at the forefront of Down's discussion of the possibilities for some degree of social class mixing in American suburbs. He notes that residential screening to exclude low income households serves to achieve relative homogeneity in school enrolments, to ensure a high predictability and acceptability of neighbourhood public behaviour patterns and to enhance the prestige of people living in certain neighbourhoods by establishing 'social distance' from others considered to be of lower socio-economic status (Downs, 1971; 1973). The preservation of urban upper class elites is the focus of an interesting discussion of some high income residential areas in Vancouver and in Westchester County, New York

## Segregation

(Duncan and Duncan, 1984)

> ... the creation and preservation of these [elite] landscapes, which have both class and ethnic connotation, serve in part as a vehicle by which the integrity of a cultural group is maintained. Landscapes and other elements of a culture are used to define membership in a culture group through reaffirmation of members' values, and exclusion of non members ... The process not only involves conscious socio-political action, but also results from the unintended consequences of collective action based on unarticulated 'take-for-granted' values. A residential landscape helps in the reproduction of a class or status group because it is an important repository of symbols of social class and ethnic heritage (Duncan and Duncan, 1984, pp. 256, 257).

Richard Harris (1984) in a comprehensive review of 'residential segregation and class formation in the capitalist city' claims that segregation facilitates and hinders social contact:

> It makes contact between members of different classes more difficult. Conversely, contacts among members of the same class are made relatively easy. Ultimately the significances of segregation for the process of class formation derives from these simple facts. (Harris 1984, p. 33).

There are a number of contradictory outcomes. For instance, the lack of inter-class contact may generate political apathy, in that there may be general ignorance between the classes of their relative states of advantage or disadvantage. On the other hand segregation, by supporting the development of distinctive class cultures, has promoted cohesion and internal class formation. This, in turn, can generate political mobilisation. Harris concludes that in order to understand how classes form themselves into coherent social and political forces it is necessary to examine all aspects of the process. The evidence and arguments reviewed by Harris suggest to him 'that segregation has played an important, albeit contradictory, role in this regard' (Harris, 1984, p. 41).

## Segregation

A Marxian perspective on residential segregation suggests that such segregation is functional for the reproduction of social class groups, including class fractions, all this being the reproduction of an appropriately structural labour power. Whether one wishes to place them in a Marxian frame or not, the suggestion I have earlier made regarding the functionality of ethnic segregation can be paralleled in the class context - the residential concentration serving as a base for class formation and maintenance, for defence against threatening intrusions, for avoidance of undesired contact and for the generation of community organization in the political, and perhaps physically, rebellious spheres.

Research work over recent years leaves little doubt that segregation performs significant functions in both the class and the ethnic contexts. Indeed class and ethnicity are themselves closely interwoven, though this is definitely not to say that one is reducible to the other. There is, however, one further perspective that is highly applicable to both contexts. This derives from Parkin's discussion and elaboration of Weber's concept of social closure, defined as the process by which social collectivities seek to maximise rewards by restricting access to resources and opportunities to a limited circle of eligibles (Parkin, 1979, p. 44). Parkin recognises two forms of social closure - 'exclusionary closure', which is really social closure as defined above, and 'usurpationary closure', where strategies are adopted by the excluded themselves as a direct response to their status of outsiders. Thus the residential concentration will be the result not only of exclusionary closure by others, but exclusionary closure by the concentrated group or groups themselves as a means of 'forging a common political entity and some measure of collective consciousness' (Parkin, 1979, p. 86). This form of exclusionary closure then becomes the basis for the operation of usurpation, which is 'that type of social closure mounted by a group in response to its outsider status and the collective experience of exclusion ... the aim of biting into the resources and benefits accruing to dominant groups in society' (Parkin, 1979, p. 74). Moreover some groups, suffering from acts of exclusionary closure by others, may in turn behave in an exclusionary manner towards other weaker groups, whilst at the same time applying upwards

## Segregation

usurpationary closure against those more advantaged
than themselves. The issue of class fractionation
might well be relevant here. A number of attempts
to apply the closure model to segregation have been
made, most of them very recent (Neuwirth, 1969;
Boal, 1981; Phillips, 1981; McDowell, 1982).

## The Classification of Segregated Residential Areas

Some attempts have been made to classify areas of
ethnic segregation into a number of relatively
distinct categories. These classifications have
usually been built on description of the dynamics
of such areas. Notions of assimilation, of
permanence or impermanence and of the relative
importance of 'choice' and 'constraint' factors
have been to the fore. Boal (1978b) has suggested
three categories for areas of ethnic segregation -
the 'colony', the 'enclave' and the 'ghetto'. This
schema has subsequently been adopted by others
including the Lamberts (Lambert and Lambert, 1982),
and Dicken and Lloyd (1981). Distinction between
these categories is made on the basis of choice/
constraint and permanence/impermanence criteria.
The colony refers to those situations where a
particular area of a city serves as a port-of-entry
for an immigrant (or migrant) ethnic group. It is
viewed as a temporary phenomenon providing a base
from which ethnic group members are culturally
assimilated and spatially dispersed. The enclave is
an ethnic concentration that stays in existence
over several generations, because the inhabitants
choose to maintain their spatial congregation.
Jewish areas in cities such as Toronto (Rosenberg,
1954), Chicago (Rosenthal, 1961) and London
(Waterman and Kosmin, 1986) exemplify this
situation very sharply. Finally the ghetto is an
area of segregation where external factors severely
limit the possibilities for dispersal - constraint
and longevity are dominant features. It is
difficult to clearly distinguish the enclave
category from the ghetto in that the two situations
will probably have elements both of choice and
constraint - indeed some of the apparent choices to
stay clustered may, in fact, be a response to
perceived external factors. More research is
needed here, but it would be useful if some agreed
framework and nomenclature could be arrived at. For
instance, in a passage quoted earlier in this
chapter, Hall et al. (1978, p. 351) wrote of the

## Segregation

West Indian 'enclave community', which they refer
to as 'colony society' with developing cultural
cohesiveness and solidarity 'inside the corporate
boundaries of the ghetto'. Thus the three labels
I have suggested for classification purposes are
all applied at one time to the same area.

Agócs (1981) has developed a typology of ethnic
communities, derived from her study of Detroit -
the Ghetto, the Recent Immigrant Reception Centre,
the Urban Village, the Residual Community, the
Transplanted Community, the New Suburban Settlement
and Community Without Neighbourhood. She concludes
that an evolving body of pluralistic theory
suggests that there may be little point in hypothe-
sizing uniform patterns of ethnic community
development and persistence, or of assimilation.
She feels it is more likely that each ethnic
community differs from every other in mode and rate
of development, under the influence of many
variables, not all of which are part of the
experience of other groups (Agócs, 1981, p. 146).

Significantly, there appears to have been no
attempt to classify areas of class segregation,
other than in terms of the predominant class
occupying them. The choice/constraint and
permanence/impermanence polarities of ethnic
segregation classification seem to have little
relevance to class, perhaps because notions of
assimilation or dispersal are taken to be inappropriate in the class situation. Social mobility
would be the equivalent of assimilation, but while
it is allowed that almost all the members of an
ethnic group might assimilate over time to the
broader, encompassing society, the possibility of
most of a social class becoming upwardly or down-
wardly mobile is unthinkable in the context of
capitalist society. This, of course, does not rule
out the possibility that a particular area may
serve as a jumping off point for socially mobile
individuals. Perhaps we may be led back to place
ethnicity in a class framework, in that much
ethnic assimilation involves social mobility.
Indeed van den Berghe sees assimilation to the
dominant ethnic group as a class mobility strategy
(van den Berghe, 1981, p. 246).


## Segregation and Intergroup Relations

The functions attributed to segregation can be
thought of as consequences of that segregation -

## Segregation

basically preservation of group characteristics
including their intergenerational reproduction.
But what of the consequences for inter-group
(inter-class or inter-ethnic) relations? Blau
(1977) claims that the influence of the spatial
distribution of people on their social relations
is, in principal, the same as that of their other
distributions among positions - 'Geographical
locations may be considered a parameter which
affects social relations as other parameters do
... People associate disproportionately with
others of their own group, and they associate
disproportionately with others in their own
locations', (Blau, 1977, p. 93). Berry (1984)
refers to the so-called contact hypothesis, which
posits that one's behaviour and attitudes towards
members of a disliked social category will become
more positive after direct inter-personal
interaction with them. However he goes on to
stress that such positive consequences will be
dependent upon the contact being equal status,
while Amir (1976, p. 264) notes that if one or
both of the interacting groups are perceived as
threatening, the chance of a positive attitudinal
change is thereby reduced.
   When we move beyond the question of the
influence of spatial segregation on intergroup
attitudes to broader issues of societal
integration, we can examine Marston and Van Valey's
(1979) discussion of the role of residential segregation in the assimilation process. Using, in
part, the framework provided by Gordon (1964) they
discuss cultural, socio-economic and structural
assimilation. Reviewing a number of mainly
American studies they claim that cultural assimilation (where a group incorporates the basic
behavioural patterns of the host society into an
ethnic way of life, and where the group conforms
to the basic values of the wider society) is
definitely retarded by segregation. Socio-economic
assimilation (defined as the degree to which the
distributions of income, occupation and education
in racial or ethnic groups are proportionate to
those in the balance of the population) is less
clearly related to segregation reduction, although
on balance they feel that reduced segregation does
contribute to socio-economic integration. In
terms of structural assimilation (the wide-scale
involvement of ethnic group members in
primary-type relationships with members of the
host society) and its relation to segregation,

111

## Segregation

Marston and Van Valey are quite adamant – 'segregation appears to be fully sufficient to prevent structural assimilation to any meaningful extent. It may even be argued that the perpetuation of minority residential segregation has been, and continues to be, one of the primary mechanisms for restricting intergroup personal contact' (1979, p. 19). It may also be worth noting that better ethnic relations seem to develop in areas where the residentially mixed populations are of relatively high economic status (Amir, 1976, p. 263). This, in turn, may relate to a further point made by Amir, when he observes that an unfavourable condition for prejudice reduction is where the contact situation produces competition between groups. Thus competition for scarce resources of housing and jobs is likely to be more intense amongst the materially less advantaged sections of a population. This, in turn, may be accentuated by a tendency towards physical expression of group opposition among lower income groups – a kind of macho-model where masculinity is expressed in the middle class by fast cars or large mortgages, but where such satisfactions are denied the working class male, being replaced by a mythology of physicality and violence (Carey, 1986, quoting Bernice Martin).

Marston and Van Valey conclude their review of the impact of residential segregation upon the assimilation process by observing that such impact is complex. They go on to claim that the residential patterning of racial and ethnic groups is clearly one of the most significant and sensitive issues facing society today. Herein lies a dilemma – persistent segregation is likely to contribute to the perpetuation of long-standing prejudices, while at the very same time contributing to the maintenance of valued group cultural attributes and providing a geographical base for political action. Act to destroy the prejudice and you may undermine a rich social plurality; preserve the social plurality and you provide a fertile environment for prejudice to thrive in.

Almost all research on the consequences of segregation refers to racial/ethnic concerns, not those deriving from social class. This may be due to the taken-for-granted nature of class segregation, where class residential desegregation is not considered to be a possible strategy for the reduction of class prejudice. Gans (1972, p. 151) has noted the importance of the concept of the socially balanced community in contemporary planning thought, while also observing the constant rejection of the concept in the housing market. Thus it is possible to conceive of ethnic residential integration being achieved by means of the creation of ethnic equality; but any corresponding effort to manufacture class residential integration by creating class equality is a logical absurdity, because that would abolish class itself. Of course it could be argued, as indeed it has been in this chapter, that the maintenance of ethnic distinctiveness is a product of ethnic inequality (in part a defensive response) and that the creation of ethnic equality would not only abolish ethnic segregation, but ethnic differentiation also.

All in all, the light that has been cast by research on the question of the relationship between residential segregation on the one hand and class or ethnic relations on the other has been very limited. In this somewhat discouraging situation, geographers have made practically no contribution at all.


Two Concepts - Territory and Critical Mass

There are two perspectives highly relevant to the study of segregation - one is the notion of 'territory' and 'territorial behaviour', the other the concept of 'critical mass'. In briefly discussing the former notion we can do no better than give Soja's definition of territoriality:

> ... a behavioural phenomenon associated with the organization of space into spheres of influence or clearly demarcated territories which are made distinctive and considered at least partially exclusive by their occupants or defines. Its most obvious geographical manifestation is an identifiable patterning of spatial relationships resulting in the confinement of certain activities in particular areas and the exclusion of certain categories of individuals from the space of the territorial individual or group (Soja, 1971, p. 19).

The link with segregation comes through the emphasis on exclusion - a situation where a territory is defined as being an area which can legitimately be occupied by persons bearing certain attributes, but which is out-of-bounds to others. Over and above notions of homogeneity of territorial occupance, Soja's statement also points to the constraining effect defined territories have on the spatial extent of social networks. Various aspects of territorial demarcation and territorial behaviour have been explored in recent years, perhaps most notable in circumstances where such behaviour is most sharply manifest - that is in contexts of highly accentuated group conflict such as the Philadelphia neighbourhood studied by Ley and Cybriwsky (Ley 1974; Ley and Cybriwsky, 1974) or the oft referred to Shankill-Falls Divide in Belfast (Boal, 1969; 1978a). Boal has extended the study of territorial behaviour in high segregation contexts beyond ethnic concerns to situations of class division (Boal, 1971), while we are given more literary references by Hoggart (1958) in his description of inner Leeds - '... they know it as a group of tribal areas. Pitt Street is certainly one of ours; just as certainly as Prince Consort Street next to it is not, is over the boundary in another parish'. Here territorial differentiation involves notions of exclusivity within a working class part of the city. Ethnicity is to the fore with the Canadian poet, Irving Layton when, recalling his boyhood in Montreal, he expressed anxiety about crossing St. Denis Street - 'The street marked the barrier between Jewish and French-Canadian territories - east of St. Denis was hostile Indian country populated with church going Mohawks somewhat older than myself waiting to ambush me'.

Territorial behaviour with concomitant spatial segregation can usefully be contrasted with what Sommer calls 'dominance behaviour', where 'both processes limit agression because an individual either refrains from going where he is likely to be involved in disputes [he behaves territorially] or based on his knowledge of who is above and below him, to engage in ritualized dominance - subordination behaviour rather than actual conflict' (Sommer, 1969, p. 12). This perspective corresponds to that of van den Berghe when he outlines what he calls paternalistic and competitive race relations. With the former a great degree of social distance between members of different groups permits close symbiosis without any threat to status inequalities - 'consequently

## Segregation

physical segregation is not prominently used as a mechanism of social control' (van den Berghe, 1967, p. 27). In a situation of competitive group relations, however, social distance diminishes and physical segregation is introduced as a second line of defence for the preservation of the dominant group's position (van den Berghe, 1967, p. 30). Thus territoriality and spatial segregation manifest one set of group relations, subservience and spatial mingling another. A further parallel to this is provided by Lofland, when she distinguishes an earlier period of 'appearential ordering' from a current phase where 'spatial ordering is predominant' (Lofland, 1973). In the pre-industrial city, status or class groups were not likely to be residentially segregated - people were categorized by how they looked. In the modern city, spatial ordering is predominant - people are categorized by spatial location - 'In the preindustrial city, a man was what he wore. In a modern city, a man is where he stands' (Lofland 1973, p. 82).

Sommer, van den Berghe and Lofland have raised some very interesting issues, albeit in a fairly general fashion. Our understanding of the nature and functions of segregation can be sharpened by viewing them in the context of alternative behavioural forms. At this point, much further research is needed.

Another conceptual framework that can be linked to territorial behaviour and questions of segregation is that provided by Hirschman - 'exit, voice and loyalty' (Hirschman, 1970). Hirschman is concerned to develop a framework for the analysis of response to decline in organizations. He suggests that exit and voice are two alternative options open to an individual. They can either quit an organization they are dissatisfied with (exit) or they can attempt to change the organization from within (voice) rather than try to escape a objectionable state of affairs. Orbell and Uno (1972) have applied this framework to an analysis of neighbourhood problem solving. They suggest that people who don't like things in a neighbourhood have three broad alternatives - they can resign themselves to doing nothing (apathy), they can leave the neighbourhood (exit) or they can stay and make some attempt to change things (voice). If the inmovement of members of a group judged by the existing occupants of a neighbourhood to be in some fashion 'undesirable' occurs, response may be triggered which can take the form of action to keep the undesirables out (voice), or which may involve abandoning the neighbourhood to relocate in a more congenial environment elsewhere. Both processes can help maintain significant levels of segregation, whether of the class or the ethnic variety, and it can be instructive, when exploring the dynamics of residential segregation, to employ the exit-voice framework. Hirschman also makes the point that the willingness to develop and use the voice mechanism is reduced by exit – that is the availability of an alternative location to escape to where one can join or create a new, pure class or ethnic territory means that there will be less resistance to invasion (voice will not be employed). Orbell and Uno make an extensive application of the exit-voice framework to the question of racial segregation in the United States, while Johnston (1982) has emphasized voice. The present author has tentatively applied exit-voice to ethnic segregation in Belfast (Boal, 1982, p. 265).

A concept that has come to the fore in recent years in discussions of residential segregation is that of 'critical mass'. Fischer (1976, p. 37) defines a critical mass as a population size large enough to permit what would otherwise be a small group of individuals to become a vital, active subculture. He goes on to link critical mass with a further concept when he notes that the larger a subculture's population, the greater its 'institutional completeness' (Fischer, 1975, p. 1331). Breton had earlier defined institutional completeness as being at its extreme 'whenever the ethnic community could perform all the services required by its members' (Breton, 1964, p. 194) and that such completeness required the formation of an 'ethnic public', such formation being dependent on the number of immigrants of a given ethnicity and the rate at which they arrived (Breton, 1964, p. 204). Thus the argument seems to be that the absolute size of a particular population group is a critical factor in the development and maintenance of the group as a cohesive entity. Sheer size enables a range of institutions to be supported, the institutions in turn providing coherence and an inward focus for the group.

Fischer's argument suggests that large urban size is likely to attract migrants from wider areas than does small urban size. However, it is also

likely that there will not only be more groups in
larger cities, but that the individual groups will
themselves be larger. Thus urban size is related
to critical mass and critical mass is related to
institutional completeness. However, Darroch and
Marston (1984) are not entirely satisfied with
this causal sequence. They argue that ethnic
residential patterns significantly mediate the
relationship between the absolute size of a given
ethnic population and the intensity of its ethnic
pluralism:

> Specifically, we have taken residential
> concentrations of ethnic populations to be the
> primary intervening variable in a process in
> which the demographic parameters affect ethnic
> pluralism, that is affect both the number of
> ethnic subcultures and their intensity
> (Darroch and Marston, 1984, p. 142).

Thus the larger the city, the larger the individual
groups that compose that city's population are
likely to be, enabling many to support a range of
group-specific institutions. If however, a large
group is not residentially concentrated, then it
will be less likely to display signs of
institutional completeness.

It appears that we are confronted with a
chicken-and-egg situation - critical mass provides
a basis for institutional completeness via the
presence of group residential concentration. On
the other hand, group residential concentration
may be supported by institutional completeness,
which, in turn, is partly built on the presence of
critical mass. Further, it has been suggested by
Marshall and Jiobu that large group size may
create a situation of threat, occurring, for
example, when the black group in an American city
becomes absolutely and/or relatively larger
vis-à-vis the white group, the latter viewing
blacks as a threat to their employment and
income. This sense of threat leads, in turn, to
discriminatory acts, with consequential residential
segregation and income and occupational differentiation (Marshall and Jiobu, 1975, p. 459).

It should be very instructive to explore the
relationships amongst the variable set critical
mass - segregation - institutional completeness -
threat. However, measurement problems will be
great and critical mass a highly variable,
contextually dependent quantity. Indeed it would be

Segregation

unfortunate if attempts to define critical mass
were to take on the attributes of the search for
the Holy Grail of the 'tipping point' (Wolf, 1963;
Schelling, 1972; Goering, 1978). To date I am
only aware of two preliminary attempts to explore
these issues - Marshall and Jiobu's 1975 paper on
black-white segregation in the United States and
Poole's examination of Catholic-Protestant
segregation in urban Northern Ireland (Poole,
1982). The latter found that Catholic-Protestant
segregation was higher in the larger urban
centres and that there was a strong positive
correlation between the absolute size of the
Catholic group and the degree of residential
segregation.

Discussion of critical mass and institutional
completeness has been carried out entirely in the
context of ethnic groups. No application has been
made to the class segregation situation. It could
be argued that critical mass in terms of class
groups is likely to be attained in a very high
proportion of urban contexts (unlike ethnic
critical mass). An examination of this critical
mass - segregation - institutional completeness
nexus from a class perspective could, however, be
a useful foil to a parallel ethnic exploration.


Conclusion

We now conclude with a question - whither
geographically focused segregation studies? It
seems desirable that segregation levels continue
to be monitored, in that these patterns are
inherently interesting and, more importantly, in
that they are both reflective of and contributory
to broader social change. Care must be taken as
to what population categories are employed and how
individuals are allocated to these categories. An
appropriate range of segregation indices should be
employed and attempts should be made to select
spatial units for the analyses that are significant
for the inhabitants. This latter requirement
will, of course, entail much painstaking work to
delineate appropriate spatial units, but we have
relied too long on the imposed spaces of census
tracts or enumeration districts.

Most segregation studies have been of
population residential distributions. The
extent to which the activity networks within which
people lead their lives display spatial segregation

## Segregation

is a much more neglected field, partly due, no
doubt, to the availability of census-type data for
the study of residential distributions, contrasted
with the need for painstaking survey to establish
network patterns. Here Wellman's work in Toronto
(Wellman, 1979, 1984) provides an excellent
framework for network studies, where he
distinguishes between what he calls 'community
saved' networks where localized communities
continue to exist in cities and 'community
liberated' networks, where such communities are
rarely organized as localized networks but are
formed of spatially dispersed linkages - a
situation that Webber (1963) would call 'community
without propinquity'. An intriguing example of
the combination of highly localized and widely
dispersed networks is provided by Watson in his
discussion of the Chinese who work in the
restaurant business in Britain:

> The economic niche that the Chinese control
> allows the migrants to live, work and prosper
> without changing their way of life to suit
> British social expectations ... The catering
> establishments are virtual islands of Chinese
> culture in the larger British society ... They
> may be enveloped by British society and
> scattered throughout the country but they
> maintain a separate culture (Watson, 1977;
> pp. 193, 195).

In a limited fashion I have explored the spatial
dimensions of Catholic and Protestant, and middle
class and working class networks in Belfast but
much remains to be done. Recently Romann (1986)
has examined the transactional dimensions of
Jewish-Arab relationships in Jerusalem. In a
situation of almost complete residential
segregation there exists a complex set of, at
times, asymmetrical relationships in the economic,
political and legal worlds. Studies carried out
within the framework presented by Romann could
greatly enrich the rather narrow perspective
provided by a focus on residential segregation
alone.
     Most studies of segregation have been
segmentary - that is they have looked at a range
of aspects of segregation rather in isolation from
each other, such as levels and spatial patterns,
networks, functions and so on. What we lack, with
a few notable exceptions, are studies that attempt

to gain an integrated view - pattern, network and function seen as interdependent dimensions. Ethnographic explorations that do provide exceptions include Ley's work on Philadelphia (1974), Suttles' on Chicago (1968), the classical examination of Bethnal Green by Young and Willmott (1957) and Burton's study of a Belfast ethnic enclave (1978). Geographers have not been notable as urban explorers, or as geographical anthropologists prepared to live in the areas they wish to study as participant observers. Bunge has tried to direct us back to the geographical tradition of exploration by way of his urban expeditions (Bunge 1971; Bunge and Bordessa, 1975). There can be little doubt that participant observation and exploration greatly enriches survey oriented or census based approaches, but unfortunately the ivory tower frequently provides the urban social geographer's own segregated enclave.

All in all what is needed is the development of sound theoretical perspectives for the study of segregation, judiciously tempered by appropriate empirical material - as C. Wright Mills declared 'social research of any kind is advanced by ideas; it is only disciplined by facts' (Mills, 1959, p. 82). We need ideas, but we also require to earth our work in the material and social worlds, by means, if at all possible, of methodologically inventive investigations.

Segregation

REFERENCES
Agócs, C. (1981) 'Ethnic Settlement in a Metropol-
     itan Area:   A   Typology   of   Communities',
     Ethnicity, 8, 127-148
Amir, Y. (1976) 'The Role of Intergroup Contact in
     Change in Prejudice and Ethnic Relations' in
     P.A. Katz (ed.), Towards the Elimination of
     Racism, Pergamon Press, New York, 245-308
Berry, B.J.L. (1971)  'Monitoring Trends, Forecast-
     ing Change and Evaluating Goal Achievement in
     the Urban Environment: The Ghetto Expansion
     Versus Desegregation Issue in Chicago as a Case
     Study' in M. Chisholm, A.E. Frey and P. Haggett
     (eds.),   Regional   Forecasting,   Butterworths,
     London, 93-117
Berry, J.W.  (1984) 'Cultural  Relations in Plural
     Societies:  Alternatives  to  Segregation  and
     their   Sociopsychological   Implications'   in
     N. Miller and M.B. Brewer (eds.), Groups in
     Contact : The Psychology of Desegregation,
     Academic Press, Orlando, 11-27
Blau, P.M.  (1977)  Inequality and Heterogeneity,
     Free Press, New York
Boal, F.W.  (1969) 'Territoriality on the Shankill-
     Falls Divide, Belfast', Irish Geography, 6,
     30-50
Boal, F.W.  (1971)  'Territoriality  and  Class: A
     Study of Two Residential Areas in Belfast',
     Irish Geography, 6, 229-248
Boal, F.W.  (1972)  'The  Urban  Residential  Sub-
     Community - a Conflict Interpretation', Area,
     4, 164-168
Boal, F.W. (1978a) 'Territoriality on the Shankill-
     Falls Divide, Belfast: The Perspective from
     1976' in D. Lanegran and R. Palm (eds.), An
     Invitation  to  Geography  (Second  Edition),
     McGraw-Hill, New York, 58-77
Boal, F.W. (1978b) 'Ethnic Residential Segregation'
     in D.T. Herbert and R.J. Johnston (eds.),
     Social Areas in Cities : Processes, Patterns
     and Problems, 57-95
Boal, F.W. (1981) 'Ethnic Residential Segregation,
     Ethnic Mixing and Resource Conflict : A Study
     in Belfast, Northern Ireland' in C. Peach, V.
     Robinson  and  S.  Smith  (eds.),  Ethnic
     Segregation  in  Cities,  Croom  Helm,  London,
     235-251

## Segregation

Boal, F.W. (1982) 'Segregating and Mixing : Space and Residence in Belfast' in F.W. Boal and J.N.H. Douglas (eds.), Integration and Division : Geographical Perspectives on the Northern Ireland Problem, Academic Press, London, 249-280

Boal, F.W. (1986) 'Ethnic Toronto: A View from the Outside', Urban History Review (forthcoming)

Boal, F.W., Murray, R.C. and Poole, M.A. (1976) 'Belfast: The Urban Encapsulation of a National Conflict', in S.E. Clarke and J.L. Obler (eds), Urban Ethnic Conflict: A Comparative Perspective, Comparative Urban Studies Monograph No. 3, Institute for Research in Social Science, University of North Carolina, Chapel Hill, 77-131

Bourne, J. and Sivanandan, A. (1980) 'Cheerleaders and Ombudsmen: The Sociology of Race Relations in Britain', Race and Class, 21, 331-352

Breton, R. (1964) 'Institutional Completeness of Ethnic Communities and the Personal Relations of Immigrants', American Journal of Sociology, 70, 193-205

Bunge, W. (1971) Fitzgerald: Geography of a Revolution, Schenkman, Cambridge, Massachusetts

Bunge, W. and Bordessa, R. (1975) The Canadian Alternative: Survival Expeditions and Urban Change, Geographical Monographs, No. 2, Department of Geography, York University, Toronto

Burton, F. (1978) The Politics of Legitimacy, Routledge and Kegan Paul, London

Cannadine, D. (1982) 'Residential Differentiation in Nineteenth-Century Towns: From Shapes on the Ground to Shapes in Society' in J.H. Johnson and C.G. Pooley (eds.), The Structure of Nineteenth Century Cities, Croom Helm, London, 235-251

Carey, S. (1986) 'Anatomy of Racial Violence', New Society, 76, 11 April, 7-9

Chudacoff, H.P. (1973) 'A New Look at Ethnic Neighbourhoods: Residential Dispersion and the Concept of Visibility in a Medium-Sized City', Journal of American History, 60, 76-93

Concise Oxford Dictionary (1976), Clarendon Press, Oxford

Darroch, A.G. and Marston, W.G. (1972) 'The Social Class Bases of Ethnic Residential Segregation: The Canadian Case', American Journal of Sociology, 77, 491-510

## Segregation

Darroch, A.G. and Marston, W.G. (1984) 'Patterns of Urban Ethnicity' in N. Iverson (ed.), Urbanism and Urbanization: Views, Aspects and Dimensions Brill, Leiden, 127-159

Dicken, P. and Lloyd, P.E. (1981) Modern Western Society, Harper and Row, London

Doherty, J. (1973) 'Race, Class and Residential Segregation in Britain', Antipode, 5:3, 45-51

Downs, A. (1981) 'Statement of Anthony Downs': Hearings before the Select Committee on Equal Educational Opportunity of the U.S. Senate, 91st Congress, 2nd Session on Equal Educational Opportunity, Part 5 - De Facto Segregation and Housing Discrimination, United States Government Printing Office, Washington, D.C., 2966-2980

Downs, A. (1973) Opening Up the Suburbs, Yale University Press, New Haven

Duncan, J.S. and Duncan, N.G. (1984) 'A Cultural Analysis of Urban Residential Landscapes in North America: The Case of the Anglophile Elite', in J. Agnew, J. Mercer and D. Sopher (eds.), The City in Cultural Context, Allen and Unwin, Boston, 255-276

Fischer, C.S. (1975) 'Towards a Subcultural Theory of Urbanism', American Journal of Sociology, 80, 1319-1341

Fischer, C.S. (1976) The Urban Experience, Harcourt Brace, New York

Gans, H. (1972) 'The Balanced Community: Homogeneity or Heterogeneity in Residential Areas' in H. Gans, People and Plans, Penguin, Harmondsworth, Middlesex, 140-159

Goering, J.M. (1978) 'Neighbourhood Tipping and Racial Transition - A Review of Social Science Evidence', Journal of the American Institute of Planners, 44, 68-78

Gordon, M.M. (1964) Assimilation in American Life, Oxford University Press, New York

Hall, S., Critcher, C., Jefferson, T., Clarke J., and Roberts, B. (1978) Policing the Crisis: Mugging, The State and Law and Order, Macmillan, London

Harris, R. (1984) 'Residential Segregation and Class Formation in the Capitalist City: A Review and Directions for Research', Progress in Human Geography, 8, 26-49

Segregation

Harvey, D. (1975) 'Class Structure in a Capitalist
    Society and the Theory of Residential Differen-
    tiation' in R. Peel, P. Haggett and M. Chisholm
    (eds.), Processes in Physical and Human
    Geography, Heinemann, London
Hirschman, A.O. (1970 ) Exit, Voice and Loyalty,
    Harvard    University    Press,    Cambridge,
    Massachusetts
Hoggart, R. (1958) The Uses of Literacy, Penguin,
    Harmondsworth, Middlesex
Jones, T.P. and McEvoy, D. (1974) 'Residential
    Segregation of Asians in Huddersfield', paper
    read at Annual Conference, Institute of British
    Geographers, Norwich
Jones, T.P. and McEvoy, D. (1978) 'Race and Space
    in Cloud-Cuckoo Lane', Area, 10, 162-166
Johnston, R.J. (1980) City and Society, Penguin
    Harmondsworth, Middlesex
Johnston, R.J. (1982) 'Voice as a Strategy in Loca-
    tional Conflict: the Fourteenth Amendment and
    Residential Separation in the United States'
    in K.R. Cox and R.J. Johnston (eds.), Conflict,
    Politics and the Urban Scene, Longman, London,
    111-126
Keane, M.C. (1985) 'Ethnic Residential Change in
    Belfast  1969-75',  Unpublished  PhD  Thesis,
    Queen's University of Belfast
Knox, P. (1982) Urban Social Geography, Longman,
    London
Lambert, J. and Lambert, C. (1982) 'Race, Ethnicity
    and  Urban  Change'  in  A.  Cochrane  and  L.
    McDowell (Block Coordinators), Urban Change and
    Conflict: Block 4 - Conflict and Stability in
    Urban Society, Open University Press, Milton
    Keynes, 71-111
Lee, T.R. (1978) 'Race, Space and Scale', Area, 10,
    365-367
Ley, D. (1974) The Black Inner City as Frontier
    Outpost, Association of American Geographers,
    Washington, D.C.
Ley, D. and Cybriwsky, R. (1974) 'Urban Graffiti
    as Territorial Markers', Annals, Association
    of American Geographers, 64, 491-505
Lieberson, S. (1972) 'Stratification and Ethnic
    Groups' in A.H. Richmond (ed.), Readings in
    Race and Ethnic Relations, Pergamon Press,
    Oxford, 199-209
Lieberson, S. (1981) 'An Asymmetrical Approach to
    Segregation' in C. Peach, V. Robinson and S.
    Smith (eds.), Ethnic Segregation in Cities,
    Croom Helm, London, 61-82

## Segregation

Lofland, L.H. (1973) A World of Strangers, Basic Books, New York

McDowell, L. (1982) 'Class Status, Location and Life-Style, in A. Cochrane and L. McDowell (Block Coordinators), Urban Change and Conflict Block 4 - Conflict and Stability in Urban Society, Open University Press, Milton Keynes, 7-44

Marger, M.N. (1985) Race and Ethnic Relations, Wadsworth, Belmont, California

Marshall, H. and Jiobu, R. (1975) 'Residential Segregation in United States Cities : A Causal Analysis', Social Forces, 53, 449-460

Marston, W.G. and Van Valey, T.L. (1979), 'The Role of Residential Segregation in the Assimilation Process', Annals of the American Academy of Political and Social Science, 441, 13-25

Massey, D.S. (1981) 'Social Class and Ethnic Segregation: A Consideration of Methods and Conclusions', American Sociological Review, 46, 641-650

Miles, R. (1982) Racism and Migrant Labour, Routledge and Kegan Paul, London

Mills, C.W. (1959) The Sociological Imagination, Penguin, Harmondsworth, Middlesex

Morgan, B.S. (1984) 'Social Geography, Spatial Structure and Social Structure', GeoJournal, 9, 301-310

Morrill, R.L. (1965) 'The Negro Ghetto: Problems and Alternatives', Geographical Review, 55, 339-361

Neuwirth, G. (1969) 'A Weberian Outline of a Theory of Community: Its Application to the Dark Ghetto', British Journal of Sociology, 20, 148-163

Office of Population Censuses and Survey (1980) Classification of Occupations 1980, H.M.S.O., London

Orbell, J.M. and Uno, T. (1972) 'A Theory of Neighbourhood Problem Solving: Political Action vs Residential Mobility', American Political Science Review, 66, 471-489

Parkin, F. (1979) Marxism and Class Theory: A Bourgeois Critique, Tavistock, London

Peach, C. (1975) 'Introduction: The Spatial Analysis of Ethnicity and Class' in C. Peach (ed.), Urban Social Segregation, Longman, London, 1-17

Peach, C. (1979) 'Race and Space', Area, 11, 82-89

Segregation

Peach, C. (1981) 'Conflicting Interpretations of Segregation' in P. Jackson and S.J. Smith (eds.), Social Interaction and Ethnic Segregation, Institute of British Geographers, Special Publication No. 12, Academic Press, London, 19-33

Peach, C. (1984) 'The Force of West Indian Island Identity in Britain' in C. Clarke, D. Ley and C. Peach (eds.), Geography and Ethnic Pluralism, George Allen & Unwin, London, 214-230

Phillips, D. (1981) 'The Social and Spatial Segregation of Asians in Leicester' in P. Jackson and S.J. Smith (eds.), Social Interaction and Ethnic Segregation, Institute of British Geographers, Special Publication No. 12, Academic Press, London, 101-121

Poole, M.A. (1982) 'Religious Residential Segregation in Urban Northern Ireland' in F.W. Boal and J.N.H. Douglas (eds.), Integration and Division: Geographical Perspectives on the Northern Ireland Problem, Academic Press, London, 281-308

Poole, M.A. and Boal, F.W. (1973) 'Religious Residential Segregation in Belfast in mid-1969: A Multi-Level Analysis' in B.D. Clarke and M.B. Gleave, (eds.), Social Patterns in Cities, Institute of British Geographers, Special Publication No. 5, Institute of British Geographers, London, 1-40

Robinson, V. (1979) 'The Segregation of Asians within a British City: Theory and Practice, Research Paper 22, School of Geography, Oxford University

Robinson, V. (1981) 'Segregation and Simulation: a Re-evaluation and Case Study' in P. Jackson and S.J. Smith (eds.), Social Interaction and Ethnic Segregation, Institute of British Geographers, Special Publication No. 12, Academic Press, London, 137-161

Romann, M. (1986) 'The Transactional Dimension of Ethnic Residential Segregation and Integration: The Case of Jewish-Arab Spatial and Economic Relationships in Jerusalem' [unpublished paper, Department of Geography, Tel Aviv University]

Rose, H.M. (1970) 'The Development of an Urban Sub-System - the Case of the Negro Ghetto', Annals, Association of American Geographers, 60, 1-17

## Segregation

Rosenberg, L. (1954) 'A Study of the Changes in the Geographic Distribution of the Jewish Population in the Metropolitan Area of Toronto, 1851-1951', Canadian Jewish Population Studies, Jewish Community Series No. 2, 1-17

Rosenthal, E. (1961) 'Acculturation without Assimilation? The Jewish Community of Chicago, Illinois', American Journal of Sociology, 65, 275-288

Schelling, T.C. (1972) 'A Process of Residential Segregation: Neighbourhood Tipping' in A.H. Pascal (ed.), Racial Discrimination in Economic Life', D.C. Heath, Lexington, Massachusetts

Shilhav, Y. (1984) 'Spatial Strategies of the "Haredi"? Population in Jerusalem', Socio-Economic Planning Science, 18, 411-418

Soja, E.W. (1971) The Political Organization of Space, Resource Paper 8, Association of American Geographers, Washington D.C.

Sommer, R. (1969) Personal Space, Prentice-Hall, Englewood Cliffs

Suttles, G.D. (1968) The Social Order of the Slum, University of Chicago Press

Taeuber, K.E. and Taeuber, A.F. (1965) Negroes in Cities, Aldine, Chicago

van den Berghe, P.L. (1976) Race and Racism, Wiley, New York

van den Berghe, P.L. (1981) The Ethnic Phenomenon, Elsevier, New York

Waterman, S. and Kosmin, B. (1986) 'The Jews of London', The Geographical Magazine, 58:1, 21-27

Watson, J.L. (1977) 'The Chinese: Hong Kong Villagers in the British Catering Trade' in J.L. Watson (ed.), Between Two Cultures, Blackwell, Oxford, 181-213

Webber, M.M. (1963) 'Order in Diversity: Community without Propinquity' in L. Wingo (ed.), Cities and Space, Johns Hopkins Press, Baltimore, 23-54

Wellman, B. (1979) 'The Community Question: The Intimate Networks of East Yorkers', American Journal of Sociology, 84, 1201-1231

Wellman, B. (1984) 'Looking for Community' Environments, 16, 59-63

Wolf, E.P. (1963) 'The Tiping Point in Racially Changing Neighbourhoods', Journal of the American Institute of Planners, 24, 217-222

## Segregation

Wolpert, J., Mumphrey, A. and Seley, J. (1972) Metropolitan Neighbourhoods : Participation and Conflict over Change', Resource Paper 16, Association of American Geographers, Washington, D.C.

Woods, R.I. (1975) 'The Stochastic Analysis of Immigrant Distributions', Research Paper 11, School of Geography, Oxford University

Yancey, W.L., Ericksen, E.P. and Juliani, R.N. (1976) 'Emergent Ethnicity: A Review and Reformulation', American Sociological review, 41, 391-401

Young, M. and Willmott, P. (1957) Family and Kinship in East London, Routledge and Kegan Paul, London

Chapter Five

SOCIAL DEVIANCE AND THE CITY

D.T. HERBERT

Geographers are relative newcomers to the study of
social deviance. Mainly due to the efforts of
other social scientists such as sociologists and
psychologists, the literature on deviance is
considerable and criminology, for example, is a
separate multi-disciplinary field of study in its
own right. Close scrutiny will reveal some
evidence of "geographies" of mental illness and
crime dating back well into the nineteenth
century; studies which have been aroused by the
observation that these forms of social deviance
tend to be unevenly distributed over space and are
often disproportionately represented in particular
places. Even this kind of analysis however is
only available for specific forms of deviance and
topics such as alcoholism, prostitution, and drugs
are almost completely neglected.

There are some advantages in being a relative
newcomer. The extant literature may serve as
framework for research, as a source of ideas,
concepts, and empirical case stuides. Data
sources and definitional issues, often the
starting points for research, have already been
studied in some detail and the caveats are well
known. If geography seeks to add a new dimension
to the study of deviance it can most readily do
this by emphasizing its traditional concerns with
space, place and environment. These concerns are
more likely however to provide a different
emphasis and perhaps another perspective rather
than a fundamentally different theoretical
position. Geographers may be best served by
working within the theoretical frameworks which
are common to the social sciences but which have
been more strongly developed in other
disciplines. In examining the ways in which these

## Social Deviance and the City

theories have evolved in relation to social deviance, geographers will find much common ground with their recent experience within social geography. The triad of positivism, humanism and structuralism which Jackson and Smith (1984) used to summarize theoretical stances in social geography has close parallels in the literature of social deviance. There is a similar eclecticism in which different and sometimes irreconcilable perspectives compete for attention. Downes and Rock (1982) describe the different epistemological positions in the sociology of deviance, such as functionalism, interactionism, phenomenology, and radical criminology, each of which has resisted decisive refutation. Of the derivative sources of ideas, the sociology of deviance is likely to be the most fruitful. It is a mature literature which has in the past moved from one source of interpretation to another and although the debate is not conclusive it can now be reviewed in a balanced way.

> The sociology of deviance is not a single undertaking which has progressed to a neat conclusion... the analysis of rule-breaking and rule enforcement has failed to be cumulative ... (it) is composed of an extended train of partially examined and partially exhausted ideas. (Downes and Rock, 1982, p. 251).

A second important lesson to emerge from this review of the sociology of deviance by Downes and Rock is the ubiquity and diversity of social deviance per se as a form of human behaviour:

> Deviance is everywhere and it leaves traces everywhere. It marks those who report it, those who attempt to control it, those who gain from it, those who imaginatively describe it and the contexts in which it is accomplished. (Downes and Rock, 1982, p. 41).

Sociologists are often reluctant to offer a definition of deviance but there is some basic agreement that it involves banned or controlled behaviour which is likely to attract punishment or disapproval. Any study of deviance enters a world of 'laws, rules, courts, criminals, rule-breakers, police and prisons'. Deviants depart from the accepted norms of a society and in so doing

130

infringe rules, many of which are legally enforced. Crime is probably the most significant form of deviance and does in itself cover an enormously wide range of human behaviours. In some forms of deviance such as mental disorders or even alcoholism and drug addiction, an individual may have very little control over forms of behaviour which may be labelled as deviant; most criminals on the other hand consciously break the rules of society.

Research in the social sciences has recognized the importance of isolating specific forms of deviance but also stresses the common features: 'The world of deviance consists of a web of relationships which must be fully explored before the separate parts are understood', (Downes and Rock, 1982, p. 41). Lee (1979) and others have argued that the very notions of deviance and social problems are inadequate starting points for an understanding of contemporary society. If deviance becomes the object of analysis it imposes a false constraint upon subsequent interpretations. A deviance approach, it is argued, is ideological as it isolates and therefore defines a series of problems through which a social system is perceived. Similar arguments are found among those who argue that the sociology of deviance is unlikely in itself to illuminate all the strategic problems of theory. It might constitute an instance of the working of deep rules, but it is not as absorbing a topic for study as those rules themselves. No review of geography and social deviance can ignore research which explores the significance of those deep rules but this chapter is written in the spirit of Weber's argument that research must progress by selecting partial aspects of the social world for study; 'not all empirical research need be drawn into the problem of the receding locus of power', (Saunders, 1981, p. 155). Although there are powerful macro forces which shape outcomes in space, 'locality' can be seen as the impact of local variations upon national systems. Social deviance may be but one instance of the working of deep rules but it is a valuable instance in which to examine key issues, methodologies and particular expressions of more general processes. Social deviance, and its links with social problems of the real world, needs the kind of research with a strong empirical base and a factual content which is in accord with the longer research traditions of social geography.

## Social Deviance and the City

The data base upon which to rest the study of social deviance is a major theoretical problem in its own right. Forms of behaviour which can be described as deviant are almost by nature covert; as Matza (1969) observed, deviance often becomes devious. This hidden nature of many forms of deviance seriously hinders any attempt to understand its incidence and affects some forms of behaviour much more than others. There are many ways of collecting information on deviance but all of them are fraught with difficulties. Sociologists of the Chicago school in the 1920s and 1930s made extensive use of participant observation methods as a means of collecting information on drug addicts, hobos, and teenage gangs among others. Shaw used such an approach in his well-known case-history of the 'Jack-roller', (Shaw, 1930). Direct studies of deviants run some risks of objectivity but can provide rare insights into the deviant's world and Bennett and Wright's (1984) investigation of burglars' attitudes towards their criminal activity provides a recent example of this kind of approach. The secondary sources from which to build up some picture of deviance are very diverse and may range from newspaper reports to official statistics. Again the hazards of relying upon these sources in an uncritical way are considerable and there are initial questions about the data collectors. Do levels and forms of recorded deviance reflect the values and practices of reporters, observers, police or court officials rather than the objective phenomenon itself? The representativeness and adequacy of official sources of data, methods used for their collection, variations in recording practice over time and space, and diversity of definition and interpretation are all questioned by analysts of statistical returns. Hindess (1973) argued that the real value of official statistics lay in their roles as indicators of the structure of society and its processes of control. Carr-Hill and Sterns (1979, p.311) state: 'We cannot use criminal statistics without asking how events became regarded as offences'. There are general principles behind the critique of offical statistics on social deviance which need to be acknowledged by all research in this field; particular circumstances which may distort those data are however, worthy of study in their own right. Lowman (1982), for example, showed how recorded offence rates are influenced by policing strategies which target specific groups, areas, or offences for close scrutiny.

Although there are other ways of gathering data on social deviance and caveats have to be acknowledged, official statistics remain the most widely used data bases. Some of the caveats need therefore to be examined in more detail. There are official sources of information for most if not all forms of deviance but some will undoubtedly be more comprehensive and efficient than others. Criminal statistics are among the most systematically collected and are published annually in the United Kingdom as 'Criminal Statistics' and in the United States as 'Uniform Crime Reports'. At a local level the police form the primary collecting unit for the many forms of social deviance that are classed as illegal. Crime is a generic term covering a very wide range of activities; Harries (1974), for example, identified over 2,800 types of Federal crime in the United States with many more defined at state or local levels. Criminal Statistics uses around 70 main classes of offence with up to 20 sub-divisions in some classes. These are clearly very detailed frameworks for the collection of data; the initial questions concern the completeness of the record.

Firstly, all researchers recognize that official statistics do not represent the total crime picture. This under-representation arises from several sources. Clear-up rates vary but are on average 40 percent of all known offences, only a minority of offenders are thus recorded. The so-called 'dark area' refers to offences which have occurred but which have not entered the official records. These are offences which are unnoticed or unreported. The police have discretionary powers and they may deal with offences which they regard as trivial in a summary manner. Estimates of the size of the dark area vary but there is some general suggestion that only 15 to 25 percent of all offences committed in the United Kingdom are officially recorded (Hood and Sparks, 1970). It must be emphasized that each type of offence has its own dark area the dimensions of which will vary. Homicides normally leave undisputed evidence and the police respond with the full force of the law. Victims of property losses have real incentives to report them to the police; not least because of the require-ments of insurance companies. For less serious offences however, and for forms of deviance such as drug addiction, the dark area is likely to be much higher. Again prostitution and pornography laws are often interpreted by the police in flexible ways and it is only through occasional 'purges' that true incidence levels are revealed.

Another problem with official statistics is the extent to which they are representative of the total deviant population. Mays (1963) argued that there was police bias against working class offenders in the production of criminal statistics. People with 'records' or other attributes which might lead to the label of 'deviant' are often targets of police scrutiny:

> It appears that both the police and the public have definite stereotypes about the type of offence and offender which should be dealt with by criminal law; seriousness of offence is certainly a major criterion for official action, but so also are persistence in offending, lack of family support, membership of street corner group, dress and demeanour. (Hood and Sparks, 1970, p.78).

The net result of selective reporting and police discretion is a set of official statistics in which males vastly outnumber females and young males of low socio-economic status are particularly over-represented. Alarming as this may seem, there is evidence that official statistics may be less fraught with error than has been previously thought. This evidence comes from research into the 'dark areas' of deviance and hidden delinquency, using self-report techniques. Gold (1966) suggested that whereas some bias against working-class youths was likely, official statistics did not seriously misrepresent their activities; Mawby (1979) showed that there was a largely uniform propensity to report crime across a range of social groups. Evidence of this kind does not provide grounds for complacency (white-collar crime and middle-class deviance may well be still hidden) but it does allow official statistics to be used with more confidence for particular types of offences and of offenders. This discussion of data sources has focused upon that deviance which is law-breaking, the problems are no less for forms of deviance which are within the law. Statistics on the mentally ill are

usually derived from hospital admission records
but as Levy and Rowitz (1973) point out, the true
incidence of mental illness would need to be
established by a count of all persons becoming ill
in a given population in a given time period and
there is no easy way of fixing the point of onset
of the illness. The alcoholic has many reasons to
hide his or her form of deviant behaviour and any
records will be considerably deficient.

. In considering ways in which social geographers
can study deviance, this review will now develop a
number of themes. Firstly, the most explicit
concern with spatial aspects of social deviance
can be found in what can be termed the ecological
tradition. This needs to be described. Secondly,
as more explicit social geographical research into
deviance has developed over the past decade, it
has both built upon this ecological base and
branched out in quite different directions; these
will be identified and assessed. Thirdly, and in
part arising from these inventories of the past
and present research record, there are issues
concerning the roles of geographical research in
the study of social deviance to be elaborated.


GEOGRAPHY AND SOCIAL DEVIANCE: THE ECOLOGICAL
TRADITION

Compared with the longevity of social science
research into deviance, the geographical
perspective is in a stage of youth if not
infancy. This is not to imply that awareness of
spatial features of deviance is absent in early
literature. Both Sutherland and Cressey (1970)
and Phillips (1972) have referred to a
'cartographic' school of criminology which existed
between 1830 and 1880 in several European
countries. Social statisticians such as Guerry in
France found the mapping of criminal statistics to
be an interesting and fruitful exercise. There
were regional variations in crime rates,
differences between urban and rural areas and
seasonal fluctuations. Mayhew (1862) performed
similar and quite detailed exercises for England
and Wales which concluded that crime rates tended
to be higher in areas of an industrial and urban
character. Nineteenth century observers of all
kinds, magistrates, statisticians and commentators
upon social conditions, noted the existence of
'crime areas' within cities which acted as breeding

grounds for criminals. These 'rookeries' were well known as this description of part of inner London suggests:

> The nucleus of crime in St. Giles consists of about six streets, riddled with courts, alleys, passages and dark entries, all leading to rooms and smaller tenements ... the lowest grade of thieves and dissolute people live in the immediate neighbourhood of the station house. (quoted in Tobias, 1967, p.131).

These were studies of the spatial incidence of crime which, whilst revealing systematic variations at different scales, were limited as conceptual frameworks. The kind of social ecology of crime and delinquency associated with Shaw and McKay (1942) and the Chicago school combined careful empirical research with more far-reaching theories for deviant behaviour. The empirical research involved mapping the homes of juvenile offenders brought before the Cook County court at various periods during the first half of the twentieth century. Using a spatial framework of square-mile grids, concentric zones and community areas, Shaw and McKay identified regular declines of delinquency rates from centre to periphery and distinctive delinquency areas in the inner city. They measured the statistical association between rates for delinquency, adult crime, recidivism and truancy and a set of social indicators for the various spatial units. The findings revealed high levels of association between deviance and substandard housing, poverty, foreign born population and mobility. Shaw and McKay argued that these correlates had no specific causal significance in themselves but were symptoms, along with delinquency and crime, of some underlying social condition. Their theory of social disorganization expressed this condition and suggested that in the absence of a stable form of society, with legalistically-based codes of behaviour and established norms and values, precipitating conditions for deviance would exist.

Although social disorganization is no longer generally tenable as a theory, it has links with other theories which are inheritors of the Chicago tradition, (Taylor, 1975). Subcultural theory for example suggesting that there were groups, within which particular sets of values, beliefs and behavioural norms prevailed, is part of this inheritance. Subculture has many expressions; for Cohen (1955) the case study was the delinquent gang in inner city areas in North America; Cloward and Ohlin (1960) argued that the content of a delinquent subculture was significantly shaped by its local milieu as working class youths reacted to their failure to achieve in middle class terms; Matza (1964) emphasized the extent to which subcultures could be integrated with the surrounding social world, delinquents are not isolated but are encircled by institutions which uphold conventional values, most young offenders retain choice and drift between these conventions and deviant behaviour.

The Chicago school offered a systematic approach to the distribution and environmental correlates of deviance which was grounded in empirical research but which used its findings to theorize the phenomena which it studied. It contained a statement on spatial models and generalizations and an appreciation of the reality of territorially-based social worlds within the city. As social geographers have developed their interest in crime and delinquency (Herbert, 1982), they have drawn heavily upon both the empirical method and the conceptual guidelines of social ecology. Contributions of the Chicago school were not confined to crime and delinquency. Thrasher's (1929) study of the gang, Anderson's (1923) study of the hobo were classic ethnographic monographs and Zorbaugh's (1929) area study of the Gold Coast and the Slum touched upon the life-styles of many deviant groups. Again, Dunham (1937) pioneered ecological studies of the mentally-ill in Chicago and mapped the spatial distribution of 7,253 schizophrenics by areas. He showed the same regular spatial patterns with clusters in the inner city which corresponded with rooming-house districts and hobohemia.


GEOGRAPHY AND SOCIAL DEVIANCE: DEVELOPING ECOLOGICAL PERSPECTIVES

As professional geographers became more directly involved in research into social deviance in the 1970s, the most obvious model was the ecological tradition. Twin foci of research were the depiction of patterns of deviance in geographical space and the measurement of association between measures of deviance and those of the social environment. Wider

awareness of statistical sources, better small
area statistics and access to the new computer
technology led to a large increase in research
output. Much of this research was descriptive
rather than analytical and was more successful at
building up an accurate portrayal of known deviance
than it was at either digging more deeply into the
real nature of a phenomenon or at seeking some
kind of causal explanation. The balance between
the empirical and the theoretical was not well
maintained and loose references to sociological
theories of deviance were not always adequate.
Crime became an active topic for geographical
study and initially carried forward the
cartographic tradition with some vigour. Other
geographies of crime in the 1970s had different
emphases. Pyle (1974) focused his attention upon
the development of a spatial referencing system as
a practical tool for the police and others
concerned with the maintenance of crime
statistics. His suggestions for a 'criminal
justice information system' involved the setting
up of basic data files on the location of
offences, details of victim and characteristics of
suspect. Each file would contain a spatial
location code in order to allow easy computer
mapping. Some research was directed more at the
justice system and spatial variations in
sentencing practice in the courts (Harries and
Brunn, 1978). The intra-urban scale attracted a
great deal of detailed research (Davidson, 1981;
Herbert, 1982). Some continuity from the work of
Shaw and McKay is evident and North American
studies tended to show that crime patterns could
still be generalized into zones and gradients. In
Britain the spatial models had less value as it
was found that crime and delinquency tended to
cluster in peripheral estates as well as in the
inner city. A distinction needed to be made
between the distributions of offenders and of
offences; both could be related to local environments but in different ways. Whereas offenders
could be linked to social conditions, both general
and specific, offences were often more usefully
seen as reactions to opportunities in environment.
Earlier studies had not always maintained this
distinction. Schmid (1960), for example, used data
for 35,000 offences and 30,000 offenders in a study
of Seattle arguing that it was important to know
not only where offenders lived but also where crime
was committed. His summary statement on crime in

## Social Deviance and the City

Seattle was that the central segment of the city contained 15 percent of the total population, 47 percent of known offences and 63 percent of offenders. Schmid's procedure of taking offences and offenders together can be justified in some circumstances, not least by the fact that most offenders are known to travel only short distances to commit an offence. More accurately however, offenders and offences need at least initially to be studied as separate distributions and indeed each type of offence, from homicide to shoplifting, tends to have its own 'geography'.

The other focal interest in the 1970s was with the ecological association between crime rates and other measures of the social demographic environment. Schmid can again be used as an early example. His factor analysis of 20 crime variables and 18 socio-demographic measures for each of 93 census tracts produced a crime dimension 'par excellence' which linked single, unemployed males with high crime rates and led him to the statement that urban crime areas were:

> generally characterised by all or most of the following factors: low social cohesion, weak family life, low socio-economic status, physical deterioration, high rates of population mobility and personal disorganisation (Schmid, 1960, p.678).

Geographers performing such statistical exercises with increasing sophistication in the 1970s found similar evidence that what might be termed a 'poor environment hypothesis' had general applicability in explaining the distribution of known offenders. There are other hypotheses. Baldwin and Bottoms (1976) produced a link between tenure and criminality in their Sheffield research in what can be termed a 'housing class' hypothesis. They also in a careful study found some support for the more general social disorganization theory though other attempts to move from statistical evidence to the support of general social theories have not always been so well founded. Lander (1954) employed multivariate statistical techniques in a study of Baltimore crime figures and, from the discovery that home-ownership and non-whites were the two significant variables, moved to support for the theory of anomie. Brown et al. (1976) in a much larger conceptual leap found evidence for the theories of anomie, working-class culture,

139

subculture, differential association (the preponderance of criminal influence in an area will increase the possibility of an individual becoming an offender), retreatism (dropping out of conventional society) and the double-failure hypothesis (resort to drugs after failure to 'succeed' by either legal or illegal means) after a cluster analysis of 35 variables for a town in Northern England. Hirschi and Selvin's (1967) justified plea for procedural rigour and circumspection in inferential analyses of this kind was well made.

These social theories of deviance are often appropriate to a geographical approach concerned with offender-residence and the general idea of some kind of precipitating conditions in the home environment which 'turns' an individual towards criminality. As a set, these traditional theories have been under considerable attack both from interactionist schools and from the radical critique; as Downes and Rock (1981) demonstrate, criminological theory has become eclectic in nature. Social geographers have used these theories as a frame of reference and have found some, such as sub-culture and social disorganization, of particular value. Again, the general principles of the radical critique are already firmly established in social geography and have found expression in relation to the geographies of crime (Peet, 1975). Whether any more purely geographical theories centred upon the interaction of time, space and place have any significant roles in the development of theory has yet to be demonstrated. Much more likely is a geographical contribution which has the effect of underlining the spatial dimension as part of a more general role in the evolution of theories of the social sciences.

Discussion so far has focused on crime as the most all-embracing form of deviance but similar developments in the ecological tradition can be found elsewhere. Research into mental illness, for example, (Giggs, 1979; 1985) has often concentrated upon the spatial clustering of some kinds of mental illness and the stability of these patterns over time. Giggs examined five types of mental disorder in Nottingham and showed their tendency to concentrate in either low-status inner city areas or in local authority estates. Schizophrenia in particular retains a broadly zonal spatial pattern with relatively high rates of incidence in virtually all inner city areas. Affective psychoses were more widely distributed with high rates in newer peripheral estates in north Nottingham. Schizophrenia was strongly related to environments of poor social and material resources, populations at risk were typically young and living in rented, furnished accommodation. Foreign born population figured prominently in the sample of schizophrenics of which they comprised one-third with a further 10.6 percent having at least one foreign-born parent. Giggs supports the concepts of anomie and social disorganization as the precipitating conditions for several forms of mental illness, though he is properly cautious about making causal inferences from statistical evidence:

> significant advances in specifically causal research will depend heavily upon carefully designed longitudinal surveys of the life histories of both hospital patients and control populations and not exclusively upon cross-sectional, aggregate (i.e. ecological) investigations (Giggs, 1979, p.102).

British research by geographers has tended to reveal divergences from simple spatial gradients for most forms of mental illness as the social geography of the city has changed. American studies, on the other hand, (Mintz and Schwarz, 1964; Levy and Rowitz, 1973) show long-term stability in those mental disorders typical of the inner city areas of deprivation. Explanations offered range between the 'drift hypothesis' which suggests that schizophrenics, for example, move into these rooming house areas after they become ill, and the 'breeder hypothesis' which suggests that their mental illness is a product of the urban conditions in which they live.

Another form of social deviance which has recently been studied by geographers is alcoholism. Data available have so far only enabled analysis at a regional scale but Smith and Hanham (1982) have classified the United States into 'wet' and 'dry' regions based upon indicators such as percentages of abstainers and heavy drinkers and per capita consumption of alcoholic beverages. Similarly, some of the recent research into prostitution has been concerned with the spatial patterning and environmental correlates of this form of social deviance. The ecological tradition persists and continues to form one ingredient to a great deal of social geographical research into deviance. More significant than this persistence however, is the gradual emergence of different emphases in research by geographers into these problems. It is to some of these new approaches that we can now turn.


NEW PERSPECTIVES

Discussion so far has reviewed the longer established major themes in the study of social deviance. As research by geographers in these fields is recent, it is perhaps inevitable that much of it is basic and draws heavily upon external sources of ideas. Research by geographers is accordingly more marked by its empirical content rather than by its conceptual rigour. The macro-micro debate (Peet, 1975; Harries, 1975) in which Peet raised the argument for a radical geography of crime which would recognize its roots in the political economy, raised some of the theoretical issues but did not develop them in any substantial way; Rengert (1981) has argued the merits of a behavioural approach which uses spatial variables in a systematic way. This is in some ways useful and effective but does not achieve any real insights and is hindered by the recognized limitations of a purely spatial perspective (Sack, 1978). Within the field of social deviance research however, there is increasing evidence of new kinds of perspectives with which geographers are strongly involved, which promise substantive progress from the traditional concerns with spatial ecology. Some examples of these are now evaluated.


Deviant Areas
Part of the geographer's stock-in-trade has been to identify areas or territories which have internal unity and which are clearly different from other areas or territories, though boundaries are often imprecise and information upon which to base them is often limited. Within the city the advent of Census-based small area statistics has enabled a great deal of research which has mainly followed traditional lines by tracing patterns and measuring environmental relationships. A study in Cardiff (Herbert, 1976) shows how these procedures

Social Deviance and the City

can be used as a base from which to develop more
detailed insights into the reasons for the
existence of 'delinquency areas' within cities and
the forms which these take. By mapping the
residences of known offenders from police data it
was clear that a number of distinctive clusters
existed in both inner city districts and
peripheral public sector estates. These high
delinquency rates corresponded with a series of
indicators of 'poor environments' such as low
socio-economic status, lack of amenities, high
unemployment, and large numbers of foreign-born.
It was also evident however, that not all areas
which were labelled as 'poor environments' also
suffered high rates of delinquency. A strategy
was devised which investigated the hypothesis that
variations in 'subjective environments' would help
understand why some areas were delinquent and
others were not. From a formal area-sampling
procedure six areas were selected for surveys;
those areas with high rates of delinquency were
compared with those which although otherwise
similar had much lower levels of delinquency. The
surveys within each of the selected areas explored
themes such as the attitudes of parents towards
education, actual educational attainment, parental
views on sanctions and punishment for
misbehaviour, and their definitions of right and
wrong forms of behaviour. Results pointed strongly
in the direction that children growing up in the
delinquency areas were exposed to 'poorer' sets of
values and attitudes of a kind which might well
underpin the fact that many more turned to
delinquent behaviour. There were laxer attitudes
towards misbehaviour, lower levels of educational
attainment, and a greater tendency to condone
illegal acts. In short, the evidence pointed
towards a sub-cultural effect in which people in
'delinquent areas' held some sets of values which
condoned some types of deviant behaviour. To relate
these values to an individual's position in an
economically-determined social class system is not
sufficient explanation, nor do housing conditions
per se or differential policing give more than
partial leads to understanding the varying
incidence of social deviance in the city. The
importance of locally-based sets of values and
attitudes has been well understood since Firey's
(1947) classic study of Beacon Hill in Boston and,
as humanistic approaches continue to develop
within geography, they will add emphasis to this

143

Social Deviance and the City

perspective:

> There is, in short, a plurality of value
> positions, intersecting in the urban arena,
> and a one-dimensional reduction to economic
> categories alone brings about an inappropriate,
> theoretical foreclosure (Ley and Mercer, 1980).

There are other kinds of deviant areas in which
geographers have recently engaged a research
interest. Ley (1974) has studied the distribution
of teenage gangs in the city and their alignment
with particular segments of inner city space; this
idea of 'turfs' has been well established since
Thrasher's (1929) classic study. Ley and
Cybriwsky (1974) explored new ground with their
study of gang graffiti in inner Philadelphia.
They showed how graffiti were used to map out
territories for particular groups, serving both as
a boundary marker and as an assertion of the
territorial rights and claims of the group. They
concluded that the graffiti-covered walls of inner
Philadelphia were much more than an 'attitudinal
tabloid' they were also a 'behavioural manifesto'.
Here again, the approach is strongly humanistic
and is far removed from formal methods of
regionalization. As another example of deviant
areas, the 'skid-rows' of North American cities
are defined as:

> any old dilapidated street or section of a
> town, containing very cheap bars, eating-
> places and flop-houses, where the permanently
> unemployed, vagrants, beggars, petty criminals,
> derelicts, degenerates, and mainly unemployed
> alcoholics hang out (Rowley, 1978, p. 211).

Such areas are in extremis the microcosms of the
deviant world. Ward (1975) examined ways in which
such areas developed and found that their central
locations in the spatially-restricted city
originally served the needs of the migrant male
workers and more latterly the male 'drop-outs'. A
strong inertial factor underpins the continuity of
'skid-rows' though there is evidence in some cities
of their decline or at least of their environmental
upgrading. Rowley (1978) studied north Main
Street in Winnipeg and found it had a continuing
role which was linked to the needs of the Indian
and Metis for whom it offered a recognized meeting
place and an oasis of familiarity in their curious

state of limbo between the reservation and the city, a behavioural sink rather than a way station.

The facts of deviant areas can be established and their internal characteristics can be examined; there are remaining questions however, on the emergence and persistence of such areas. The first of these questions is often difficult to resolve as historical evidence may not be available. Common locational features may typify skid rows or red-light districts but detailed studies of their origins are rare. A more recent problem area in British cities is the 'difficult-to-let' estate in the public sector of housing. As they are relatively recent, the opportunities to understand ways in which they acquired bad reputations are more realistic. When Baldwin (1975) reviewed the problems of problem estates, he cited high rates of tenant turnover, paucity of recreational facilities and some evidence that local authority housing managers had followed a practice of 'dumping' problem families in particular estates. The issue is contentious but a significant number of studies do attribute key roles in the creation of problem estates to the managers who control the allocation of housing as a resource. Gill (1977) for example, scrutinized housing officials' records of tenants of the Luke Street area of Liverpool and found them liberally sprinkled with phrases such as 'not suitable for new property', 'suitable for the Dock area only', and 'not suitable for the Corporation to rehouse'. 'It was local planning and housing department policy that produced Luke Street,' (Gill, 1977, p.187).

Others such as Wilson (1963) have argued that there is a strong self-selection process operative among potential residents of problem estates which is related to the image of the estate, levels of rent, proximity to family and friends, and expectations of the quality of housing and estate life. On problem estates the tenant with any kind of social aspiration was attempting to leave, those who stayed were either indifferent to the estate's reputation or were desperate for housing. Labels given to problem estates are influenced by the initial occupants and in their Sheffield study, Bottoms and Xanthos (1979) showed how one estate was used to rehouse a number of notorious gang leaders and their associates in the 1950s whilst another was tenanted by people displaced by slum clearance. In Cardiff (Herbert, 1979) an

estate was given distinctiveness by the fact that
its occupants were largely Roman Catholic. Once
labelled, estates have reputations which are
difficult to change even if actual behaviour no
longer matches up to expectations. Damer (1974)
studied Wine Alley in Glasgow, a place labelled by
municipal officials as being typified by rent
arrears, vandalism, crime and socio-psychiatric
problems. His enquiry pointed strongly to the
negative effect of a labelling process which was
based far more upon past rather than present
events.

## Environmental Criminology

Environmental criminology offers an example of an
approach to the study of social deviance which is
less concerned with theories of causation and more
focused on measures for prevention and control and
with what Davidson (1981) termed 'coping with
crime'. Environmental criminology focuses upon
criminal events and the places at which they occur,
the thrust is the offence rather than the offender.
One assumption is that criminal events, especially
those involving property, are reactions to opportunities in the environment. There is a good deal
of evidence to suggest that many burglaries and
thefts from dwellings are not carefully planned in
advance. Davidson (1981) concluded that the
professional thief in Christchurch was numerically
swamped by his 'brash, young, opportunist
colleagues'. For some time it has been argued
that there are cues or stimuli in local environments to which offenders respond. The nature of
these 'cues' varies. Newman's (1972) concept of
defensible space was constructed mainly around the
need to counteract opportunities offered by bad
design of buildings and space; Carter (1974)
identified 'soft targets' for burglars as environments which lacked security and surveillance and
were well-known to potential offenders. Environmental criminologists argue that all people are
likely to commit some kind of offence and that
there is no sharp distinction between criminal and
non-criminal populations. Because of a particular
assemblage of opportunities, access, low
surveillance, weak control or poor security, some
places are more vulnerable and become the loci
of criminal events. These places are 'vulnerable
areas' and although they may vary by type of
offence, there is a generally higher likelihood of

being victimized in such areas. The example of research into environmental criminology described below involves the testing of some hypotheses which seek to understand why vulnerable areas emerge. This example is specific to residential burglary.

It has already been shown that most offenders travel short distances to commit offences and a first hypothesis is that places close to where known offenders live will be vulnerable - this is termed the offender-residence hypothesis. It was possible for a study of Swansea, using data collected for 1975 and 1980, to examine the movement of offenders among 'planning cells' which were areas identified by the City Planning Department as approximations of neighbourhoods (Herbert and Hyde, 1985). The data showed that 44 percent of offences were committed in the same planning cell within which the offender lived and a further 33 percent of offences were committed in the adjacent cell. Over three-quarters of the offences involved very short trips from the offender's home. The weight of evidence from this and other studies (see for example, Baldwin and Bottoms, 1976) is that the offender-residence hypothesis is valid and that areas become vulnerable if they contain, or are close to areas which contain, large numbers of offenders.

The border-zone hypothesis suggests that the edges of a well-defined neighbourhood are more vulnerable to burglary than their cores. In the original study (Brantingham and Brantingham, 1975) an algorithm was used to define neighbourhoods and clear differences were found between central and peripheral blocks in the neighbourhoods of Tallahassee. Burglary rates in the edge-blocks were typically two to three times higher. When this hypothesis was applied in Swansea the effect was discernible but inconsistent; in the southern part of the study area which comprised a mixture of local authority estate, rented subdivided dwellings and stable terraced-row houses, the edges of the 'planning cells' did have higher burglary rates; in the northern part however, comprising a large municipal estate, there was little evidence of variation along these lines.

The area variability hypothesis suggests that heterogeneous or mixed areas are more likely to suffer from a high incidence of offence rates. A key question concerns the kind of heterogeneity which is critical and how it can be measured. In the Swansea study a composite measure based upon census variables was used which included indicators of social class, demographic composition and household features. Whereas this measure captures some of the main features of residential structure, it is less effective as a measure of the juxtaposition of people, land-uses and activities. Results of the application of this procedure to Swansea (Figure 5.1) show some support for area variability in the sense that 60 percent of the planning cells support the hypothesis if means are taken as thresholds and 73 percent if medians are taken. This is a useful finding but there is still a need for a more refined measure of variability. The significance of juxtaposition is that it is relative rather than absolute deprivation that conditions offenders' aspirations and relative rather than absolute wealth that provides tempting local opportunities for crime.

The final hypothesis to be considered, that of local social control, suggests that areas in which social cohesion is low and where there is little sense of community, are more vulnerable to crime. Tests of the significance of the level of social cohesion within neighbourhoods in this context have obtained mixed results. Reppetto (1974) found that in Boston neighbourhoods with low levels of social cohesion suffered five to six times the burglary rates of neighbourhoods with high social cohesion; Ley and Cybriwsky (1974) found that pockets of offences in inner Philadelphia tended to correspond with places where social control was weak. The Swansea study employed a range of techniques to test neighbourhood cohesion and found no consistent relationship between cohesion and crime rates. Whereas parts of the inner city fitted the hypothesis well in the sense that very cohesive areas experienced little crime and areas with low cohesion experienced far more, there were problem estates with high crime rates which still scored well on indices of social cohesion. By distinguishing between the objective opportunities for crime and those which offenders perceive as being available, it was possible to devise a framework into which the study areas in Swansea could be placed (Figure 5.2). Area type A was typified by one of the inner city districts that had subdivided properties, transient populations, and mixed land-uses; area type B was the problem

148

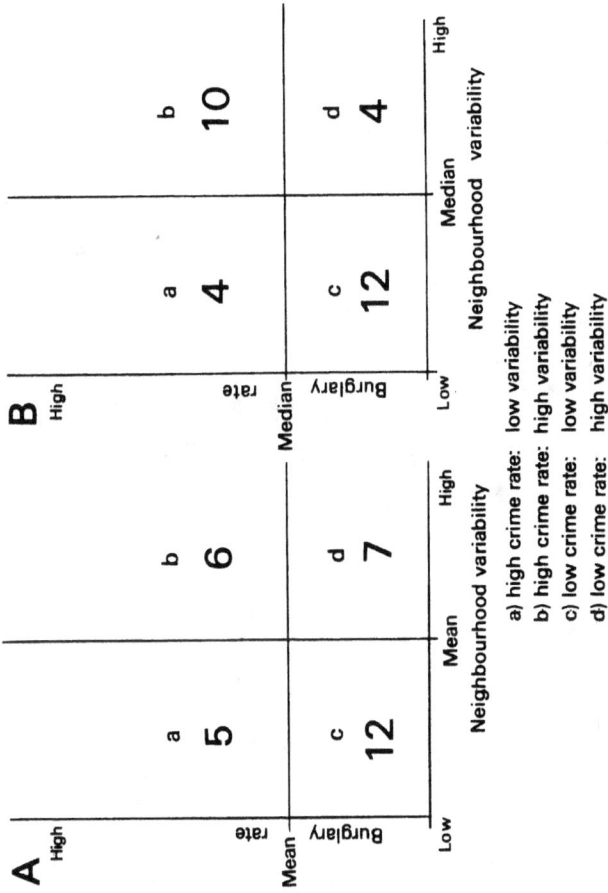

A

| | Neighbourhood variability | |
|---|---|---|
| | Mean | |
| a 5 | | b 6 |
| Burglary rate | Median | |
| c 12 | | d 7 |

B

| | Neighbourhood variability | |
|---|---|---|
| | Median | |
| a 4 | | b 10 |
| Burglary rate | | |
| c 12 | | d 4 |

a) high crime rate: low variability
b) high crime rate: high variability
c) low crime rate: low variability
d) low crime rate: high variability

Figure 5.1 Classifying Residential Areas by a Measure of Variability and Residential Burglary Rates

Social cohesion and crime:   A typology of areas

| Area type | Degree of cohesion | Residential crime rate | Interpretation | Examples of areas |
|-----------|--------------------|-----------------------|----------------|-------------------|
| A | Low | High | Opportunities exist and are perceived as available to offenders   Low social cohesion affects this image | Transient inner city |
| B | High | High | High social cohesion co-exists with a subcultural effect which condones some forms of criminality: delinquent norms outweigh effects of cohesion | Problem estate |
| C | High | Low | Opportunities are few and high cohesion suggests to the offender that they are not available | Stable inner city |
| D | Low | Low | Generally social cohesion is low but either opportunities are few or individual security practice makes them unavailable | Private suburb |

Figure 5.2  Classifying Residential Areas by Levels of Social Cohesion and Residential Burglary Rates

estate where although social cohesion was high a sub-cultural effect condoning some forms of criminality still led to high offence rates; area-type C fitted the stable inner city district with little crime; and area-type D was represented by the private suburb where although social cohesion was low, strict security practice kept levels of crime under control.

Environmental criminology is an example of one approach to a type of deviant behaviour. One of its merits is its close affinity to crime prevention policy as an arm of policing strategy. If some of the things which make for vulnerability can be identified, this is clearly an aid to policy prescription. Neighbourhood Watch schemes are a case in point. Designed to involve residents in crime prevention, they make use of the social cohesion idea. People are encouraged to work together in neighbourhoods and in collaboration with the police, to reduce burglary and some other crimes. Elsewhere, areas have been selected for target-hardening exercises whereby householders are encouraged to improve dwelling security. The effectiveness of such schemes needs to be carefully monitored as they often have short-term effects and the success of crime prevention is notoriously difficult to measure. Close attention by police or residents to crime in a specific area, for example, may well result in greater awareness of offences which would otherwise go undetected. Several projects have followed the principles of Newman's (1972) defensible space ideas by introducing better design standards into housing areas. Coleman (1985) detailed ways in which the design of flats and apartments in London could be improved in ways which should influence the incidence of crimes and also improve quality of life. Tata et al. (1975) studied the design of a privately-owned, low income housing project in Florida and found that it violated six of the eight Newman principles. They also found that many of the residents suffered from intense feelings of frustration, alienation, insecurity, and helplessness and judged these to be linked to a depressing, residential environment.

## Facilities and Social Deviance

There is little doubt that deviant groups make very heavy demands upon the resources of the societies within which they live, or at least that

they incur heavy costs for those societies. A
whole hierarchy of law-makers, court officials,
police and social services exists as a direct
consequence of the need to 'deal with' social
deviance. Drug addicts and alcoholics make heavy
demands upon medical services, the mentally-ill
occupy large numbers of hospital beds and
institutional places, serious criminals require
long-term commitals to prisons which need large
staffing establishments. Over recent years one
main thrust in the treatment of many forms of
deviance has had the effect of reducing the burden
upon the state. Penal reform groups advocate less
use of custodial sentences and new forms of prison
which involve greater continuity of interaction
with the community for a wide range of offenders.
The policy towards the mentally-ill has focused
upon the discharging of many individuals from
hospitals and institutions. In the United States
in 1955 there were 559,000 mentally-ill patients
in State and County hospitals, by 1975 this had
been reduced to 193,000. As Dear (1981) argues,
the history of the treatment of the mentally-ill
is a study of isolation and exclusion; in medieval
Europe the mad were driven outside the city walls
and the formal institution of the asylum began to
appear by the end of the eighteenth century. This
new policy of reducing isolation and enabling the
integration of many of the mentally-ill into
communities has attracted a great deal of
geographical research. In addition to the
empirical issues of the volume and extent of
de-institutionalization, this research has
addressed the questions of the effectiveness of
new policies and their impact upon communities.
Phillips and Radford (1985) in a review of
British experience in this field, suggest that
there is a gap of some significance between the
ideal of the beneficial effects that provision of
a normal, integrated, source-rich environment
brings to the mentally-ill and the reality of
failure to meet even modest targets of
community-care. In Britain at least, with its
National Health Service, there is a powerful
incentive to reduce costs in the 'bottomless pit'
of medical care, in addition to socio-medical
reasons for de-institutionalization. Dear (1981,
p.495) is more cynical: 'The objective of the
service profession frequently seems less directed
towards client care and more concerned with
regulating and managing the flow of clients through

the case network'. The process of discharging
mentally-ill people from institutions has to be
selective. There is a range of mental illness
from the relatively common to more serious chronic
conditions; the more serious the illness the more
likely the need for institutional treatment.

In the United States where de-institutionalization has proceeded apace, there is evidence of new
kinds of problems being created for both clients
and professionals. Professionals face the problem
of keeping track with patients once they have left
the secure world of the institution. Dear and
Witman (1980) found that of a sample of 169
patients discharged from a Hamilton, Ontario
psychiatric hospital, one-quarter had changed
address at least once within six months and many
were lost track of; Smith (1976) showed that of
130 patients discharged from a state hospital in
Ypsilanti, Michigan almost half were back in the
institution within twelve months. The main
general concern is that many mentally-ill patients
will be discharged without sufficient planning to
ensure that they have a supportive system of home,
family or friends to protect them. Much stress
has been placed upon the role of community as an
informal care system and upon the establishment of
a hierarchy of facilities from formal institutions
at one end, to day-centres and domiciliary
care-units which may be community-based. Phillips
and Radford (1985) described the evolution of a
'core and cluster' scheme in South-west England in
which the core area contains essential services
whilst the clusters are composed of domiciliary
units in which the patients are housed. In the
United States the Community Support Program has
set out to co-ordinate formal services with those
which are offered by friends, relatives and
volunteer help. Wolpert (1979) questioned the
ability of communities to give and to accept
deviants into what he termed 'normal places'. Most
research indicates that whilst community attitudes
to deviants are not simple they are mostly
exclusionary. Dear, Taylor and Hall (1980)
recognize that the location of mentally-ill
persons and facilities causes fear of externality
effects, especially in better-off areas:

It is important to realise that individuals
and groups have different stakes in their
daily life environment. A resource-rich,
middle class neighbourhood is likely to be

defended more vociferously than is a transient, resource-deficient area (1980, p.343).

Their study of Toronto questioned over a thousand residents and found that a strong minority (31 percent) anticipated no adverse effects from the siting of a facility for the mentally-ill. When respondents were asked to rate the impact of a facility upon property value, traffic generation, propensity to migrate, general satisfaction with neighbourhood, and some other factors, they showed more negative than positive attitudes. Those with greater awareness of the nature of mental illness were more likely to soften their attitudes and proximity to a facility was a critical factor. 25.7 percent of those surveyed thought that a facility within one block's distance would be undesirable compared with only 11.1 percent if the facility was to be more than six blocks away. Most evidence points to the fact that popular myths such as the negative effect of a facility are in fact unfounded; in Toronto there was no evidence of effects on either levels of sales or house prices.

Allied to the fact that suburban communities are more alert to the likelihood of negative externalities and produce stronger resistance to the siting of facilities, is the observation that distance has limited influence on the extent to which facilities are used. Whereas suburbs tend to close ranks, this is less evident in parts of the inner city and Trute and Segal (1976) found that more successful facility locations occurred in neighbourhoods with low social cohesion. This experience tends to be general and is leading to 'institutional saturation' of parts of the inner city. What Dear (1981) identifies as an 'asylum without walls' arises from the process by which the mentally ill end up in poor inner city areas, either in institutions which are located there or through an informal 'drift' whereby they seek out like persons in similar kinds of inner city areas. Dear regards this as a manifestation of the requirements of a capitalist process of reproduction and, although the class relations involved are not simply economic, the relation-ship between community and client remains, exclusionary. The mentally ill have exchanged a custodial, safe environment for an open, less safe environment but in neither were their health-care needs being fully met. In whatever terms the

154

process of de-institutionalization is explained, the reproduction needs of a capitalist society, the cost efficiency aims of health-care managers, or the prejudices of middle-class suburbanites, most evidence to date suggests that the outcomes do not favour the mentally ill.

## Rule-Makers and Rule-Breakers

There are several areas in which research can most usefully be focused upon those who make the rules rather than those who break them. Some involved in the debate on the production of criminal statistics might argue that this should be the central thrust of any analysis of deviance. This section will focus on questions relating to the use of police discretion and the effect of policing strategies upon visible crime rates. There is a common belief that some police bias exists against low-income offenders and recent research suggests that this may be reflected in the quality of police-community relations in many working-class areas. Lea and Young (1984) identify an areally selective dichotomy in police-community relations. In the respectable suburbs the policing is based on consensus, in non-respectable parts of the inner city it is more likely to be based on force and coercion. As some research literature emerges on this theme it has initially produced some contradictory findings. Mawby (1979) came to the conclusion that there was no evidence to support the idea that differential policing affected relative offender rates in contrasting residential areas nor that offence rates had been affected by a police presence. Lowman (1982) on the other hand was critical of this finding and argued that: 'an understanding of criminal justice and legal policy is necessary to understand certain kinds of socio-spatial behaviour, particularly criminal behaviour' (Lowman, 1982, p. 32).

Some recent research into prostitution can be used as an example of the impact of changes in legal policies upon the spatial incidence of a form of social deviance. Symanski (1974) argued that the location of brothels and the activity spaces of prostitutes in Nevada could not be understood apart from the legal and quasi-legal regulations. In the most detailed available case-study, Shumsky and Springer (1981) examined the red-light district of San Francisco between

Social Deviance and the City

1880 and 1934. Noting the movements of both
brothels and prostitutes over time, Shumsky and
Springer argued that there was an indisputable
relationship between the changing spatial
distribution of prostitution and legal attitudes.
As the laws or the areas within which anti-prosti-
tution laws were enforced were changed, so
prostitutes moved their places of activity in
order to avoid being arrested. This move in turn
relocated the zone of prostitution.

Shumsky and Springer showed that in common
with many American cities, San Francisco developed
a red-light district in the nineteenth century
which was located close to the city centre and
Chinatown and which had links with the Chinese
underworld. The red-light district of 1880, an
elongated district west of the C.B.D., contracted
as new laws were introduced. As new orders were
imposed in the 1890s their effects could be seen
on individual streets. The number of brothels in
Moore Street declined from 37 in 1886 to 1 in
1900; comparable figures for Quincey Street showed
a change from 26 to 0. In 1909 the Police
Commission decided to enforce a policy of street
segregation of prostitutes with controls for
health, and between 1911 and 1913 San Francisco
tolerated prostitution within the circumscribed
red-light area. After 1913 this tolerance
disappeared as a result of political in-fighting
and new legislation led to the dispersal of
prostitutes. Shumsky and Springer concluded that
changes in laws and in law-enforcement practice,
brought about largely by changing social
attitudes, led to the changing 'geography' of
prostitution. It was the rule-makers who formed
this 'geography' and not the rule-breakers.

Lowman (1982) made a similar study of street
prostitution in Vancouver. Until 1975 there were
three areas of street prostitution in the central
part of the city; one was adjacent to Chinatown
and the other two were in 'skid-row type' areas.
After 1975, two new areas appeared in
densely-used, prestigious areas in the central
city. The single event of significance in 1975
seemed to be the closure of clubs which had served
as bases for prostitutes and the displacement of
their clients onto the streets. By Canadian law,
prostitution is legal but the act of soliciting
is not; with the closure of the clubs
prostitution became visible and the police set up
a special task force to prosecute prostitutes.

Social Deviance and the City

Between September 1977 and February 1978 there were 240 vice-related or soliciting charges as a result of task force activities. This police operation against prostitutes was confounded however, by a series of court decisions which negated its policy objectives and strategies. For example, the court allowed the argument that the interior of a car was a private (legal) and not a public (illegal) place for the purposes of prostitution. Again, the question of 'who was soliciting whom?' was raised when undercover police officers seeking convictions sought to trap prostitutes with prompts and key-phrases. More significantly, the court did not accept that when a woman offered her services and quoted a price she was soliciting; in the court's interpretation she had to harass the client by not accepting no for an answer, something which prostitutes rarely do. Over one hundred charges for soliciting were dropped and the legal environment in Vancouver became highly conducive to the practice of street prostitution. Fluctuations in this form of social deviance in Vancouver were strongly influenced by changing definitions of legal behaviour; once again the spatial incidence of a form of social deviance could best be understood by a scrutiny of those who made the rules rather than those who infringed them.


CONCLUSIONS

Geographers studying social deviance have the advantage of an existing literature which is both considerable and diverse and the disadvantage of seeking to establish a niche in what is well-trodden ground for research. The most obvious and traditional niche for a geographer would be one which focuses upon patterns in space and links with environments, but this is not likely to add any significant new conceptual insights to the study of social deviance. What those approaches might more usefully offer are empirical research tools for those concerned with coping with deviance. Accurate spatial statistics and classifications of the type suggested by Pyle et al. (1974) have much to commend them to law-makers, law enforcers and the caring agencies. The mere addition of spatial references to crime reports, for example, would allow the application of a range of computer-mapping techniques both to

Social Deviance and the City

depict the patterns of crime and to show changes over time. Such information would have considerable value to policing strategies aimed at crime prevention. Similarly, optimal location models could have a useful application in terms of a range of facilities from day care-centres to police stations.

The significant theoretical contributions which geographers might make may lie less in specifically 'spatial' roles than in providing an input to the general concepts of the social sciences and in testing their accuracy. As shown in the topics selected for case studies, the range of possibilities is great. Whereas traditional ecology may appear to have a limited role, a research strategy which delves more deeply into subjective environments has more potential for development. This approach in some ways returns us from the scientism of ecological association to the richest heritage of the Chicago school, the ethnographic studies of particular groups and the territories that they occupy within the city.

Environmental criminology has been developed as an example of practical research. Its methods and perspectives are very suited to a form of applied geography which is concerned with crime prevention. Many of the recent analyses of mental illness by geographers have amounted to evaluations of the effects of a de-institutionalization policy and have commented upon practical issues such as the location of community-based facilities and the effects which these might have upon both the patients and the local populations. The whole concept of spatial externalities is clearly central to much of this research. Finally, studies of the rule-makers open up new avenues for geographical research. The police and the legal system may not only decide what is right and what is wrong but can also 'create' geographies of social deviance through the control strategies which they define and implement.

Social deviance covers many forms of human behaviour and is more created than it is inherited. Whilst some forms of mental illness are clearly genetic, most deviance is the product of protest, carelessness or wilful action against the rules of society. Geographers must be interested not only in the 'where' of social deviance but also in the 'why' of deviance in the first place. Not only in the deviants themselves but also in those who seek to control, administer and service their

158

## Social Deviance and the City

activities. Social deviance is a recognized if not accepted part of human behaviour and as such it needs to be studied, understood and catered for.

Social Deviance and the City

REFERENCES

Anderson, N. (1923) The Hobo, University of Chicago Press, Chicago

Baldwin, J. (1975) 'Urban criminality and the problem estate', Local Government Studies, 1, 12-20

Baldwin, J. and Bottoms, A.E. (1976) The Urban Criminal, Tavistock, London

Bennett, T. and Wright, R. (1984) Burglars on Burglary, Gower, Aldershot

Bottoms, A.E. and Xanthos (1979) Housing policy and crime in the British public sector, Discussion paper, University of Sheffield

Brantingham, P.J. and Brantingham, P.L. (1975) 'Residential burglary and urban form', Urban Studies, 12, 273-284

Brantingham, P.J. and Brantingham, P.L. (1981) Environmental Criminology, Sage, London

Carr-Hill, R.A. and Sterns, N.H. (1979) Crime, the Police and Criminal Statistics, Academic Press, London

Carter, R.L. (1974) The Criminal's Image of the City, unpublished doctoral thesis, University of Oklahoma at Norman

Cloward, R.A. and Ohlin, L.E. (1960) Delinquency and Opportunity, Free Press, Chicago

Cohen, A.K. (1955) Delinquent Boys, Free Press, Chicago

Coleman, A. (1985) Utopia on Trial: Vision and Reality in Planned Housing, Hilary Shipman, London

Damer, S. (1974) 'Wine Alley: the Sociology of a Dreadful Enclosure', Sociological Review, 22, 221-248

Davidson, R.N. (1981) Crime and Environment, Croom Helm, London

Dear, M. (1981) Social and Spatial reproduction of the mentally ill, in M. Dear and A.J. Scott (eds.) Urbanization and Urban Planning in Capitalist Society, Methuen, London

Dear, M., Taylor, S.M. and Hall, G.B. (1980) 'External effects of mental health facilities', Annals, Association of American Geographers, 70, 342-352

Dear, M. and Wittman, I. (1980) 'Conflict over the location of mental health facilities', in D.T. Herbert and R.J. Johnston (eds.) Geography and the Urban Environment, Wiley, London, 3, 345-362

Downes, D. and Rock, P. (1982) Understanding Deviance, Clarendon Press, Oxford

Social Deviance and the City

Dunham, H.W. (1937) 'The ecology of the functional psychoses in Chicago', American Sociological Review, 2, 467-479

Firey, W. (1947) Land-use in Central Boston, Harvard University Press, Cambridge, Mass.

Giggs, J.A. (1979) 'Human health problems in urban areas', in D.T. Herbert and D.M. Smith (eds.), Social Problems and the City: Geographical Perspectives, Oxford University Press, London, 84-116

Giggs, J.A. (1985) 'Mental disorders and ecological structure in Nottingham', Proceedings Joint A.A.G/I.B.G. Symposium in Medical Geography, University of Nottingham

Gill, O. (1977) Luke Street, Macmillan, London

Harries, K. D. (1974) The Geography of Crime and Justice, McGraw-Hill

Harries, K. D. (1975) 'Rejoinder to Richard Peet: the geography of crime, a political critique, Professional Geogr., 27, 280-282 New York

Harries, K.D. and Brunn, S.D. (1978) The Geography of Laws and Justice, Praeger, New York

Herbert, D.T. (1976) 'The study of delinquency areas: a social geographical approach', Transactions, Institute of British Geographers, 1, 472-492

Herbert, D.T. (1982) The Geography of Urban Crime Longman, London

Hirschi, T. and Selvin, H.C. (1967) Delinquency Research: An Appraisal of Analytic Methods, Macmillan, London

Hood, R. and Sparks, R. (1970) Key Issues in Criminology, Weidenfeld and Nicolson, London

Jackson, P. and Smith, S. (1984) Exploring Social Geography, George Allen and Unwin, London

Lea, J. and Young, J. (1984) What is to be Done about Law and Order, Penguin, Harmondsworth

Lee, R. (1979) 'The economic basis of social problems in the city', in D.T. Herbert and D.M. Smith (eds.) Social Problems and the City: Geographical Perspectives, Oxford University Press, London, 47-62

Levy, L. and Rowitz, L. (1973) The Ecology of Mental Disorder, Behavioural Publications, New York

Ley, D. (1974) The Black Inner City as Frontier Outpost, A.A.G. Monograph 7, Washington D.C.

Ley, D. and Cybriwsky, R. (1974) 'Urban graffiti as territorial markers', Annals, Ass. of Amer. Geographers, 64, 491-505

Lowman, J. (1982) 'Crime, criminal justice policy and the urban environment', in D.T. Herbert and R.J. Johnston (eds.) Geography and the Urban Environment, 5, Wiley, London, 307-341

Matza, D. (1964) Delinquency and Drift, Wiley, New York

Matza, D. (1969) Becoming Deviant, Prentice Hall, Englewood Cliffs

Mawby, R (1979) Policing the City, Saxon House, Farnborough

Mayhew, H. (1862) London Labour and the London Poor Griffin-Bohn, London

Mintz, N.L. and Schwarz, D.T. (1964) 'Urban ecology and psychosis', Int. Jnl of Soc. Psychiatry, 10, 101-118

Newman, O. (1972) Defensible Space, Macmillan, New York

Peet, R. (1975) 'The geography of crime: a political critique', Professional Geographer, 27, 277-280

Phillips, D. and Radford, J. (1985) 'Any fool can close a long-stay hospital: de-institutionalisation and community care for the mentally handicapped - a study of South-west England', Proceedings, Joint A.A.G./I.B.G. Medical Geography Symposium, University of Nottingham

Phillips, P.D. (1972) 'A prologue to the geography of crime', Procs. Ass. of Amer. Geogs., 4, 59-64

Pyle, G. et al. (1974) The Spatial Dynamics of Crime, Geography Department Research Paper 159, Chicago

Rengert, G.F. (1981) 'Burglary in Philadelphia: an opportunity structure model', in P.J. Brantingham and P.L. Brantingham, (eds.) Environmental Criminology, Sage, London, 189-201

Reppetto, T.A. (1974) Residential Crime, Ballinger, Cambridge, Mass.

Rowley, G. (1978) 'Plus ça change... a Canadian skid-row', Canadian Geographer, 22, 211-224

Sack, R.D. (1978) 'Geographic and other views of space', in K. Butzer (ed.) Dimensions of Human Geography, Geography Department Research Paper 186, University of Chicago, 166-184

Saunders, P. (1981) Social Theory and the Urban Question, Hutchinson, London

Schmid, C.F. (1960) 'Urban crime areas', Amer. Soc. Rev. 25, 527-554

Shaw, C.F. (1930) The Jackroller, University of Chicago Press, Chicago

Social Deviance and the City

Shaw, C.F. and McKay, H.D. (1942) Juvenile Delin-
    quency and Urban Areas, University of Chicago
    Press, Chicago
Shumsky, N.L. and Springer, L.M. (1981) 'San Fran-
    cisco's zone of prostitution, 1880 to 1934',
    Jnl. of Hist. Geog. 7, 71-89
Smith, C.J. (1976) 'Distance and the location of
    community mental health facilites: a divergent
    viewpoint', Economic Geography, 52, 181-191
Smith, C.J. and Hanham, R.Q. (1982) Alcohol Abuse:
    Geographical Perspectives, Resource Publica-
    tions in Geography, A.A.G., Washington
Sutherland, E.H. and Cressey, D.R.(1970) Principles
    of Criminology, Lippincott, Philadelphia
Symanski, R. (1974) 'Prostitution in Nevada',
    Annals Ass. of Amer. Geogs., 64, 357-377
Tata, R.J., van Horn, S. and Lee, D. (1975)
    'Defensible space in a housing project: a case
    study from a South Florida ghetto',
    Professional Geographer, 27, 297-307
Taylor, L. (1973) 'The meaning of environment', in
    C. Ward (ed.) Vandalism, Architectural Press,
    London
Thrasher, C. (1927) The Gang, University of Chicago
    Press, Chicago
Tobias, J.J. (1967) Crime and Industrial Society in
    the Nineteenth Century, Penguin, Harmondsworth
Trute, B. and Segal, S.P. (1976) 'Census tract
    predictors and social integration of sheltered-
    care residents', Social Psychiatry, 11, 153-161
Ward, J. (1975) Skid-row as a geographical entity:
    skid-row in six cities, Professional Geographer
    27, 286-296
Wilson, R. (1963) Difficult Housing Estates,
    Tavistock, London
Wolpert, J. (1976) 'Opening closed spaces', Annals,
    Ass. of Amer. Geographers, 66, 1-13
Zorbaugh, H.W. (1929) The Gold Coast and the Slum,
    University of Chicago Press, Chicago

Chapter Six

COLLECTIVE CONSUMPTION AND SOCIO-SPATIAL CHANGE

P. L. KNOX

The social geography of cities and regions in economically advanced nations has long been conditioned by a complex array of public sector activity: from legal codes, regulations, electoral systems and government employment to the allocation of welfare benefits and the provision of a wide variety of services. With the transition to 'postindustrial' (or 'advanced' or 'corporate') capitalism, the influence of the public sector on many aspects of social geography has become critical. Welfare systems, along with the rest of the public economy, have increased in size, extent and sophistication; but the ability and, in recent years, the willingness of governments to fund them has been called into question. At the same time, the transition to the postindustrial era has itself brought about certain spatial transformations and realignments which have created or reinforced a variety of socio-economic disparities. The net result is that the interactions of socio-spatial processes with changes in welfare systems now represent important dimensions of the social geography of cities and regions of the developed nations. In this chapter, attention is focused on the interactions between socio-spatial change and one particular component of welfare systems: collective consumption.

Collective consumption is taken here to include all collectively organized and managed services that are consumed via non-market mechanisms and at least partly paid for through the public purse (Fig. 6.1). Collective consumption therefore includes both 'pure' public goods such as libraries, parks, museums and fire services which are (theoretically) available to all members of society, and 'impure' public goods

## Collective Consumption and Socio-Spatial Change

(or 'merit' goods) such as education, public housing and welfare services that are restricted to particular subgroups of the population (Pinch, 1985). While this clearly involves a wide range of activity which does not lend itself to neat or watertight definitions, it does facilitate the examination of interactions between socio-spatial change and public service provision without becoming ensnared in the taxonomic niceties of the pure theory of public goods as articulated by Samuelson (1954), Musgrave (1959), Margolis (1968) and others. In particular, it allows us to view spatial factors - jurisdictional partitioning, tapering effects (the effects of distance on the net benefits derived from fixed-point services), and externality effects - as something more than sources of theoretical impurity; and so it encourages us to link them to a variety of broader economic, social and spatial processes.

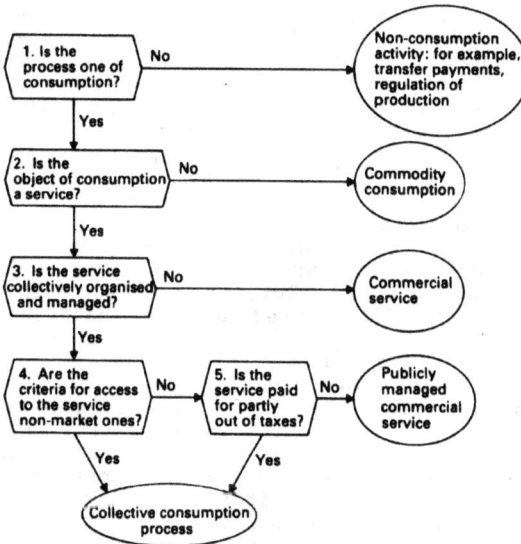

Figure 6.1   Criteria for Determining Whether a Social Process can be included within Collective Consumption

## Collective Consumption and Socio-Spatial Change

One of the overarching socio-economic processes of concern here is the evolution of welfare systems in response to the changing needs and capacities of postindustrial economic systems. On the one hand, expenditure on welfare in general and collective consumption in particular has accounted for a large and increasing share of the GNP of most of the economically advanced social democracies. On the other hand, this growth in welfare expenditures has in general been directed more towards 'average' employees and their families than towards low-income groups or disadvantaged households. Welfare expenditure has thus tended to redistribute income horizontally within similar income groups, leaving significant gaps in service provision for the disadvantaged (George and Lawson, 1980; OECD, 1976). The European Community's programme of pilot schemes and studies on poverty (Europe Against Poverty) has highlighted three major gaps in European welfare states: (i) the educational neglect of lower working-class children, (ii) the inadequacy of pensions for women and those with an interrupted record of social insurance contributions, and (iii) the housing needs of immigrants and ethnic minorities (Room, 1982). In addition, the programme has pointed to the ways in which the expansion of welfare states has created new forms of deprivation and disadvantage: the socially incapacitating effects of many institutionalized forms of health care, for example, and the socially disruptive effects of urban redevelopment schemes and housing projects.

Inasmuch as the victims of these shortcomings are unevenly distributed geographically, so the operation of the welfare state has involved a spatial differential, with a net transfer of benefits to more prosperous citizens and localities. Yet, as these shortcomings began to emerge as serious theoretical and political issues, they were compounded and complicated by a change in the economic environment which occurred in the mid-1970s. The dilemma facing most governments was that the deepening economic recession accentuated the vulnerability of more people while making it increasingly difficult, economically and polit-ically, to finance existing welfare programmes. As a result, it has been suggested that Western welfare states have entered a new stage of reformulation and retrenchment (Heclo, 1981; Navarro, 1982), and a good deal of attention

Collective Consumption and Socio-Spatial Change

has been given to the 'new conservatism' associated with the orientation of central and local governments in the wake of recession. Electoral victories of right-of-centre parties in Australia, Belgium, the Netherlands, Sweden, New Zealand, the United Kingdom and the United States were associated with an ideological stance based on the belief that the welfare state had not only generated unreasonably high levels of taxation, budget deficits, disincentives to work and save, and a bloated class of unproductive workers, but also that it may have fostered 'soft' attitudes toward 'problem' groups in society. Ironically, the electoral appeal of this ideology can largely be attributed to the success of welfare states in banishing the spectre of material deprivation through illness, bereavement, unemployment and old age: consequently, the priority afforded to welfare programmes has receded (though the logic and, critically, the costs of maintaining them have not).

Meanwhile, the transition to the postindustrial era has been accompanied by several major processes of spatial change. The internationalization of the corporate economy has brought about a new international division of labour and, within the world's core economies, a consequent restructuring and redeployment of corporate tasks. Routine production and assembly jobs have been decentralized to peripheral regions and non-metropolitan settings where labour is less expensive and less organized; new jobs in producer services and high-tech manufacturing have become localized in accessible, high-amenity settings; and administrative and managerial jobs have become concentrated in national and international 'control centers' (Castells, 1985; Hicks and Glickman, 1983; Stanback and Noyelle, 1982). Meanwhile, most metropolitan regions have themselves experienced large-scale decentralization as investments have been withdrawn from inner-city settings and redirected towards the more congenial, less expensive and less restrictive settings of the metropolitan fringes and certain non-metropolitan environments. What is important about these processes in the present context, of course, is that their outcomes inevitably have significant implications for patterns of public collective consumption.

# Collective Consumption and Socio-Spatial Change

## Territorial unjustness: hypotheses and explanations

Central to the geography of collective consumption, and encapsulating many of the conceptual and analytical issues associated with public sector activity, is the notion of territorial justice (Davies, 1968; Smith, 1977). Although widely accepted as a laudable objective for collective consumption, it begs several important questions (Heald, 1980; Ircha and Sundarajan, 1984; Merget and Berger, 1982; Rich, 1982a).

1. What is the yardstick of justice or equity? Needs? Preferences? Effort? Willingness to pay?
2. What is to be equitably distributed? Inputs? Activities? Outputs? Outcomes? Potential outcomes?
3. What is the appropriate territorial unit? Jurisdictions? Wards? Neighbourhoods? Blocks?

For Davies, territorial justice is essentially a spatial extrapolation of Marx's dictum of 'to each according to his needs' (1968, p. 16). The object of territorial justice Davies took to be the provision of services, or expenditure on them; the appropriate territorial unit, in the context of his research, has been the local administrative area (Davies et al., 1971, 1972). Davies, however, has been mainly concerned with personal social services, personal health services and other services directly available to individuals. In this context, individual needs may justifiably be aggregated to the scale of service-providing jurisdictions to provide a yardstick of territorial need. But there are many aspects of collective consumption for which territorial needs cannot be gauged from the aggregation of individual needs: local services whose spatial range is limited, for example, and indivisible services such as parks, mass transit systems, and fire services.

Moreover, the justness of patterns of collective consumption can be related to criteria other than need. Lucy (1981) discusses four others:

1. Equality
2. Demand (the notion that active interest in a service - e.g. willingness to travel or to wait for a service - should be rewarded)
3. Preferences
4. Willingness to pay

168

## Collective Consumption and Socio-Spatial Change

In practice, however, these criteria overlap with one another, often raising more questions than they resolve. As Lucy puts it:

> Each service has objectives involving serving populations and influencing social conditions. This is done by using resources (expenditures, personnel, facilities, equipment) and engaging in activities having results (direct consequences, intended and unintended) and leading to impacts (changes in social conditions). (Lucy, 1981, p.451)

As a result, Lucy suggests, the justness of patterns of service provision can only be gauged once multiple measures of distribution (as illustrated in Table 6.1) have been used in conjunction with demographic and social indicators to clarify the nature of existing inequalities.

This, in turn, points to another important issue: the degree to which justness has to be traded off against efficiency. Immediately, we are faced with the problem of defining efficiency. Bebbington and Davies (1983), for example, suggest that territorial justice in the allocation of personal social services can be gauged in terms of the 'efficiency' with which services are targeted on the persons most in need of them. Efficiency here is of two types: horizontal efficiency (the proportion of persons judged in need who receive services), and vertical efficiency (the proportion of services allocated to persons judged in need). It is more common, however, for efficiency to be viewed in terms of the marginal costs of service provision.

In short, we are still some way from being able to make unambiguous, normative statements about patterns of collective consumption. Nevertheless, it is clear that many aspects of collective consumption are unjustly distributed, whatever criteria, yardsticks or spatial graticules are employed. Moreover, some degree of unjustness in the provision of collective services seems to be inevitable. Tuckman (1984) argues that this inevitability stems from three main sources. First there is the 'failure of preference' which occurs when governments produce a different mix of collective services than its citizens desire: usually as a result of biased electoral systems or the systematic distortion of public opinion. Second is the 'failure of production'

Table 6.1 Examples of service indicators

| Resources | Expenditures | dollars per 1000 population or 100 households; dollars per phenomenon, such as dollars per serious crime |
| | Personnel | number per 1000 population; number per phenomenon, such as per serious crime |
| | Equipment | playground swings per 100 children aged twelve and under |
| | Facilities | neighbourhood park acres per 1000 residents |
| Activities | Frequency | refuse pick-up per week: hours swimming pools are open per week |
| | Duration | response time for police or fire department from receipt of call for service to arrival on scene |
| Results | Intended consequences | arrests per 100 serious crimes reported; street cleanliness rating after refuse collection; water pressure on tap |
| | Unintended consequences | number of missed refuse collections per week per 100 households; complaints about unnecessary use of force per 100 arrests for serious crimes |
| | Use of service by amount | number of branch library books circulated per year; number of swimmers per day; number of park users per week |
| | Use of service by rate | Number of branch library books circulated per year per population in service area; number of mass transit riders per day per population in service area |
| | Use of service by reason | percentage of persons not using a park because of anxiety about their personal safety when using the park; percentage of persons not using mass transit for the journey to work because the relationship between transit and work schedules requires waits of 15 minutes or more |
| Impacts | Changes in social conditions | partially identifiable using experimentation or elaborate and complex calculations |

Source: Lucy (1981, p. 452).

170

Collective Consumption and Socio-Spatial Change

which occurs when the cost effectiveness of public
services is less than it could be.  This includes
'failures of setting' which occur when the
institutional framework of service delivery
adversely affects the costs and quality of the
services provided.  It also includes 'failures of
output' (the failure of governments to provide
sufficient funds to fully operationalize a
service), 'failure of incentive' (resulting from
the internal dynamics of the bureaucratic
administration of public services), and 'failures
of information' (which precipitate inappropriate
decisions about service allocation).  Third, there
are 'failures of delivery', which arise from
unexpected patterns of service utilization,
demand, or take-up, from misunderstandings about
the distributional effects of particular services,
and from unintended externality effects.
     Given the inevitability of inefficiencies and
disparities and, therefore, of unjustness (however
defined) in the distribution of public services,
the question arises as to whether they exhibit,
individually or in aggregate, systematic patterns
in relation to the social geography of cities and
regions.  Several hypotheses have been developed
in relation to this question, including the
so-called 'underclass hypothesis': the idea that
economically disadvantaged groups and areas are
actively discriminated against in terms of service
provision.  As articulated by Lineberry (1976),
this subsumes three overlapping hypotheses: the
existence of a power elite capable of manipulating
the distribution of public resources, the 'race
preference' hypothesis (which points to
discrimination against blacks), and the 'class
preference' hypothesis (which points to
discrimination against low-income communities in
general).  A variant of the underclass hypothesis
is the 'inverse care law' proposed by Tudor-Hart
(1971) in relation to medical care services in the
United Kingdom, whereby 'the availability of good
medical care tends to vary inversely with the need
of the population served' (p.412).  Note that the
suggestion here is that it is the quality as much
as the quantity of service provision that is at
issue.  Qualified support for the underclass
hypothesis can be found in some studies of urban
service provision in the United States (see, for
example, Levy et al., 1974; Mladenka and Hill,
1977; Nivola 1978), while qualified support for
the inverse care law can be found in some studies

## Collective Consumption and Socio-Spatial Change

of medical care provision in Britain (Knox, 1978; Phillips, 1981). For some observers, however, the number of exceptions to the underclass hypothesis is sufficient to make the case for an entirely different hypothesis: that unjustness in patterns of collective consumption is, overall, 'unpatterned inequality' (Lineberry, 1977; Mladenka, 1978). In other words, some service delivery patterns favour middle class communities, some favour working class communities, some favour black communities, some favour inner-city neighbourhoods irrespective of their class or ethnicity, and so on. Support for this hypothesis can be found in studies of municipal services in San Antonio, Texas (Lineberry, 1977), Houston (Mladenka and Hill, 1977, 1978; Antunes and Plumlee, 1977), and Chicago (Mladenka, 1980). From here, however, it is a short step to hypotheses which associate different categories of services with different outcomes. Gibson et al. (1985), for example, suggest that a distinction can be made in terms of services which are publicly funded and publicly provided and those which are publicly funded but provided through private organizations. They suggest that the former will tend to be geographically centralized (because of bureaucratic centralization) whereas the latter will be more decentralized. More plausible, perhaps, is the hypothesis that property-related services (e.g. fire protection, sanitation, parks) will tend to be regressively distributed, whereas welfare-related services will tend to be progressively distributed (Boyle and Jacobs, 1980; Goschel et al., 1982).

In terms of the research paradigms in which these hypotheses have been developed and tested, it seems that the single most dominant perspective has been derived from the pluralist viewpoint of public choice theory. In essence, the public choice perspective is based on an analogy with private markets, with local politics envisaged as a political marketplace in which elected representatives respond to the demands of the public in a similar manner to the way in which entrepreneurs are supposed to respond to consumer preferences (Archer, 1981; Buchanan and Tullock, 1969; Reynolds, 1981). Politicians are interpreted as offering particular expenditure packages to voters in order to maximize the votes they receive: the imperatives of obtaining and retaining office, it is assumed, will ensure that

Collective Consumption and Socio-Spatial Change

politicians are sensitive to people's preferences.
At the same time,

> voters make electoral choices and through
> these electoral choices give elected
> office-holders power and legitimacy. Elected
> office-holders make allocational decisions
> which may be different from those which would
> have been made had an alternative set of
> representatives been elected. Voters, observing
> the allocational decisions of elected represen-
> tatives, act in the next election at least
> partially on the basis of their satisfaction
> or dissatisfaction with the decisions made
> (Glassberg, 1973, p.342).

A variant of public choice theory which is set
specifically within the framework of metropolitan
jurisdictions is Tiebout's (1956) theory that the
demand for public goods is reflected in residential
behaviour, with consumer-voters expressing their
preference for particular tax/service packages
through their choice of metropolitan jurisdiction.
This idea, in turn, has formed the basis of a more
general theory in which municipalities are seen as
being in competition with one another for those
residents and industrial land users that are least
demanding of public services relative to the tax
base they bring (Ostrom et al., 1961).

The public choice approach is implicit in much
of the vast literature on patterns of public
expenditure (see, for example, Dye, 1966; Boaden,
1971; Danziger, 1978). These 'outputs' studies
have generally conceptualized the political arena
as a mediating mechanism between social, economic
and environmental factors (the 'inputs' of the
whole process) and expenditures on service
provision (the 'outputs'). This conception of
events is portrayed in Fig 6.2 and by model A in
Fig 6.3. Most of the empirical research in this
field, however, has been operationalized in terms
of model B in Fig 6.3, with socio-economic inputs
and political variables both exercising independent
effects on outputs (Pinch, 1985). The fact that
the results of this empirical research have shown
that political variables do not exercise important
independent effects has led to the hypothesis that
socio-economic conditions have some direct effect
on outputs that are not related to the political
arena, as in model C (Figure 6.3). Pinch (1985,
p. 77) observes that 'this, in turn, has

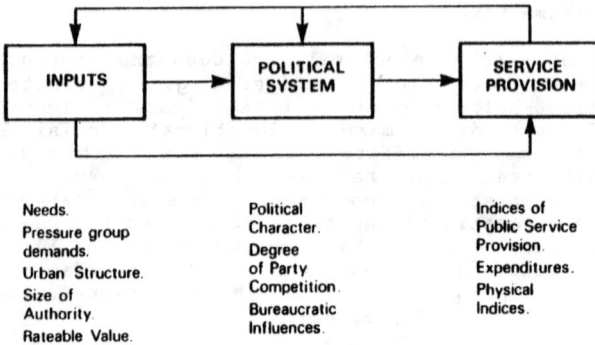

| INPUTS | POLITICAL SYSTEM | SERVICE PROVISION |
|---|---|---|
| Needs. Pressure group demands. Urban Structure. Size of Authority. Rateable Value. | Political Character. Degree of Party Competition. Bureaucratic Influences. | Indices of Public Service Provision. Expenditures. Physical Indices. |

Figure 6.2   A Model of the Local
Government System

MODEL A.

MODEL B.

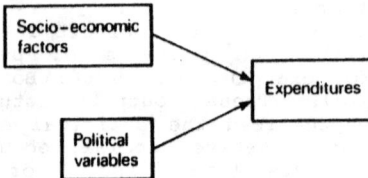

MODEL C.

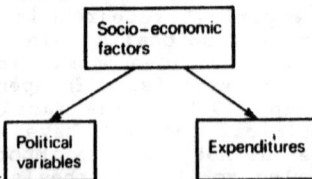

Figure 6.3   Interpretations of the
Policy-Making Process in Local Government

## Collective Consumption and Socio-Spatial Change

prompted the near panic and intense effort to prove that politics is important after all' (see, for example, Sharpe, 1981; Sharpe and Newton, 1984).

The inconclusiveness of the results of statistical analyses of socio-economic inputs, political variables and expenditure outputs has also prompted some different kinds of research. A good deal of attention has been given to the institutional settings of public bureaucracies, in an attempt to investigate some of the 'failures' of the mechanisms central to public choice theory (Tuckman, 1984). Lineberry, for example, argued that bureaucratic activities are the 'missing link' between expenditure allocations and actual service distributions. Most of the work on bureaucractic influence has its roots in Weberian theory, with bureaucrats being seen as key managers or gatekeepers whose expertise and institutionalized roles allow them systematically to influence allocations and outcomes in ways that are consonant with their own professional self-interests and world views (Pahl, 1970; Lipsky, 1980; Saunders, 1981). The influence of the bureaucracy has been shown to extend even to the setting of 'machine' politics which has for many years used public services to reward loyal supporters/neighbourhoods and to punish enemies/opponents (Mladenka, 1980). A good deal of recent research effort, however, has been directed towards the 'decision rules' or 'service delivery rules' that are established within bureaucracies in order to codify the repetitive decisions they must make in dealing with recurring situations (Jones et al., 1980). In this context, it is argued that there are four central questions:

1. Who demands? What are the sources of citizen demands for government service action? How are demands related to demographic characteristics of citizens and their neighbourhoods? To what degree are demands rooted in the need for service intervention?
2. Who receives? What definable social, economic, racial, or geographic groupings receive the services that municipal bureaucracies provide?
3. How? By what institutionalized methods are service delivery decisions made?
4. What difference does it make? What are the impacts of the municipal service effort?

175

## Collective Consumption and Socio-Spatial Change

> Are the impacts different for different
> social, economic, racial or geographic
> groupings of citizens? (Jones et al.,
> 1980, p.6)

Another area of research with strong Weberian
influences has focused on the politics of location
that attach to the distribution of public service
outputs. Here, the emphasis is on citizen
reactions to, and influence upon, political and
bureaucratic decision-making (Burnett, 1984;
Burnett and Hill, 1982; Rich, 1979a; Seley, 1983),
with particular attention being given to the
process of 'demand-making' (the first of the
issues raised by Jones et al.). It is clear that
these aspects of public service delivery involve
complex behavioural patterns. In a study of
policymaking in the London borough of Kensington
and Chelsea, for example, Dearlove (1971) found
that councillors responded to citizen pressure
groups not only in relation to the nature of their
demands but also in relation to their comportment.
The groups which had the most influence on public
service outputs were those whose demands passed
the test of acceptability and whose styles of
action did not affront officials through overly
vocal or disruptive tactics.

More comprehensive approaches to the conflicts
(and suppressed conflicts) surrounding collective
consumption are provided by the neo-Marxist
research paradigm, though the scope of this
paradigm is such that only brief reference can be
made here to some of the salient themes that have
been developed. Among these we should note the
view that the service/tax packages of different
local government jurisdictions represent key
mechanisms of class conflict and social
reproduction (Markusen, 1984), the view that
collective consumption itself arises from the
contradictions of urbanized capitalism (Castells,
1977; Lojkine, 1976), the view of localized
conflicts over collective consumption - 'turf
politics' - as part of the overall relations of
commodity production (in particular, the
'commodification' of neighbourhood space that has
come with widespread owner-occupation (Cox, 1984),
and the view that the failure of the state
effectively to tax the profits that accrue to
private industry from the provision of collective
services results in fiscal stress (O'Connor, 1973).

## Collective Consumption and Socio-Spatial Change

Finally, we should note that some research has focused on the effects of urban structure and ecology on patterns of collective consumption. Three themes are important here. First is the suggestion by McLafferty (1982) that the typical spatial structure of Western cities is such that low-income, inner-city communities are inevitably favoured by the location of public services: the geometry of cities, in other words, is an important constraint on the territorial justness of patterns of collective consumption. Second is the suggestion that patterns of municipal service provision are conditioned by the overall process of metropolitan expansion. In particular, it is argued, the metropolitan periphery has now taken over from the central city as the 'hub of daily activity', with the result that new patterns of municipal expenditure have been initiated in both central cities and peripheral rings (Sly and Tayman, 1980). Finally, there are the reciprocal relationships between some public services and their clientele which have been emphasized by Wolch (1980, 1981, 1982) in her examination of the spatial linkages between the service-dependent poor and their support services. She attributes the localization of both clients and services in inner-city neighbourhoods to: (i) the dominance of housing and transportation-to-services costs in the locational decisions of service-dependent households, (ii) the desire of service facility administrators to minimize clients' transportation costs, and (iii) the budgetary constraints of both clients and services, which dictate low-rent, inner-city locations.

Between them, these research paradigms have spawned what Kirby and Pinch (1983) described as a 'seemingly chaotic' mass of studies. These have been reviewed in detail elsewhere (Kirby, 1982; Kirby, Knox and Pinch, 1984; Pinch, 1985; Rich, 1979b, 1982a, 1982b). What is at issue here are the interactions between collective consumption and socio-spatial change. In the absence of any single, generally-accepted theoretical framework, a crude but nevertheless useful framework for discussion is provided by the different spatial scales and settings in which these interactions can be observed. In the following sections, the existing literature on collective consumption is reviewed in terms of the dominant aspects of socio-spatial change at four scales/settings: rural, inter-urban, metropolitan and intra-urban.

177

## Collective Consumption and Socio-Spatial Change

The final section will then point to the implications of the retrenchment of collective consumption in response to the conditions of economic austerity and political antagonism that have affected public service provision in the past few years.

### Collective consumption and rural change

Aspects of collective consumption have come to represent an important dimension of the social geography of rural settings of all kinds in the advanced economies. In essence, this is because most public services (and, in particular, health care, electricity supply, education, postal services, public transport and telecommunications) cost more to provide to rural populations, while the fiscal resources of rural regions tend to be relatively thin (Cloke, 1983; Lonsdale and Enyedi, 1984). Moreover, the problem of per capita costs has been increasing in response to the increasing sensitivity of rural services to economies of scale. Thus in Britain during the 1970s the number of rural service outlets declined by around one per cent per year, despite a growth in rural populations of around one per cent per year (Moseley, 1984). The result, of course, is that rural residents have to travel farther for services; and this at a time (since the 1973 oil crisis) when increases in petrol prices have significantly increased the friction of rural distances. Moreover, it seems that mobile and delivery services are unlikely to redress the trend, since the force of market thresholds affects this kind of service organization just as it does fixed services (Broder, 1979; Moseley and Packman, 1983, 1985).

It is against this overall background that we have to consider the interactions of socio-economic change and collective consumption. In general, we can think in terms of two kinds of rural change: decline and recovery. In distressed or declining rural regions, the major issue concerns the withdrawal of public services consequent upon outmigration. Though the residual population may contain particularly high proportions of the service-dependent, the economics and politics of rural service provision have consistently made for the reduction and closure of key services (Nelson et al., 1984; Phillips and Williams, 1984). This, in turn, tends

178

to hasten outmigration and diminish the prospects for economic recovery (Fisher and Rushton, 1979).

In rural regions characterized by population growth and economic expansion the issues are rather different and the conflicts and cleavages over collective consumption are more sharply defined. Whether growth and expansion are the result of the arrival of an adventitious population of ex-metropolitan households or of some new exploitation of the local resource base, the demand for public services inevitably outstrips the capacity of governments to supply and deliver them. Moreover, the incoming (and returning) population not only requires more services; it typically expects a greater range and quality of service provision; and it typically gives priority to different types of services (Holmes, 1984; Smit and Joseph, 1984; Forsyth, 1980). The demand-making processes associated with these expectations often make for conflict between established households and newcomers. It is the housing market which is the principal arena for conflict. The supply of rural housing is usually very limited, so that the intervention of newcomers in the housing market, at any level, tends to displace indigenous households and inflate prices, creating a kind of rural gentrification (Berger, 1980). In these circumstances, established low-income households are made more dependent on public housing. Yet middle-class incomers often oppose the expansion of the local housing stock (especially if proposals include public housing) on the grounds that it would be 'detrimental to the character of the rural environment' (Rodgers, 1983).

## Collective consumption and urban systems
In overall terms, patterns of collective consumption are a function of the size, role and prosperity of cities. These characteristics are brought together under the notion of centrality, and in recent years a number of sociologists and political scientists have suggested that central place theory can be of powerful potential when it comes to explaining variations in levels of collective consumption, particularly for indivisible public services such as parks, libraries, fire services and police protection (Aiken and Deprè, 1980; Aiken and Martinotti, 1984; Hansen, 1984; Newton, 1981, 1984). Following

# Collective Consumption and Socio-Spatial Change

Newton (1981, pp. 128-9), we can summarize the influence of centrality on patterns of collective consumption as follows:

Centrality→large population size→diseconomies of scale→high service costs

Central places also have a high proportion of shops, offices and other commercial property, and this type of property generally has a high tax yield. The wealth of the general population of the city may also be enhanced by the importance of central places in the national economy, and by the amount of business they do for surrounding areas. These relationships can be expressed as follows:

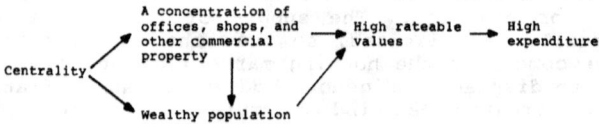

Centrality → A concentration of offices, shops, and other commercial property → High rateable values → High expenditure

Centrality → Wealthy population → High rateable values

In addition, local government, no less than the private sector, provides central place services, particularly libraries, museums, art galleries, sports facilities, parks, botanical gardens, zoos and special educational facilities. The need for parks and sports facilities is further increased by the fact that open countryside is relatively inaccessible in those central places which are at the centre of large urban agglomerations:

Centrality──────────► high expenditure on public central place services, namely libraries, museums, art galleries, sports facilities, parks, etc. special education

## Collective Consumption and Socio-Spatial Change

Lastly, central places attract large numbers of commuters and visitors who use them for business and pleasure. The more important the central place, the heavier the demands placed upon some of its services, including police, planning and highways:

Centrality →large population flows →high expenditure on police planning highways

Figure 6.4 combines these relationships into a single diagram which helps to specify the relationships between dependent and independent variables, thus helping to create theoretical coherence in a research area which at present is dominated by isolated empirical findings.

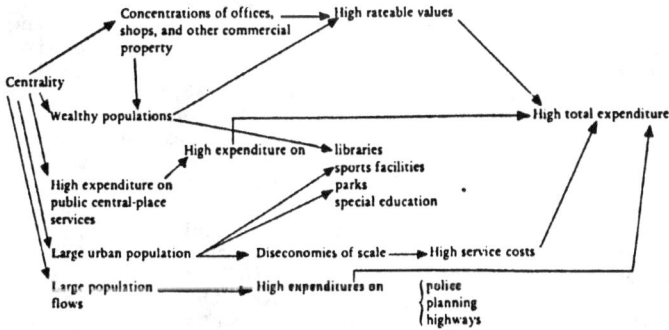

Figure 6.4  A Causal Model Relating to
Urban Centrality and Local
Public Expenditure

## Collective Consumption and Socio-Spatial Change

But although patterns of centrality are by definition relatively stable, they do change, and these changes will have significant implications for patterns of collective consumption. In the advanced economies, the major changes affecting urban systems have been related to structural economic change, to the changing locational logic of both new and established industries, to the redeployment of economic activity (at the level of both international and national urban systems) by large conglomerates as functional reorganization is reflected in spatial reorganization, and to the 'catch-up' urbanization of certain regions. The net results are reflected in the urban distress - and loss of centrality - of cities in the 'rustbelts' of northeastern United States, northern England, central Scotland, the Ruhr, etc.; in the new affluence - and increased centrality - of 'sunbelt' cities in the United States, southern England and Mediterranean Europe; and in the intensification of the control functions - both corporate and public - of the most dominant administrative and financial central places: Brussels, Chicago, London, Los Angeles, New York, Paris, San Francisco, Zurich, etc. The point is that each of these trajectories of change is associated with rather different sets of issues in relation to collective consumption. Distressed cities like Liverpool and Detroit must cope with the downward spirals set in motion by a declining economic base, a weakened tax base, and increasing concentrations of service-dependent households (Hill, 1984; Rose and Page, 1982); while in affluent cities like Houston, Vancouver and San Jose the issues are focused on responses to new needs and new demands that are articulated with varying degrees of success by different groups (Feagin, 1984; Ley and Mercer, 1980; Saxenian, 1984); and in the likes of London and New York the issues are often dominated by the intensifying burdens of traditional (public) central place functions (Glassberg, 1980). All these issues, in turn, have to be set in the context of fiscal relationships between central and local governments (Bennett, 1980; Clark and Dear, 1984; Kennett, 1980), and the interaction of both with private money markets (Boast, 1980).

## Collective Consumption and Socio-Spatial Change

### Collective consumption and metropolitan change

At the metropolitan scale, the decentralization of jobs and residences has been the dominant aspect of spatial change for the past 40 years, though we should also recognize the importance of other, inter-related processes such as gentrification, downtown redevelopment, and the localization of service-dependent sub-groups in inner-city neighbourhoods. What is particularly important, in the present context, about these processes is that they have often (nearly always, in the US) been operating across jurisdictional boundaries, thus making for enormous problems of service delivery and generating intense conflict between jurisdictions and service-delivery agencies (Cox and Nartowicz, 1980; Nathan and Adams, 1976; Oakland, 1979). The outcome, in general terms, has been that central city jurisdictions have increasingly been faced with the problems associated with the dilemma of increasing service commitments and decreasing tax bases, while suburban jurisdictions have been able to exclude the service-dependent poor and attract residential and/or industrial activities which generate higher tax yields (It should be noted, however, that only the more affluent upper-middle class communities have been able to enjoy high levels of service provision and relatively low tax rates: most middle class suburbs have to make a relatively high tax effort and take on significant debts in order to maintain desired levels and packages of collective consumption (Schneider and Logan, 1981). In addition, it is clear that the magnitude of the service burden carried by central city jurisdictions is influenced by a wide variety of factors, including the ease of annexation, tax laws, metropolitan homogeneity, and the policies of higher-tier governments (Benton and Rigos, 1985). In the United States, the suburban protectionism inherent to these differences has been challenged in the Supreme Court, but for the most part judicial interpretations of the Federal Constitution have supported the status quo (Johnston, 1981, 1982, 1983).

Meanwhile, the predicament of central city jurisdictions has reached crisis proportions and, with the crisis, a variety of important changes to patterns of collective consumption. The public-choice explanation of this urban fiscal crisis rests on the idea that public expenditure has grown by adding the wrong functions, especially

## Collective Consumption and Socio-Spatial Change

those that serve a limited (but vocal and electorally critical) clientele (Buchanan, 1977; Savas, 1982). The neo-Marxist explanation, on the other hand, argues that urban fiscal crisis is a product of:

1. The exodus of middle class taxpayers
2. The influence of local pro-growth business groups that have encouraged central city governments to spend heavily on redevelopment projects that serve businesses, on police and fire services (that serve property owners), and on services that train people for jobs and, hence, serve business
3. The availability of central government grants which hid or delayed fiscal stress, leaving local governments more dependent and desperate for revenues (O'Connor, 1973)

Different again is the interpretation of the interactions between urban change and patterns of collective consumption offered by Friedland (1981), who argues that fiscal crisis has not been the result of economic decline but of the nature of economic growth. In particular, he suggests, it has been the growth of new kinds of private economic activity that has imposed high costs on the public sector. In general, the growth of new kinds of urban economic activity has been expensive because (1) it has failed to provide employment and income for central city residents, and (2) it has made demands on the public sector for infrastructure expenditures which were self-financing:

> On the one hand, new economic growth in the central cities did not provide sufficient employment and income benefits to the central city's residents. Industrial jobs were taken by suburbanized union workers. Construction work was dominated by restrictive craft unions. And the new office economy was drawing on the better educated, better heeled, suburban workforce. Industrial investments were now part of vast multilocational networks of plants, thus weakening the local multipliers from local plant investments. This export of the income benefits of local economic growth meant a continuous reservoir of poor, structurally unemployed people who turned to city governments for jobs and services.

## Collective Consumption and Socio-Spatial Change

On the other hand, the rising economy of the central city required a restructuring of urban space to move people and information most efficiently. This required a massive investment in public capital for mass transit, parking, urban renewal, and the more traditional forms of infrastructure (Friedland, 1981, pp. 370-1).

These infrastructural investments were insulated from conflict, Friedland argues, through the exploitation of new forms of administration and financing: autonomous special districts, banker committees, and new forms of revenue and tax bonding. As a result, there emerged two worlds of local expenditure: one oriented to providing services and public employment for the city's residents, the other to constructing the infrastructure necessary to profitable private development. 'These two worlds - of social wage and social capital - were structurally segregated. The former was governed by electoral politics and the excesses of patronage. The latter was housed in bureaucratic agencies, dominated by men of business who survived by their efficiency' (Friedland, 1981, p.371).

### Collective consumption and intra-urban change

It follows from the classification used here that some of the issues and interactions described in relation to urban systems and metropolitan areas will also be worked out within individual municipal jurisdictions. At the same time, we must recognize the importance of processes whose imprint is to be found mainly at the intra-urban scale. It is at this scale, for example, that urban politics, managerial influences and community activism conspire to produce expenditure allocations and service locations that may or may not be sensitive to evolving social ecologies (Cox and McCarthy, 1980; Cox and Johnston, 1982; Goschel et al., 1982; Whitehead, 1983). Another example of changes at the intra-urban scale is the rupture of the spatial linkages between the service-dependent poor and the 'service hubs' of inner city neighbourhoods (Wolch and Gabriel, 1984, 1985). This seems to have been a result of (i) imbalances that have developed between local labour and housing markets, (ii) the consequent gentrification of some inner-city neighbourhoods, (iii) downtown

## Collective Consumption and Socio-Spatial Change

redevelopment projects, and (iv) political pressure to reduce service capacity. Consequently, the service-dependent poor have begun to disperse, to become reinstitutionalized, or have been unable to receive services for which they are eligible. In addition, it is at this scale that patterns of collective consumption are conditioned by the 'local resources squeeze' arising from the increasing conflict in recent years between, on the one hand, forces which have contributed to rising municipal expenditures and, on the other, forces which have restricted municipal incomes. A cross-national study of Newton et al. (1980) identified six major sets of factors that have contributed to rising levels of expenditure on collective consumption:

1. An expansion of existing services, partly because of social, economic and demographic changes (e.g. the effects of ageing and of increased female participation in the labour force, which require, respectively, more sheltered housing and more day care centres)

2. Increases in the quality of services provided, as a result of rising expectations and an increasing disposition toward the idea of social justice

3. Increases in the range of services, to include, for example, environmental protection, consumer protection, and the provision of special services for groups such as migrants and the handicapped

4. The replacement of social capital, which is simply a legacy of the early start experienced by some municipalities in terms of modern economic development. Outworn and inadequate schools, housing, roads, etc. have had to be replaced as they reached the end of their life cycle

5. The increased costs of services arising from the fact that municipal services include many activities that have suffered disproportionately from inflation because they are labour-intensive.

6. The costs of urbanization, both for central city municipalities that have had to cope with congestion and agglomeration diseconomies, and for suburban municipalities that have had to cope with the high costs of initial urban development: new sewers, water supplies, roads, schools, etc.

## Collective Consumption and Socio-Spatial Change

In relation to the constraints on local government incomes, Newton et al. identify, in addition to the constraints arising from imbalances at the metropolitan scale, three major factors:

1. The lack of buoyancy of many local taxes, especially those that are related to land and property and which are less sensitive to inflation and more difficult to manipulate or adjust.
2. The high visibility of many local taxes, especially those which are paid in a lump sum: it is argued that this makes it difficult, politically, to increase tax levels.
3. The political sensitivity of local financial matters.

The net result is that many municipalities have had to resort to curbs on collective consumption that have been more stringent than any since war-time conditions. Moreover, though the 'local resources squeeze' has been experienced by almost all municipalities, the impact has been most severe in central city jurisdictions where resource squeeze has slid into fiscal crisis. In Rome, local officials talk of the 'monthly miracle' which enables the city to pay its operating expenses and to avoid bankruptcy yet again. In Liege, local government employees were put on subsistence wages when the city went bankrupt in 1983 and had to negotiate a massive loan from the central government in order to bail itself out. Such problems, coming as they have during a period of economic stagnation, have contributed to the movement towards the retrenchment of entire welfare systems described at the beginning of this chapter. We conclude, therefore, with a brief consideration of the implications of these changes.

### Retrenchment and reorganization

Although the current phase of retrenchment and reorganization which characterizes public service delivery has been seen at its starkest in the United Kingdom and the United States under the Thatcher and Reagan administrations, the phenomenon is widespread and dates from the early 1970s when it became clear that service-dependent households (particularly single-parent families,

187

Collective Consumption and Socio-Spatial Change

children in care, and the elderly) were increasing
much faster than the general population and that
expenditure on welfare systems was increasing much
faster than GNP (Derthick, 1975; Judge, 1978;
Richan, 1981). As a result, Labour and Democrat
administrations in the United Kingdom and the
United States had begun to curb expenditure on
collective consumption as early as the mid-1970s.
By this time, however, cyclical economic
depression had begun to bite, and for many
right-wing economists and policy advisors the
Malthusian nightmare became a real prospect:
societies in which welfare so subverts the
operation of the labour market that more and more
people drop out of the workforce, leaving a
shrinking proportion of productive workers to
support a growing burden of unproductive social
expenses (Bacon and Eltis, 1976; Campbell, 1977;
Hague, 1980). This vision first acquired
ideological legitimacy with the popular support
for California's Proposition 13 (1978), which
reduced local government spending by $7 billion
and led to a ceiling of four per cent per annum on
local government spending (Stumpf and Terrell,
1979). Shortly afterwards, electoral victories for
conservatives at the national level in both the
United Kingdom and the United States brought a
vigorous commitment to substantial cutbacks in the
size and scope of welfare systems (Adams and
Freeman, 1982). In addition to having their
budgets cut, agencies responsible for various
aspects of collective consumption were strongly
encouraged to find ways of 'load shedding', most of
which have amounted to various forms of privatization (Hatry, 1983; Savas, 1982). These include:

1. Contracting out, which can range from the
   contracting out of particular functions
   (e.g. hospital laundry work) to the
   contracting out of whole services (as in
   Danish municipalities' private contracts
   for fire and ambulance services)
2. Franchises, which require citizens to pay
   private firms directly for services. The
   most common examples are franchises for
   the collection of refuse and garbage
3. Vouchers, which enable citizens to choose
   the organization(s) (public or private)
   from which to buy services. The most
   well-known examples have been the use of
   vouchers in elementary education, housing,

and transport for the elderly, though most have been experimental in character

4. Self-Help for individuals or groups (such as neighbourhood associations). A good example here is the Housing Corporation set up in the UK to foster the activities of voluntary housing groups (Kirby, 1985)

5. Public-Private partnerships formed for the purposes of effecting major developments such as downtown revitalization (see, for example, Fosler and Berger, 1982)

6. De-marketing, or reducing the demand for public services through marketing techniques, e.g. campaigns to reduce litter, to encourage private carpools, to install fire- or crime-prevention devices, and so on.

7. Voluntarism, including the use of volunteer labour in public schools, libraries, fire stations, etc. (in Virginia Beach, Virginia, (population 260,000) a total of 1776 volunteers provided an average of 30 hours free labour each during July-September 1981: a scale of voluntarism which is typical for many communities in the state); and the encouragement of voluntary donations of time and money to private (usually non-profit) service delivery organizations (which now amount to between five and nine per cent of GNP in the US as a whole).

These changes cut across all of the spatial processes described in earlier sections, bringing with them new socio-geographical patterns and posing new research questions. Which regions, cities and neighbourhoods are being affected most? What aspects of collective consumption are being affected most? What types of household are being affected most? What are the specific effects of load-shedding and privatization? In some areas the picture is beginning to emerge. Bassett (1980), Barke (1983), English (1982), Forest and Murie (1984), Harloe (1981) and others have described how the retreat from public housing in the United Kingdom is rapidly leaving a residual service for residualized households; Reynolds (1984) and Honey and Sorenson (1984) have surveyed the implications of school budget retrenchment and school closings in the United

## Collective Consumption and Socio-Spatial Change

States; and Wolch 1983; Wolch and Geiger, 1983, have explored the spatial implications of voluntarism. Perhaps the best-documented example of retrenchment is the UK National Health Service, where rigid cash limits have been imposed, a tier of the administrative hierarchy has been removed, revenue funds have been withheld, performance indicators have been introduced, some functions have been contracted out, and some facilities have been closed down. At the same time, private medical services have been actively encouraged by relaxing controls and planning regulations on private hospitals, allowing private medical insurance premiums as corporate tax deductions, and revising medical consultants' contracts in order to make it easier for them to work in the private sector (Klein, 1982; Mohan and Woods, 1985; Mohan, 1985). It is clear that these changes involve marked spatial inequalities. What is not clear is how these inequalities may be interacting with other consequences of retrenchment and with other dimensions of social and economic life. Such themes must be near to the top of social geographers' research agendas, for they seem certain to become important components of the social geography of cities and regions by the end of present decade.

Collective Consumption and Socio-Spatial Change

REFERENCES
Adams, P. and Freeman, G. (1982) 'Social Services under Reagan and Thatcher', in N. Fainstein and S. Fainstein (eds.) Urban Policy Under Capitalism, Sage Beverly Hills, pp. 65-82

Aiken, M. and Depre, R. (1980) 'Policy and politics in Belgian cities', Policy and Politics, 8, 73-106

Aiken, M. and Martinotti, G. (1984) 'Left politics, the urban system and public policy', British Journal of Political Science, 14, 87-103

Antunes, G. and Plumlee,J. (1977) 'The distribution of an urban public service: ethnicity, socio-economic status and bureaucracy as determinants of the quality of neighborhood streets', Urban Affairs Quarterly, 12, 313-332

Archer, C. (1981) 'Public choice paradigms in political geography', in A.D. Burnett and P.J. Taylor (eds.) Political Studies from Spatial Perspectives, Wiley, Chichester, pp. 73-90

Bacon, R. and Eltis, W. (1976) Britain's Economic Problem: Too Few Producers, St Martin's New York,

Barke, M. (1983) 'The sale of council houses in Newcastle upon Tyne: some early results', Northern Economic Review, 8, 2-12

Bassett, K.A. (1980) 'The sale of council houses as a political issue', Policy and Politics, 8, 290-307

Bebbington, A.C. and Davies, B. (1983) 'Equity and efficiency in the allocation of personal social services', Journal of Social Policy, 12, 309-330

Bennett, R. J. (1980) The Geography of Public Finance, Methuen, London,

Benton, J.E. and Rigos, P.N. (1985) 'Patterns of Metropolitan service dominance', Urban Affairs Quarterly, 20, 285-302

Berger, M. et al. (1980) 'Reurbanisation and the analysis of peri-urban space', L'Espace Geographique, 9, 303-314

Boaden, N. (1971) Urban Policy Making, Cambridge University Press, Cambridge

Boast, T. (1980) 'Urban resources, the American capital market, and federal programs', in D.E. Ashford (ed.) National Resources and Urban Policy, Methuen, London

Boyle, J. and Jacobs, D. (1980) 'The intracity distribution of services: a multivariate analysis', American Political Science Review, 76, 371-9

191

Broder, J.M. (1979) 'Bringing services to people versus bringing people to services', in A.R. Bunker and T.Q. Hutchinson (eds.) Roads of Rural America, USDA, Washington DC, pp. 34-40

Buchanan, J.M. (1977) 'Why does government grow?', in T. Borcherding (ed.) Budgets and Bureaucrats Duke University Press, North Carolina, pp. 3-18

Buchanan, J.M. and Tullock, G. (1969) The Calculus of Consent, Ann Arbor, University of Michigan Press

Burnett, A.D. (1984)'Neighbourhood participation, political demand-making and local outputs in British and North American Cities', in A. Kirby, P.L. Knox and S. Pinch (eds) Public Service Provision and Urban Development, Croom Helm, London, pp. 316-62

Burnett, A.D. and Hill, D.M. (1982) 'Neighborhood organizations and public services', in R.C. Rich (ed.) The Politics of Urban Public Services, Lexington Books, Lexington, Mass., pp.189-206

Campbell, C. D. (1977) Income Redistribution, American Enterprise Institute, Washington, DC

Castells, M. (1977) The Urban Question, Arnold, London

Castells, M. (1985) High Technology, Space and Society Vol 28, Urban Affairs Annual Reviews, Sage, Beverly Hills

Clark, G. and Dear, M. (1984) State Apparatus: Structures and Language of Legitimacy, George Allen and Unwin, Boston

Cloke, P. (1983) An Introduction to Rural Settlement Planning, Methuen, London

Cox, K.R. (1984) 'Social change, turf politics and concepts of turf politics', in A. Kirby, P.L. Knox and S. Pinch (eds) Public Service Provision and Urban Development, Croom Helm, London, pp.283-315

Cox, K.R. and Johnston, R.J. (1982) Conflict, Politics and the Urban Scene, Longman, London

Cox, K.R. and McCarthy, J.J. (1980) 'Neighborhood activism in the American city: behavioral relationships and evaluation', Urban Geography, 1, 22-38

Cox, K.R. and Nartowicz, F.Z. (1980) 'Jurisdictional fragmentation in the American metropolis: alternative perspectives', International Journal of Urban and Regional Research, 4, 196-211

Danziger, J.N. (1978) Making Budgets: Public Resource Allocation, Sage, Beverly Hills

Davies, B. (1968) Social needs and resources in local services, London, Joseph

Davies, B., Barton A., McMillan I. and Williamson, V.K. (1971) Variations in services for the aged, Bell, London

Davies, B., Barton, A. and McMillan, I (1972) Variations in children's services among British urban authorities, Bell, London

Dearlove, J. (1971) 'Councillors and interest groups in Kensington and Chelsea', British Journal of Political Science, 1, 129-153

Derthick, M. (1975) Uncontrollable Spending for Social Service Grants, Brookings Institution, Washington, DC

Dunleavy, P. (1980) Urban Political Analysis, Macmillan, London

Dye, T. R. (1966) Politics, Economics and the Public, Rand McNally, Chicago

English, J. (1982) The Future of Council Housing, Croom Helm, London

Feagin, J. R. (1984) 'Sunbelt metropolis and development capital. Houston in the era of late capitalism', in W.K. Tabb and L. Sawers (eds.) Sunbelt/Snowbelt, Oxford University Press, New York, pp.99-127

Fisher, H.B. and Rushton, G. (1979) 'Spatial efficiency of service locations and the regional development process', Papers of the Regional Science Association, 42, 83-97

Forrest, R. and Murie, A. (1984) 'Residualization and council housing', Journal of Social Policy, 12, 453-468

Forsyth, D. (1980) 'Urban incomers and community change, the impact of migrants from the city on life in an Orkney community', Sociologia Ruralis, 20, 287-307

Fosler, R.S. and Berger, R.A. (eds.) (1982) Public-Private Partnership in American Cities. Seven Case Studies, Lexington Books, Lexington, Mass.

Friedland, R. (1981) 'Central city fiscal strains, the public costs of private growth', International Journal of Urban and Regional Research, 5, 356-375

George, V. and Lawson, R. (eds.) (1980) Poverty and Inequality in Common Market Countries, Routledge & Kegan Paul, London

Glassberg, A.(1973) 'Linkage between urban policy output and voting behaviour', British Journal of Political Science, 3, 341-361

Collective Consumption and Socio-Spatial Change

Glassberg, A.(1980) Responses to fiscal crisis: Big city government in Britain and America, Studies in public policy No 55, Centre for the Study of public policy, University of Strathclyde, Glasgow

Gibson, D.M., Goodwin, R.E and Le Grand, J. (1985) 'Come and get it: distributional biases in social service delivery systems', Policy and Politics, 13, 109-125

Goschel, A., Herlyn, U., Kramer, J., Schardt, T., and Wendt, G.(1982) 'Infrastructural inequality and segregation', International Journal of Urban and Regional Research, 6, 503-532

Hague, D. (1980) 'Why the public expenditure cuts must go on', London Times, July 20, p.7

Hansen, T. (1984) 'Urban hierarchies and municipal finances', European Journal of Political Science, 14, 39-46

Harloe, M.(1981) 'The recommodification of housing' in M. Harloe and Lebas, E. (eds.) City, Class and Capital, Arnold, London, pp.17-50

Hatry, H. P. (1983) A Review of Private Approaches for Delivery of Public Services, The Urban Institute Press. Washington, DC

Heald, D. (1980) Territorial equity and public finances. Studies in public policy No 75, Centre for the Study of Public Policy, University of Strathclyde, Glasgow

Heclo, H. (1981) 'Toward a new welfare state?' in P. Flora and Heidenheimer, A.J. (eds.) The Development of Welfare States in Europe and North America, Transaction Books, New Brunswick, New Jersey, pp.383-406

Hicks, D. A. and Glickman, N. J. (eds.) 1983, Transition to the 21st Century. JAI Press, Greenwich, CT

Hill, R.C. (1984) 'Economic Crisis and Political Response in Motor City', in W. K. Tabb and Sawers, L. (eds.) Sunbelt/Snowbelt, Oxford University Press, New York, pp.313-38

Holmes, J.H. (1984) 'Australia: the dilemma of sparse population and high expectations', in R. E. Lonsdale and Enyedi, G. (eds.) Rural Public Services. International Comparisons, Westview Press, Boulder. CO, pp. 163-84

Honey, R. and Sorenson. D. (1984) 'Jurisdictional benefits and local costs: the politics of school closings', in A. Kirby, Knox, P.L. and Pinch, S. (eds.) Public Service Provision and Urban Development, Croom Helm, London, pp.114-30

Ircha, M.C. and Sundarajan, D. (1984) Municipal service distribution: equity concerns, Journal of Urban Planning and Development, 110, 34-40

Johnston, R.J. (1981) 'The management and autonomy of the local state: the role of the judiciary in the US', Environment and Planning A, 13, 1305-1315

Johnston, R.J. (1982) 'The local state and the judiciary: institutions in suburban America', in R. Flowerdew (ed.) Institutions and Geographical Patterns, Croom Helm, London, pp.255-88

Johnston, R.J. (1983) 'Texts, actors and higher managers: judges, bureaucrats and the political organization of space', Political Geography Quarterly, 2, 3-19

Jones, B.D., with S. Greenberg and J. Drew (1980) Service Delivery in the City, Longman, New York

Judge, K. (1978) Rationing Social Services, Heinemann, London

Kennett, S.(1980) Local Government Fiscal Problems: a context for inner areas, Social Science Research Council, London

Kirby, A.(1982) The Politics of Location, Methuen, London

Kirby, A. (1985) 'Voluntarism and the state funding of housing: political explanations and geographical outcomes in Britain', Tigdschift voor Economische en Sociale Geografie 76, 53-62

Kirby, A., Knox, P. L. and Pinch, S. (1984) 'Changing emphases in public services research', in A. Kirby, P.L. Knox and S. Pinch (eds.) Public Service Provision and Urban Development, Croom Helm, London, pp.1-17

Klein, R. (1982) Performance, evaluation and the NHS , Public Administration, 80, 385-407

Knox, P.L. (1978) 'The intra-urban ecology of primary medical care', Environment and Planning A, 10, 415-435

Levy, F.S., Meltsner, A.J. and Wildavsky, A. (1974) Urban Outcomes, University of California Press, Berkeley

Ley, D. and Mercer, (1980) 'Locational conflict and the politics of consumption', Economic Geography, 56, 89-108

Lineberry, R.L. (1976) 'Equality, public policy and public services: the underclass hypothesis and the limits to equality', Policy and Politics 4, 67-84

Collective Consumption and Socio-Spatial Change

Lineberry, R.L. (1977) Equality and Urban Policy, Sage, Beverly Hills

Lipsky, M. (1980) Street-Level Bureaucracy, Sage, Beverly Hills

Lojkine, J. (1976) Contribution to a Marxist theory of capitalist urbanization , in C. Pickvance (ed.) Urban Sociology: Critical Essays, Tavistock, London, pp.119-46

Lonsdale, R. and Enyedi, G. (1984) Rural Public Services: International Comparisons, Westview Press, Boulder, Co

Lucy. W. (1981) 'Equity and planning for local services', Journal of the American Planning Association, 47, 447-457

McLafferty, S. (1982) 'Urban structure and geographical access to public services', Annals, Association of American Geographers, 72, 347-354

Margolis, J. (1968) 'The demand for urban public services' in H. Perloff and L. Wingo (eds.) Issues in Urban Economics, Johns Hopkins University Press, Baltimore

Markusen, A. (1984) 'Class and urban social expenditure: a Marxist theory of metropolitan government , in W.K. Tabb and L. Sawers (eds.) Marxism and the Metropolis. 2nd edition, Oxford University Press, New York, pp.82-100

Merget, A. E. and Berger, R.A. (1982) 'Equity as a decision rule in local services', in R. C. Rich (ed.) Analyzing Urban-Service Distributions, Lexington Books, Lexington, Mass., pp.21-44

Mladenka, K. (1978) 'Organizational rules, service equality, and distributional decisions in urban politics, Social Science Quarterly, 59, 192-146

Mladenka, K. (1980) 'The urban bureaucracy and the Chicago political machine', American Political Science Review, 74, 991-998

Mladenka, K. and Hill, K.Q. (1977) 'The distribution of benefits in an urban environment: parks and libraries in Houston', Urban Affairs Quarterly, 13, 73-94

Mladenka, K. and Hill, K.Q. (1978) 'The distribution of urban police services', Journal of Politics, 40, 112-133

Mohan J. (1985) 'Independent acute medical care in Britain: its organization, location and future prospects', International Journal of Urban and Regional Research, 9, 467-84

Mohan, J. and Woods, K.J. (1985) Restructuring health care: the social geography of public and private health care under the British conservative government, International Journal of Health Services, 15, 197-215

Moseley, M. (1984) Service decline and policy response: rural Britain in the 1980s , in R.E. Lonsdale and G. Enyedi (eds.) Rural Public Services. International Comparisons, Westview Press, Boulder, Co, pp. 105-12

Moseley, M. and Packman, J. (1983) Mobile Services in Rural Areas, University of East Anglia, Norwich

Moseley, M. and Packman, J. (1985) The distribution of fixed, mobile and delivery services in rural Britain, Journal of Rural Studies. 1, 87-95

Musgrave, R.A. (1959) Theory of Public Finance, McGraw-Hill, New York

Nathan, R.P. and Adams, C.F. (1976) 'Understanding central city hardship', Political Science Quarterly, 91, 47-62

Navarro, V. (1982) 'The crisis of the international capitalist order and its implications for the welfare state', International Journal of Health Services, 12, 169-190

Nelson, J. R., Tweeten, L. and Doeksen, G. (1984) 'The economics of rural community services in the US', in R.E. Lonsdale and G. Enyedi (eds.) Rural Public Services: International Comparisons, Westview Press, Boulder, Co, pp.53-88

Newton, K. (1981) 'Central places and urban services' in K. Newton (ed.) Urban Political Economy, Frances Pinter, London, pp.117-36

Newton. K. (1984) 'Urban systems theory and urban policy and expenditures in England and Wales, European Journal of Political Research, 12, 357-369

Newton, K. et al. (1980) Balancing the Books, Sage, Beverly Hills

Nivola, P.S. (1978) 'Distributing a municipal service: a case study of housing inspection', Journal of Politics, 40, 59-81

O'Connor. J. (1973) 'The Fiscal Crisis of the State, St Martin's, New York

Oakland, W. H. (1979) 'Central cities: fiscal plight and prospects for reform', in P. Mieszkowski and M. Straszheim (eds.) Current Issues in Urban Economics, Johns Hopkins University Press, Baltimore, pp.322-58

197

OECD (1976) Public Expenditure on Income Maintenance Programmes, OECD, Paris

Ostrom, V., Tiebout, C.M. and Warren, R. (1981)
'The organization of government in metropolitan
areas: a theoretical enquiry'. American
Political Science Review, 40, 831-42

Pahl, R.E. (1970) Whose City?, Penguin, Harmondsworth

Phillips, D. R. (1981) Contemporary Issues in the
Geography of Health Care, Geo. Abstracts,
Norwich

Phillips, D. R. and Williams, A. (1984) Rural
Britain: A Social Geography, Blackwell, Oxford

Pinch, S. (1985) Cities and Services: the geography
of collective consumption, Routledge and Kegan
Paul, London

Reynolds, D.R. (1981) 'The geography of social
choice', in A.D. Burnett and P.J. Taylor
(eds.) Political Studies from Spatial
Perspectives, Wiley, Chichester, 91-110

Reynolds, D.R. (1984) School budget retrenchment
and locational conflict: crisis in local
democracy? in A. Kirby, P.L. Knox and S. Pinch
(eds.) Public Service Provision and Urban
Development, Croom Helm, London, pp.96-113

Rich, R.C. (1979a) 'Neglected issues in the study
of urban service distributions: a research
agenda', Urban Studies, 16, 143-156

Rich, R. C. (1979b) 'The roles of neighborhood
organizations in urban service delivery',
Urban Affairs Papers, 1, 81-93

Rich, R. C. (1982a) 'Problems of theory and method
in the study of urban-service distributions'
in R.C. Rich (ed.) Analyzing Urban-Service
Distributions, Lexington Books, Lexington,
Mass., pp.3-18

Rich, R.C. (ed.) (1982b) The Politics of Urban
Public Services, Lexington Books, Lexington,
Mass.

Richan, W.C. (1981) Social Service Politics in the
United States and Britain, Temple University
Press, Philadelphia

Rodgers, A.W. (1983) 'Rural Housing' in M. Pacione
(ed.) Progress in Rural Geography, Croom Helm,
London

Room, G. (1982) 'Understanding poverty' in J.
Dennett et al., Europe Against Poverty,
Bedford Square Press, London, pp. 163-84

Rose R. and Page, E.G. (eds.) (1982) Fiscal Stress
in Cities, Cambridge University Press,
Cambridge

Samuelson, P.A. (1954) 'The pure theory of public expenditure', Review of Economics and Statistics, 36, 387-389

Saunders, P. (1981) 'Community power, urban managerialism and the "Local State"', in M. Harloe (ed.) New Perspectives on Urban Change and Conflict, Heinemann Educational, London, pp.27-79

Savas, E.S. (1982) Privatizing the Public Sector, Chatham House, New Jersey

Saxenian, A-L. (1984) 'The urban contradictions of Silicon Valley', in L. Sawers and W. K. Tabb (eds.) Sunbelt/Snowbelt. Oxford University Press, New York, pp.163-97

Schneider, M. and Logan, J. R. (1981) 'Fiscal implications of class segregation: inequalities in the distribution of public goods and services in suburban municipalities', Urban Affairs Quarterly. 17, 23-36

Seley, J. E. (1983) The Politics of Public Facility planning, Lexington Books, Lexington, Mass.

Sharpe, L.J. (1981) 'Does politics matter?', in K. Newton (ed.) Urban Political Economy, Frances Pinter, London, pp. 1-26

Sharpe, L.J. and Newton, K. (1984) Does Politics Matter?, Oxford University Press, London

Sly, D.F. and Tayman. G. (1980) 'Changing metropolitan morphology and municipal service expenditures', Social Science Quarterly, 61, 595-611

Smit, B. and Joseph, A. (1984) 'Identifying service priorities of rural consumers', in R.E. Lonsdale and G. Enyedi (eds.) Rural Public Services: International Comparisons Westview Press, Boulder, CO, pp.39-50

Stanback, T. M. Jr. and Noyelle, T.J. (1982) Cities in Transition, Allanheld, Osmun, Totowa, NJ

Stumpf, J. and Terrell, P. (1979) Proposition 13 and California Human Services, National Association of Social Workers, Millbrae, CA

Tiebout, C.M. (1956) 'A pure theory of local expenditures', Journal of Political Economy, 64, 416-424

Tuckman, H. P. (1984) 'Social efficiency and the provision of collective services', American Journal of Economics and Sociology, 43, 257-267

Tudor-Hart, J. (1971) 'The inverse care law', Lancet, i, 405-412

Whitehead, P. (1983) 'Intraurban spatial variations in local government service provision: 2. Application and results, Environment and Planning C, 1, 229-248

Wolch, J. (1980) 'Residential location of the service-dependent poor , Annals, Association of American Geographers, 70, 330-340

Wolch, J. (1981) 'The location of service-dependent households in urban areas', Economic Geography. 57, 52-67

Wolch, J. (1982) 'Spatial consequences of social policy: the role of service-facility location in urban development patterns', in R.C. Rich (ed.) The Politics of Urban Public Services, Lexington Books, Lexington, Mass., pp.19-36

Wolch, J. (1983) 'The voluntary sector in urban communities', Environment and Planning D. Space and Society, 1, 181-190

Wolch, J. and Gabriel, S.A. (1984) 'Development and decline of service-dependent population ghettos', Urban Geography, 5, 111-129

Wolch, J. and Gabriel, S.A. (1985) 'Dismantling the community-based human service system', Journal of the American Planning Association, 51, 53-62

Wolch, J. and Geiger, R.K. (1983) 'The distribution of urban voluntary services : an exploratory analysis', Environment and Planning A, 15, 1067-1082

Chapter Seven

POVERTY, DEPRIVATION AND SOCIAL PLANNING

J. EYLES

Introduction

It is the purpose of this chapter to examine some
of the ideas and evidence concerning the nature
and extent of poverty and deprivation in a variety
of societal contexts and at different geographical
scales.  It is necessary, therefore, to begin by
looking at the definitional problems of the nature
of poverty.  It will be noted that poverty is more
than a lack of income, being related to command
over resources as well as social expectations with
respect to needs, wants and expenditure.  This
deprivation view of poverty leads to a general
consideration of the standards of living and
quality of life.  Reference will be made to the
work of social geographers and others who have
used a number of approaches to attempt to measure
quality of life, eg single and multiple indicators
of deprivation or well-being, objective and
subjective indicators and the use of formal survey
instruments as opposed to that of ethnography. But
what this research mainly does is identify the
incidence and extent of deprivation.  As Harvey
(1974) asked, before the main endeavours of social
indicators research, do we really need further
documentary evidence of some people's inhumanity
to others?  Perhaps the answer is a qualified yes
with the main qualification being what, if
anything, is to be done about the identified
inequalities?  In other words, what is or should
be the policy response to the patterns of poverty
and deprivation?  The answer to this question is
not straightforward because policy response is
strongly linked to how poverty and deprivation are
viewed and explained. This chapter will, therefore,

go on to examine some of the theories of deprivation for the practical reason that therein lie an understanding of which particular policy options are put forward, which are put into practice, which rejected and which not even considered. Having looked at why particular policies are practised, the chapter will conclude by exemplifying policy by social planning from different societies. In the main, it will be noted that social planning is directed at changing environments rather than changing people's attitudes, the ways in which resources are allocated or the way the social system is structured. But social planning is not an isolate; its context is vital for evaluating its nature, form and impact.

## Poverty

It must be recognised that by its very nature poverty is a comparative term. Wealth and poverty only have meaning in terms of a scale on the basis of which some are richer and some poorer than others. Even then comparison is not particularly easy as a scale that is appropriate to compare the living standards of individuals within one country may be less useful in terms of comparing individuals between countries. To suggest that a valid comparison may be made between the citizens of Bangladesh and those of Britain is to point to the existence of an absolute poverty. Such a poverty means an insufficiency in basic necessities - inadequate food, clothing, shelter - such that life itself is threatened. Those deemed poor in any Western society are indeed well off compared with those in countries where starvation and disease are common. As Coates & Silburn (1970) point out, the coexistence of rich nations and those existing at the barest imaginable level of living cannot be morally defended. Figure 7.1 shows calories available per head as a proportion of estimated requirements. It points up the North-South division in this crucial arena of survival, although it also demonstrates that some Western countries - Netherlands, Scandinavia - have, by and large, instituted healthy regimes. But malnutrition captures only one aspect of our idea of poverty (see Sen, 1982). It was, however, used by Rowntree (1901) to define primary poverty in York. Being in primary poverty means being unable to maintain physical efficiency. And

202

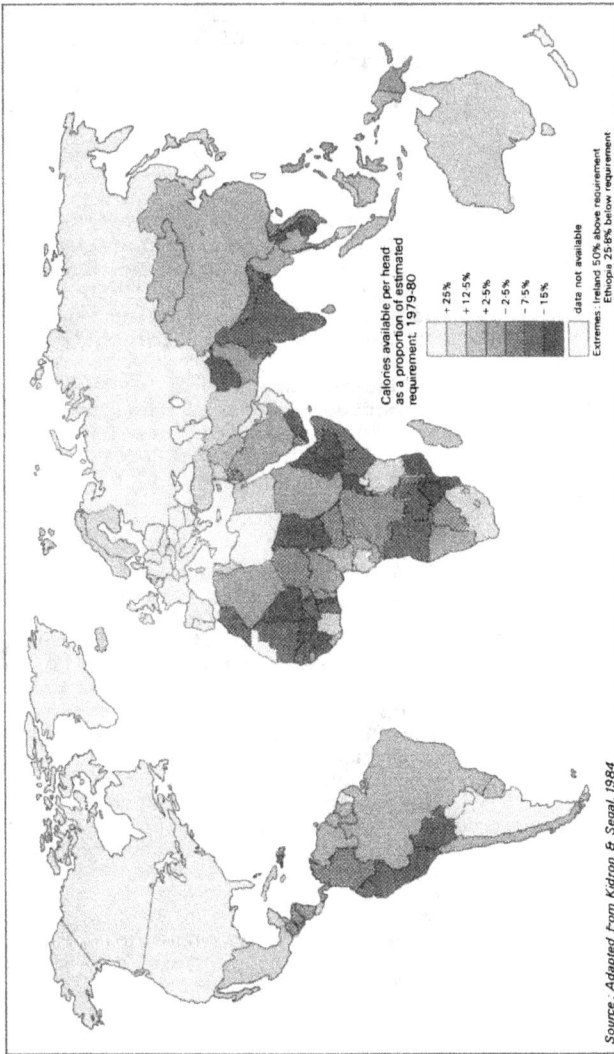

Source: Adapted from Kidron & Segal, 1984

**Figure 7.1  Deprivation at the World Scale: Malnutrition 1979–80**

Calories available per head
as a proportion of estimated
requirement, 1979–80

+ 25%
+ 12.5%
+ 2.5%
− 2.5%
− 7.5%
− 15%

data not available

Extremes : Ireland 50% above requirement
Ethopia 25.6% below requirement

Poverty, Deprivation and Social Planning

identifying such poverty - to have an absolute standard - defines a minimum level of subsistence which can be used as the basis of social security payment scales (see Townsend, 1979). It also means that to avoid primary poverty, adequate nutrition must be obtained at the lowest possible cost.

To consider only primary poverty and levels of subsistence is to misunderstand the nature of poverty and the attempts to alleviate its effects. First, it assumes that the poor will spend their incomes as efficiently and as rationally as indicated by the experts compiling the list of necessities (see Townsend, 1954). Such rationality is assumed by the New Right advocates of an absolute and minimum level of support for the poor:

"An absolute standard means one defined by reference to the actual needs of the poor and not by reference to the expenditure of those who are not poor. A family is poor if it cannot afford to eat" (Josephy & Sumption, 1979, pp. 27-8)

But this absolutist notion is not rejected by a more relativistic approach. The approach of relative deprivation supplements rather than competes with this concern with absolute poverty (see Sen, 1978). Thus the second difficulty posed by a consideration of primary poverty alone is to consider the necessities of life as somehow lying outside of their containing societal context. Indeed, it is now some 150 years ago that both Adam Smith and Karl Marx argued that necessities are in part determined by 'the custom of the country' and that our needs spring from society itself. If needs are customarily and socially determined then poverty is best seen as a relative phenomenon (see Galbraith, 1958; Harrington, 1962). As Crosland (1964, p. 89) argued:

"Poverty is not, after all, an absolute, but a social or cultural concept ... This demands a relative, subjective view of poverty, since the unhappiness and injustice it creates, even when ill-health and malnutrition are avoided, lies in the enforced deprivation not of luxuries indeed, but of small comforts which others have and are seen to have, and which in the light of prevailing cultural standards are really 'conventional necessities'."

# Poverty, Deprivation and Social Planning

Once physical survival is assured, therefore, what is deemed necessary becomes a matter of convention. Unlike Coates and Silburn (1970), we also assert that these necessities are matters of principle because without a notion of social justice (and its concomitant just distribution), it will soon cease to be conventional to regard certain conditions as necessary. This 'conventional' view is well summarised by Townsend (1979, 31):

> Individuals, families and groups in the population can be said to be in poverty when they lack the resources to obtain the types of diet, participate in the activities and have the living conditions and amenities which are customary, or are at least widely encouraged or approved, in the societies to which they belong. Their resources are so seriously below those commanded by the average individual or family that they are, in effect, excluded from ordinary living patterns, customs and activities.

Key elements in this definition of poverty are living patterns - called styles of living by Townsend - and resources. For both, a measure of substitutability is possible. Individuals can as their resources are reduced alter their living patterns, by buying cheaper foods and clothing, cutting down on heating their living space, or by not going on holidays. But there may come a point at which individuals are forced to withdraw from participating in culturally sanctioned customs and activities. Indeed, many of the unemployed and the elderly who spoke to Harrison (1985) in Hackney and Seabrook (1982) in Sunderland and Birmingham withdraw by staying in their homes for as long as they possibly can.

Resources are also variable. It is not, as Titmuss (1962) pointed out, just a matter of cash income. There are also housing and other capital assets, employment benefits in kind (fringe benefits), and public services in kind (eg health and education). But perhaps more crucial to the poor in terms of resource substitutability are those identified by, amongst others, Harvey (1973) and Townsend (1979), namely relative location or accessibility and private income in kind (through home production, gifts and social support networks). It is important for the poor to be close to public services and job opportunities, although high accessibility may be 'bought' at the cost of negative externalities. Further, the support resource provided by family, friends and neighbourhood may make the difference between muddling through and sinking into a mire of increasing debt and stress. Hoggart (1957) describes cases of people joining forces to make do with what they had in the deprived working class communities in Britain in the 1950s. Pahl (1984) has reviewed how at various times and in various societies households have formulated work strategies to make the best use of resources under their particular social and economic circumstances. Wallman (1983) in her study of Battersea has shown how resources need not be material objects but can be time, skill, knowledge and organisation. These 'resources' may make the difference between chronic poverty and unemployment and occasional bouts of difficulty and, say, integration into the informal economy.

If a relativistic approach is adopted to poverty, resources, styles of living, it is difficult to know where to stop. It is in this regard that critics on the New Right have attacked the notion of relative poverty. They suggest that people's demands are insatiable. We must note, however, that these demands are socially determined and constrained. It may be that Townsend's (1979) deprivation index contains items which are debatable measures (eg cooked breakfasts, afternoons or evenings out, children's friends for tea), especially in the context of his search for an objective measure of poverty. His index omits consideration of choice. Those who are poor have little or no opportunity to take a holiday or eat a cooked breakfast (see Piachaud, 1981). His work also tries to be scientifically prescriptive and while it informs greatly on inequality, it does not necessarily tell us why the lack of particular resources is the basis of poverty and deprivation. The resonances between the measures and people's experiences and perceptions are not demonstrated.

Thus while Townsend approvingly cites the work on feelings of deprivation carried out by Merton (1957) and Runciman (1966), he is concerned with the conditions of deprivation. But as Sen (1982) notes, the choice of conditions cannot be made independent of feelings. Social perceptions of needs are themselves determined by social conditions but in such terms poverty may be seen as the enforced lack of socially perceived necessities (see Mack and Lansley, 1985), with the perceptions being established by use of large-scale public opinion sampling.

In any event, it is necessary to draw a line below which individuals are considered to be in poverty or deprived. In the UK, that line is governmentally determined and is based on supplementary benefit (SB) rates. For his 1968-9 investigations, Townsend (1979) used three measures to identify the extent of poverty. First, there is the state's standard and Townsend calculated that those whose net disposable household income was less than 100 per cent of SB scales plus housing costs totalled 3.3 million people. This differs from the DHSS's own calculations which estimated the number at around 2 million from 1960 to 1977 rising to 2.64 million in 1983 (Mack and Lansley, 1985). Townsend also calculated those on the margins of poverty (100 to 139 per cent of SB scales plus housing costs) at 11.85 million. This level of 140 per cent of the SB rate is taken to allow for the fact that most claimants have income higher than basic rates, this resulting from special needs allowances and earned income (see Abel-Smith and Townsend, 1965). Some 15 million people are in or on the margins of poverty by the state's standard - a number remaining constant as the 1981 figures indicate (Mack & Lansley, 1985). Townsend's other measures, a relative income standard which sets household income against the mean household income of the type concerned and his deprivation standard, show respectively 21.1 million in or on the margins of poverty and 12.46 million in poverty. Whatever measure is used, between 23 and 39 per cent of the population is in or on the margins of poverty. Mack and Lansley concur with this finding in their study, suggesting that 30 to 40 per cent of British society are vulnerable to deprivation. They do, however, try and make adjustments for spending patterns, smoking, low expectations and the intensity of deprivation. They conclude that while 12.1 million are in or on the margins of poverty (22.2 per cent), 7.5 million are in poverty, including 2.5 million children (13.8 per cent) and 2.6 million (4.8 per cent) are in intense poverty. Those more likely to be poor are the unemployed, the low paid, the sick, the disabled, the elderly and single parents. There is of course likely to be a coincidence of characteristics. Furthermore, poverty is not uniformly distributed over space. The geographical distribution of poverty depends greatly on the scale of analysis. On a regional scale, Townsend found that in 1968-9 its highest incidence was in Northern Ireland, followed by the North-West, Wales, the South-West and Scotland, and lowest in Greater London. In 1983, Mack and Lansley found a sharp north-south divide, with over two-thirds of those in poverty living in Scotland, Northern England and the Midlands, while under half of the comfortably off lived in these areas. Regionally, poverty marches south but, within prosperous regions, there are areas of intense poverty and deprivation, eg Tower Hamlets and Hackney in Greater London, and areas with high levels of well-being in deprived parts. More will be said concerning the impact of scale later. But we conclude by stating that poverty means a lack of resources to participate fully in the style of living sanctioned and approved by society in general in a context of little or no choice over how life is lived. In this regard, poverty is not only defined by conditions of deprivation but by feelings too. Poverty is always relative, implying a sense of deprivation. To sense deprivation is to feel not part of society. As we have seen, who determines what is necessary to be deemed a fully integrated member of society is the subject of debate which finds echoes in quality of life research and policy responses.


Deprivation and Quality of Life
Even if we accept the relativistic approach to poverty and deprivation, we are still left with the fraught problem of what constitutes deprivation. Should it be defined by government fiat (SB scales), expert opinion or popular consensus or community survey? Consideration of government responses will be left until the policy section. The remaining definitional problem is encapsulated in social indicators research, particularly in the issue of whether objective and/or subjective dimensions of deprivation or well-being are to be measures. Indeed, if we define deprivation as a lack of resources (relative to others or not), we are seeing the

Poverty, Deprivation and Social Planning

phenomenon primarily in objective terms. By
pointing to the resources that people have or
lack, we are describing the conditions in which
they live and work. What they think of, say,
their housing, health care or the safety of their
neighbourhood, is ignored. To concentrate on the
objective description of conditions usually
through using secondary, census-based data means
highlighting only one of the three dimensions of
well-being identified by Allardt (1973, 1975) and
also referred to by Smith (1977). The one
emphasised is having, involving that needed to
survive. It largely corresponds to standard of
living. There are further dimensions, namely
loving, ie conditions of belonging, solidarity and
affection often found in interpersonal relations,
and being, ie whether an individual feels
alienated or able to find a purpose in life. To
assess these dimensions requires a subjective
evaluation by the individual concerned, although
it must not be suggested that loving and being are
somehow independent of having. They are not, but
their relationships are variable.

There has though, been a concentration in
social indicators research on having, on objective
and descriptive analyses of well-being and
deprivation. This is perhaps understandable. Not
only are data readily available on a range
ofliving conditions from national censuses and
other sources, but there was also a clear policy
link in the development of social indicators
research. Social indicators may be seen as
numerical measures of social conditions. They are
attempts to measure aspects of quality of life of
an identified group of people or territories. They
convey the present state of affairs with respect
to the incidence of a particular condition or
problem. These measures have been used since the
1930s in the United States to discover the role of
social factors on public policy, although such
social accounting becomes of greater significance
in the 1960s as an element in the debates about
the 'Great Society' (see Gross, 1966; Smith,
1973). As such, social indicators were a means of
judging whether conditions had improved or whether
people were better off. The need for objective
measures to evaluate social changes over time and
space is, therefore, self-evident. The changing
political and economic climate in the United States
and other capitalist societies since the late

Poverty, Deprivation and Social Planning

1960s-early 1970s has meant that the relation between social indicator research and policy has been largely severed. Inequalities and differential levels of living and deprivation continue to be monitored because they (and the data) are there.

This is not to belittle such monitoring, although it must be noted that it is fraught with technical and substantive problems. What variables and indicators are to be employed and what is the basis of their selection? Smith (1973, 1977) and Knox (1975) provide full discussions on how different aspects of well-being may be measured and the type of compromises that are necessary. See, for example, Smith's (1973) detailed exposition of how to represent his seven general criteria of well-being, namely income, wealth and employment; the living environment; health; education; social order (or disorganisation); social belonging (alienation and participation); and recreation and leisure. Different variables can of course result in different pictures of well-being and deprivation emerging and Pacione (1982a) notes how the two studies of US states by Liu (1973) and Wilson (1969) indicate rank order differences of up to 32 places for education (New Jersey) and 26 places for health and welfare (New Hampshire). There has in fact been little consideration in the geographical literature as to what type of indicators particular variables represent. Thus, for example, Carlisle (1972) identifies four main types of indicator, namely informative, the purpose of which is to describe parts of the social system and monitor and describe changes taking place in those parts; predictive, which are informative but are often an integral part of a theoretical construction or model of the social system; problem-orientated, which are designed to point the way to potential policy solutions or required actions through particular programmes; and programme evaluation, which are usually operationalised goals or targets against which the progress or effectiveness of a particular programme can be monitored. The lack of direct policy input precludes the last two-named, while the lack of theory seems to militate against the second (see also Walmsley, 1980). It thus seems that virtually all indicators in geographical research are informative. This is not in itself terribly informative and it may be better to refer to Thunhurst (1985) who establishes

210

three types of indicator: direct, consisting of deprivations in themselves, eg severe overcrowding, single parent families, unemployment; indirect, which allow the existence of deprivation to be inferred but do not necessarily constitute deprivations in themselves, eg households without a car, large households, numbers of children and pensioners and perhaps even those of New Common-wealth and Pakistani descent; and interpretative, which are not measures of deprivation but which assist the geographical analysis of the distribution of direct and indirect measures eg the number of in-migrants during the previous year, the number of publicly rented houses and the amount of furnished and unfurnished rented accommodation. This differentiation is important for interpretation. It enables an answer to the question 'what is being measured?' to be formed. Thus not all objective measures of deprivation are direct measures. If they are not direct what do they inform on the nature and extent of deprivation? Such a question is particularly pertinent when a single indicator of deprivation is employed. (Multiple or composite indicators present other difficulties.)

Because a coexistence of deprivations is often assumed (or is it a powerlessness to resist data availability?), single indicators are seldom used. Many studies of what are in effect single indicators have taken the form of examining the phenomenon as a social problem. Large-scale housing problems are now mainly problems of the past as great efforts have been made to try and ensure decent housing for all households. There do, however, remain households that are overcrowded or that are forced to share their accommodation. In the UK these households are found particularly in inner city areas, especially those of London and Glasgow (see Holterman, 1975; Danson, 1984; Conway, 1984). In the case of London, Conway (1984) estimates that there are over 100,000 households forced to share their dwelling. In addition, over 130,000 households are living at densities of over one person per room and over 180,000 households may be at least one bedroom short of their needs. This is a large problem compounded by the poor condition of much of London's housing with nearly one in four dwellings being unfit, lacking some basic amenity or in a serious state of disrepair (GLC, 1981). But there are about 2.7 million dwellings and households in

211

Poverty, Deprivation and Social Planning

London (although there is a shortage of around
120,000 dwellings). Thus, under 4 percent of
households in London now share their dwellings.
(see also Cullingworth, 1972; Robson, 1979:
Donnison and Ungerson, 1982). The problem of old
housing stock often lacking in such basic
amenities as inside toilet, bath or shower and
central heating is not however, confined to
Britain. In many European cities, the majority of
dwellings date from before the Second World War,
while the percentage of dwellings with basic
amenities varies from 27 in Utrecht to 97 in Arhus
(Knox, 1984). While these phenomena may be
regarded as direct indicators of deprivation,
housing tenure is an interpretative one. Those
renting their accommodation are often considered
to be more likely to be deprived than
owner-occupiers. While the raison d'être of
public housing in particular is unclear (see
Cullingworth, 1972), it has political and moral
implications. The political may be most readily
seen in Britain in the period immediately after
the First World War when a housing shortage and
the returning forces conspired to produce a
feeling of political necessity to organise and
control housing supply. The moral may be
exemplified in the attempts to provide
accommodation for poor or vulnerable individuals
and families. In fact, in the UK with its longish
history of public housing, tenure would until
recently have been a poor indicator of
deprivation. Public housing was not by and large
a low-income ghetto, although there were the 'dump
estates' to which housing officers in their
subjective grading of tenants direct the
'undesirable', eg those with rent arrears,
'problem' families and so on (see Gray, 1976;
English, 1979'). Such grading and dumping can also
be found in, for example, France and the
Netherlands (see Scobie, 1975) and lead to the
localisation of certain types of deprivation (eg
single parent families, the chronically sick and
the long-term unemployed who possess low
rent-paying ability) and their stigmatisation
(Damer, 1974; Taylor, 1979). The recent event,
however, that has resulted in tenure becoming a
better interpretative indicator is the Housing Act
of 1980 which enshrined 'the right to buy'. The
result of this and subsequent legislation and
directives has been the sale of many of the most
sellable properties, ie those constructed as
houses in the post-1945 periods, particularly in

212

suburban locations. Those remaining as tenants
are the poor and those in flatted accommodation.
Public housing tenure now indicates those most
likely to suffer from stress and from a series of
medical and psychological problems (see Eyles &
Donovan, 1986.). Public housing in the UK may
indeed become like that in the US where it is
restricted to very limited groups of people. Not
only are its locations limited by the zoning
powers of middle class communities but strict
means testing also ensures that only the poorest
are found therein. Public housing in the US
reinforces economic and racial segregation.
Housing is primarily allocated on the basis of
ability to pay, as it is in Australia where only
about 5 per cent of households are in public
housing (Neutze, 1981). This notion means that
the idea of housing classes (Rex and Moore, 1967),
despite its difficulties (Pahl, 1975; Saunders,
1979), remains a pertinent way of summarising
housing deprivations. Further, it takes us from
description to explanation (see below).

A further direct indicator of deprivation is
unemployment. Many studies have shown how the
changing nature and structure of employment has
resulted in different employment and unemployment
patterns. Jobs are increasingly concentrated in
the service sector where they can often be
performed on a part-time basis by women. There
has been an increase in employment opportunities
in small towns often at the expense of older,
manufacturing areas. Industrial restructuring has
hit the inner cities particularly severely and job
losses are not simply transferred from one
location to another but losses to the economy
itself. Unemployment changes have been analysed
for a variety of cities in Britain and Australia
(see for example, Danson et al., 1980; Metcalf,
1975; Walker, 1981; Burnley and Walker, 1982;
Forster, 1983; Vipond, 1981). The effects of
industrial restructuring have been examined for
the British economy (Jordan, 1982; Massey and
Meegan, 1983) and for the inner city (Massey and
Meegan, 1978; Stilwell, 1979; 1980), although the
more positive side - unequal growth - is explored
by Fothergill and Gudgin (1982). It is in the
inner city that we may perhaps see the closest
link between unemployment and deprivation. Parts
of the inner city with their inadequate infrastruc-
tures, differential patterns of outmigration and
labour forces with long histories of unionisation

Poverty, Deprivation and Social Planning

represent poor prospects for private investors.
Unemployment is, therefore, a major reason why
much ameliorative policy has been directed at the
inner city (see below). Unemployment itself,
because it is so closely related to the level of
resources available to an individual, household or
population in an area, is often regarded as a good
surrogate measure for deprivation (see Powell,
1986). Figure 7.2, based on 1981 Census data,
shows that those towns with better-than-average
male unemployment rates (eg Stoke, Plymouth) have
better-than-average social and environmental
conditions, while those with worse-than-average
rates have far more deprived conditions (eg
Liverpool, Manchester, Sunderland). Redfern
(1982) can only conclude that the unemployment
rate is a good measure of deprivation in general
after examining in detail multiple indicators of
well-being. And while it is possible to document
other single indicators such as the relationship
between race and deprivation (see, for example,
Runnymede Trust 1980; de Vise, 1976; Castles,
1984), so many of the indicators demonstrate the
interrelated nature of facets of deprivation that
it is perhaps best to turn to the use of multiple
indicators.

The studies of well-being, levels of living
and deprivation employing many indicators often
gleaned from national censuses and multiple
analyses are legion. A guiding principle in such
studies appears to be data availability because
they have been carried out at a variety of spatial
scales. Their links with theory and policy have,
for the most part, been minimal. So, for example,
many investigations have looked at the major
administrative entities in a country. Smith's
(1973, 1977) work on American states using a
variety of social, economic and environmental
variables has recently been updated by Cutter
(1985). Knox (1975), employing similar measures
to Smith, derived levels of living for English
counties. A similar exercise was carried out for
the Australian states by Walmsley (1980). Figure
7.3 shows the factor scores for social affluence
and social pathology for the prefectures of Japan,
demonstrating that the former is highest in the
industrial areas such as South Kanto, Tokai, Kinki
and Sanyo, while high levels of pathology are
mainly in the peripheral districts. As Shen and
Young (1984) note, these findings are similar in
kind to those derived for the US. A similar

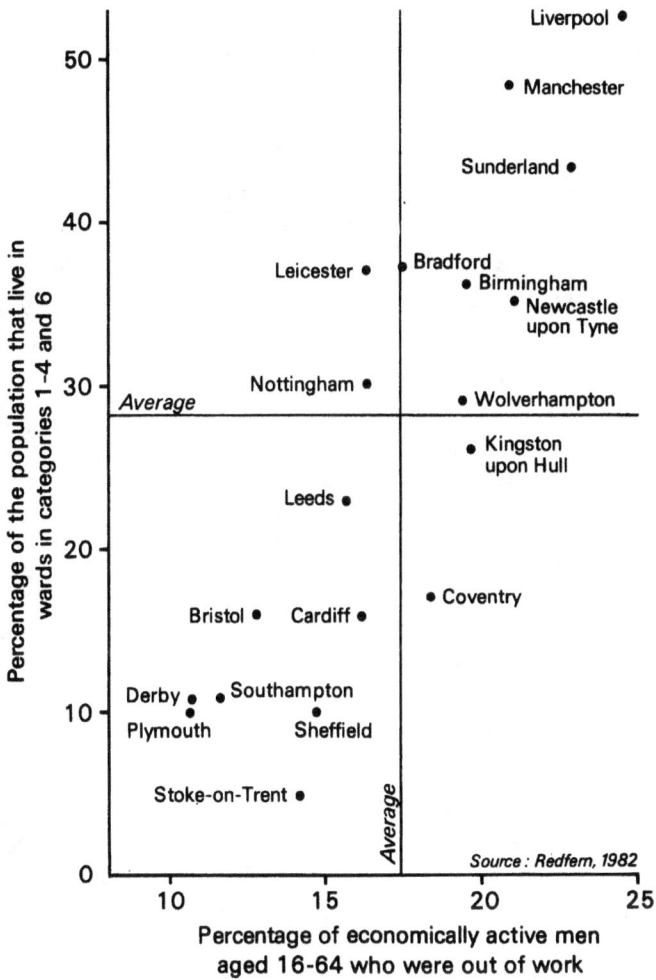

Figure 7.2  Relationship Between Unemployment and the Proportion of the Population that live in Wards that Suffer Poor Conditions

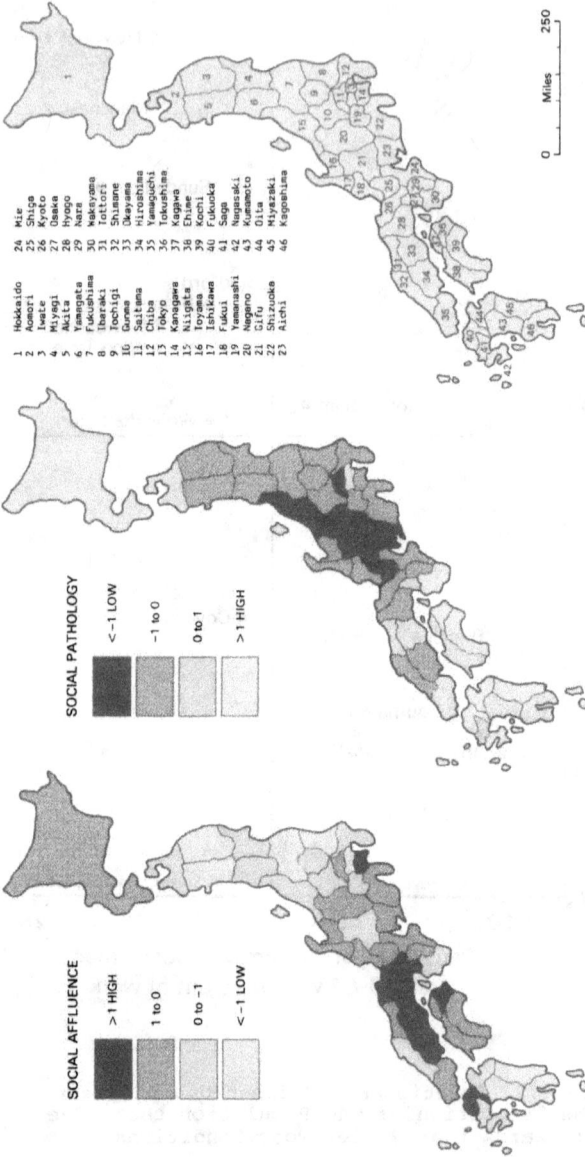

Source: Adapted from Shen & Young, 1984

SOCIAL PATHOLOGY

< -1 LOW
-1 to 0
0 to 1
> 1 HIGH

SOCIAL AFFLUENCE

> 1 HIGH
1 to 0
0 to -1
< -1 LOW

| 1 | Hokkaido | 24 | Mie |
| 2 | Aomori | 25 | Shiga |
| 3 | Iwate | 26 | Kyoto |
| 4 | Miyagi | 27 | Osaka |
| 5 | Akita | 28 | Hyogo |
| 6 | Yamagata | 29 | Nara |
| 7 | Fukushima | 30 | Wakayama |
| 8 | Ibaraki | 31 | Tottori |
| 9 | Tochigi | 32 | Shimane |
| 10 | Gunma | 33 | Okayama |
| 11 | Saitama | 34 | Hiroshima |
| 12 | Chiba | 35 | Yamaguchi |
| 13 | Tokyo | 36 | Tokushima |
| 14 | Kanagawa | 37 | Kagawa |
| 15 | Niigata | 38 | Ehime |
| 16 | Toyama | 39 | Kochi |
| 17 | Ishikawa | 40 | Fukuoka |
| 18 | Fukui | 41 | Saga |
| 19 | Yamanashi | 42 | Nagasaki |
| 20 | Nagano | 43 | Kumamoto |
| 21 | Gifu | 44 | Oita |
| 22 | Shizuoka | 45 | Miyazaki |
| 23 | Aichi | 46 | Kagoshima |

0    Miles    250

Figure 7.3  Deprivation at the Regional Scale:
Social Affluence and Pathology in Japan

Poverty, Deprivation and Social Planning

conclusion may be drawn from a study of 'family welfare' in Italian regions (Giampaglia and Young, 1980). High levels of affluences tend to be found in the northern regions of Piemonte, Lombardia and Liguria (containing Turin, Milan and Genoa) and the lowest not in the South but in Molise, Abruzzi and Marche (east central). There is no social pathology factor and indeed many of the variables loading highly on the affluence factor also load highly on the second one, demonstrating the difficulties of aggregation of variables and interpretation. Interestingly, though, the third factor ('basic consumption') shows a pattern of household expenditure and basic amenities on which Puglia and Basilicata score lowest and Lazio (including Rome) and Toscana highest. This leads the authors to speculate as to the role of the state in ensuring high levels of living close to the centre of administration, a point which may also be debated in the British context (see CSO, 1985).

While interesting in itself, this level of analysis masks as much as it reveals, involving as it must the combination of urban and rural populations, inner and outer cities and so on. Much social indicator research has, therefore, been carried out at the city scale. This has involved either a comparison of cities or more commonly intra-urban patterns within one metropolitan area. As examples of the former, it is possible to cite Liu's (1976) monumental study of metropolitan US, Flax's (1972) of 18 American cities, Bentham's (1985) of British inner cities and Redfern's (1982) of 19 large British towns. For the latter, investigations of Atlanta (Bederman, 1974), Tampa (Smith, 1973), Sydney (Vinson and Homel, 1976), Cardiff (Herbert and Thomas, 1982), and Belfast (Boal et al., 1978) may be noted. It must not, however, be assumed that the deprivations found in one city are similar in type or pattern to those found in another. Edwards (1975) has pointed to the shifting nature and character of deprivation which makes the attempts to operationalise social indicators extremely difficult. Indeed many of the intra-urban analyses are reliant on data availability, forming a deprivation-oriented sub-set of general studies of residential differentiation and sub-area classification. Further, what Knox (1984) calls different syndromes of disadvantage can be found to be associated with different types of neighbourhood,

Poverty, Deprivation and Social Planning

as evidenced by studies of Scottish cities,
Stockholm, London and Paris (see Knox & MacLaran,
1978; Peters, 1979; Bentham & Moseley, 1980; Madge
& Willmott, 1981). But nearly all neighbourhoods
manifest some form and level of deprivation. And
herein of course lies one of the major
difficulties of the geographical approach to
social problems. Geographical analysis pertains to
area while deprivation is a characteristic of
individuals or households. There is the danger of
the ecological fallacy, of imputing individual
characteristics from areal data so that all
individuals in a deprived neighbourhood are
labelled 'deprived'. While few, if any,
geographers remain unaware of such a possibility,
the fallacy is still a basis for scapegoating and
stigmatising particular districts and individuals.

A further problem arises from a consideration
of individuals in areas. It is possible that an
area suffers from multiple disadvantages. This
need not be true of the individuals within the
area. If an area's population is 50 per cent
unemployed and 50 per cent black, the range of
possible combination runs from a complete
coincidence of the deprivations to complete
separation. Indeed Shaw (1979) remarks that this
issue is particularly noticeable in rural areas.
Further, deprivation studies are also problematic
because of the urban bias of their indicators.
These indicators reflect urban problems, notably
the condition and age of the physical fabric and
the changing economic base. Rural areas certainly
suffer from economic changes, particularly the
falling demand for agricultural labour. They also
have to deal with the changing locational requirements of service activity, associated with growing
personal mobility (see Moseley, 1979, Nutley,
1980; Phillips & Williams, 1984). Shaw (1979)
thus identifies three different but related types
of deprivation: household (income, housing),
opportunity (employment, education, health and
recreation) and mobility (transport costs and
accessibility).

In studies of both urban and rural areas, the
coincidence of deprivations remains unknown. So
too does the relative importance of the difference
dimensions of deprivation. If analysis relies
entirely on secondary data sources, the only way
to weight these dimensions is through statistical
manipulation, with both Z scores (Smith, 1973; Liu,
1976) and factor analysis (Wilson, 1969; Gordon &

Whittaker, 1972) being used. It is possible to ask experts how they would rank the dimensions. Figure 7.4 shows the areas of poverty to emerge in Sheffield after social, welfare, environmental and police personnel were asked for their opinions. The figure also demonstrates the extremely complex picture of deprivation that emerges at the local level: the smaller the spatial scale, the less clear will be the emergent pattern. In other words, if analysis is based on individual lives, it will reflect the complexity of those lives. And an aid to understanding that complexity and to weighting dimensions of deprivations may be found in community survey and the employment of subjective social indicators.

Although these indicators are costly and difficult to obtain (see Dalkey and Rourke, 1973) they seek to discover directly the quality of life experienced by people rather than assume a link between objective conditions and well-being or deprivation (Schneider, 1975). Indeed, the problem of this link is demonstrated by a study of a slum in Oldham, which found people to be happy in and satisfied with their objectively defined deprived conditions (Ministry of Housing & Local Government, 1966). Subjective indicators measure satisfactions, reflecting feeling, reactions to life and perceptions of events. Various national surveys in the US, Britain, Australia and Western Europe (see, for example, Andrews & Withey, 1976; Abrams, 1973; Hall, 1976; Headey, 1981; Andrews and Inglehart, 1979) have identified various life concerns or life domains (eg job, home life, standard of living, neighbourhood) about which people can express their feelings. The individual life domains can be broken down into their constituent parts. Neighbourhood, for example, can include consideration of home, clean air, refuse collection, street safety, open space and neighbours (see Pacione 1982b; Eyles, 1985). Such indicators see well-being and deprivation in relative terms. They are not without problems, with perceptions being strongly influenced by social background (see Andrews, 1974; Dale, 1980). Further, the relationships between objective and subjective indicators have been variable. This is not surprising given that few studies have utilised both (for exceptions see Stipak, 1977; MacLaren, 1981) and there is disagreement on what exactly constitutes a subjective dimension. Kuz (1978) in a study of

# Poverty, Deprivation and Social Planning

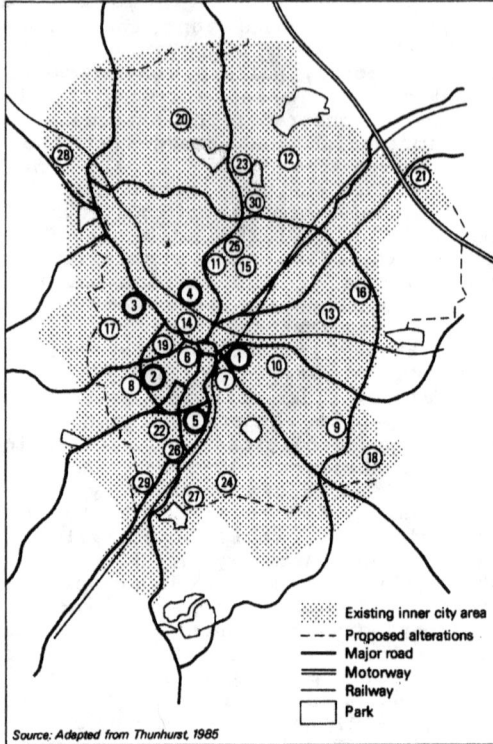

Source: Adapted from Thunhurst, 1985

AREAS OF ACUTE POVERTY

1   Hyde Park
2   Broomhall Flats
3   Kelvin
4   Pye Bank
5   Cromford Street

AREAS OF POVERTY

6   Crofts Buildings/Townhead/
    Hawley Street
7   Park Hill
8   Havelock
9   Manor
10  Wybourn
11  Nottingham Street
12  Flower Estate

13  Staniforth Road
14  Moorfields Flats/
    Gibralter Buildings
15  Ellesmere
16  Greenland-Darnall
17  Crookesmoor
18  Woodthorpe
19  Edward Street
20  Parsons Cross
21  Tinsley
22  Sharrow Street
23  Brushes Estate
24  Hallyburton Road
25  Abbeyfield
26  Wolseley Road
27  Albert Road
28  Winn Gardens
29  Machon Bank
30  Firvale

Figure 7.4    Deprivation at the Regional Scale:
              Poverty in Sheffield

220

Poverty, Deprivation and Social Planning

Manitoba used such measures as 'belong to an organisation', and 'attend meetings' as subjective indicators. Kuz in fact found no correlation between the two measures. Schneider (1975) in his study of US cities found no consistent relationship while a positive and statistically significant correlation was found by Knox & MacLaren (1978) for Dundee. In a Norwegian study, Dale (1980) noted that indicator correspondence varied according to the spatial scale employed and went on to suggest that lack of correspondence may be also caused by the failure to define objective and subjective indicators clearly and to take account of the relationship between indicator and life-domain. Indeed Pacione (1982a) is surely correct when he suggests that the heterogeneity within the sets of indicators is such that a debate on the superiority of one over the other is quite sterile. They may, however, measure different aspects of well-being and deprivation. To ignore subjective indicators because they are costly, difficult to apply and open to several interpretations would mean failing to examine deprivation in the context that really matters: the life of the deprived person.

This context has also been addressed by in-depth interviews with different groups of people employing ethnographic methods or qualitative methodologies (see Jackson, 1985; Eyles, 1986). While we must assume that people talk honestly about their lives, the accounts derived from these sources enhance our understanding of what deprivation is and what it means. While full accounts of people who live in poverty or on the dole may be found in Townsend (1979) and Seabrook (1982), these quotations illuminate the conditions, angry resignation, demoralisation and making do of the poor and deprived:

> It's very bad with damp, the rain coming in through the window, the mice, the rats, the bugs, beasts, the lot. And it's tiny in here. I can't get room to move about, I can't put my child on the floor to play ... And when it rains in here, the floor gets soaking wet ... It's just ridiculous to have ended up in a rubbish dump, that's what I call it, a rubbish dump (Pamela, quoted in Mack & Lansley, 1985, 137).

221

> Christ what a summer eh? Really gets me
> down. Been off bleeding work six fucking
> months now, it does it really gets me down.
> Sit on my arse and take the sick, that's all
> I'm good for. Forty-fucking-two and that's my
> lot. Gets you down you know ... Bear with a
> sore head, that's what the wife says I am ...
> Sheer fucking frustration in every sense of
> the expression - you know what I mean? (Brian,
> quoted in Parker, 1985, 334).

> We're getting low now. We've got food for
> today, but there's none for tomorrow. Last
> week we ran out of money for the electric
> meter. We had to hunt round the house for
> pennies to make up 50p. I make sure the kids
> eat all right, they get fish fingers and
> beefburgers ... I just have one meal a day ...
> I've had to get the little one out of nappies
> - I couldn't afford them any more ... We're
> going steadily downhill. This week I started
> thinking of things I could sell to be a bit of
> money. (Terry, quoted in Harrison, 1985, 153)

While they could be replicated many times, these
quotations bring home the despair of deprivation.
It affects individuals and prevents them living
full lives. Deprivation is experienced: it is
not merely a statistical phenomenon, although this
point seems lost in some of the theories developed
to help formulate policy to deal with poverty and
deprivation.

## From Deprivation to Policy

Policy is not developed in a societal or
theoretical vacuum. Descriptive studies continue
to demonstrate the existence of deprivation. So
what? If anything is to be done about poverty and
deprivation, the views and explanations of policy-
makers and other key groups are central. We must
remember that one option is to do nothing. Another
is to increase the disparities in levels of living
between groups and territories: such may occur
under authoritarian regimes as, for example, in
military-run Argentina (see Escudero, 1981). There
are then several policy options which are
predicated on different views and explanations of
deprivation. This relationship is most clearly
expressed in Townsend (1979). He identifies
alternative policies according to three distinct

principles, namely conditional welfare for the few; minimum rights for the many; and distributional justice for all.

Conditional welfare for the few assumes that not only is poverty necessary but that it is the result of moral inadequacy on the part of the deprived. Poverty is needed to motivate individuals to work and inequalities themselves cannot and should not be removed because they are necessary to allow the economic system to flourish. They motivate individuals to try and achieve the most demanding jobs which carry with them the highest material rewards (see Davis and Moore, 1945). This approach to poverty allows its societally advantageous side to be shown. Poverty ensures, for example, that dirty, dangerous and menial jobs get done, that substandard housing is rented and that shoddy and damaged goods get bought (see Gans, 1972). The existence of the poor also legitimises dominant values by providing often stereotyped examples of the lazy, spendthrift and dishonest. Indeed, this view of poverty regards the issue as much one of morality as of material conditions. People are poor or deprived because they lack the will to improve their lot. They may also be improvident or feckless. Indeed, the poor may be divided into the deserving and undeserving poor, the former poor because of low wages or sickness, the latter because of unemployment, 'irrational' spending habits and so on. The distinction was forcibly made by Rowntree (1901) with his distinction between primary and secondary poverty, while its effects, particularly the marginalisation of families, groups and districts, are graphically portrayed in Stedman Jones' (1971) study of the East End of London. In general terms, this view of poverty and welfare is allied with one that sees virtue in a market society in which virtue itself is carefully linked with work. Not only is public expenditure on social policy (excluding mandatory unemployment benefits) kept low, but public policy is also seen as interfering with the market. In theory, the minimalist state is advocated (see Jordan, 1976; Sawer, 1983) although in practice there tends to be a transfer of interest and expenditure away from social policy to social control as evidenced in H.M. Treasury (1985) and discussed by Eyles and Woods (1986).

No one theory is of course the complete base for policy and a policy itself may given credence to several distinct, if related, explanations. Allied to the view that poverty is caused by moral inadequacy are the notions of the culture of poverty and the cycle of deprivation. Their alliance may be seen in that all these explanations derive from a liberal interpretation of social policy (see Room, 1979). Room in fact distinguishes between market and political liberals, the former suggesting that policy must not damage market principles and that although a minimum standard of welfare should be provided on the grounds of compassion and political stability, it should be based on merit, work performance and productivity (see Titmuss, 1974). The latter emphasise the need to reintegrate the work force into the mainstream of society. Social policy is necessary to tame the violence of the market. Both groups of liberals, however, point to a minimum provision. Note, therefore, how even market advocates may encompass minimum rights for the many, although in the 1980s on the grounds of cost containment, there has been a move towards conditional welfare for the few in both the UK and the US and the encouragement of individual enterprise, either through the provision of vocational training as in Headstart or the Youth Training Scheme or through fostering conditions for growth as in enterprise zones (see below).

The culture of poverty explanation was developed by Lewis (1956; 1968) in his work based originally on fieldwork in Mexico. The poor form a distinctive culture within society. This culture is 'both an adaptation and a reaction of the poor to their marginal position in a class-stratified, highly individuated, capitalistic society. It represents an effort to cope with feelings of hopelessness and despair which develop from the realisation of the improbability of achieving success in terms of the values and goals of the larger society' (Lewis, 1968, p. 54). The poor thus possess certain 'trait characteristics' - present centredness, fatalism, resignation, demoralisation, acquiescence. It is 'a design for living' passed on from generation to generation. It flourishes in low-wage, profit-oriented economies with inadequate government assistance to the poor. But it is suggested, particularly by those advocating the related cycle of deprivation view, that this assistance is best concentrated on helping people to help themselves, to break the inherited spiral

Poverty, Deprivation and Social Planning

of decline. The cycle of deprivation view in fact
notes that the problems of one generation are
passed to another. Poor housing and low incomes
undermine the chances of self improvement from
generation to generation. With inadequate
parental upbringing and home background, children
of deprived families are doomed to an uphill
struggle. But as poverty is seen as primarily a
residual and family problem, it may be tackled by
casework by social services and improved
educational opportunities. Despite much evidence
that most poverty is not intergenerational (see
Rutter & Madge, 1976), policy concentrates
resources on treating individual conditions and
providing some skills training, advice centres and
so on. We may indeed note a close relationship
between cycle of deprivation explanations and area
based policies to assist particularly the inner
city (see below and Eyles, 1979; Lawless, 1981;
Berthoud and Brown, 1981).

The second of Townsend's (1979) principles -
minimum rights for the many - was the basis of
social and welfare policy in Britain for the 30
years or so immediately after the Second World
War. It was based on a 'social democratic
interpretation' of policy (Room, 1979) in which
need was a key to entitlement. Also important was
the notion of citizen rights (see Marshall, 1965)
by which individual members of a society possess,
as of right, entitlement to a minimum standard of
living. Based on the reforming legislation of the
late 1940s, the aim of policy was to cover those
who became unemployed, who could not or were not
expected to work (eg the sick and the elderly and
children) and who could not afford the 'basic'
necessities of life because of low wages, large
families and so on. Poverty was thus seen as a
significant but manageable problem. It was caused
by individual misfortune due to certain individual
attributes. These did not point to moral failings
but to such characteristics as age, employment
status, family size, level of income, sickness and
disability. Poverty was explained in terms of
these minority group characteristics. Policy to
cover concomitant deprivations clashed, however,
with the principle of universal provision, the
outcome of basing entitlement on citizen rights.
Social and deprivation policy became, therefore,
in the British context, a mixture of universal
provision, eg general practitioner and hospital
care under the National Health Service and special,

225

means-tested payments to particular population groups (eg one parent families, low income households). Indeed, the policy response to poverty as misfortune is of necessity ad hoc as new misfortunes and their lobbies receive attention. Such policy is dependent upon the identification of needs and the creation of bureaucratic arrangements to meet those needs. Townsend (1979) documents the growth of the groups covered by anti-deprivation legislation in the early 1970s. The ad hocery of such policy resulted in criticisms in the UK, the US and elsewhere (see King, 1975; Friedmann, 1977; Mishra, 1984) of public policy which was seen as crowding out enterprise and individual freedom. 'Government
overload' and its apparent high levels of taxation and social wages were salient features in the conservative electoral victories in several advanced industrial nations. Policy moved in direction from minimum and towards conditional welfare.

As Townsend (1979) readily admits, his third principle - distributional justice for all - has not yet been clearly articulated in Britain. The poor are seen as those denied their potential share of societal resources or access to activities generally available within society. It is perhaps a principle to strive towards and is likely brought about by nationally based policies. As Berthoud and Brown (1981) point out, these policies may take three forms: those involving institutional reorganisation to achieve more equitable access, as tried in the 1960s and 70s in the health and social services; interventions in the market, as with housing policies and wage councils to ensure, respectively, a supply of housing for those unable to compete for credit and a minimum income level in poorly unionised or structured industries; and the redistribution of incomes and resources through the taxation and social security systems. Of course, none of these nationally-oriented policies need favour the deprived and in the 1980s interventions in the market have mainly benefited owner-occupiers through mortgage tax relief, and resource redistribution has mainly been in favour of the wealthier sections of society.

Further, while national policies must be seen as the primary means of tackling poverty and deprivation, especially if these are seen as structural phenomena, deriving from the nature of the social

system itself, policies which favour certain
population groups and areas must not be entirely
discounted. Poverty may indeed be concentrated,
not necessarily in the entire belt known as the
inner city but in particular parts of it.
Inaccessibility may create mobility deprivation
which demands spatial policies. In fact, the
resource allocation formulae for obtaining a more
equitable distribution of hospital and community
health resources have a built-in 'sparsity factor'
to favour Scotland, Wales and Northern Ireland.
Similarly, the rural health regions of New South
Wales are also favoured (Eyles, 1985b). But
whatever their type all state responses to
deprivation are underpinned by the notion of
citizen rights, related to how those in power view
society and the functions of the state. From 1945
to the mid-1970s, policy was formulated mainly in
terms of the moral obligations of the state to
citizens: now, a minimum standard, safety net
approach is applied. Whether a social democratic
interpretation with the state responding to the
perceived and articulated needs and demand of its
citizens (see Lockwood, 1974; Reisman, 1977) or a
neo-marxian one with the state needing to ensure
the loyalty of its citizens for the social
stability necessary to ensure the conditions for
capital accumulation (see Habermas, 1976; Gough,
1979; Offe, 1984) is adopted is a moot point.
Anti-deprivation policies vary and the basis of
that variation may be in part seen in explanations
of poverty. These explanations (as well as
resources) also shape the thrust of policy, ie the
mix of population group, area and national
strategies. All are employed, although for the
remainder of this paper emphasis will be placed on
areal policies, especially those which may be seen
as forms of social planning.

Social Planning as Policy

In some ways, it is possible to regard all forms
of spatial planning as social. Regional policy
and state economic strategy (or their lack) affect
individual lives and the social structures of
places. But social planning need not have a
spatial dimension. In the US, it often refers to
the social welfare role of public bodies,
particularly social service departments. Walker
(1984, p. 3) sees it as 'the process of development, implementing and evaluating social policies..

227

those that determine the distribution of resources, status and power between different groups'. In sum, it concerns the distribution of welfare and determination of social priorities and hence the levels of well-being enjoyed by different groups. There is much to recommend this approach; it is in line with a great deal of the material already discussed in this paper. It is a view shared, with different emphasis, by many writing from a physical planning perspective. Cullingworth (1972) sees social planning as the process of integrating physical, financial, manpower and management programmes with social ends in mind, while Cherry (1970) suggests that it deals with social implications of the statutory planning process. Similarly but with more of an advocacy flavour, Eversley (1973) regards it as being based on the aims of public agencies, the activities of which are geared to the pursuit of improvements in living standards. Social planning, therefore, concerns the ways in which the welfare of different groups and the distribution of goods and bads are determined. While social planning is, by and large, interventionist, a possible strategy is to leave the determination and distribution of welfare to the market. This may, though, be regarded as a planning strategy for it is in an attempt to ensure that the future takes a specific shape through the employment of particular means. Such stategies will be examined but, in the ensuing discussion, we shall limit social planning to socio-spatial planning, seeing this as a lacuna in recent attempts to develop social strategies. It is then planning for people (and their welfare) in space, unlike physical planning which plans space in which people happen to be (see Jones and Eyles, 1977).

While, as Knox (1984) does for West European cities, it is possible to devise a temporal classification of post-war planning, namely re-construction, 'heroic' planning and the period of reappraisal and rehabilitation, a two-fold division will suffice. Social remedial and social development planning are seen as separate but related policies. Rather than being pursued independently, one may be more dominant than the other at a particular time or phase or in a particular place or society. Social remedial planning is primarily reactive planning. It is an attempt to react to problems and remedy defects. In Offe's (1976) terms, it is a crisis management strategy which may on occasion through forward action also be a crisis avoidance technique. On the other hand, social development planning is creative planning. It is an attempt to create or engineer the future or social arrangements through design or service provision strategies. It is interesting to note that most planners see their role in social development terms. Two of the three planning 'ideologies' (sic) identified by Foley (1960) are promoting a better way of life by improving the quality of the physical environment and providing a better physical design for a better community life. (The third is as umpires, reconciling competing land claims.) Most social planning is, however, of the remedial kind.

In Britain, the most obvious form of social remedial planning in the post-1945 period was the replacement of dilapidated housing stock and the refurbishment of the environment. Comprehensive redevelopment schemes were initiated to improve living conditions, although the programme moved slowly because of the massive cost of housing replacement. Large areas of cities were cleared as Paris (1977) documents for Birmingham and Mason (1977) for Manchester. But several events conspired to bring an end to comprehensive redevelopment as a national solution. Short (1982) points to the general malaise of the British economy which reduced housing expenditure during the late 1960s. There was a further financial implication in the fact that clearance was not a once-and-for-all answer. As housing continually ages, it will always need replacement and repair (see Cullingworth, 1960). The programme had also been successful so large areas needing improvement were no longer easily found. The wide scatter of housing needing improvement meant that an area approach was less helpful than in the past. Further, improvement and rehabilitation booame major aspects of housing policy not only for reasons of cost containment but also to attempt to retain established communities and social networks, to eliminate urban blight and to satisfy the demand for low-cost housing (Eyles, 1979). Indeed as Jones (1979) points out, financial stringency ensured that the destruction of the inner Melbourne suburb of Carlton did not take place. In Great Britain, the number of dwellings cleared as slums declined dramatically from 88,713 in 1972-3 to 20,919 in 1982-3 (see DoE, 1984). The decline was especially noticeable in Scotland with a sixfold decrease over the same period.

Poverty, Deprivation and Social Planning

The raison d'etre of improvement policy gradually led to its shift from concentrating on individual houses to being directed at areas of poor housing and their total environments. The Housing Act of 1969 introduced the general improvement area (GIA) to concentrate rehabilitation. Grants were available to households and landlords to improve their properties while environmental schemes such as traffic management and tree planting were initiated by local authorities. Improvement grant take-up was not, however, limited to inhabitants or properties in GIAs. In fact, in 1973 only 9 per cent of grants were for properties in GIAs despite this being the year of the greatest number for the 1970s. While improvement grants have led to an improvement in the quality of housing stock, their numbers are low in inner city areas. GIA designations failed to improve conditions in the worst areas. We should though, not expect otherwise. The policy was intended to concentrate improvement effort where it was likely to have its greatest effect. As Roberts (1976) commented, the GIA is too limited a device to tackle the national housing problem and too broad to tackle areas of housing stress. The latter were, though, one of the subjects of the 1974 Housing Act which introduced housing action areas (HAAs). These could be declared in areas suffering from multi-occupation and shared facilities, housing disrepair, dilapidated private rented accommodation and unattractive surroundings. As Short (1982) notes, some 272 HAAs were declared between 1974 and 1978. While their suggested size was 300 to 400 dwellings, the range was 14 to over 1250 (Eyles, 1979). Further, only 9 per cent of improvement grants in 1976 were concentrated in GIAs and HAAs. The rate of progress was slow as Bassett and Short (1978) demonstrate in their study of HAAs in Bristol. And this progress was further reduced by the financial crisis that led to public expenditure cuts in Britain from the mid-1970s onwards. Housing has been particularly badly affected. In England, the number of improvement grants fell from around 290,000 in 1973 level to 104,000 in 1977 (see DoE, 1984). It was not until 1983 that the 1973 level was again exceeded. The number of dwellings renovated per year in GIAs and HAAs was static from 1978-9 to 1981-2. The market increase in the year 1982-3 may not only reflect an easier financial climate but also the re-emergence in governmental consciousness

Poverty, Deprivation and Social Planning

of the inner city and its problems after the 1981 riots. Riots indeed concentrate attention. Those of 1985 have resulted in the establishment of task forces in certain inner areas to try and improve job opportunities through state and private actions.

It was, however, American riots of the 1960s as well as various reports on delinquency, education, racial tension and social service delivery that helped focus attention in the late 1960s on the inner city and its social problems. It was seen that there were social defects to remedy as well as environmental ones. Government concern was first given concrete expression by the recommendations of the Plowden report (DES, 1967) which reported a coexistence of deprivations and saw education as one of the ways to alleviate such deprivation. In other words, a cycle of deprivation explanation was adopted and a policy of positive discrimination to make schools in the most deprived areas as good as the best in the country was instigated. The policy introduced the educational priority area (EPA) with community schools, special payments for teachers, attached social workers and so on. Funding was low and thinly spread and did little to affect the crucial relationship between educational attainment and home background. Further by adopting an area approach, resources did not reach the right children or schools. In Inner London, resources for EPA schools reached 13.6 per cent of all children but only 20.2 per cent of the most disadvantaged children (Barnes, 1975).

In other schemes, low funding was also thinly spread. The urban aid programme introduced in 1968 was supposed to provide money for education, health, housing and welfare in inner city areas of special need. The projects funded were small-scale: holiday schemes, day nurseries, play groups, advice centres. The key problem was in fact seen as one of access to resources which were often provided on a poorly co-ordinated basis, a point emanating from the Seebohm report on personal social services (Home Office, 1968). The urban aid programme is the most extensive and expensive of the British anti-poverty strategies (see Batley and Edwards, 1974; Edwards and Batley, 1978 and Berthoud and Brown, 1981 for full appraisals). It has been predicated on a view of poverty as a marginal or personal phenomenon. Such a view suggests that all that is required are

## Poverty, Deprivation and Social Planning

better access to and co-ordination of services, a breaking of the cycle of deprivation, and the participation of the poor so that they may help themselves and become more self reliant and less resigned to their lot. A series of experiments were, therefore, instigated to suggest solutions without large financial outlay. One of these - the community development projects (CDP, 1977a, 1977b) - bit the hand that fed it, suggesting that poverty did not arise just from individual failings and inefficient management and provision of services. But effective management and co-ordination of services and experimentation remain cost-effective options to inner city problems. In April 1985, city action teams were launched with no extra resources but with the aim of using money more effectively by co-ordinating the activities of public bodies and private enterprise. To date a craft centre has been opened in Newcastle.

In the late 1970s, however, social planning for the inner cities became entwined with the needs for economic regeneration and job creation. A White Paper on the inner city (DoE, 1977) stated that industrial, environmental and recreational issues would be covered as well as social problems. To this end, seven partnership schemes (that is based on a close relationship between central and local governments) were established in Lambeth, London Docklands, Hackney-Islington, Newcastle-Gateshead, Manchester-Salford, Birmingham and Liverpool. The emphasis on economic revival can be seen in the expenditures on industrial estates and factory units (Nabarro, 1980). Few additional resources have in fact been made available (Laurence and Hall, 1981) and most of the finance for partnership schemes comes from the grant from central to local government, the rate support grant (RSG). A result of the 1979 Conservative victory was to transfer funds through this device from the inner cities to the country areas - to their power basis, although the indications are that from 1986 the resource transfer will again operate to the advantage of the inner city, the riots of 1985 being an apparent initiator of policy change.

Before the changes initiated by the Conservatives are considered, a rather separate economic scheme must be mentioned. Under the Scottish Development Agency (SDA) Act of 1975, the SDA was enabled to establish area projects to foster local economic development. It has several types of project (see Gulliver, 1984), including the setting up of task forces after plant closure as at Garnock Valley and Clydebank. Perhaps the most import scheme is one of comprehensive urban renewal in Glasgow - the Glasgow Eastern Area Renewal scheme (GEAR). The aim is, however, regeneration, social, economic and environmental and unlike earlier comprehensive schemes, GEAR does not involve wholesale housing clearance. Between 1976 and 1984 over £202 m of public money had been expended, with nearly 60 per cent being spend on new housing and the refurbishment of existing stock. Thirteen per cent had been spent on factory building and site preparation and 6 per cent on environmental improvements (Leclerc and Draffan, 1984, Pacione 1985). There has also been £117 m of private investment, over two-thirds of which is in housing. The 'greening' of eastern Glasgow is important and as Donnison (1985) points out, GEAR is adopting an important economically-oriented approach that also has an area focus (concentrating and coordinating resources on particular areas and groups) and a community base (involving and responding to local people). But with respect to employment, McArthur (1985) notes that much of the emerging industry would have existed anyway. He estimates that by the spring of 1982, GEAR probably initiated 400 new jobs of which one half would have gone to local people - important but a small dent in the local unemployment total of 4000.

The creation of employment is in fact the spur of social planning under the Conservatives. Employment, however, is created by wealth generation not by state aid. State policies were seen to have failed. It was now capitalism's 'turn' to provide recovery to inner city areas by stimulating an increase in the number of small business operating in such areas and thus increase available jobs (see Butler, 1981). The significance of small businesses in this process has been documented by Birch (1979) in the US where two-thirds of all new private sector jobs in the period 1969-76 had been created by firms with 20 or fewer employers. To attract such firms to the inner city was difficult and so Hall (1977) suggested a 'freeport' solution with the aim of creating the Hong Kong of the 1950s and 1960s inside the inner city. Hall recommended it as a model, an experiment, because planning controls, health and safety and welfare notions would have to

233

Poverty, Deprivation and Social Planning

be relaxed. A paler version of this proposal
emerged in practice as the enterprise zone (EZ) in
which certain planning and tax controls would
cease to apply and in which there would be tax
exemptions (see Butler, 1981; Badcock, 1984). The
concept itself has been the subject of much
debate, especially with respect to who gains and
at what cost. As Massey (1982) points out, those
to gain most are landowners and property-developers
inside the zones. Further, firms establishing
themselves in a zone benefit not from the market
but from the state interference in the development
process. Industry located outside the boundaries
of an EZ is thus disadvantaged, along with workers
within who are meant to allow wages and conditions
to reduce to a level to make London competitive
with Seoul or Port-au-Prince (see Goldsmith, 1982).

What has happened to EZs in practice? EZs do
not seem to be the best ways of stimulating
manufacturing jobs. Their property-based
incentives appear to favour the development of
retail outlets, hotels and offices (Tyme &
Partners, 1983; 1984; Anderson, 1983). It has
also been questioned whether the emphasis on small
firms can generate sufficient jobs to replace
those lost in redundancies (see Anderson, 1983;
Storey, 1983). The number created is indeed
small. Bromley and Morgan (1985) point out that
less than 500 new jobs had been created in the
Lower Swansea Valley EZ up to December 1983.
Further, new developments account for 60 per cent
of all enterprises established in the EZ between
June 1981 and December 1983, but these in turn
account for only 45 per cent of the jobs created.
These jobs are also expensive to create. Many of
the jobs created inside the EZ are relocations from
outside the zone. In a study of Belfast EZ,
O'Dowd and Rolston (1985) estimate that 55 per
cent of new zone jobs could be seen in these
terms, the vast majority being from within the
Belfast urban area. Even where new jobs have been
created, it is difficult to separate the effect of
EZ policy from other public investments. In
Belfast, Clydebank, Swansea and Corby, regional or
urban assistance has been of great importance. In
Speke, Liverpool, little such aid has been
available. This variation makes evaluation of EZ
policy difficult and as O'Dowd and Rolston (1985)
comment, it leaves ample scope for 'success
stories' to be emphasised as justifying the
policy, while failures can be explained in terms of

local conditions such as the lack of enterprise. The emphases within EZ policy - relaxed planning controls, the envouragement and use of private investment, employment creation - appear to be likely to receive wider application than at present with the suggested creation of simplified planning zones (SPZs).

As with all remedial planning policies, EZs are not peculiar to Britain. They have proved attractive in the US because of their low cost and their apparent role in creating jobs in depressed neighbourhoods, encouraging local enterprise and social improvement and expanding the economy in general. Enacted in 1983, the zones must be seen against a backdrop of falling real expenditure on urban policy (see Clarke, 1984). In fact, urban outlays declined from a peak of 12.4 per cent of all federal outlays in 1978 to 7.8 per cent in 1984 (Glickman, 1984) in the light of a policy of decentralisation and 'recapitalisation' of the political and economic systems (see Piven and Cloward, 1978; Tomaskovic-Devey and Miller, 1984). The parallels between American and British experience are perhaps now most marked because of a coincidence in ruling opinion and practice. In the past, while British policy has often been inspired by American practice (Eyles, 1979), American practice itself has been piecemeal. Goldsmith and Jacobs (1982) point out that there exists no coherent national policy in the US to deal with urban problems. They suggest that in only two periods have there been partially co-ordinated policies, namely in the 1930s when economic crisis led to housing sector collapse and foreclosures and in the 1960s when social crisis pointed to the fiscal and social demise of inner city neighbourhoods. This latter period led to the development of the Model Cities programme to allow for the rebuilding or restoring of blighted areas. As in so many policies, money was spread very thinly (Eyles, 1979). From the Model Cities idea emerged the notion of general entitlement to funds but decentralisation of decision-making for expenditure. It underpinned funds from the General Revenue Sharing Act (1972) and Community Development Block Grants (CDBGs) (1974). In these, eligibility was determined by overcrowding, poverty and blighted conditions. Most of the cities and neighbourhoods assisted were in the industrial North East and on a per capita basis two-and-a-half times more aid went to the central cities than the suburbs (Schwartz, 1981). While other forms of assistance particularly to housing must not be ignored (see Downs, 1973; Feiss, 1985), much aid, including CDBGs, failed to target problem cities. It also tended to be used to reduce local taxes rather than improve or expand services. But CDBGs did have citizen participation built in which allowed for a grass roots impact into neighbourhood planning, with Atlanta providing a pertinent example (see Silver, 1985). But the Federal neighbourhood manifesto of 1978 was seen as too little too late (Barry, 1980) and the movement was riven with divisions between those favouring self-reliance and those wanting structural change (see Goering, 1979). Further, the political and economic climate was changing. The role of the private sector becomes more obvious again. It may be seen in the partnerships between private companies and government programmes as with the People's Development Corporation in South Bronx, (Schwartz, 1981). Private developers are also used by the non-profit-making redevelopment organisations created to undertake comprehensive community development, eg the Bedford-Stuyvesant Restoration Corporation in Brooklyn, New York. The changed circumstances also saw greater emphasis placed on the management of cities, for the primary aims of urban policy were now to minimise additional expenditure, encourage the states to do more, conserve the existing rather than undertake new federal investment, provide incentives for private investment in blighted neighbourhoods and stimulate self-help and voluntary organisations. As in Britain, the result of such policy is a widening gulf between suburban populations with their mortgage subsidies and the inner city with its welfare service-dependent populations, minority groups and high rates of unemployment and social distress.

While similarities may be seen in social remedial policies, there are then bound to be differences. The similarities result from common political philosophies and explanations detailed in the previous section, while the differences arise from specific local conditions that demand particular responses and practices. These local conditions may spawn resistances to the policies of New Right as In Dundee (Elliot and McCrone, 1984) and other British cities (eg Liverpool, London, Edinburgh) and certain French municipalities (Lojkine, 1984). Von Einem (1982), for example, shows how in West Germany there are conflicts between redevelopment and rehabilitation and between urban policy and anti-recession economic policy. The latter tension means that variable sums of money are available for urban improvement dependent on the state of the German economy. In the Swedish context, Goldfield (1982) notes the importance of conservation and local, decentralised initiative in urban policy. Social and environmental considerations have been compromised in recent years because of financial exigencies. Similar exigencies affect social and housing expenditures in Australia (Jones, 1983) where general spatial planning has followed a pattern of urban renewal, rehabilitation and concerns with inequalities and job creation (Jones, 1979). In Australia, however, there is a greater emphasis on social development planning, particularly in new cities (see Scott, 1978), although Canberra seems to absorb most Australian energy and finance on this issue.

Social development planning is the attempt to create or engineer social arrangements (present or future) mainly through the physical planning process. By laying out housing and industrial estates and so on, physical planning of course directly impinges on social goals such as creating equal life chances, combating poverty and unemployment and providing adequate housing (see Simmie, 1971). In new and expanded towns in Britain, the process has gone further. Not only is good quality housing provided but so also are social and leisure facilities and welfare, advice and information services. Such communities possess a well-structured management system to co-ordinate these matters as well as act as catalysts for job creation through attracting firms to the area concerned. While this is not the place to re-tell the story of new town development (see Osborn and Whittick, 1977; Golany, 1978), it should be noted that, like remedial policies, new communities are not immune from changing economic circumstances and ruling political philosophy. In the late 1970s when the problems of the inner cities re-emerged, the policy of attracting people and jobs to the new communities was slowed down. It proved impossible to reverse as people wanted to live and work in pleasant environments. Industry also saw the benefits of establishing its factories and offices

237

in green field sites. In the early 1980s, many of
the development corporations, set up to instigate
and manage the new communities, were wound up.
Their land banks were gradually sold as was some
of their housing stock. Private enterprise became
more dominant in new community settings. Private
house-building rose from 52 to 67 per cent of the
total between 1981-3 and 1983-5 (Potter, 1985). In
the same period, all private investment has risen
from 52 to 65 per cent of the total. But as
Potter (1985) comments, the economic success of
the new towns has not been achieved by 'rolling
back' the state but by an extreme form of state
intervention - the development corporation. Indeed,
it may be proof of the significance of such
organisations in that they have been established
to guide the redevelopment of dockland areas in
London and on Merseyside. Indeed, if GEAR is an
attempt to use remedial policies for development
purposes, the London Docklands Development
Corporation (LDDC) may be seen as a means of
employing development strategies for remedial
purposes. In London, however, LDDC has cut across
long established political boundaries and
authorities. Its non-elected nature has led to
charges of secrecy and lack of democracy (GLC,
1984) which LDDC (1985) has tried to counter. The
Corporation's industrial strategy and its emphasis
on the Isle of Dogs enterprise zone in job creation
and on private housing have also been criticised.
Of the 3500 jobs created between 1981 and 1984
only some 500 can be associated with LDDC activity
(GLC, 1984). Few benefit local people (see JDAG,
1984). In housing, private schemes obtain
precedence almost by default as the reduction in
the housing investment programmes lead to
reduction in expenditure on new housing and
repairs. The search for private enterprise
schemes can also be seen in LDDC's pursuit of the
financial futures market operation for a site at
Canary Wharf. But the importance of the private
sector in social development planning is not
restricted to the Docklands. Private new towns
and estates are being planned, despite local
opposition, in London's green belt at such places
as Tillingham Hall, Essex and Leybourne, Kent.
Public inquiries to be held during 1986 will
determine whether private enterprise and home
ownership are victorious over conservation and
urban containment.

   Finally, it must be noted that with social

development planning there resides the assumption
that the expert, the policy-maker, knows best and
is in fact capable of successfully engineering the
future. Such policy is guided by a particular
vision which is at least paternalistic (see
Ambrose and Colenutt, 1975). It may be geared to
institutional interests as Simmie's (1981) study
of Oxford shows. The vision is also fired by the
belief that changing physical design or environmental conditions can materially alter social
arrangements and hence future behaviour. The
evidence for judging the validity of this belief
is inconclusive. This belief certainly influenced
such builders of utopian communities as Robert
Owen. His construction of New Lanark, Scotland,
was based on the view that the provision of jobs
and good housing along with educational pursuits
to fill leisure time would improve the social and
moral lives of working people. They did not,
however, share his views on the conditions which
fostered a happy and contented life. Work
opportunities in the developing industries of
Glasgow provided an escape. Even before Owen, the
sanitary reformers thought that their improvements
to city conditions would affect for the better not
only health but also social behaviour. In less
extreme but more modern guise, planners, by
designing and providing particular small-scale
arrangements of dwellings, have tried to engender
a spirit of neighbourliness and increasing social
inter-action (Jones and Eyles, 1977; Mercer, 1975;
Keller, 1968; Golany, 1976). Neighbourhood
planning is seen then, as a way of developing
primary relationships and community co-operation
and reliance (see Downs, 1981; Hallman, 1984;
Silver, 1985). There was debate over whether this
might best be achieved with a socially homogeneous
or mixed population (Mann, 1959; Gans, 1968). But
for those in poor housing conditions, particularly
in the 1950s and 1960s, the main purpose came to
be to provide them with materially improved living
conditions. Even then architecture and planning
were seen as agents of social reform. 'Streets in
the sky' would produce improved living and social
conditions. Such social engineering has had
unfortunate consequences. The high-rises and
housing estates have often assisted in the
development of anti-social behaviour through their
unprotected, amorphous, public spaces. As Newman
(1972) put it, their environments were not
defensible. In other words, rather than improve

social conditions and relationships certain designs may be associated with high levels of crime and vandalism. Despite criticism of Newman's work (see Hillier, 1973; Mayhew, 1979), it has formed the basis of studies of the great social engineering experiments of the 50s and 60s (see Newman, 1982; Coleman, 1985). These studies, while not being deterministic, suggest how the restructuring of living space may make cities more livable.

What this social development planning, which these studies criticise, does point to, however, is the underlying importance of theoretical explanations and moral evaluations in guiding policy. We cannot doubt the optimistic, if utopian, sentiments of these planning reformers who saw people as essentially good and deprivation as material and residual. It is indeed these explanations of deprivation and views on human nature that link the two parts of this paper. Social geography has concentrated much of its energy on the cataloguing of states and distribution of poverty and deprivation. Since the early 1970s, there has been, more often implied than stated, an undercurrent of evaluation and prescription. Yet there is not merely one prescription. These prescriptions are competing policy options emanating from different political philosophies and practices. As we have seen, policy reflects in part these philosophies and explanations (as well as local and material conditions). Our discussions and evaluations of policy would be advised to always recognise that. From it, we may learn about the views of the world that underpin our own work, and the fact that no policy is 'naturally right'.

Poverty, Deprivation and Social Planning

REFERENCES

Abel-Smith, B & P Townsend (1965) The Poor and the
    Poorest, Bell, London
Abrams, M (1973) 'Subjective social indicators',
    Social Trends 4, 35-50
Allardt, E (1973) 'About dimensions of welfare.
    University of Helsinki, Research Group for
    Comparative Sociology, Research Report 1
Allardt, E (1975) 'Dimensions of welfare in a
    comparative Scandinavian study', University of
    Helsinki, Research Group for Comparative
    Sociology, Research Report 9
Ambrose, P & R Colenutt (1975) The Property
    Machine, Penguin, Harmondsworth
Anderson, J (1983) 'Geography as ideology and the
    politics of crisis', in J. Anderson et al.
    (eds) Redundant Spaces in the Cities and
    Regions, Academic Press, London
Andrews, F M (1974) 'Social indicators of perceived
    life quality', Social Indicators Research 1,
    279-99
Andrews, F M & R F Inglehart (1979) 'The structure
    of subjective well-being in nine western
    societies', Social Indicators Research 6, 73-90
Andrews, F M & S B Withey (1976) Social Indicators
    of Well-being, Plenum Press, New York
Badcock, B (1984) Unfairly Structured Cities, Basil
    Blackwell, Oxford
Barry, J. T. (1980) 'The National Commission on
    neighbourhoods, in D Rosenthal (ed) Urban
    revitalization, Sage, Beverly Hills
Barnes, J A (1975) Educational Priority vol 3,
    Heinemann, London
Bassett, K & J Short (1978) 'Housing improvement in
    the inner city', Urban Studies 15, 333-42
Batley, R & J Edwards (1974) 'The urban programme',
    British Journal of Social Work 4, 305-31
Bederman, S. H. (1974) 'The stratification of
    'quality of life' in the black community of
    Atlanta, Georgia. South-eastern Geographer
    14, 26-37
Bentham, C G (1985) 'Which areas have the worst
    urban problems?' Urban Studies 22, 119-31
Bentham, C G & M Moseley (1980) 'Socio-economic
    changes and disparities within the Paris
    agglomeration'; Regional Studies 14, 55-70
Berthoud, R & J C Brown (1981) Poverty and the
    Development of Anti-poverty Policy in the
    United Kingdom, Heinemann, London

Birch, D (1979) The Job Generation Process, MIT Press, Cambridge, Mass

Boal, F W, P Doherty & P G Pringle (1978) 'Social problems in the Belfast urban area', Queen Mary College, Department of Geography, Occasional Paper 12

Bromley, R D F & R H Morgan (1985) 'The effects of enterprise zone policy', Regional Studies 19, 403-13

Burnley, I & S Walker (1982) 'Unemployment in metropolitan Sydney', in R V Cardew et al. (eds) Why Cities Change, Allen & Unwin, Sydney

Butler, S M (1981) Enterprise zones, Heinemann, London

Carlisle, E (1972) 'The conceptual structure of social indicators', in A Shonfield & S Shaw (eds) Social Indicators and Social Policy, Heinemann, London

Castles, S (1984) Here for Good, Pluto Press, London

CSO (Central Statistical Office) (1985) Regional trends, HMSO, London

Cherry, G (1970) Town Planning in its Social Context, Leonard Hill, London

Clarke, S E (1984) 'Neighbourhood policy options', Journal, American Planning Association 50, 439-501

Coates, K & R Silburn (1970) Poverty - the Forgotten Englishmen, Penguin, Harmondsworth

Coleman, A (1985) Utopia on Trial, Hilary Shipman, London

CDP (Community Development Project) (1977a) Gilding the ghetto, CDP, London

CDP (1977b) The costs of industrial change, CDP, London

Conway, J (1984) Capital decay, Shelter, London

Crosland, C A R (1964) The Future of Socialism, Cape, London

Cullingworth, J B (1960) English Housing Trends, Bell, London

Cullingworth, J B (1972) The Social Content of Planning, Allen & Unwin, London

Cutter, S (1985) Rating Places, AAG, Washington

Dale, B (1980) 'Subjective and objective social indicators in studies of regional social well-being', Regional Studies 14, 503-15

Dalkey, N C & D L Rourke (1973) The quality of life concept, Environmental Protection Agency, Washington

Damer, S (1974) 'Wine alley', Sociological review 22, 221-48

Danson, M (1984) 'Poverty and deprivation in the west of Scotland', in M Pacione and G Gordon (eds) Quality of life and human welfare, GeoBooks, Norwich

Danson, M, W. F. Lever & J F Malcolm (1980) 'The inner city employment problem in Great Britain, 1952-76', Urban Studies 17, 193-210

Davis, K & W E Moore (1945) 'Some principles of stratification', American Sociological Review 10, 242-49

DES (Department of Education and Science) (1967) Children and their primary schools 2 vols (Plowden Report), HMSO, London

DoE (Department of the Environment) (1977) Policy for the inner cities, HMSO, London

DoE (1984) Housing and construction statistics 1973-83, HMSO, London

Donnison, D (1985) 'What can we learn from GEAR?' The Planner, 17, 53-4

Donnison, D & C Ungerson (1983) Housing in Britain, Penguin, Harmondsworth

Downs, A (1973) Federal Housing Subsidies, D C Heath, Lexington

Downs, A (1981) Neighborhoods and Urban Development Brookings Institution, Washington

Edwards, J (1975) Social indicators, urban depriva- tion and positive discrimination. Journal of Social Policy 3, 127-35

Edwards, J & R Batley (1978) The Politics of positive discrimination, Heinemann, London

Einem, E von (1982) 'National urban policy - the case of West Germany', Journal, American Planning Association 48, 9-23

Elliot, B & D McCrone (1984) 'Austerity and the politics of resistance', in I Szelenyi (ed) Cities in recession, Sage, Beverly Hills

English, J (1979) 'Access and deprivation in local authority housing', in C Jones (ed) Urban deprivation and the inner city, Croom Helm, London

Escudero, J C (1981) 'Democracy, authoritarianism and health in Argentina', International Journal of Health Services 11, 559-72

Eversley, D E C (1973) 'Problems of social planning in inner London', in D Donnison & D E C Eversley (eds) London: urban patterns and policies, Heinemann, London

Eyles, J (1979) 'Area-based policies for the inner city', in D T Herbert & D M Smith (eds) Social problems and the city, Oxford, London

243

Eyles, J (1985a) Senses of Place, Silverbrook Press, Warrington

Eyles, J (1985b) 'From equalisation to rationalisation', Australian Geographical Studies 23

Eyles, J (1986) 'Qualitative methods: a new revolution?' in J Eyles (ed) Qualitative approaches in social and geographical research, Queen Mary College, Department of Geography and Earth Science, Occasional Paper 26

Eyles, J & J Donovan (1986) Regional variations in perceptions of health and health care, ESRC End of Research Report, London

Eyles, J & K J Woods (1986) A Geography of the National Health, Croom Helm, London

Feiss, C. (1985) 'The foundations of federal planning assistance. Journal, American Planning Association 51, 175-84

Flax, M J (1972) A study in comparative urban indicators, Urban Institute, Washington

Foley, D L (1960) 'British town planning: one ideology or three?', British Journal of Sociology 11, 211-31

Forster, C (1983) 'Spatial organisation and local employment rates in metropolitan Adelaide', Australian Geographical Studies 21, 33-48

Fothergill, S & G Gudgin (1982) Unequal Growth, Heinemann, London

Friedman, M (1977) From Galbraith to economic freedom, Institute of Economic Affairs, London

Galbraith, J K (1958) The Affluent Society, Hamish Hamilton, London

Gans, H J (1968) People and Plans, Basic Books, New York

Gans, H J (1972) 'The positive functions of poverty', American Journal of Sociology 72, 275-89

Giampaglia, G & F W Young (1980) 'The structural context of family welfare in the regions of Italy', Social Indicators Research 7, 443-62

Glickman, N J (1984) 'Economic policy and the cities', Journal American Planning Association 50, 471-78

Goering, J M (1979) 'The national neighbourhood movement. Journal, American Planning Association 45, 509-14

Golany, G (1976) New Town Planning, Wiley, Chichester

Golany, G (1978) International Urban Growth policies, Wiley, Chichester

Goldfield, D R (1982) 'National urban policy in Sweden', Journal, American Planning Association 49, 24-38

Poverty, Deprivation and Social Planning

Goldsmith, W W (1982) 'Enterprise zones', Interna-
tional Journal of Urban and Regional Research,
435-42
Goldsmith, W W & H M Jacobs (1982) 'The improba-
bility of urban policy', Journal, American
Planning Association 49, 53-66
Gordon, I R & R M Whittaker (1972) 'Indicators of
local prosperity in the south-west region',
Regional Studies 6, 299-313
Gough, I (1979)The Political Economy of the Welfare
State, Macmillan, London
Gray, F (1976) 'Selection and allocation in council
housing', Transactions, Institute of British
Geographers 1, 34-46
GLC (Greater London Council) (1981) The Greater
London housing condition survey, GLC, London
GLC (1984) London docklands, GLC, London
Gross, B M (1966) The State of the Nation,
Tavistock, London
Gulliver, S (1984) 'The area projects of the
Scottish Development Agency', Town Planning
Review 55, 322-34
Habermas, J (1976) Legitimation Crisis, Heinemann,
London
Hall, J (1976) 'Subjective measures of quality of
life in Britain 1971-5', Social Trends 7, 47-60
Hall, P (1977) 'Green fields and grey areas', in
Proceedings of Royal Town Planning Institute
Annual Conference, RTPI, London
Hallman, H W (1984) Neighbourhoods, Sage, Beverly
Hills
Harrington, M (1962) The Other America, Penguin,
New York.
Harrison, P (1985) Inside the Inner City, Penguin,
Harmondsworth
Harvey, D (1973) Social Justice and the City,
Arnold, London
Harvey, D (1974) 'What kind of geography for what
kind of public policy?', Transactions,
Institute of British Geographers 63, 18-24
Headey, B (1981) 'The quality of life in
Australia', Social Indicators Research 9,
155-81
Herbert, D T & C Thomas (1982) Urban Geography,
Wiley, Chichester
H M Treasury (1985) Government expenditure plans
1987-8, HMSO, London
Hillier, D (1973) 'In defence of space'. RIBA
Journal 80, 539-44
Hoggart, R (1957) Uses of Literacy, Penguin,
Harmondsworth

Poverty, Deprivation and Social Planning

Holterman, S (1975) 'Areas of urban deprivation in Great Britain', Social Trends, 6, 33-47

Home Office (1968) Report of the Committee on Local authority and allied personal social services, HMSO, London

Jackson, P (1985) 'Urban ethnography', Progress in Human Geography 9, 157-76

JDAG (Joint Docklands London) (1984) Stifling the island's enterprise, JDAG, London

Jones, E & J Eyles (1977) An Introduction to Social Geography, Oxford UP, London

Jones, M (1979) 'Australian urban policy', Politics 14, 295-303

Jones, M (1983) The Australian welfare state, Allen & Unwin, Sydney

Jordan, B (1976) Freedom and the Welfare State, RKP London

Jordan, B (1982) Mass Unemployment and the Future of Britain, RKP, London

Joseph, K & J Sumption (1979) Equality, Murray, London

Keller, S (1968) The Urban Neighborhood, Random House, New York

King, A (1975) 'Overload', Political Studies 23

Knox, P (1975) Social Well-being, Oxford UP, Oxford

Knox, P (1984) The Geography of Western Europe, Croom Helm, London

Knox, P & A MacLaren (1978) 'Values and perceptions in descriptive approaches to urban social geography', in D T Herbert and R J Johnston (eds) Geography and the Urban Environment, vol 1, Wiley, Chichester

Kuz, T J (1978) 'Quality of life, an objective and subjective variable analysis', Regional Studies 12, 409-17

Laurence, S & P Hall (1981) 'British policy responses', in P Hall (ed) The Inner City in Context, Heinemann, London

Lawless, P (1981) Britain's Inner Cities, Harper & Row, London

Leclerc, R & D Draffan (1984) 'The Glasgow eastern area renewal project', Town Planning Review 55, 335-51

Lewis, O (1956) Children of Sanchez, Penguin, Harmondsworth

Lewis, O (1968) La Vida, Panther, London

Liu, B C (1973) The quality of life in the US, Midwest Research Institute, Kansas City

Liu, B C (1976) Quality of Life Indicators in US Metropolitan Areas, Praeger, New York

246

Poverty, Deprivation and Social Planning

Lockwood, D (1974) For T H Marshall. Sociology 8, 363-67

Lojkine, J (1984) 'The working class and the state', in I Szelenyi (ed) Cities in recession, Sage, Beverly Hills

LDDC (London Docklands Development Corporation) 1985 Memorandum, LDDC, London

Mack, J & S Lansley (1985) Poor Britain, Allen & Unwin, London

MacLaran, A (1981) 'Area based discrimination and the distribution of well-being', Transactions, Institute of British Geographers 6, 53-67

Madge, C & P Willmott (1981) Inner city in Paris and London, RKP, London

Mann, P (1959) 'The socially balanced neighbourhood unit', Town Planning Review 30, 91-97

Marshall, T H (1965) Class, Citizenship and Social Development, Doubleday Anchor, New York

Mason, T (1977) Inner city housing and renewal policy. Centre for Environmental Studies, London

Massey, D (1982) 'Enterprise zones: a political issue', International Journal of Urban and Regional Research 6, 429-34

Massey, D & R Meegan (1978) 'Industrial restructuring versus the cities', Urban Studies 15, 273-88

Massey, D & R Meegan (1983) The Anatomy of Job Loss Methuen, London

Mayhew, P (1979) 'Defensible space', The Howard Journal 18

McArthur, A (1985) 'GEAR: jobs and incomes', The Planner

Mercer, C (1975) Living in Cities, Penguin, Harmondsworth

Merton, R K (1957) Social Theory and Social Structure, Free Press, New York

Metcalf, D (1975) 'Urban unemployment in England', Economic Journal 85, 578-89

MHLG (Ministry of Housing and Local Government) (1966) Living in a slum, HMSO, London

Mishra, R (1984) The Welfare State in Crisis, Wheatsheaf, Brighton

Moseley, M (1979) Accessibility, Methuen, London

Nabarro, G (1980) 'Inner city partnerships', Town Planning Review 51, 25-38

Neutze, M (1981) 'Housing', in P N Troy (ed) Equity in the City, Allen & Unwin, Sydney

Newman, O (1972) Defensible Space, Macmillan, New York

Newman, O (1982) Review and analysis of the Chicago
    housing authority and implementation of recom-
    mended changes, Institute of Community Design
    Analysis, New York
Nutley, S D (1980) 'Accessibility, mobility and
    transport related welfare', Geoforum 11, 353-62
O'Dowd, L & B Rolston (1985) 'Bringing Hong Kong to
    Belfast?', International Journal of Urban and
    Regional Research 9, 218-32
Offe, C (1976) 'Political authority and class
    structures', in P Connerton (ed). Critical
    sociology, Penguin, Harmondsworth
Offe, C (1984) Contradictions in the Welfare State,
    Heinemann, London
Osborn, F J & A Whittick (1977) New Towns, Leonard
    Hill, London
Pacione, M (1982a) 'The use of objective and
    subjective measures of life quality in human
    geography', Progress in Human Geography 6,
    495-514
Pacione, M. (1982b) 'Evaluating the quality of the
    residential environment in a deprived council
    estate', Geoforum 13, 45-55
Pacione, M. (1985) 'Inner city regeneration:
    perspectives on the G.E.A.R. project',
    Planning Outlook 28, 65-69
Pacione, M (1986) 'Quality of Life in Glasgow: an
    applied geographical analysis', Environment
    and Planning A 18, 1499-1520
Pahl, R E (1984) Divisions of Labour, Blackwell,
    Oxford
Paris, C (1977) Birmingham, Centre for Environ-
    mental Studies Review 1, 54-61
Parker, T (1985) The People of Providence, Penguin,
    Harmondsworth
Peters, B G (1979) 'Dimensions of quality of life
    in an urban area', in M C Romanos (ed) Western
    European cities in crisis, D C Heath, Lexington
Phillips, D & A Williams (1984) Rural Britain,
    Blackwell, Oxford
Piachaud, D (1981) 'Peter Townsend and the holy
    grail', New Society 10 September
Piven, F F & R A Cloward (1984) 'The new class war
    in the US', in I Szelenyi (ed) Cities in
    recession, Sage, Beverly Hills
Potter, S (1985) 'How the new towns changed', Town
    and Country Planning 54, 284-90
Powell, M (1986) 'Territorial justice and primary
    health care', Social Science and Medicine 20
Redfern, P (1982) 'Profile of our cities', Popula-
    tion Trends 30, 21-32

248

Reisman, D (1977) Richard Titmuss: Welfare and Society, Heinemann, London

Rex, J R & R Moore (1967) Race, Community and Conflict, Oxford UP, Oxford

Roberts, J T (1976) General Improvement Areas, Saxon House, Farnborough

Robson, B T (1979) 'Housing, empiricism and the state', in D T Herbert and D M.Smith (eds) Social problems and the city, Oxford UP, London

Room, G (1979) The Sociology of Welfare, Martin Robertson, Oxford

Rowntree, S (1901) Poverty, Macmillan, London

Runciman, W G (1966) Relative Deprivation and Social Justice, RKP, London

Runnymede Trust (1980) Britain's Black Population, Heinemann, London

Rutter, M & N Madge (1976) Cycles of Deprivation, Heinemann, London

Saunders, P (1979) Urban Politics, Hutchinson, London

Sawer, M (1983) 'From the ethical state to the minimalist state', Politics 18, 26-35

Schneider, M (1975) 'The quality of life in large American cities', Social Indicators Research 1, 495-509

Schwartz, G G (1981) 'Urban policy and the inner cities in the US', in G G Schwatz (ed) Advanced Industrialisation and the Inner Cities, D C Heath, Lexington

Scobie, R S (1975) Problem Tenants in Public Housing. Praeger, New York

Scott, P. (1978) Australian Cities and Public Policy, Georgian House, Melbourne

Seabrook, J (1982) Unemployment, Granada, St Albans

Sen, A K (1978) Three Notes on the Concept of Poverty, International Labour Organisation, Geneva

Sen, A K (1982) Poverty and Famines, Oxford UP, Oxford

Shaw, J M (1979) 'Rural deprivation and social planning', in J M Shaw (ed) Rural deprivation and planning, GeoBooks, Norwich

Shen, C H & F W Young (1984) 'The structural context of social indicator differentials in Japanese prefectures 1965-75', Social Indicators Research 15, 17-42

Short, J R (1982) 'Urban policy and British cities', Journal, American Planning Association, 48, 39-52

Silver, C (1985) 'Neighborhood planning in historical perspective', Journal, American Planning Association 51, 161-74

249

Poverty, Deprivation and Social Planning

Simmie, J M (1971) 'Physical planning and social
    policy', Journal of the Town Planning
    Institute 57, 450-53
Simmie, J M (1981) Power, Property and Corporation,
    Macmillan, London
Smith, D M (1973) Geography of social well-being in
    the US, McGraw-Hill, New York
Smith, D M (1977) Human Geography, Arnold, London
Stilwell, F J B (1979) 'The current economic
    depression and its impact on Australian
    cities', Australian Quarterly 51(2), 5-16
Stilwell, F J B (1980) Economic Crisis, Cities and
    and Regions, Pergamon, Rushcutters Bay
Stipak, B (1977) 'Attitudes and opinions concerning
    urban services', Public Opinion Quarterly 41,
    41-55
Storey, D (1983) 'Small firms and economic develop-
    ment', Town and Country Planning 52, 183-84
Taylor, P J (1979) "Difficult-to-let", "difficult-
    to-live-in", and sometimes "difficult-to-get-
    out-of", Environment and Planning A 11, 1305-20
Thunhurst, C (1985) 'The analysis of small area
    statistics and planning for health', The
    Statistician 34, 93-106
Titmuss, R M (1962) Income Distribution and Social
    Change, Allen & Unwin, London
Titmuss, R M (1974) Social Policy, Allen & Unwin,
    London
Tomaskovic-Devey, D & S M Miller (1984) 'Business
    rationality and barriers to recapitalisation',
    in I Szelenyi (ed) Cities in Recession, Sage,
    Beverly Hills
Townsend, P (1954) 'Measuring poverty', British
    Journal of Sociology 5, 130-37
Townsend, P (1979) Poverty in the UK, Penguin,
    Harmondsworth
Tyme, R & Partners (1983) Monitoring enterprise
    zones: year 2 report, Tyme, London
Tyme, R & Partners (1984) Monitoring enterprise
    zones: year 3 report, Tyme, London
Vinson, J & R Homel (1976) Indicators of community
    well-being, AGPS, Canberra
Vipond, J (1901) 'Change in unemployment differen-
    tials in Sydney', Australian Geographical
    Studies 19, 67-77
Vise, P de (1976) 'The suburbanisation of jobs and
    minority employment', Economic Geography 52,
    348-62
Walker, A (1981) 'South Yorkshire: the economic and
    social impact of unemployment', Political
    Quarterly 52, 74-87

Poverty, Deprivation and Social Planning

Walker, A (1984) *Social Planning*, Blackwell, Oxford
Wallman, S (1983) *Eight London Households*, Tavistock, London
Walmsley, D J (1980) *Social Justice and Australian Federalism*, University of New England, Armidale
Wilson, J O (1969) *Quality of Life in the US*, Midwest Research Institute, Kansas City

Chapter Eight

GEOGRAPHICAL LOCATIONS AND SOCIAL RELATIONSHIPS
AMONG THE ELDERLY

A.M. WARNES

Academic studies of the elderly tend to focus on
the special difficulties and needs of the most
disadvantaged and disabled. If it is justifiable
and understandable that the concern of social
welfare policy is with those who require intensive
medical, nursing or residential care, or
domiciliary support, such emphases need on occasion
to be balanced by consideration of the other
elderly. In western countries only about one in
twenty are resident in any kind of institution
and, in England, only about one in ten receive
visits from any public social service (Hunt,
1978). Most of the elderly are in good health,
active, socially involved and fiercely proud of
their independence. Earlier retirement, increasing
life expectancy and rising real incomes in old age
have combined to make obsolescent the view of
retirement as a brief, inactive, passive and
unrewarding phase of life. While no clear
template exists of the roles and activities to be
pursued after work, individual elderly people are
exploring their individuality and their social
positions in an extending 'third-age' of life. Much
more study and consideration of normal,
non-pathological, ageing is required, for the
obstacles and problems that face the majority of
people in late life have become submerged by the
information concerning the more acute but rarer
difficulties (Johnson, 1982). We need, for example,
to turn our attention more to health education and
promotion in late life, perhaps by preventive
screening. We need to foster improved, less costly
and more convenient dwellings for the majority of
the elderly in general housing, as well as to
continue to expand the provision of specialised
dwellings.

## Geographical Locations and Social Relationships

The geographical setting in which older people lead their lives is of great importance. While detailed knowledge of the time budgets and spatial activity patterns of older people is scant, some key elements are clear. Most elderly people remain self-supporting and socially integrated. Convenient access to basic services such as shops, health centres and to social, entertainment and religious activities are minimal requirements. The activity patterns of most people remain highly localised, and this phenomenon may intensify in later life. Certainly mobility is often restricted, even among the generally healthy and young elderly, by reduced income, car ownership, impaired eyesight or preference.

Most prescriptions for the housing location and residential setting of older people tend to be biased by a conception of the old as inactive and frail. Much has been done during the third quarter of this century to improve the elderly's housing conditions and amenities, but notwithstanding the poor standards and disgraceful accommodation still endured by a minority, it will soon be time for our environmental and housing objectives to be built from a more positive appreciation of normal ageing. What kinds of housing and what kinds of locations will promote the elderly to develop their own activities and social relationships? To what extent would a deeper knowledge of the lives of older people enable us to remove existing impediments to better third age lives?

This essay turns away from a conventional synthesis of the several features of the elderly's situation which have attracted geographical research, partly because a number of comprehensive reviews have recently been published (Golant, 1984a, 1984b; Rowles, 1978, 1986; Warnes, 1981, 1982). The valuable and detailed studies of migration, distribution, access to services, reactions to neighbourhood change, and mobility problems can be found in this literature. Instead this takes up two highly contrasting but less frequently discussed aspects of the social geography of the elderly. The first is a topic of global and macrosocietal interest, the impacts of the imminent rapid ageing of the populations of many developing countries. Until now western social scientists have tended to see the problems of demographic ageing in the context of resource-rich politically mature societies. The economic and human consequences of rapid ageing will be very different and possibly more severe elsewhere. The second objective is to explore the geographical contribution to a better understanding of normal ageing. It will examine the relationships between changing households among elderly people, the nature and importance of extra-household social relationships and the spatial characteristics of social networks. It will develop the argument that an elderly person's location has a very strong influence on the nature and frequency of their social contacts, and hence on their morale. Its essence is that the geographies of friendship and of consanguineal relationships have been much neglected, with the result being the durability of myths concerning the modern dispersal of families, the low amount of contact between generations, and the social isolation of elderly people.

It is not yet possible to write a rounded account of the social geography of the elderly, either from the functional perspective of the social networkposition of individuals, or from chorographic perspectives at different scales, of the diverse social complexes which form the sociogeographical and living environments of elderly people. This tries to set out the importance of adopting a wider range of scales of analysis in the social geography of the elderly. Macrosocietal and microsociological perspectives can be added to existing approaches, which for the most part has focused on specific attributes and characteristics of elderly people at the scale of national and regional aggregates. Some indications of an agenda for worthwhile lines of study are expressed within the final sections of the paper.

## Ageing in society

There are multiple ageing processes: endogenous biochemical and physical changes traject throughout the life-span; fertility, mortality and regional migration histories structure the numeracy and relative youthfulness or longevity of each cohort as well as the likelihoods at any time of its members having surviving parents, children, grandchildren and age-peers; and different societal and political-economic structures construct different roles and status for persons of advanced age (de Beauvoir, 1970; Goody, 1976; Phillipson, 1982). In traditional societies, an

individual's transitions between age-related
ascriptive roles are normally marked by rituals
which, in modern western societies, have been
largely supplanted by impersonal and restrictive
rules concerning the periods of compulsory
education and retirement or employment. These
have institutionalised a third-age of life with
ambiguous standing and little function. It is
left to individuals and nuclear family groups to
work out their own activities and social roles in
retirement: the 1980s are at but the beginning of
the exploration of third-age lives. Whatever is
presented in this or other accounts of the current
social conditions of the elderly and of their
geographical contexts, they are transitory and can
be only a partial guide to the future. If the
family, material and social situations of older
people have been revolutionised since 1914, most
gerontologists anticipate even greater changes by
the middle of the next century.

Given the multiplicity of ageing processes it
is an expedient simplification to regard a
specified age as defining the socially ascribed
status of 'an old person' - 60 or 65 years are
commonly used in this way. In western societies
the early sixties put a lower bound on a fifth of
the population as elderly, but in pre-industrial
demographic conditions, as continue in large parts
of Africa, people of forty years or more
constitute one-fifth. While 'elderly', like
childhood, adolescence and middle age, is a
socially constructed term with only a partial
basis in chronological age, in modern societies a
fundamental characteristic which links the vast
majority of persons aged 65 years or more is their
exclusion from gainful employment. Their material
support depends upon the productivity of younger
persons, not primarily through direct remittances
or services from their own relatives, but either
through state pensions and benefits or through
investment income derived from accumulated
assets. Although elderly people are enormously
diverse and although they do not constitute a
functional social group in the manner of a family,
religious sect or political party, the elderly
have no less systemic or interconnected existence
than the familiar occupationally-defined social
classes. Notwithstanding the definitional
problems, a logical and an applied sociological
basis exists for enquiry focused upon the diverse
social and geographical situations of the elderly.

Geographical Locations and Social Relationships

The diffusion of demographic ageing
During this quarter of the twentieth century the
world is passing through an interesting stage in
the spatial diffusion of the fertility and
mortality transitions associated with modernisation. The demographic transition model is well
known among population and social geographers but
fewer appreciate the later stages of the
age-structure changes which accompany and follow
the sequential decline of mortality and fertility
(Rowland, 1984). These can be represented on
conventional diagrams of the demographic
transition or presented as a tabular summary
(Table 8.1) (Warnes and Law, 1984).
     As theoretical models of stable populations
with different levels of fertility and of
mortality show, it is only after the onset of
declines in fertility from the very high levels of
pre-industrial or pre-modern conditions that there
are significant increases in the share of the
population aged 60 years or more (Coale and
Demeny, 1966; Spengler, 1974). The earliest
declines of mortality during the transition, by
reducing infant death, lower the median age, and
in any case have little impact on the elderly's
share if fertility is high. The demographic
ageing of a population continues for approximately
three generations after fertility has ended its
decline and reached approximately replacement
levels. Thereafter the elderly share may increase
moderately with further falls in mortality but, to
take the example of Great Britain, even with the
most optimistic assumptions about the likely
decline of mortality over the next forty years,
the pensionable age population would increase only
from 18 per cent now to 27 per cent by the middle
of the next century: if recent mortality declines
do not accelerate, the share will be only 21 per
cent (Benjamin and Overton, 1981).
     While demographic ageing in Britain and other
developed nations continues diminuendo, many less
developed countries are only now entering the
phase of crescendo which in exceptional cases such
as China may be of unprecedented rapidity. The
elderly share among 22 world regions in 1980
ranged from 4.3 per cent in both Eastern and
Western Africa to 19.6 per cent in Northern Europe
(Figure 8.1). Among individual countries the
share ranged from 3.0 per cent in Kenya and less
than four per cent in Malawi, Tanzania, Botswana
and Nicaragua, to 21.9 per cent in Sweden and over

Table 8.1 The stages of the demographic transition in relation to age structure

| Demographic characteristic | Phases of the Demographic Transition | | | | | |
|---|---|---|---|---|---|---|
| | Before | Early | Peak | Late | After | Future |
| Mortality | High, fluctuating with pandemics | Decline accelerating | Decline decelerating | Low, irregular age-specific differentials in slow decline | | Slow declines irregular? decelerating? |
| Fertility | High fluctuating | | Decline accelerating | Decline decelerating | Low fluctuating | ? |
| Population change | Slow, irregular growth | Growth accelerating | Very high growth | Growth decelerating | Fluctuating | Fluctuating |
| Elderly share | Low ( 5%) | | Growth accelerating | Growth decelerating | High ( 15%) | Fluctuating slow increase? decelerating increase |

nineteen per cent in Norway, East Germany, Denmark, the United Kingdom, Austria and Switzerland (United Nations, Department of Economic and Social Affairs, 1985). In 1980 a slim majority of the world's elderly lived in the less developed regions but by 2000 AD the number will increase to 595 million; 61 per cent will live in the less developed nations and only 17 per cent in Europe. The extended projections for 2025 suggest that 14 per cent of the world's population will be aged 60 or more years, that 71 per cent of these 1,135 million elderly people will be in the less developed regions and fewer than 12 per cent in Europe. Among the 22 world regions the mean increase of the elderly population from 1980 to 2000 will be 66 per cent, with a range from 95 per cent in Central America to just 2.7 per cent in Northern Europe (Figure 8.2). Awareness of the implications of these projections has encouraged social gerontologists and social demographers to write evaluative prognoses of ageing in the less developed nations (Binstock et al., 1982; Hauser, 1976; Meegama, 1982; Myers, 1978, 1983, 1985).

While UN demographic projects have a history of both dramatic representations and of autodestruction, it is undeniable that for the most part European and American social gerontologists and social geographers have been disgracefully purblind in their studies of the elderly. There is little geographical literature on the situation of elderly people in third world settings. To their credit, several governments, international agencies and charitable organisations like Help the Aged have been more aware.

### The elderly in less developed nations

Demographers, social administrators and government officials also have a growing awareness of the imminence of a rapid ageing of their populations. One sign has been the priority adoption of the subject by the Department of International Economic and Social Affairs of the United Nations, which since 1975 has been publishing a Bulletin on Aging. Representatives from the developed and developing worlds first came together to exchange experience and understanding at the World Assembly on Aging in Vienna in 1982 (Neysmith and Edwardh, 1984). The report of the first African conference on gerontology, held in Dakar in December 1984,

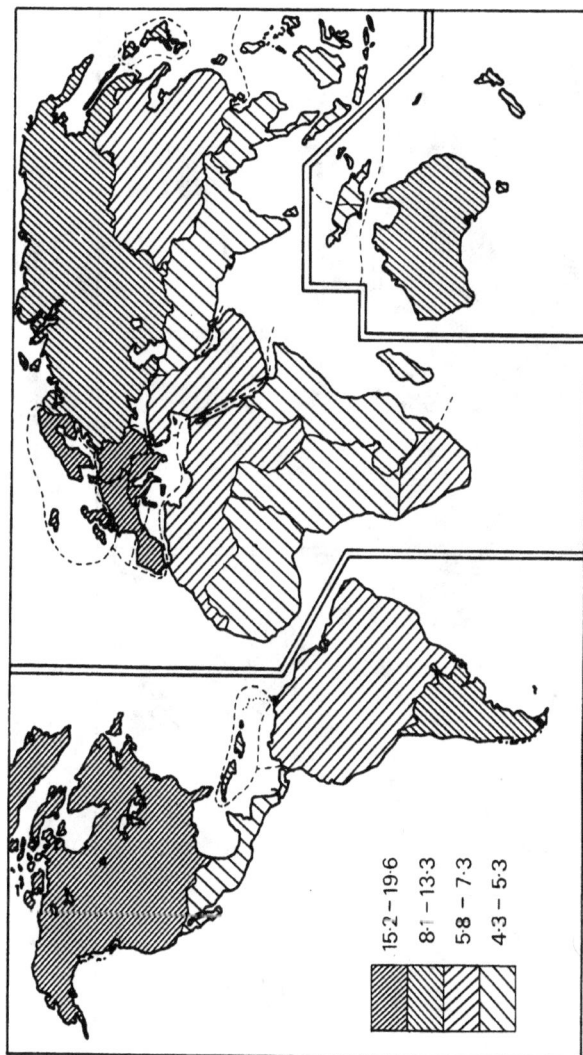

Figure 8.1 Persons Aged 60 Years or More as a Percentage of the Population, 22 World Regions, 1980

15·2 – 19·6

8·1 – 13·3

5·8 – 7·3

4·3 – 5·3

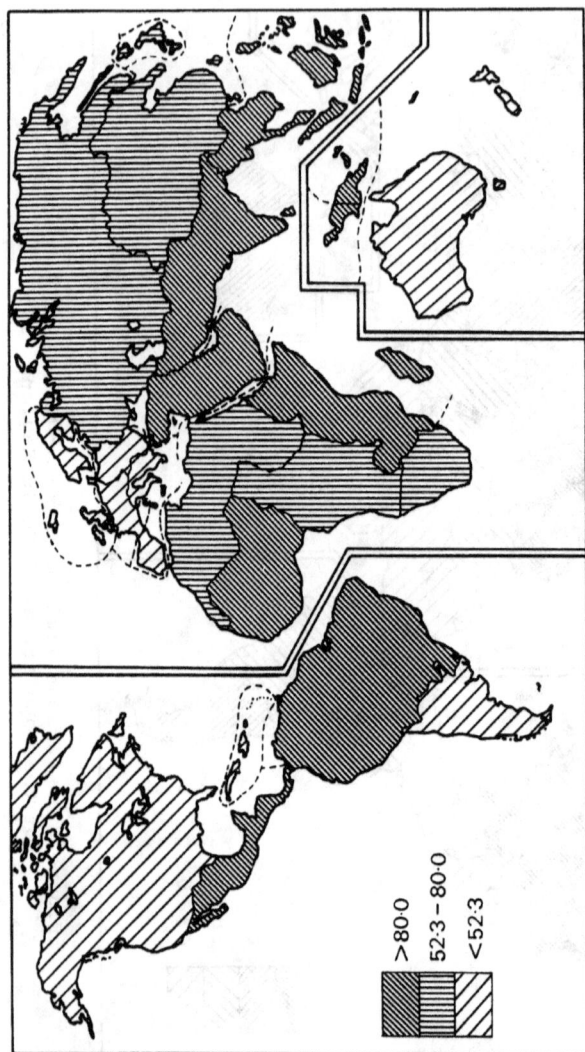

Figure 8.2 Projected Percentage Increase of
the Population Aged 60 Years or More, 1980–2000

>80·0

52·3 – 80·0

<52·3

highlights the effect of drought and persistent agricultural failure on premature ageing. Its recommendations recognise the continent's severe economic and disease problems and focus on the deficiencies of demographic information, medical and nutritional needs, social and cultural issues, and training and education. From this and other publications, it is clear that much more study is required to promote both understanding and effective policy measures (Gracia, 1985; International Center of Social Gerontology, Paris, 1985). In July 1985 more than 100 papers on the elderly in developing countries were delivered at the thirteenth Congress of the International Association of Gerontology in New York. Most publications to date are either contributions to strategic policy debates or theoretical and aggregative speculations, e.g. about whether family support systems for the elderly will be more enduring in the third than the first world (Beattie, 1978; Myers, 1982).

At present there is more ignorance than understanding of the present situation and social geography of the elderly in the third world. Of course there is immense diversity and generalisations may be more likely to perpetuate myths, particularly among westerners, than to provide illumination. Most of the facts that can be stated are denials of unfounded but common assumptions. It is not true, for example, that all parts of the third world are characterised by a high prevalence of multi-generational households and close-knit extended families or by a low incidence of the elderly living alone. The principal topics which have been investigated to date have been the impact of rural-urban migration on the ageing population of rural areas, the impact of the modern employment sector and of primary education on the attitudes of young people towards the elderly, and the urban-rural and social class differentials in the provision of pensions, health care and social services.

A selection of these issues will be considered, mainly by drawing upon recent reviews of the situation in central America and Nigeria. While at the present time the sources of the care and financial support of elderly people are mainly autogenous and while state pensions, retirement benefits, municipal social services and subsidised medical care are the exception rather than the rule, these same conditions applied among European

nations well into the twentieth century. The
ability of the nations of Asia, Africa and Latin
America to elaborate a range of social welfare
institutions and services, which seem an essential
prerequisite of the improvement of the material
and health standards of their prospectively
burgeoning elderly populations, will depend
fundamentally on the progress of their economic
development and its accompaniment by more stable,
democratically-inspired governmental institutions.
In limited ways they may be able to learn some
lessons from the path-breaking of European
nations. At the present time, however, the
diverse situations of elderly people range from
those who continue to be socially integrated and
economically active in traditional agricultural
family units and communities, to those who have
been abandoned on degraded farms by the
out-migration of younger people, and to those who
having moved to towns now find by reason of their
age or a lack of skill, that they are excluded
from employment and neither socially integrated
nor with institutional social service or medical
support (Hampson, 1985; Neysmith and Edwardh,
1984; Tapio-Videla and Parrish, 1982).

The republics of central America sustain some
of the world's highest birth rates although
substantial declines have recently occurred in
Costa Rica, Mexico and Panama (International
Program of Laboratories for Population Studies,
1980). Denton (1981) has provided a general
review and an assessment of the situation in Costa
Rica. Panama and Nicaragua have adopted the
extension of social security coverage to their
entire populations as policy goals and in the
former Canal Zone of Panama, only the most recent
migrants from Darien and other interior areas and
marginalised families are not given some
protection. The considerable social unrest in El
Salvador means that little progress has been made
towards the expansion of medical and social
programmes. In Honduras, ageing has not yet
emerged as a problem for decision makers: for the
forseeable future the family will continue to be
the principal social mechanism providing life time
care for the aged. In Guatemala, the Indian
population cares for its own aged and, to the
extent that village life survives, this will
continue. In the urban areas the picture is
different, for any Indian who moves from the
village and assumes western dress is dubbed a

ladino and 'no matter how well or how poorly a ladino does he cannot return to the village to live'. Unless the political structure finds resources for old age programmes and support, the future is not a positive one for the largest nation of the isthmus (Denton, 1981).

In Costa Rica, clear differences between the partially modernised elderly population of the capital region around San José and the rural elderly have been shown by a social survey of 952 persons aged 60 years or more, conducted in 1979 by the Institute of Social and Population Studies of the National University (Denton, 1981, p 91). Although the income of the elderly was little different to that of younger adults, 47 per cent of those answering in San Jose and 69 per cent of those elsewhere received monthly less than 100 dollars. Almost 90 per cent of the Costa Rican elderly lived with spouses and/or relatives and only 7 per cent lived alone or in institutions. More claimed to be employed (16%) or unemployed (28%) than retired (8%). Denton is at pains to emphasise the widespread geographical distribution of rural health centres and social security clinics and that health services are universally available, but he also reports that the country had only one specialist geriatrician and no nurses or other professionals trained in the care of the elderly. In 1979 there were no state nursing homes and no domiciliary social services. An attitude survey of younger people suggested that the family will increasingly withdraw from its role of caring for the elderly and already the majority of the elderly reported receiving from them no assistance and, to the surprise of the researchers, nearly one-third stated that they would prefer to live in an old-age home or institution: 'it was presumed that virtually all the aged would desire to reside with their families (but they) may well live in such hardship conditions that even the impersonality of an institution would seem more desirable: perhaps they are not eating well or fight with their family' (Denton, 1981, p. 102). In 1979 there were in fact 21 homes for the aged accommodating 1,477 of the nation's 110,000 persons aged 60 or more years, but most of these were relatively affluent.

Although many county councils were pressing for a residential homes construction programme, in 1981 the government was against this policy and favoured the provision of intermediate health centres and

day centres. Denton presents a brief picture of
the very restricted activity patterns and lives of
the elderly in Costa Rica. While few live alone,
this appears to be mainly a consequence of income
constraints, and a picture comes through of the
strains of their intergenerational living
arrangements and of the irrelevance of their
skills and experience in the labour market and to
younger people. While a Presidential Commission
on Policies for the Elderly was established in
1978 and while Denton tends to be optimistic about
the prospects of building services for the
elderly, the lack of resources, other priorities
and the tendency, which has been seen in more
developed countries, to diminish the importance of
the elderly's needs point to a less promising
future.

If we turn from central America to the most
populous nation of Africa, other perspectives on
the elderly in less developed countries are
gained. While the oil wealth and turbulent recent
political history of Nigeria are special factors,
recent studies by Adeokun (1982, 1984) place these
well in a broad analysis of the relationship
between modernisation and the social situation of
older people. He is also able to draw on some
detailed empirical studies (Adebagbo, 1978;
Odekunle, 1978; Olusanya, 1975). Until recently
in Nigeria the attainment of old age was itself a
mark of distinction:

> To live long was to accumulate the wisdom of
> coping with the human and physical environment
> in a non-literate society. The rule of the
> elder or gerontocracy and the privileges
> attached to age were necessary and sensible
> responses to demographic and socio-economic
> circumstances. But since the second world war
> the integration of the developing countries
> into a worldwide process of modernisation is
> producing both a demographic and social
> transition ... (there is a) deterioration of
> traditional status and prestige of old age as
> society moves from gerontocracy to that of
> franchise which often effectively excludes the
> elderly on the basis of literacy, formal
> education, modern sector education or some
> other acquired trait (Adeokun, 1984, p.69).

Adeokun concludes his 1984 monograph with brief
biographies of three contrasting elderly people,

each affected by aspects of Nigeria's political
transformations and modernisation. The first is a
75 year old traditional chief living in a family
compound with his four wives. Although some of
his children had entered modern professions and he
uses modern, specialist hospitals, his children's
marriages were arranged in time-honoured fashion
so that his patronage extends to at least three
other titled families. 'Although the reduced
political power of the native chieftaincy system
is obvious, his control of substantial family land
and his many linkages give him a leading position
in local affairs ... he is one of the very
fortunate elderly persons'.

The second case study of a widow in her late
sixties illustrates the universal consequences of
premature widowhood and the more specific
dissolution of a household as a result of rural
urban migration. Although the lady continued to
live in a traditional compound with others and was
sent remittances by one son of her four surviving
children, they had all moved away and rarely
visit. She considers the other members of her
household to be tenants rather than relatives and
felt a pervasive sense of loss. The third case
study is of a man whose equally difficult
circumstances are partly the consequence of
youthful migrations. He grew up in a large family
on a small farm and left home to live in northern
Nigeria where he learnt and practised carpentry
for forty years. In the 1960s the political
situation placed strains on southerners in the
northern region, and he returned to his native
region, leaving his northern wife and completely
losing contact with his children and other
relatives. He has lost the influence his age
would normally entitle him to and complains about
the separation from his northern family. He has
had few opportunities to practise his trade since
returning and is not integrated with his native
family, living not in the compound but in a
'modest house' nearby. Adeokun states that these
cases are by no means exceptional and illustrate
the range of factors that influence the social
status and living arrangements of the elderly in
Nigeria. Few have received any formal education
or spent any time in paid employment; consequently
they have no retirement benefits and lifetime
activity is for most a necessity and the only
viable alternative to privation. He concludes:

## Geographical Locations and Social Relationships

As a result of current investment in mass
formal education the future cohorts of elderly
will present planners with people who by their
education have migrated and disengaged
physically if not emotionally from their
family networks. Even when such persons have
not passed through a period of paid
employment, limited opportunities for lifelong
occupation outside agriculture or crafts will
force some of this generation into urban
destitution. (This phenomenon) has already
attracted voluntary organisations to respond
(as) in the developed countries (Adeokun,
1984, p. 109).

The diverse circumstances of elderly people in
central America and in Nigeria only hint at the
variation throughout the world. The contrasts
between the extreme indigence of millions of
elderly Africans and the pampered hedonism and
valetudinarians of some rich elderly in Palm
Beach, Marbella and Monte Carlo could not be
greater. In all countries the family situations
of the elderly range from isolation to a
plentitude of descendents, while living
arrangements vary from primary independence, now
endemic in affluent nations, to multigenerational
and multi-household dwellings which are common in
parts of Africa and south-east Asia. There is no
less diversity in older people's daily activity
patterns, from the peasant's relentless tasks on
the land and the wife's unchanging household and
often intensifying caring duties, to the contrived
recreations and socially competitive entertaining
of high-income retirement communities.
Millions of elderly never stray beyond their
village or township, while others provide the
mainstay of the passenger lists of world cruises
and of off-peak resort hotel trade. Within this
range only a few sociogeographical complexes have
been studied and published in English. The
interesting and rapidly changing situation of
elderly people in Japan has been particularly well
covered (Japan Institute for Gerontological
Research, 1978; Palmore, 1975). Relatively little
is available on the elderly's welfare, roles and
living arrangements in the Soviet Union or eastern
block countries (but see Synak and Taylor, 1984;
Szwarc, 1983). The vast bulk of the literature
deals with the elderly in north-west Europe, north
America and Australia and, so as not to try the

concentration of many readers any further, the rest of the paper will focus on these regions.

The principal geographical feature of the present stage in the diffusion of demographic ageing from the more to the less developed nations is the unprecedented and temporary concentration of the world's elderly in Europe, north America, Japan and the temperate southern hemisphere nations. Within the lifetimes of today's students, this distribution is most likely to be radically transformed. By the end of the first quarter of the next century it is possible that only one-quarter of the world's population aged 60 years or more will be citizens of the developed nations. Current western perceptions of the characteristics and social and geographical situations of the elderly are narrowly ethnocentric. It is paradoxical that a wide public awareness of the social and economic problems produced by demographic ageing has only recently gained ground, but this reflects in part our governments' preoccupations with the costs of support for the elderly and their awareness of the continuing growth of the numbers in extreme old age. As the family, household and residential situations of elderly people in the mid-1980s have a great deal to do with an interaction between changing demographic structures and the population's rising material standards and health expectations, it is instructive to begin with a brief review of current demographic developments.

## Future ageing in western countries

The latest official projections of the numbers of people of different ages are founded on the current schedules of fertility and mortality, with some allowance for the continuation of recent mortality improvements. During this century in Britain there have been substantial fluctuations in annual births. A significant fall during the First World War was followed by a sharp baby-boom from 1919 to 1923. Annual births then declined from a peak of nearly one million to 0.6 m by 1941. Another post-war peak in 1947 of nearly 0.9 m was followed by a trough during the early 1950s but a further strong rise to 0.85 m births in 1964. These remarkable fluctuations will have a substantial influence on the size and age structure of the nation's elderly population well into the next century (Craig, 1983; Great Britain,

267

Office of Population Censuses and Surveys, 1984a).
They have a large bearing on the ratio of elderly
people to the working age groups and, along with
the recent history of fertility, influence the
frequency of an elderly person's relatives of
different ages.

The population of statutory pensionable age is
projected to increase in England and Wales from
9.0 millions in 1981 to 10.8 millions in 2021
(Table 8.2). This growth will be interrupted by a
fall of around 200,000 during the 1990s,
reflecting the low birth rates during the First
World War. The young elderly (aged less than 75
years) will decrease during the 1980s and 1990s.
Those aged 75-84 years have been increasing very
strongly since 1971 but their numbers will
stabilise during the 1990s and decrease during the
first decade of the next century. The 85 plus
years population is growing during the 1980s at
the exceptional annual rate of 3.8 per cent but
this will moderate during the 1990s to 2.2 per
cent. By the 2010s their numbers will be almost
stable.

In the United States, Canada and Australia,
the more consistent population growth through the
twentieth century, partly as a consequence of net
international migration gains and partly through
higher fertility, means that they are at a less
advanced stage of demographic ageing and that their
elderly populations for several decades will grow
absolutely and relatively at a greater rate than
in north west Europe. In the United States the
population aged 62 years or more has been projected
to increase from 28.4 m in 1976 to 36.1 m by 1991.
For a decade thereafter growth will be slow but a
very rapid increase to 55.8 m will occur during
the first twenty years of the next century
(Siegel, 1980; USA Bureau of the Census, 1977;
Warnes, 1983).

The scope and detail of population projections
have recently been extended in Britain both to
regions, counties, districts and London boroughs
and to household composition (GB, OPCS, 1984b; GB,
Government Statistical Service, 1985). For the
smaller regions migration gains and losses are far
more influential in population change but because
the volume of migrations fluctuates in response to
employment, housing market and urban development
factors, local projections are less reliable than
national forecasts. Even with conservative
assumptions concerning the loss of population from

Table 8.2   The elderly by age group in England and Wales, 1981–2000 (millions)

| Age | Sex | 1981 | 1991 | 2001 | 2011 | 2021 |
|---|---|---|---|---|---|---|
| 65–74 | male | 2.0 | 2.0 | 1.9 | 2.0 | 2.3 |
| | female | 2.6 | 2.5 | 2.3 | 2.4 | 2.8 |
| 75–84 | male | 0.8 | 1.0 | 1.1 | 1.0 | 1.2 |
| | female | 1.6 | 1.7 | 1.7 | 1.6 | 1.8 |
| 85+ | male | 0.1 | 0.2 | 0.3 | 0.3 | 0.4 |
| | female | 0.4 | 0.6 | 0.7 | 0.8 | 0.8 |

Source: GB, OPCS (1984a)

urban areas and the growth of new suburbs,
substantial variations in growth are projected,
e.g. during the 1980s the pensionable population
of the Greater London Council area is expected to
decline annually by 0.5 per cent whereas in
Buckinghamshire it will increase by 1.5 per cent.
Similar differentials are projected for the 1990s
by the OPCS figures (Table 8.3). It should be
emphasised however that these extrapolations are
based on conservative assumptions about the
continuation and reduction of long term net
migration for smaller areas. The redistribution
of the elderly population by this process was at a
high level during the 1960s but with the recession
since 1973 has declined (Warnes and Law, 1984,
1985). It may revive strongly in a period of
economic growth. As revealed by the changing
distribution from 1971 to 1981 of the decennial
cohort which aged from 50–59 to 60–69 years, local
changes can be considerable. Wimborne County
District, north west of Bournemouth, and several
other Districts experienced increases of a third
or more in this cohort during the decade, while
there were decreases of more than a quarter in the
City of Glasgow and a dozen London boroughs
(Warnes and Law, 1985).

Since the late 1960s there has been a renewed
period of declining mortality at later ages in
Britain and in the United States of America. This
has stimulated an interesting debate among
demographers, epidemiologists, clinicians and
biologists about the future course of mortality
and ageing. Essentially the opposing views are on
the one hand that human life expectancy cannot
reach substantially more than the 80 or so years
now attained in the healthiest and wealthiest
regions of the developed world. Further progress
in combating cancers and heart disease and in
eliminating smoking will · enable a larger
percentage of future cohorts to reach these ages
but will not radically prolong life. It is
proposed that we are reaching the upper limit of
survival potential. The result will be a
reduction of both mortality and morbidity among
people in their later sixties and seventies and an
increase in the percentage of all deaths occurring
among persons in their eighties. The age profile
of deaths will become more rectangular (Fries,
1980). The opposing school suggests that further
substantial increases in life expectancy can be
anticipated. It is argued that because demographic

270

analyses frequently consider all persons aged more
than 75 (or some other) years as a single
category, they have been insensitive to the
changes in mortality rates within these ages and
to increases in longevity. A recent commentary
has also claimed that there is no conclusive
evidence that the incidence of physical or mental
disorders is decreasing among people in their
sixties and seventies (Benjamin and Overton, 1981;
Brody, 1985; Manton, 1982; Myers and Manton,
1985a, 1985b).

The outcome will have profound implications
not only for the social welfare and health status
of elderly people and therefore for expensive
areas of social policy, but also be a strong
determinant of the future social geography of the
elderly. In the first case, one anticipates a
decreasing incidence of disabilities and widowhood
among the retired population and therefore a
growing number of active, healthy elderly people
well able with their spouses or household
companions to support themselves. In the second
case, the prospect is for substantial increases of
very elderly people and, as in the most
pessimistic appraisals, for quite startling
increases of the numbers who will be disabled,
widowed, socially isolated, and suffering from
specific disorders requiring either expensive
surgery, such as hip replacements, or long term
intensive care, as with dementia. Even the august
USA Bureau of the Census has published projections
of the number of hip fractures rising from 0.2 m
now to nearly 0.7 m in 2050. The personal
situation of elderly people and their interaction
with their local environments may therefore be
increasingly characterised either by the active,
independent and fit person, the kind who so
frequently say with pride that in their retirement
they are busier than ever, or by those persons on
whom the pathological stereotype of the elderly is
based, of people constrained by physical
disabilities, low income and decayed social
networks to dependency and to restricted, mainly
sedentary and passive lives.

## The political economy and the social construction
of old age

The demographic future and the course of morbidity
is not the only set of long term factors
conditioning the situation of the elderly; the

Table 8.3  Pensionable population projections, 1981-2001, selected districts of England

| District | Population (000s) | | | Annual change (%) | |
| --- | --- | --- | --- | --- | --- |
| | 1981 | 1991 | 2001 | 1981-91 | 1991-2001 |
| Greater London | 1272 | 1216 | 1082 | -0.5 | -1.2 |
| Camden LB | 38 | 35 | 32 | -0.8 | -0.9 |
| Lewisham LB | 46 | 43 | 36 | -0.7 | -1.8 |
| Harrow LB | 38 | 35 | 33 | -0.8 | -0.6 |
| Buckinghamshire | 80 | 93 | 104 | +1.5 | +1.1 |
| Dorset | 153 | 175 | 181 | +1.4 | +0.3 |
| Norfolk | 145 | 152 | 150 | +0.5 | -0.1 |

Source: GB, OPCS (1984b)

other is those societal, cultural, legal,
political, economic and administrative arrangements
which have a fundamental effect on the wealth,
income, housing, opportunities and employment
status of people of different ages. Brief
reference to these factors was made in the
discussion of the elderly in less developed
countries, but it is no less the case in western
nations that an elderly person's position and
treatment is in some part structured at the
societal level. This point may be illustrated
from the field of employment. Whether a person
aged 63 years has been encouraged to remain
economically active at different dates in the
twentieth century has been related to fluctuations
in the demand for and supply of labour. Contrary
views have always coexisted, with spokesmen of the
young seeking work and of trade unions normally
advocating early mandatory retirement, and those
concerned about the income and morale of the
elderly normally counselling flexibility and
choice (Fogarty, 1980, 1982). Which view prevails
at any one time has been a matter of political
influence. Within a few months in 1983, France,
Belgium and Spain lowered the pension age, while
in Japan it was increased, and in the United
States legislation paved the way for financial
inducements to later retirement and of a two-stage
raising by 2027 of the statutory pensionable age
to 67.

All too frequently in modern times,
governments have adopted a brace of non-positive
attitudes to the old. Only a few regimes have
broken the rule that contemporary western
governments accept a final responsibility to
support financially the destitute elderly and to
provide health care, social services and
specialised or institutional accommodation for
those socially isolated persons who cannot live
independently. Humanitarian and collectivist
motives have reinforced each other to persuade
governments to elaborate and improve services
beyond an unavoidable minimum. These responsible
measures however, commonly coexist with a
perception of the majority of the elderly that is
overwhelmed by the pecuniary calculations of the
costs of their support. A large fraction of
government welfare expenditure is spent on the
income maintenance of elderly people, and the
costs of treatment and services for elderly people
dominate health spending (Clark and Spengler,

1980). It is these facts that lead administrators and ministers, particularly those with financial responsibilities, to describe the elderly as unproductive and a 'burden': a usage that rarely occurs in relation to children or to unwaged mothers.

These 'pathological' and 'economic-dependency' perceptions of the elderly combine to an unattractive and predominantly negative response to the ageing of western populations. While the last Labour government explored policy measures to encourage A Happier Old Age, largely through an expansion of specialised housing and social services, and the recent Conservative administrations have advocated self-reliance and community, effectively family, care; both positions have coexisted with the too common presentation of the ageing process as itself a problem, rather than as a magnificent biomedical and social achievement with attendant difficulties (Fogarty, 1982; GB Department of Health and Social Security, 1978, 1981; Tinker, 1981). One extreme manifestation of an expedient government response has been the recent dramatisation by the Reagan administration of the forecasts of social welfare and state medical costs for older people. The resulting concern has helped to diffuse opposition to the substantial trimming of these programmes (Estes, 1981; Estes et al., 1982; Neugarten, 1982; Rix and Fisher, 1982).

The last decade has seen a resurgence of interest in the political economy and macrosocietal conditioning of the situation of elderly people. Historical scholarship is investigating the neglected but instructive ideological and political background to the foundation and development of the western welfare states (Guillemard, 1980; Johnson and Laslett, 1984; Laslett, 1984; Quadagno, 1982; Stearns, 1977). British academic social administration has an enviable record of trenchant if atheoretical critiques of social policy and welfare practice, but recently it has adopted a more macrosocietal scale of analysis. Peter Townsend's work exemplifies the trend: from his early empirical studies of family life in working class districts and in residential institutions, he has progressed through an impressively detailed and comprehensive analysis of poverty in Britain (among which the elderly population features), to more historical and theoretical discussions of the elderly's present position (Townsend, 1957, 1962,

274

Geographical Locations and Social Relationships

1979, 1981; Townsend and Wedderburn, 1965). Other British social gerontologists and historians have enthusiastically and critically developed the structural scale of analysis and are producing notably stimulating and original contributions (Phillipson, 1982; Smith, 1984; Walker, 1980, 1981, 1983).

## Geographical contributions to gerontology

While a comparable sequence of approaches and scales of analysis has characterised social geography over the last quarter century, studies of specified population groups have given particular attention to the disadvantaged, the poor, ethnic minorities, women and criminals but not commonly featured the elderly (Jackson and Smith, 1984; Ley, 1983; Warnes, 1984). Too few geographers have worked in social gerontology for their work to replicate the serial methodological and philosophical changes of the social sciences. So far, only the surface has been explored of the geographical and spatial aspects of ageing and of the circumstances of the elderly: no particular approach has received sufficient attention from sufficient people to have been exhausted. Several literature reviews have recorded a large number of studies, either by geographers or of geographical questions, but collectively the research has been dominated by information gathering and organisation (Golant, 1984b; Rowles, 1986; Rudzitis, 1984; Warnes, 1981; Wiseman, 1978). Leading American social geographers have added a substantial attempt to elucidate behavioural and experiential facets of the relationships between elderly people and their urban and residential environments, while the few British scholars have adopted interests shared by their colleagues in social administration, taking up applied research in welfare policy and service delivery (Barnard, 1982; Bernard, 1985; Golant, 1984a; Peace et al, 1985; Pinch, 1980; Radford and Phillips, 1985; Rowles, 1978, 1984; Warnes and Law, 1985).

Several specific features of the human geography of the elderly have been extensively researched, including their distribution and the selectivity, patterns and motivations of their migrations. Other topics which have attracted

some attention include the elderly's housing
conditions and satisfactions, accessibility to
primary health care, accessibility to shops and
services and geographical aspects of the elderly's
family and social relationships. Encyclopaedic
bibliographies of this research have been provided
in the cited literature reviews and in the
excellent bimonthly New Literature on Old Age,
published by the Centre for Policy on Ageing,
which covers applied British work. This account
adopts a less bibliographically-led approach to
the current understanding of the contemporary
social geography of the elderly. There is space
only to examine the basic features of the
elderly's living circumstances and geographical
contexts.

Living arrangements, social integration and morale
One starting point for an examination of the
social situation of an older person is his or her
household or living arrangement. The societal
pattern of these is closely related to demographic
facts through nuptuality, the differential
longevity of the sexes and the twentieth-century
trends towards smaller families and a younger age
at which the last child is born. Twenty-seven per
cent of all women in England and Wales in 1981
were widows by age 65 years and a majority of 72.
Widowers did not outnumber married men until age
85 (GB, Office of Population Censuses and Surveys,
1983b. There have been substantial declines
during this century in the percentage of elderly
people who share a household with their children
or others, although the levels of co-residence
found in nineteenth century industrialising
nations may have exceeded those of pre-industrial
conditions (Table 8.4).

In western countries today an elderly person is
most likely to live either alone or with only their
spouse. There are variations among the developed
countries but in general no more than five per cent
live in institutions (Shanas et al., 1968; Wall,
1984). In 1976, 30 per cent of the non-institu-
tionalised population aged 65 or more years in
England lived alone, 44 per cent lived with their
spouse and no others, 6 per cent lived with their
spouse and others, and 3 per cent lived with
siblings only. Partly included in the third group
were the 13 per cent of the elderly who lived with
their children and or children's spouses      (Hunt,

Table 8.4 Historical comparisons of Household arrangements among persons aged 60 years or more in Europe and the United States of America

| Location | Date | Non-married persons | | | Married persons coresiding with: | | |
|---|---|---|---|---|---|---|---|
| | | Living alone | Coresiding with child | others | Spouse only | Spouse & child | Spouse & others |
| Graz, Austria | 1857 | 9 | 30 | 62 | 21 | 46 | 33 |
| Graz, Austria | 1900 | 6 | 43 | 52 | 15 | 52 | 33 |
| Vienna | 1963 | 57 | 25 | 18 | 75 | 20 | 5 |
| United States | 1880 | 9 | 64 | 27 | 25 | 57 | 17 |
| | 1900 | 11 | 64 | 24 | 29 | 58 | 13 |
| | 1962 | 48 | 34 | 18 | 79 | 17 | 4 |
| | 1975 | 66 | 17 | 16 | 84 | 12 | 6 |
| England | 1684-1796 | 21 | 54 | 25 | 44 | 49 | 7 |
| GB | 1962 | 43 | 37 | 19 | 68 | 28 | 4 |
| | 1980/81 | 71 | 17 | 12 | 83 | ----17---- | |

Source: Wall (1984) Table 4. For further details of the sources, sample sizes, definitions and estimates, Wall's paper should be consulted.

1978). The considerable variations by gender and by age-group should be noted, e.g. 50 per cent of women aged 85 or more years lived alone but only 14 per cent of men aged 65-74 years (Figure 8.3). Recent years have seen higher rates of the elderly living without others in 'minimal household units' as married couples or as single, divorced or widowed persons. The higher income and occupational groups of the elderly are least likely to live with others, attesting to the fact that most people prefer independent living arrangements (Ermisch and Overton, 1984).

Residential isolation cannot be directly equated with loneliness, although surveys do repeatedly establish its relationship with low morale, depression and even short life expectancy. 'Some isolates are happy, satisfied with their lives and feel far from lonely; and at the same time some of those leading highly gregarious lives are not immune from a sense of loneliness and depression' (Abrams, 1978, p. 38; 1982). When a sample of the elderly living in England was asked whether they agreed with seven statements describing loneliness, of those living alone, affirmative replies came from about a quarter of the respondents aged 65-74 years and from 30 per cent of those who were older. Among those living with others, only 11 per cent of the younger elderly and 12 per cent of the older agreed (Table 8.5).

The majority of the elderly in Britain lead localised lives. Whether this is an ageing effect of their reduced means, social roles and physical capacities, or whether it is a cohort effect arising from their comparatively low levels of education, youthful mobility and restricted previous geographical experience, is difficult to assess. One well established ageing effect is that car driving amongst elderly people is curtailed at night or to familiar routes, but it is also known that only a minority of the present female elderly cohorts have ever learnt to drive. The principal extramural activities for most elderly people are shopping and personal services trips, visits to relatives and friends, and trips to places of worship and to communal groups (Abrams, 1980; Daniels and Warnes, 1980; Hanson, 1977; Kutter, 1973; Little, 1984).

The social networks and social integration of elderly people have been major themes in social gerontology. Interest includes the similarities

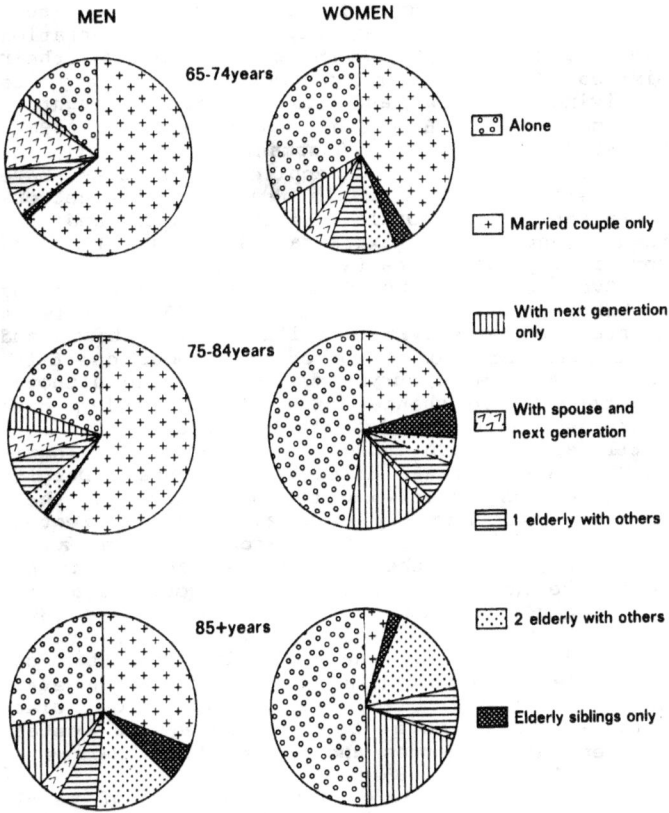

MEN          WOMEN

65-74years

Alone

Married couple only

With next generation only

75-84years

With spouse and next generation

1 elderly with others

2 elderly with others

85+years

Elderly siblings only

Source: Hunt (1976) Table 4.6.1 p.16

Figure 8.3  Living Arrangements of Elderly
People by Age and Sex, England 1976

and differences in attitudes and values between generations. Many studies have examined the situational family changes produced by declining fertility, earlier marriage, less extended childrearing and increasing life expectancy: such as the relative frequency of five-generation families or the prevalence among women in their sixties of dual caring responsibilities, e.g. to surviving mothers and to divorced daughters (Abrams, 1985; Bengtson and Robertson, 1985; Hagestad, 1981, 1985; Sussman, 1976; Troll and Bengtson, 1979). More applied approaches have considered the relationship between social network characteristics, morale, mental health and the requirements for extra-familial support and domiciliary facilities (Wenger, 1984).

Even among elderly married couples living without others in England in 1983, nearly a quarter had no surviving children in contact, and a further third only one child. About one-fifth had three or more surviving children, so although the demographic changes of the last century have increased the number of extant generations in many families, the norm among the ever-married elderly is for two or fewer direct descendants. Despite quite common assertions to the contrary, these children are normally proximate and in frequent contact. Although the phenomenon of living a few doors away, or in the same or next street, is now rare, the mutual accessibility of households from adjacent generations is high. Over a third (36%) of the retired married couples in our recent survey had at least one child living within one kilometre. The variation in proximity is however, considerable and there are strong social class effects which have been analysed in detail (Warnes, 1986; Warnes and Howes, 1984; Warnes et al., 1984, 1985a, 1985b).

In England in 1976, five per cent of people aged 65 or more years in private households had no relatives living with them; another five per cent were never visited by their relatives. One third received visits from relatives several times each week, and a majority were visited at least once a week. The elderly make visits less frequently, only a fifth visiting relatives at least once a week and nearly a quarter, including the bedfast and housebound, never visiting relatives. For well over half, their children were the most common visitors and the most frequently visited, and in both cases they were

Table 8.5  Residential isolation and loneliness, England 1976: percentage of survey respondents agreeing with statements describing loneliness

| Description of loneliness | Sex | 65-74 years | | 75+ years | |
|---|---|---|---|---|---|
| | | Living alone (%) | Others % | Living alone (%) | Others % |
| Never dreamed could .. be this lonely | m | 28 | 7 | 53 | 4 |
| | fm | 28 | 8 | 32 | 8 |
| Feel lonely and remote .. from others | m | 22 | 10 | 36 | 6 |
| | fm | 23 | 12 | 29 | 13 |
| Average over .. seven statements | m | 25 | 11 | 34 | 9 |
| | fm | 23 | 12 | 27 | 14 |

Source: Abrams (1978) Tables 52 and 54

followed in frequency by siblings, nephews or
nieces, and adult grandchildren. Increasing age
was found to change the relative pattern of
visits, siblings giving way to adult grandchildren
and nephews or nieces, but the variation in
association with marital status is greater, the
most distinctive group being the never-married who
maintain frequent contact with friends, siblings,
nephews and nieces (Hunt, 1978 95-100; Wenger,
1984). Hunt's survey also discovered that a
quarter of the elderly would like relatives to
visit more often: nearly two-thirds of this
group believed that the distance of separation was
the reason for the lowest frequency. Distance was
also cited as the reason by a quarter of those who
never visited their relatives.

Many survey reports include references to an
elderly person's location and distance from
friends and relatives as a factor in their social
contacts and integration. 'Proximity is a
necessary condition for the satisfaction of
instrumental and affective needs in later life,
but it is not a sufficient condition for effective
family support' (Swain, 1984). The inclusion of
an aged person in a kinship network is related to
both the geographical and the social distance
between the members. Simultaneously, culturally
prescribed attitudes, such as the norm of
intergenerational autonomy, a belief in public
responsibility and the importance of reciprocity,
can limit the nature and level of exchanges.
Personalities, the history of the social
relationship and other idiosyncracies are also
important. These factors have been extensively
studied in family sociology, but although the
strong influence of distance is frequently
recognised, relatively few analyses of any depth
have been undertaken (but see Adams, 1968;
Kerckhoff, 1965; Litwak, 1960; McAuley and Nutty,
1985). A realisation that the spatial influence
was being neglected, to the extent that improbable
generalisations were gaining currency within the
social sciences about the effects on family
dispersion and disintegration of growing
geographical mobility, led the author to undertake
a focused empirical study. This has corroborated
that there is significant suppression of visiting
frequencies and of social integration by
residential separation. In the sense that about a
fifth of elderly married couples with children
wish to live nearer to them, there is 'excess'

separation, but the unavailability of accommodation, the costs and difficulty of moving and
other ties all deter desired moves (Warnes, 1986;
Warnes et al., 1985a, 1985b). Surveys of the
elderly residents of new owner-occupied sheltered
and general housing have found similar expressions
of unsatisfactory location with respect to friends
and relatives (Fleiss, 1985).

Conclusions: social relationships and housing
location
The trend in affluent nations towards smaller
households suggests that extra-household social
relationships are of increasing importance in
life-satisfaction: if this is the case, the
spatial attributes of social networks will become
more critical. This assertion would not be
weakened by continuing improvements in personal
mobility or by increases in the characteristic
geographic extent of an elderly person's social
network. Indeed the further spread of
white-collar occupations, higher education, job
insecurity and serial monogamy are likely to
maintain the trend towards smaller households, so
long as real incomes continue to rise, and to
loosen the present localisation of families and to
increase the social implications of a person's
location. These possibilities direct attention to
the locational implications of present trends in
housing investment and policy.
     Since 1980 public sector housing investment in
Britain has been emasculated, bringing to a close
a twenty year expansion of small, specialised and
sheltered dwellings for the elderly. The Housing
Corporation continues to support the work of
specialist Housing Associations in providing
accommodation for the socially isolated and frail
elderly, and now encourages them to build for sale
(full or partial equity). The main thrust of
present policy with respect to housing for the
elderly is, however, to promote private sector
investment but, so far, the level of investment
has been too small, it has served mainly
relatively affluent owner-occupiers and has been
confined to the southern and prosperous urban
regions of the country (Age Concern Scotland,
1985; Butler et al., 1983; Ermisch, 1983; Warnes
and Law, 1905). By tolerating an inadequate scale
of new construction, conversion and improvement,
and by making no attempt to ensure the widespread
availability of small dwellings, too little is

being done to assist the elderly to adjust their housing to their changing requirements and reducing means, and to relocate to more convenient and socially promising locations. Official policies towards the elderly, too often dominated by the pathological and dependency models, are not adopting a positive approach to either the promotion of satisfactory social relationships and roles in third age, or to the morale of our increasingly healthy, active and educated elderly population.

One valuable result of the wider participation of social geography in the study of ageing processes and of the circumstances of the elderly is likely to be a fuller understanding of the impacts of occupational, marital and reproductive changes on individual and household transitions through the lifespan. This would result if geographical studies add to their present strength in particular fields, such as residential mobility, migration and environmental relationships, an increased and evaluative interest in the social relationships and the dominant activities of people at different ages and particularly in their later years. Our attention will rightly continue to be given to the most disadvantaged and impoverished elderly people, but there are also applied social welfare, as well as academic, reasons for a concerted effort to elucidate normal ageing.

If, in western situations, social geography's approach to gerontological questions would benefit from the adoption of larger and smaller scales of analysis, the same recommendation would be underlined as part of a call for a less ethnocentric presentation of the geographical and social implications of demographic ageing. The final word must be to reiterate that the poverty, ill-health, social isolation and emotional deprivation of millions of elderly people in several less developed world regions is the overwhelming feature in a global assessment of the situation of the elderly. Given the probability that rapid ageing will take place in some of these regions in a quickly changing social environment, a valuable response from geographers would be to initiate detailed and careful studies of the situation of elderly people in a wide selection of diverse urban, rural, cultural and economic settings. It may be possible to play a small part in raising the consciousness of governments, and of those with political influence and economic power, about the implications of ageing, and thereby to accelerate the vital development of programmes of education, pensions legislation and development, housing, medical facilities and social services.

## Acknowledgements
Research studies which have formed the background to this paper have been funded by the Economic and Social Research Council and the Irwin Fund of the University of London. I am most grateful to Clare Peppercorn and to Roma Beaumont and Gordon Reynell for their excellent secretarial and cartographic help.

## REFERENCES

Abrams, M. (1978) <u>Beyond Three-Score and Ten: A First Report on a Survey of the Elderly</u>, Age Concern England, Mitcham, Surrey.

Abrams, M. (1980) <u>Beyond Three-Score and Ten: A Second Report on a Survey of the Elderly</u>, Age Concern England, Mitcham, Surrey.

Abrams, M. (1982) <u>People in Their Late Sixties: A Longitudinal Survey of Ageing: 1, Survivors and Non-Survivors</u>, Age Concern England, Mitcham, Surrey.

Abrams, M. (ed.) (1985) <u>Social Change and Social Values</u>, Macmillan, London.

Abrams, B.N. (1968) <u>Kinship in an Urban Setting</u>, Markham, Chicago.

Adebagbo, S.A. (1978) 'Institutional care of the aged: a study of a Lagos City institution for the aged', <u>Nigerian Behavioural Sc. Jl.</u> 1, 150-161.

Adeokun, L.A. (1982) 'Demographic determinants of intra-family support for the aged in Nigeria'. Paper presented at the 10th International Conference on Social Gerontology, Deauville, France, 25th-29th May.

Adeokun, L.A. (1984) <u>The Elderly in Nigeria</u>, Centre International de Gerontologie Sociale, Paris. (in English and French)

Age Concern Scotland (1985) <u>Housing Facts and Figures</u>, Age Concern Scotland, Edinburgh.

Barnard, K.C. (1982) 'Retirement housing in the United Kingdom: a geographical appraisal', in Warnes, A.M., <u>Geographical Perspectives on the Elderly</u>, Wiley, Chichester, pp. 161-90.

Beattie, W.M. (1978) 'Aging: a framework of characteristics and considerations for cooperative efforts between the developing and developed regions of the world', Expert Group Meeting on Aging, United Nations, New York, 3-5 April.

Bengtson, V.L. and Robertson, J.(eds) (1985) <u>Grandparenthood: Research and Policy Perspectives</u>, Sage, New York.

Benjamin, B. and Overton, E. (1981) 'Prospects for mortality decline in England and Wales', <u>Pop. Trends</u> 23, 22-28.

Bernard, M. (ed.) (1985) <u>Leisure in Later Life: Examples of Community Based Initiatives</u>, Beth Johnson Foundation, Stoke on Trent.

Binstock, R.H., Chow, W.S. and Schulz, J.H. (eds.) (1982) <u>International Perspectives on Aging: Population and Policy Changes</u>, United Nations

Fund for Population Activities, New York.

Brody, J.A. (1985) 'Prospects for an ageing population', Nature 315, 463-466.

Butler, A., Oldman, C. and Greve, J. (1983) Sheltered Housing for the Elderly Allen & Unwin, London.

Clark, R.L. and Spengler, J.J. (1980) The Economics of Individual and Population Ageing, Cambridge University Press, Cambridge.

Coale, A.J. and Demeny, P. (1966) Regional Life Tables and Stable Populations Princeton University Press, Princeton.

Craig, J. (1983) The growth of the elderly population', Pop. Trends 32, 28-33.

de Beauvoir, S. (1970) La Vieillesse, Gallimard, Paris.(1972) English translation Old Age, Andre Deutsch, London.

Daniels, P.W. and Warnes, A.M. 1980) Movement in Cities, Methuen, London.

Denton, C.F. (1981) The Elderly of Costa Rica and Central America, Centre International de Gerontologie Sociale, Paris. (in English and French).

Ermisch, J. (1983) The Political Economy of Demographic Change, Heinemann, London.

Ermisch, J. and Overton, E. (1985) 'Minimal household units: a new approach to the analysis of household formation', Population Studies, 39, 33-54.

Estes, C.L. (1981) Political Economy, Health and Ageing, Winthrop. Cambridge, Mass.

Estes, C.L., Swan, J.H. and Gerard, L.E. (1982) 'Dominant and competing paradigms in gerontology: towards a political economy of ageing', Ageing and Society 2, 151-63.

Fleiss, A. (1985) Home Ownership Alternatives for the Elderly, Her Majesty's Stationery Office, London.

Fogarty, M.P. (1980) Retirement Age and Retirement Costs, Policy Studies Institute, London.

Fogarty, M.P. (ed) (1982) Retirement Policy: The Next Fifty Years, Heinemann, London.

Fries, J.F. (1980) 'Aging, natural death and the compression of morbidity', New England J. Med. 303, 130-35.

Golant, S.M. (1984a) A Place to Grow Old: The Meaning of Environment in Old Age, Columbia University Press, New York.

Golant, S.M. (1984b) 'The geographic literature on aging and old age: an introduction', Urban Geography, 5, 262-72.

Goody, J. (1976) 'Aging in non-industrial societies', in Binstock, R. and Shanas, E. (eds.) Handbook of Aging and the Social Sciences, Van Nostrand Reinhold, New York.

Gracia, M. (1985) 'Research findings in Cameroon: older persons in villages in the district of Dibombari', African Gerontology No. 3, 25-40.

Great Britain, Department of Health and Social Security (DHSS) (1978) A Happier Old Age: A Discussion Document on Elderly People in Our Society, Her Majesty's Stationery Office (HMSO), London.

GB, DHSS (1981) Growing Older, HMSO, London (Cmnd 8173).

GB, Government Statistical Service (1985) 1981-Based Household Projections 1981-2001. HMSO, London.

GB, Office of Population Censuses and Surveys (OPCS) (1983) Census of England and Wales, 1981: Persons of Pensionable Age, HMSO, London.

GB, OPCS (1984a) Population Projections 1981-2021, HMSO, London.

GB, OPCS (1984b) Population Projections: Area, 1981-2001, HMSO, London.

Guillemard, A.M. (1980) Old Age and the State, Presses Universitaires de France, Paris.

Hagestad, G.O. (1981) 'Problems and promises in the social psychology of intergenerational relations, in Fogel, R., Hatfield, E., Kiesler, S.B. and Shanas, E. (eds.) Aging: Stability and Change in the Family, Academic Press, New York.

Hagestad, G. O. (1985) 'Continuity and connectedness', in Bengtson, V.L. and Robertson, J. (eds.) Grandparenthood: Research and Policy Perspectives, Sage, New York.

Hampson, J. (1985) 'Elderly people and social welfare in Zimbabwe'. Ageing and Society 5, 39-68.

Hanson, P. (1977) 'The activity patterns of elderly households', Geografiska Annaler, 59B, 109-25.

Hauser, P.M. (1976) 'Aging and worldwide population change', in R.H. Binstock and E. Shanas (eds.) Handbook of Aging and the Social Sciences, Van Nostrand Reinhold, New York, pp. 58-86.

Hunt, A. (1978) The Elderly at Home: A Study of People Aged 65 and Over Living in the Community, Her Majesty's Stationery Office, London.

International Center of Social Gerontology, Paris (1985) Recommendations Adopted by the African Conference on Gerontology, Dakar, 10-14

December 1984m ICSG, Paris (ISBN 2-901653-13-8)
International Program of Laboratories for Popula-
tion Studies (1980) The 1979 Mexico National
Fertility and Mortality Survey: A Summary of
Results, IPLPS, Chapel Hill, North Carolina.
Jackson, P. and Smith, S.J. (1984) Exploring Social
Geography, Allen & Unwin, 1984.
Japan, Institute for Gerontological Research (1978)
Ageing in Japan, Institute for Gerontological
Research, Tokyo.
Johnson, M.L. (1982) 'The implications of greater
activity in later life', in Fogarty, M.P.
(ed.) Retirement Policy, Heinemann, London,
pp. 138-56.
Johnson, M.L. and Laslett, P. (eds.) (1984) History
and Ageing, special issue, Ageing and Society
4, 379-524.
Kerckhoff, A.C. (1965) 'Nuclear and extended family
relationships: normative and behavioral
analysis', in Shanas, E. and Streib, G. (eds.)
Social Structure and the Family: Generational
Relations, Prentice-Hall, Englewood Cliffs,
New Jersey.
Kutter, E. (1973) 'A model for individual travel
behaviour', Urban Studies 10, 235-58.
Laslett, P. (1984) 'The significance of the past in
the study of ageing', Ageing and Society, 4,
379-89.
Ley, D. (1983) A Social Geography of the City,
Harper & Row, New York.
Little, V.C. (1984) 'An overview of research using
the time budget methodology to study ageing
behaviour', Ageing and Society, 4, 3-20.
Litwak, E. (1960) 'Geographic mobility and extended
family cohesion', Am. Sociol. Rev. 25, 385-94.
Manton, K.G. (1982) 'Changing concepts of morbidity
and mortality in the elderly population',
Milbank Memorial Fund Quarterly, 60, 183-244.
McAuley, W.J. and Nutty, C.L. (1985) 'Residential
satisfaction, community integration and risk
across the family life cycle', J. Marriage
and the Family, 47, 125-30.
Meegama, S.A (1982) 'Aging in developing countries'
World Health Statistics Quarterly 35, 239-245.
Myers, G.C. (1978) 'Cross-national trends in mortality rates among the elderly', The Gerontologist, 18, 441-48.
Myers, G.C. (1982) 'Demographic and socio-economic
aspects of population ageing', Paper presented
to the CICRED Conference, Montreal, 4-7
October.

Myers, G.C. (1983) 'Mortality declines, life exten-
    sion and population aging', International
    Population Conference, Manila, 1981, volume 4,
    International Union for the Scientific Study
    of Population, Liege.
Myers, G.C. (1985) 'Aging and world-wide population
    change', in Binstock, R. and Shanas, E. (eds.)
    Handbook on Aging and the Social Sciences, 2nd
    edtn, Van Nostrand, New York.
Myers, G.C. and Manton, K.G. (1985a) 'Morbidity,
    disability and mortality: the aging
    connection', In Gaitz, C.M., Niederehe, G. and
    Wilson, N.L. (eds.) Aging 2000: Our Health
    Care Destiny, volume 2, Springer-Verlag, New
    York, pp. 25-39.
Myers, G.C. and Manton, K.G. (1985b) 'The rate of
    population aging: new views of epidemiological
    transitions',. Paper presented at the XIIIth
    International Congress of Gerontology, New
    York.
Neugarten, B.L. (ed.) (1982) Age or Need? Public
    Policies for Older People, Sage, Beverly
    Hills, California.
Neysmith, S.M. and Edwardh, J. (1984) 'Economic
    dependency in the 1980s: its impact on third
    world elderly', Ageing and Society 4, 21-44.
Odekunle, F.F. (1978) 'Nigeria's social welfare
    services: past, present and future', Nigerian
    Behavioural Sc. Jl. 1, 174-93.
Olusanya, P.O. (1975) 'Population growth and its
    components: the nature and direction of
    population change'. In J.C. Caldwell et al.
    (eds.) Population Growth and Socio-Economic
    Changes in West Africa, Columbia University
    Press, New York, pp. 251-274.
Palmore, E. (1975) The Honorable Elders: a Cross-
    Cultural Analysis of Aging in Japan, Duke
    University Press, Durham, North Carolina.
Peace, S.M., Willcocks, D.M. and Kellaher, L.A.
    (1985) Living in Homes: A Consumer View of
    Residential Alternatives, British Association
    for Service to the Elderly, Keele,
    Staffordshire.
Phillipson, C.R. (1982) Capitalism and the Con-
    struction of Old Age, Macmillan, London.
Pinch, S.P. (1980) 'Local authority provision for
    the elderly: an overview and case study of
    London', in Herbert, D.T. and Johnston, R.J.
    (eds.) Geography and the Urban Environment,
    Vol. 3, Wiley, Chichester, pp. 295-344.

Quadagno, J. (1982) Ageing in Early Industrial Society: Work, Family and Social Policy in Nineteenth Century England, Academic Press, London.

Radford, J.P. and Phillips, D.R. (1985) 'Closure of major institutions for the mentally handicapped: geographical evidence from a case study in south west England', South West Papers in Geography, 10, The University, Exeter.

Rix, S.E. and Fisher, P. (1982) Retirement Age Policy: An International Perspective, Pergamon, New York.

Rowland, D.T. (1984) 'Old age and the demographic transition', Pop. Studs 38, 73-87.

Rowles, G.D. (1978) Prisoners of Space? Exploring the Geographical Experience of Older People, Westview, Boulder, Colorado.

Rowles, G.D. (1984) 'Aging in rural environments', in Altman, I., Wohlwill, J. and Lawton, M.P. (eds.) Human Behaviour and Environment: The Elderly and the Physical Environment, Plenum, New York, pp. 129-52.

Rowles, G.D. (1986) 'The geography of ageing and the aged: toward an integrated perspective', Progress in Human Geography 10, forthcoming.

Rudzitis, G. (1984) 'Geographical research and gerontology: an overview', The Gerontologist, 24, 536-42.

Shanas, E., Townsend, P., Wedderburn, D., Friis, H., Milhoj, P. and Stehower, J. (1968) Old People in Three Industrial Societies, Atherton, New York.

Siegel, J.S. (1980) 'On the demography of ageing', Demography 17, 345-64.

Smith, R.M. (1984) 'The structured dependence of the elderly as a recent development: some sceptical historical thoughts', Ageing and Society 4, 409-28.

Spengler, J.J. (1974) Population Change, Modernisation and Welfare, Prentice-Hall, Englewood Cliffs, New Jersey.

Stearns, P.N. (1977) Old Age in European Society, Croom Helm, London.

Sussman, S.B. (1976) 'The family life of old people', in Binstock, R. and Shanas, E. (eds.) Handbook of Aging and the Social Services, Van Nostrand, New York.

Geographical Locations and Social Relationships

Swain, C. (1981) Family roles and support, in Howe, A.L. (ed.) Towards an Older Australia, University of Queensland Press, St Lucia, Queensland, pp. 205-20.

Synak, B. and Taylor, R.C. (1984) The current state of social gerontology in Poland. Ageing and Society 4, 219-28.

Szwarc, H. (1983) The Elderly in Poland, Centre International de Gerontologie Sociale, Paris, (in English and French).

Tapio Videal, J. and Parrish, C.J. (1982) Ageing, development and social service delivery systems in Latin America: problems and perspectives. Ageing and Society 2, 31-56.

Tinker, A. (1981) The Elderly in Modern Society, Longman, London.

Townsend, P. (1957) The Family Life of Old People, Routledge & Kegan Paul, London.

Townsend, P. (1962) The Last Refuge, Routledge & Kegan Paul, London.

Townsend, P. (1979) Poverty in the United Kingdom, Penguin, Harmondsworth, Middlesex.

Townsend, P. (1981) The structured dependency of the elderly: a creation of social policy in the twentieth century. Ageing and Society 1, 5-28.

Townsend, P. and Wedderburn, D. (1965) The Aged in the Welfare State, Bell, London.

Troll, L.E. and Bengtson, V.L. (1979) Generations in the family, in Burr, W.R., Hill, R., Nye, F.I. and Reiss, I.L. (eds.) Contemporary Theories About the Family, Free Press, New York.

United Nations Organisation, Department of International Economic and and Social Affairs (1985) Periodical on Aging No. 1 1984, UNO, New York.

United States of America, Bureau of the Census (1977) 1976 Base Population Projections of the United States:Current Population Reports, Series P-25, No. 704, Government Printing Office, Washington D.C.

Walker, A. (1980) The social creation of poverty and dependency in old age. J. Social Policy 9, 49-75.

Walker, A. (1981) Towards a political economy of old age. Ageing and Society 1, 73-94.

Walker, A. (1983) The social production of old age. Ageing and Society 3, 387-95.

Wall, R. (1984) Residential isolation of the elderly: a comparison over time. Ageing and Society 4, 483-503.

Warnes, A.M. (1981) Towards a geographical contribution to gerontology. Progress in Human Geography 5, 107-48.

Warnes, A.M. (ed.) (1982) Geographical Perspectives on the Elderly, Wiley, Chichester.

Warnes, A.M. (1983) Migration in late working age and early retirement. Socio-Economic Planning Sciences, 17, 291-302.

Warnes, A.M. (1984) Places and people: reflections on their study in social geography. GeoJournal, 9, 261-71.

Warnes, A.M. (1986) Microlocational issues in housing for the elderly, in Maddox, G.L. and Busse, E.W. (eds.) Proceedings of the XIII International Association of Gerontology Congress, Springer, New York, forthcoming.

Warnes, A.M. and Howes, D.R. (1984) A social survey of retired married couples and their family units. Department of Geography, King's College London. Occasional Paper, 20.

Warnes, A.M., Howes, D.R. and Took, L. (1984) Residential separation and visiting between retired parents and their sons and daughters, in Bromley, D.B. (ed.) Gerontology: Social and Behavioural Perspectives, Croom Helm, Beckenham, pp. 213-219.

Warnes, A.M., Howes, D.R. and Took, L. (1985a) Residential locations and inter-generational visiting in retirement. Quarterly Journal of Social Affairs, 1, 231-247.

Warnes, A.M., Howes, D.R., and Took, L. (1985b) Intimacy at a distance under the microscope, in Cutler, A. (ed.), Ageing: Recent Advances and Creative Responses, Croom Helm, Beckenham, pp. 98-112.

Warnes, A.M. and Law, C.M. (1980) The characteristics of retirement migrants, in Johnston, R.J. and Herbert, D.T. Geography and the Urban Environment Vol. III, Wiley, Chichester, pp. 175-222.

Warnes, A.M. and Law, C.M. (1982) The destination decision in retirement migration, in Warnes, A.M. (ed.) Geographical Perspectives on the Elderly, Wiley, Chichester, pp. 53-81.

Warnes, A.M. and Law, C.M. (1984) The elderly population of Great Britain: locational trends and policy implications. Trans. Inst. Brit. Geogr. N.S. 9, 37-59.

Warnes, A.M. and Law, C.M. (1985) 'Elderly popula-
    tion distributions and housing prospects in
    Britain: a review', Tn. Plann. Rev. 56,
    292-314.
Wenger, C.G. (1984) The Supportive Network, Allen &
    Unwin, London.
Wiseman, R.F. (1978) Spatial Aspects of Aging,
    Resource Paper 78-4, Association of American
    Geographers, Washington D.C.

Chapter Nine

THE FEMINIST CHALLENGE TO SOCIAL GEOGRAPHY

S. R. BOWLBY AND L. McDOWELL

## Introduction

The late 1960s and early 1970s saw the emergence
of many of the current approaches to social
geography. The development of these approaches
arose from the debate within geography about the
relationship between academic work, public
policies and personal political beliefs. This
'relevance' debate within geography reflected
wider social and political changes in Europe and
North America – in particular, the growth of
'radical' protest movements around such issues as
the Vietnam war, environmental damage and
pollution and critiques of the materialistic
values of capitalist society (Johnston, 1979).
These social and political changes also included
the resurgence of feminist politics after three
decades of quiescence, and the re-establishment
of the Women's Movement. During the 1970s,
questions about women's inequality were both put
on the political agenda and debated within many
academic disciplines. In this chapter we examine
the impact of feminist ideas and practice on
social geography since 1970 and suggest ways in
which future developments in the subject could
draw on and contribute to feminist analyses. In
particular, we argue that feminism challenges the
very definition of what is 'social' about social
geography.
In this introductory section we briefly
describe some features of the early development
of the current Women's Movement, and then
consider the emergence of new approaches within
social geography in the late 1960s and early
1970s.

The Feminist Challenge to Social Geography

The growth of the Women's Movement. There are a
number of reasons for the re-emergence of feminism
as a significant social and political force in
Europe, North America and Australia in the late
1960s (Wilson, 1980; Bouchier, 1983; Banks, 1981),
but one of the most important was the rapid
increase in the number of women in the labour
market. But although women's share of the
workforce in these countries rose rapidly between
1950 and 1970 their share of well paid jobs and of
career opportunities hardly increased at all. Most
women worked in a restricted range of poorly paid,
semi-skilled manual or service occupations, with
a high proportion in part-time work (Coote &
Kellner, 1980; West, 1980; Joseph, 1983). This
inequality between women and men in the workplace
led to industrial action and political pressure
for equal pay and employment opportunities from
both working- and middle-class women in a number
of advanced capitalist countries during the late
1960s and early 1970s.
    A second important influence on the growth of
the Women's Movement was the experience of
married women workers. One of the most striking
features of the increase in women's participation
in waged work was the increase in the numbers of
married women in the workforce. To use the
example of Britain, in 1950 only 38% of women in
the labour force were married, by 1970 the figure
was 63%. Some of these women began to relate
their inequality in the workplace to their
inequality within the home.
    There was, however, a further important
ingredient in the development of the Women's
Movement: the growing anger of women who worked
actively in the new left-wing politics in both
North America and Europe. These women found
themselves being used by their male 'comrades'
only as "secretaries, tea-makers and sexual
partners" (Bouchier, 1983, p. 52). The concern
of the male-dominated left with imperialism,
racism and the alienating charcter of industrial
capitalism did not extend to issues of sexism,
which was treated as at best irrelevant and at
worst laughable. As a result women began to
organise independently. In Britain, the first
national meeting of groups involved in the Women's
Movement took place in 1970 and formulated four
demands: equal pay for equal work; equal
opportunities and education; free contraception
and abortion on demand; free 24-hour child-care.

# The Feminist Challenge to Social Geography

Associated with the formulation of these political demands was a growing body of empirical and theoretical analyses. These sought to explain the origins and maintenance of women's inequality and oppression. Although many different strands of intellectual and political thought were represented in these analyses, they all emphasised, first, the need to recognise and respect women's experience and to accord women's understanding and conceptions of the world as much social importance as those of men. Secondly, they suggested that the differences between men and women are socially constructed rather than biologically determined. Thirdly, they argued that male sexual, economic and ideological power and dominance within the family – and the consequent unequal division of child care and domestic work responsibilities between men and women – were central to an understanding of women's unequal position in society. Fourthly, they argued that women's inferior position in the labour market was also crucial to women's continued position of dependence within the family and to their lack of social power. Thus these analyses stressed both the links between social relations in the home and in the workplace and the significance of ideological as well as physical and economic power.

Within these broad areas of agreement there were major differences between liberal, socialist and radical feminists over what they identified as the principal 'cause' of women's subordination and over strategies for achieving gender equality. While liberals emphasised reform of existing institutions to give equality of opportunity, socialist feminists emphasised the need to integrate feminist struggles with those against capitalism, and radical feminists stressed the necessity of challenging male power in both the public and the private spheres. Radical feminists have, perhaps, laid more emphasis on the need to explore women's own experiences and subjectivity than have liberal or socialist feminists. However, all agree that 'the personal is political', that personal relationships and encounters are part of political struggle. (Further details of contrasting feminist ideas and literature are available in WGSG, 1984; Bouchier, 1983; Oakley, 1972, 1981.)

Some parallels and contrasts can be drawn between these differing approaches and those developed during the same period in other areas of

297

social analysis and political practice. In
particular, as we shall point out, the contrast
between liberal and socialist feminist analyses
has many similarities to the contrast between, on
the one hand, the 'welfare' and neo-Weberian
approaches to social geography, and on the other,
political economy approaches. There are also
points of contact between the approaches (although
not the content) of some radical feminists and of
humanistic geographers.

Changes in social geography. As we have already
mentioned, the late 1960s saw the start of rapid
changes within geography in general, and in social
geography in particular. One of the first
pressures for changes was a reaction to what was
seen as an over-emphasis in geography on abstract
spatial processes and the search for regularities
in spatial distributions. There was a feeling
that 'people' should be put back into geography.
In the 1960s this reaction led to the early
'behavioural' approach which stressed the
importance of the individual, and of individual
cognition, perception and choice (Cox & Golledge,
1969; Gould and White, 1974). This initial
concern with individual behaviour led, for some,
into work in the time-space geography of the Lund
school (Hagerstrand, 1967; Pred, 1981). Others
reacted to the concentration of the early
behavioural approach on individuals and on overt
behaviour by turning to the cultural and
historical tradition in geography and the
philosophies of phenomenology and existentialism,
to develop the humanistic approach to geography
(Relph, 1970, 1977; Ley, 1977, 1978, 1981; Ley and
Samuels, 1977). Workers in this humanistic school
have stressed the importance of understanding
people's lived experiences, the subjective
meanings of places and the nature of socially
shared cultural and symbolic systems.
These developments in humanistic geography
were attempts to challenge what was seen as the
narrow scientism and materialism of earlier
approaches in geography. A rather different
reaction was the development of welfare geography
(Smith, 1974; 1977). Geographers, reflecting the
general social mood, became increasingly concerned
with problems of inequality. In the general field
of social geography this led to a variety of
studies of spatial variations in social well-being
and social conflicts over spatial externalities

## The Feminist Challenge to Social Geography

(Smith, 1973; Knox, 1975; Cox, 1973; Harvey, 1971; Coates & Rawstron, 1971; Morrill and Wohlenberg, 1971).

A second popular approach, deriving from Weberian theory, emphasised the <u>constraints</u> on individual choice and a view of society as made up of conflicting groups defined in terms of their 'market situation' in relation to scarce urban resources (Eyles, 1974; Pahl, 1969; 1970a; 1970b; 1975). Thus, the work in both the welfare geography tradition and the neo-Weberian, conflict/constraint school emphasised the need to examine the differential 'market capacity' of social groups and the distributional impacts of changes in the built environment and in the location of social facilities. Their policy implications were essentially reformist, emphasising the need for redistributive action and bureaucratic reform to create equality of access.

An alternative reaction to the concern with 'relevance' and with social inequality was the development of analyses drawing on the Marxist tradition (Harvey, 1973). This development followed changes within other disciplines, particularly in sociology and political science. These analyses emphasised the fundamental opposition of interests and of power between capital and labour and the need for radical change in the organisation of society. Within the field of social geography, one major focus of Marxist work has been the process of capital accumulation in relation to housing (Harvey and Chatterjee 1974; Broadbent, 1975; Scott, 1976; Ball, 1978). A second major focus, deriving from the work of Castells, has been 'community'-based struggles over 'collective consumption' (Castells, 1977, 1978). A particularly important aspect of this Marxist work from the point of view of social geographers has been its emphasis on the fundamental importance of relations of production. This led to a questioning amongst social geographers of the accepted separation of the 'social' from the 'economic' and to arguments for integrating analyses of production with those of distribution (Asheim, 1979; Duncan, 1979): arguments which, as we shall show in the next section have been greatly strengthened by developments within feminist thought.

Our brief sketch of the different approaches to social geography that developed during the 1970s should have indicated that two concepts that came to prominence and around which arguments were focused were those of 'inequality of opportunity' and of 'power relations within society'. Two other important areas for debate were, first, the role and significance of experiential accounts of human action and, second, the relationship between the 'economic' and the 'social', between the realm of 'production' and the realm of 'consumption'. The debates over these issues continue today and are by no means resolved. As we have suggested above, these were also issues of central concern to the Women's Movement.

We may ask therefore, first, how far has work carried out in social geography within these various 'schools' of thought over the past 15 years been influenced by or contributed to an understanding of women's inequality and lack of power? Secondly, we may ask what potential contribution have feminism and social geography to make to one another? We will now examine each of these questions in turn.

Representing Women

As we have emphasised, the social changes in the sixties outlined in the last section had a marked impact on geography – both on the scope of the subject, leading to new definitions of what were appropriate areas of study for geographers, and also on the theoretical development of the discipline. The scope of the subject was influenced by one of the major demands of the Women's Movement – that women's experience should be recognised, as distinct from men's, and that the invisibility of women in much public discourse should be challenged. This began to influence geography from the beginning of the seventies (see McDowell, 1983, for a review of some of the resulting work in urban and regional studies).

At first, it was the perceived disjunction between the everyday experiences of women and the few representations of women's lives offered by the geographic literature that provided the impetus for unearthing, describing and 'adding in' specifically female experiences to conventional geographic analysis. An enormous number of studies now exist carried out by researchers of different theoretical persuasions, working in a variety of areas of social geography, that focus on women, both as individuals and in groups. Among these there are included studies of shopping behaviour, of access to facilities such as health

## The Feminist Challenge to Social Geography

and childcare provision, of women in the suburbs, women in city centres, of single women, elderly women, black women, women as mothers, women as workers, women in the home and in the community, of women as activists or designers, as criminals and as victims of crime. Many of these studies are North American, perhaps since in the U.S.A. there was more public, governmental emphasis on the need for equal opportunities for women and on women as a 'problem' group. In most of this work, however, women tend simply to be substituted for men or for households as the object of study and their behaviour and attitudes are analysed in conventional geographic ways.

An assumption that informs the majority of these studies is that women's activities are based in the home, since their main roles are those of wives and mothers or, slightly less commonly, that women perform the dual role of wage earner and home maker. It was not until later in the decade that these assumptions were subjected to more rigorous analysis and the idea that distinct gender roles could be described was replaced by work that examined how gender relations produced such gender roles.

By gender relations we mean the system of social relations between men and women that leads to and reflects the subordination of women. These gender relations relate to the social organisation and interpretation of biological reproduction and sexual differences. The latter are often represented as having necessary or 'natural' social effects (for example, the view that because women bear children they cannot be the equal of men at work). However, feminists argue that biological differences between men and women do not determine their social roles and use the term 'gender' to refer to the socially created distinctions between them. They argue that these distinctions are created through gender relations which are relations of power of men over women. One of the aims of feminist theory is to analyse the maintenance and various sources of this power. It is important to stress that although the representation of gender characteristics as derived from the biological nature of men and women is 'ideological' to the extent that gender differences do not have a real basis in reproduction, this does not mean that general divisions do not have 'real' material effects and involve 'real' material practices (Anthias and Yuval Davis, 1983).

301

# The Feminist Challenge to Social Geography

The substitution of the idea of roles by relations has led to a clearer understanding of the underlying structures of women's oppression and a shift away from description towards theorisation in the geographic literature. But we are getting ahead of ourselves. The changes that have occurred in the last decade and a half are of major importance and deserve outlining in greater detail. We therefore will now examine how far and why women have been 'added in' to different types of social geographic study.

In behavioural and humanistic geography, despite the parallel emphasis in this tradition and in feminism on individual behaviour and subjective experience, women's behaviour and beliefs have seldom been examined. Women have occasionally been the objects of analyses but the specificity of their views, and the reasons for differences between men's and women's images and behaviour have not been explored or questioned (see Gold, 1980 and Ley, 1983 for good summaries of work undertaken from the behaviour and humanistic perspective). One feature of this perspective that must be emphasised is the way in which an opposition between the public world of the city, and the communities within it, between the worlds of work, community and politics, and the private world of the home is accepted without challenge. The assumption is then made that only the former spheres are part of the discourse of geography. Moreover, they are seen as the worlds of men. By implication, women are limited to the world of the home and excluded from study. Even if it were accepted that this distinction between men's and women's worlds approximated to reality at a particular moment, we would argue that the reasons for this should have been examined and arguments for excluding the home from geographic study put forward. However, we consider that social and spatial relations based in the home cannot be kept separate and distinct from those in the community and the workplace. Indeed, we would agree with Saunders and Williams (1986), that much of what goes on in the home is hardly 'private' but strongly influenced by 'public' institutions and relations.

Work in the neo-Weberian and welfare tradition has focused more directly on women, if only because women were often the key users of the resources and services whose allocation was under consideration. Thus a sizeable literature has

302

grown and expanded over the last fifteen years documenting in many towns, cities and rural areas, the difficulties facing women in gaining access to scarce gods and resources. Excellent summaries of this work, a great deal of it North American, can be found in Monk and Hanson (1982), Zelinsky, Hanson and Monk (1982) and, with specific reference to urban areas, in the special issue of Sociological Focus edited by Van Vliet (1984). However, there remains a problem with many of these studies; while they convincingly demonstrate and document the difficulties women face in gaining access to facilities, most of them fail to integrate an analysis of the source of women's inequality with their study of its effects.

There is a strand of the welfare – constraint type approach that was more aware of the importance of women's generally socially inferior position as a key explanatory variable of the differences between women's and men's behaviour. This work drew on the ideas of space–time constraints developed by the Swedish geographer, Hagerstrand, to suggest that women's social roles were a key constraint on their spatial behaviour. Thus Tivers (1978) argued that gender role ideology, the ascription of particular tasks and activities to women or to men, is a structural constraint on spatial behaviour. In North America, Palm and Pred (1978) adopted a similar approach to show how women with domestic and childcare responsibilities face space and time constraints that tend to limit their activities to a narrow spatial sphere. In the British context, Pickup (1984) has demonstrated the importance of these 'gender role constraints' on women's access to employment.

During the late seventies and early eighties, both in urban geography and in feminist analyses of women in the labour market, arguments were being developed that began to meet some of our criticisms and tok challenge conventional academic divisions between home and 'work', between repro- duction and production. In urban geography, as we suggested earlier, the reorientation of the subject towards the analysis of the structure of collective consumption created a new overlap with social geography. However, yet again goods and services provided in the home, in the main by women, were defined out of the analysis. Geographers, in common with other social scientists, ignored the links between domestic servicing and collective provision as an area for academic debate despite their own experience of such interpenetration in their everyday lives. Yet for an increasing number of households in Britain today, the decline in collective provision and an increasing reliance on the family to provide essential 'social' services is creating all kinds of problems in the home. Thus the recession, high rates of unemployment and increasing costs in state expenditure throughout the eighties are making the area of women's domestic labour harder to ignore.

Feminists, however, have not ignored domestic work. Feminist economists argued that despite definitions of 'the economy' that exclude the activities that dominate many women's lives – cooking, shopping, cleaning, child care – these activities are essential to the operation of the capitalist economy and cannot be left out of account. Feminist analyses of the integration of women into waged work, for example, started from the perspective of women's domestic roles and family obligations. Women's oppression in the patriarchal family was seen as an essential part of the explanation of their position in the labour market: as a reserve of labour to be drawn into and pushed out of the market as conditions dictated (Beechey, 1978; Breugel, 1979). As waged workers, women occupy low paid, often part-time and insecure positions in a limited range of jobs and semi-professions that tended to be seen as appropriate to their caring and nurturing role in the family or as a reflection of their domestic duties. These jobs include nursing, secretarial and clerical work, hospital ancillary work and a range of unskilled and semi-skilled occupations. These feminist analysts emphasised that it was the social characteristics of women as women – their supposed femininity, their economic dependence on men – that allowed a set of jobs and occupations with characteristics that 'suited' women to be developed. It was not simply a demand for a particular type of labour. Thus, they suggested that the owners of the means of production deliberately created 'jobs for women'. Similarly, they have reversed arguments about occupational skills. Rather than it being the characteristics of the labour process that determine whether a job is semi-skilled or skilled, feminist economists have forcibly argued that skill definition depends on the gender of the labourer (Phillips and Taylor, 1980).

## The Feminist Challenge to Social Geography

More sophisticated analyses of women's waged labour are now beginning to suggest that the relationships between home and work are not one-way but are mutually reinforcing. While oppression in the home is a key explanatory variable in any analysis of waged labour, specific forms of oppression and the exploitation of socially constructed attributes of femaleness also occur in the labour market and feed back into the construction of gender relations in the home and in the community (Foord et al., 1985; Westwood 1984). These studies have also emphasised that the significance of the inter-relations between home, community and work in creating and sustaining particular gender identities and roles have been ignored.

This type of analysis has not yet had a significant impact on geographical studies where, except in a small number of cases outlined below, economic geographers have steadfastly ignored other aspects of workers lives and social geographers have failed, except at the broadest scale, to relate the organisation of everyday life to changes within the economy. The few exceptions to the analytical separation of home and waged labour include the work of Lewis (1984) and Massey (1984), writing about women's lives in the cities of advanced capitalist societies. Many other geographers, almost all without exception both feminists and women, are also now trying to draw out the significance of the new understanding that production and reproduction - the conventionally accepted subjects of economic and social geography respectively - cannot analytically be separated. We will now therefore turn our attention to a discussion of how recent feminist research and ideas could influence social geography in the future.

### Gender relations and social geography: directions for the future

Feminist geographers, in common with other feminist social scientists see an analysis of gender relations as essential to an understanding of the roles played by men and women in different areas of social life. Gender relations, relations of power between men and women, permeate all areas of social life. It is our contention that if social geographers continue to ignore gender divisions, they will exclude significant issues from their

The Feminist Challenge to Social Geography

analysis. We are not suggesting that a focus on gender divisions should replace other perspectives, rather that it must become part and parcel of analyses of social divisions, just as class and race have become. By neglecting gender, a key structuring element of the division of space and the allocation of resources is defined out of the analysis and so the power of existing explanatory frameworks is reduced.

There are some areas of human activity in which the salience of gender relations is more immediately evident than in others. We suggest that in all the areas of activity traditionally covered by social geography, gender relations are highly salient. The substantive topics covered by the other authors in this volume illustrate the point: for example, gender relations are central to the interaction of social groups; they affect the different social situations of elderly men and elderly women; they influence the differing patterns of crime and delinquency amongst women and men or girls and boys and the family and educational situations which are often held responsible for producing or preventing 'social deviance'. Gender relations and the institution of the family are of profound significance to all aspects of housing and residential segregation. The incidence of poverty and the prescriptions of social planners for the combat of deprivation are also linked to family and employment structures in which gender relations affect men's and women's ability to earn and the household strategies available to escape poverty. Finally, the type and territorial distribution of collective consumption resources are influenced by and influence what tasks are performed within or outside the household and they affect differentially the welfare of men and women.

In the rest of this section we will show how a feminist perspective and a recognition of the importance of gender relations suggest new ways of looking at the field of social geography by considering two areas: - first, work concerned with relations in the home and, secondly, work concerned with relations in the community. We have selected these two areas both because of their centrality in social geography as it is currently constituted and because of their importance as arenas in which gender relations are played out and gender identities constituted and negotiated. It is now generally accepted by social and urban geographers that the built environment in general and the nature of housing and residential areas in particular both reflect and affect social attitudes, identity and behaviour. However, the links between the two are only just beginning to be explored in detail. Houses and communities are as much social constructions as the concepts of gender and family and both types of social construction direct and order activities and relationships in profound ways. At any particular time in history, ideas about gender and the family help to determine the physical design and location of dwellings, of places of work, open spaces and other designed settings. These environments then support and reinforce the ideas of gender and family that generated them. The design of environments translates into physical form society's expectations of what activities should take place where, who should pursue those activities, and how they should relate to one another. Sometimes, of course, there are time lags. Expectations attached to the concepts of gender and family may change more quickly than the physical form, making it difficult to enact new expectations without considerable hardship.

Gender relations and housing. The nature, style, allocation and location of housing in Britain both reflects and affects past and present ideas about the respective roles of men and women and the relations between them. These include the ideas that men are the primary wage earners and responsible for their dependants - both women and children; that as wage earners, men should have the support of women, in the home, to take care of non-wage earning necessities of life; that the home is a place of leisure, a haven from the brutal realities of capitalist wage relations, so ignoring the coincidence, for women, of the home as both a work place and a rest place. Finally, the idea that an 'Englishman's home is his castle' sums up a whole set of power relations between men and women that assume men have control over not only women's domestic labour but also over their bodies; and, perhaps to a lesser extent, control over their children. Hence the reluctance of the state to intervene in what it sees as personal and domestic issues, such as wife battering, incest and child abuse. In fact, despite the control men exert in their homes, the domestic sphere is very much construed as a woman's place - which perhaps explains the neglect of internal power relations, domestic design, domestic labour and so on by most geographers. Rising rates of male unemployment, however, may lead to greater attention to domestic divisions in gender roles. Despite the horrors of mass unemployment, the increasing visibility of men in the home may have an academic benefit in assisting in a new focus on housing as a site where a complex set of social relations between men and women, and between adults and children, are in part both composed and contextualised. But, whatever the impetus, it is vital that geographers move beyond their present theoretical and empirical treatment of housing solely as a commodity or as a set of tenure relations.

We would argue as feminist social geographers that the following set of issues should and must in future become part of any analyses of housing. First, we must explore how the physical design, layout and location of housing confirms social expectations of the roles of women and men and views about the family. Austerberry and Watson (1981), for example, have attempted to reveal the patriarchial assumptions on which present housing policies in Britain are based. They have looked at the type of provision within each tenure category and the ways in which housing structure and design affect women's lives. They argue that current policies are based on an assumption of a male headed nuclear family as the norm - indeed housing constructed specifically for other types of household is labelled 'special need' housing - and show how a range of issues, from security of tenure, through access to owner occupation, to housing managerial practices, systematically discriminate against women.

Secondly, housing design and location are also a significant element in an understanding of women's experience of everyday life in advanced societies. Because the home is their workplace, women, on average, tend to spend more time there than men and children. But because the home is regarded as a private sanctuary rather than a workplace there is no legislation that protects the health and safety of domestic workers. As domestic workers women have too little control over the design and layout of their home. Architects and planners are usually men and, in the case of local authority housing, men who themselves seldom live in the type of accommodation that they design. It is women who have to cope on

308

The Feminist Challenge to Social Geography

a daily basis with estates with no play space, broken lifts, inadequate laundry facilities, dangerous balconies and stairwells - conditions that make childcare and domestic work more difficult than it need be. In other ways, too, trends in the internal design of modern houses make housework more time consuming than is necessary. Plate glass windows, open plan houses, galley kitchens all add to the visibility of domestic labour and act to enforce high standards of cleanliness and tidiness. In a time budget study of housework, Oakley (1974) has revealed the almost absurdly high standards, and consequently long hours spent in attaining them, aspired to by many women in their domestic labour.

Although there is already literature on housing design written from a feminist perspective (Matrix, 1984), there is little work by geographers, although Saunders and Williams (1986) argue forcibly that such work is needed. We suggest that geographers, with their interest in relations between environment, space and social life, could make a useful contribution to this area. They could explore both the implications of different divisions of housing space for the ways of life of women and men and the sense of identity with and safety in the house and its immediate environs felt by people of different gender, class and race whose everyday working lives provide different patterns of behaviour relating to the home.

The location of housing, too, has a significant effect on women's lives - on their opportunities to combine domestic labour with other activities, including a range of social activities as well as waged labour (Signs, 1980; Holcomb, 1984). The great expansion of suburban developments in the interwar and postwar periods not only removed many families from their networks of friends and kin but also increased journeys to work for men and so increased the isolation felt by many women. For the women themselves access to waged labour was made difficult by few local opportunities, at least in the initial phases of suburban expansion, and by inadequate public transport facilities, especially at off-peak hours. Here again there is already existing work (Rothblatt et al., 1979; Wekerle et al., 1980), but more needs to be done to tease out the relations between the effects of gender, class and racial or religious affiliations on the experience of living

309

in different housing environments. The techniques of time geography combined with interviewing women and men about their experiences of and feelings about their housing location is well suited to the empirical investigation of this area.

Thirdly, the cult of domesticity, the ideal of the home as a haven for men based on a 'female angel of the hearth', that was embodied in suburbanisation in Britain, North America and other advanced industrial nations has also had implications for the structure of the economy. It is here that feminists' insistence on the reciprocation of productive and reproductive activities improves our understanding of issues that conventionally are considered separately: viz. housing and the economy. The development of a privatised suburban life-style on the urban fringes based on individual households' consumption of an ever-growing range of consumer durables has supported the rise of vast new industries. The domestic ethic has been manipulated since World War II to encourage the purchase and use of a new range of products. Women are presented by advertisers as creative and scientific managers of modern homes, busy 'choosing' between products that will improve the quality of life of their men and their children as long, of course, as they themselves remain fit, healthy and, above all, beautiful to welcome back the toilers from the industrial jungle. To purchase this ever-growing list of apparent necessities, however, women have entered the formal waged labour force in increasing numbers and from here there are important links to be made between the changing spatial location of light industries in the post war period and the entry of women living in suburbs into the labour market. These jobs were often on a part-time basis, while children were at school, or in the evening, and as women's earnings were assumed to be 'secondary' to the family wage, rates of pay were low. Thus women's economic dependency and the ideology of domesticity were used and reinforced by capital to produce a flexible and cheap source of new labour. The burdens of dealing with the contradictions in time and space of integrating domestic and waged labour fell on the shoulders of individual women. Another example of the links between housing and labour markets that remains to be teased out in detail, is the shift towards female-employing service industries, often in city-centres. This raises questions about spatial accessibility but also about the implications for class and gender roles in those households increasingly dependent on women's waged labour.

Research on the different ways in which the ideal of domesticity has changed and been renegotiated in different places and situations, on the links between this ideal and women's and men's involvement in different types of paid and unpaid work needs to be carried out. While literature on such relationships at the national levels exists (Davidoff et al., 1976; Mackenzie and Rose, 1983) and there is some case study work, we still have little knowledge of how such relations may vary over space.

Fourthly, while we have emphasised the home as the site of domestic labour, it is quite clear that the common distinction, accepted unquestioningly by many social geographers, between the home and the market, between reproduction and production, and the association of the former with women, is not a complete or watertight distinction. Within the home a wide range of activities takes place that blurs the boundaries between domestic and waged labour. These include the obvious example of 'home work' that is employment for wages undertaken in the home. Approximately 1 in 7 of all women working for wages work at home (Hakim, 1984) and in addition there are a substantial number of casual and so unregistered workers who also engage in home work. It is argued that this informal sector of the economy currently is expanding in advanced industrial nations (Huws, 1984; Mitter, 1986), and it has long been recognised as an essential part of the economy of Third World countries (Redclift and Mingione, 1984). A further range of activities, such as activities for reciprocal exchange between households outside the cash economy or DIY tasks that replace market services or goods are also based in the home. These activities bridge the gap between the economy and the home and are an essential part of any analysis of gender divisions of labour. The recent work of Pahl (1984) has begun to explore these areas but, once again, further studies in localities with different social and economic histories need to be carried out.

These are the type of issues that we believe should become part of the subject matter of social geography. We also believe that there are a

311

further set of activities, a set of social relations between men and women, parents and children, that occurs within the home that should also become part of the subject matter of a social geography of housing. As we argued at the beginning of this section, the home is an important location for the social construction of gender identities, the socialisation of children and the development of a sense of individual identity. Geographers, and others, have devoted a great deal of attention to issues of class and status identity, housing form and the urban environment and the appropriation and use of space by different class, ethnic and age groups. However, the development of gender identities, of power relations between household members and the socialisation of male and female children into idealised masculine and feminine individuals have been neglected. The use of space within the home and the domestic division of labour between household members are part and parcel of this socialisation process. We also suggest that gender relations and perceptions of appropriate masculine and feminine behaviour vary between places and over time. In these spatial variations, a broader set of social processes that occur within the community, at the level of neighbourhoods, play an important part. In the next section, therefore, we shall move up a scale to consider how a feminist analysis raises a new set of issues within studies of the community - a spatial scale with which social geographers are more familiar than they are with analyses of behaviour within the home.

Gender relations and the community. Part of the stock in trade of social and urban geography is the demarcation and study of the mosaic of different residential 'communities', with their different socio-economic composition and life styles, that make up so much of the fabric of our cities (Knox, 1982). Existing studies of such activities as neighbouring and friendship, of styles of material consumption and recreational behaviour, and of involvement in voluntary societies hint at how different are the roles played by men and women in these local activities (Keller, 1968; Michelson, 1970; Short et al., 1986). However, few of these studies consider in any depth the reasons for and the implications of such gender differentiated behaviour.

312

# The Feminist Challenge to Social Geography

One important consequence of these different social experiences of men and women is that 'gender identities' are learned and constructed in part through such experiences. By 'gender identities' we are referring to the idea that people learn what sorts of behaviour and attitudes are appropriate to people of different genders. To use two simple examples, men learn that it is 'unmasculine' to play Bingo, women learn that it is 'unfeminine' to play snooker. However, as these examples suggest, these characteristics of 'masculinity; and 'femininity' are not fixed but can be and are renegotiated as circumstances and experiences change. As a result gender identities will vary not only over time but also over space.

Not only may gender identities vary over space, the different spatial patterns of social interaction of men and women form part of the experiences through which such identities are learned. For example the separation of home and work has divorced many men from the daily routines of domestic life. Some of these routines, such as taking children to school or going shopping, usually performed by women, do lead to social contacts within a neighbourhood. It is often women, rather than men, who thus control and manage the social contacts of other household members. Men's social contacts within a locality may, in contrast, centre around leisure activities - the pub, the sports centre - or such outdoor domestic tasks as the ritual of the weekend car wash. These contacts help both to define certain activities and interests as 'masculine' or 'feminine' and to create social spaces dominated by one gender. The control and manipulation of such spaces are part of the processes of power negotiation between men and women. Obvious examples here are the 'masculine' territories of the working men's club, the rugby club or the street-corner of a boy's gang and the 'feminine' territories of the playgroup, the keep-fit class or children's ballet classes. As Chabaud and Fougeyrollas, (1978) argue, certain spaces - for example parks - can only be used by women without fear of verbal or physical attack from men at certain times or provided women are exhibiting appropriately 'female' behaviours such as child care. Moreover, 'inappropriate' use of space is an important method by which gender identities are challenged and changed. For example, women in male clubs or men at playgroups.

313

## The Feminist Challenge to Social Geography

We have suggested that the nature of the contrasting gender identities found in different areas is bound up with the contrasting activities of and use of space of women and men in the community. But these contrasting activities in part derive from gender relations in the home and in the workplace. Clearly, the gender identities constituted in the community themselves are both influenced by and influence home-based relations. They are also related to the particular form of the built environment within which they are constituted. As we suggested earlier, this built environment will itself partly reflect the ideas about gender identities of those involved in its planning and construction. Thus there is a complex web of interactions which produce the contrasts between the gender identities specific to particular places. As yet we have very little knowledge of how different combinations of the physical form of the built environment, and the history of gender and class relations within an area work to create gender identities specific to different localities. This is clearly an area of study to which social geographers could make a significant contribution.

Gender identities are also closely bound up with ethnic and class identities; Anthias and Yuval Davis (1983). The enaction of certain behaviours by women or men and the relations between them are often part of the self-conscious identity and culture of particular ethnic groups or classes. The residential spatial segregation of such groups within urban areas may involve attempts to preserve these distinctive gender identities while conflicts between groups with different beliefs about what constitutes appropriate male or female behaviour is a common feature of urban life. The recent arguments in various British communities over the provision of single-sex schools for Asians spring to mind as one example. Residential spatial segregation often involves attempts to prevent intermarriage and to encourage the physical reproduction of an ethnic minority as well as the reproduction of its culture. Gender relations and gender identities are thus intimately bound up in the spatial patterning of residential areas as well as with the activities that take place within them. However, we still have almost no detailed understanding of how gender relations are linked with class and ethnic relations in the creation of residential

314

differentiation and segregation. Here again is an area in which social geographers could make a significant contribution.

Another important area of investigation which falls within the sphere of social geography is that of community conflict and community based politics (Cox, 1973, 1978; Saunders, 1979; Castells, 1983). Despite the commonly held view that women operate largely outside the 'public' world of political action, in both past and contemporary 'community politics' women have played an important part in struggles over food prices, health care, housing, education, planning and state-welfare as well as in work-based action (Mayo, 1977; Hyman, 1980; Lees and Mayo, 1984; Bondi and Peake, 1984). Indeed, one of the distinctive features of women's involvement in such action is that their daily lives provide constant evidence of the links between home and workplace, so that women appear to make such links in their political struggles more often than men (Lawrence, 1977; Cockburn, 1977; Ackelsberg and Breitbart, 1985). Women may thus play a significant role in the generation of 'urban social movements' and their political activities challenge the view that movements which create fundamental social change must be workplace based.

An aspect of women's political action has been the attempt to change the form or use of the built environment within which home, community and work-based activities take place and to challenge the spatial as well as the social divisions between such activities (Hayden, 1981; Taylor, 1983). In other cases, spaces have been used as a 'refuge' within which to experiment with unconventional life styles and family relationships (Ettorre, 1978; Breitbart, 1984; Hayden, 1981; Taylor, 1983). The relationship between locally based conceptions of masculinity and femininity and the form and goals of locally based political action is another topic where geographical research is needed. Social geographers should also have a particular interest and skill in exploring how political action in the community relates both to the physical form and use of the built environment and to the nature of gender relations.

## Conclusions

We have argued in this paper for feminist analysis in social geography. Analysis of gender and of gender relations, however, means more than doing work on women. Men too are gendered beings. This implies that 'taking gender into account is "taking men into account" and not treating them - by ignoring the question of gender - as the normal subjects of research' (Morgan, 1981, p.95). Vital as studies of women's lives have been and are in showing that gender does matter and ensuring that male views of the world are not treated as the norm, a feminist analysis should not and, indeed, cannot be confined to the study of women alone. Thus existing methods and topics of research in social geography which are directed at 'masculine' areas of life need to be re-evaluated no less than those concerned with 'feminine' ones. Furthermore, we contend that such a re-evaluation must analyse how power relations between men and women relate to the organisation of and power relations within capitalist society.

We have indicated above that one element of the 'feminist challenge to social geography' is to include recognition and analysis of gender relations within social geographical research. However, the second element of this challenge is to the very conception of social geography and its sphere of concern. This challenge is not unique to feminism, in both the Weberian and the Marxist traditions we find arguments for the importance of links between the 'economic' and the 'social' and for the significance of relations within both arenas to the maintenance of the social power of dominant groups. Nevertheless, in practice, most research in social geography is confined to relations within the sphere of reproduction. Thus the topics covered within this reader are an accurate reflection of the type of work currently felt to constitute social geography. Feminist research and practice, however, indicate the necessity of focusing on the relations between the spheres of reproduction and production since these relations and the conflicting demands they place on individuals are so evidently part and parcel of the everyday experience of most women. These relations and demands are also part of the everyday experience of men - a part that is perhaps too rarely acknowledged or considered but is nonetheless important. Thus we argue that social geographers must analyse the socially created power relations and systems of meanings involved in and affected by the human creation and use of places and environments. Such a project must include the environments of work, home and

316

community and the ties between social relations within each. It must also in our view include those power relations and systems of meanings relating to the subordination and oppression of women.

# The Feminist Challenge to Social Geography

REFERENCES

Acklesberg,M.A. and Breitbart, M.(1985) Terrains of
protest: reappropriation of space and trans-
formation of consciousness in urban struggle,
Unpublished Ms, Smith College. and Hampshire
College, U.S.A.

Austerberry, H. and Watson, S. (1981) 'A woman's
place: a feminist approach to housing in
Britain', Feminist Review, 8, Summer, 49-62

Anthias, F. and Yuval-Davis, N. (1983) 'Contextual-
ising feminism — gender, ethnic and class
divisions', Feminist Review, 15, 62-75

Asheim, B.T. (1979) 'Social geography — welfare
state ideology or critical social science?',
Geoforum, 10, 1, 52-68

Ball, M.J. (1978) 'British housing policy and the
house building industry', Capital and
class, 4, 78-99

Banks, O. (1981) Faces of Feminism, Martin
Robertson London

Beechey, V. (1978) 'Women and production: a
critical analysis of some sociological
theories of women's work', in Kuhn, A. and
Wolpe, A. (eds.) Materialism and Feminism:
Women and modes of production, Routledge and
Kegan Paul

Bondi, L. and Peake, L. (1984) Gender and urban
politics, Paper presented at the Women and
Geography Group Conference on Women and the
city, Newcastle University, Autumn

Bouchier, D. (1983) The Feminist Challenge,
Macmillan, London

Breitbart, M. (1984) 'Feminist perspectives in geographic theory and methodology', Antipode, 16,3

Broadbent, T. (1975) 'An attempt to apply Marx's
theory of ground rent to a modern urban
economy', Research paper 17, Centre for
environmental studies, London

Breugel, I. (1979) 'Women as a reserve army of
labour', Feminist Review, 3

Castells, M. (1977) The urban question, Edward
Arnold, London

Castells, M. (1978) City class and power, (trans:
E. Lebas), Macmillan, London

Castells, M. (1983) The City and the Grassroots,
University of California Press, Berkeley

Chabaud, D. and Fougeyrollas, C. (1978) 'Travail
domestique et espace-temps des femmes',
International Journal of Urban and Regional
Research, 2, 3, 421-431

The Feminist Challenge to Social Geography

Coates, B. E. and Rawstron, E. M. (1971) Regional Variations in Britain: essays in economic and social geography, Batsford, London

Cockburn, C. (1977) The Local State, Pluto Press, London

Coote, A. and Kellner, P. (1980) Hear this brother: women workers and Union power, New Statesman Report No: 1, London

Cox, K. (1973) Conflict, Power and Politics in the City, McGraw-Hill, New York

Cox, K. (1978) Urbanization and Conflict in Market Societies, Methuen, London

Cox, K. and Golledge, R. (1969) Behavioural problems in geography: a symposium, Northwestern University Studies in Geography, No. 17

Davidoff, L., L'Esperance and Newby, H. (1976) 'Landscape with figures: home and community in English society', in Mitchell, J. and Oakley, A. (eds.) The rights and wrongs of women, Penguin, Harmondsworth

Duncan, S. S. (1979) 'Qualitative change in human geography', Geoforum, 10, 1, 1-4

Ettorre, E.M. (1978) 'Women, urban social movements and the lesbian ghetto', International Journal of Urban and Regional Research, 2, 3, October

Eyles, J. (1974) 'Social theory and social geography', in Board et al., (eds.), Progress in geography, 6, Edward Arnold, London

Foord, J., McDowell, L. and Bowlby, S. (1985) 'For love not money: gender relations in local areas', Discussion Paper: Centre for Urban and Regional Studies, University of Newcastle-upon-Tyne

Gold, J. (1980) An Introduction to Behavioural Geography, Oxford University Press, Oxford

Gould, P. and White, R. (1974) Mental Maps, Penguin, Harmondsworth

Hagerstrand, T. (1967) Innovation Diffusion as a Spatial Process, (trans A. Pred) University of Chicago Press, Chicago

Hakim. C. (1984) 'Homework and outwork: national estimates from two surveys', Employment Gazette, January

Harvey, D. (1971) 'Social processes, spatial form and the redistribution of income in an urban system', in Chisholm, M., Frey, A.E. and Haggett, P. (eds.) Regional Forecasting, 270-300, Butterworth, London

Harvey, D. (1973) Social Justice and the City, Edward Arnold, London

319

The Feminist Challenge to Social Geography

Harvey, D. and Chatterjee, L. (1974) 'Absolute rent
    and the structuring of space by governmental
    and financial institutions', Antipode, 6,22-36
Hayden, D. (1981) The Grand Domestic Revolution,
    M.I.T Press, Cambridge
Holcomb, B. (1984) 'Women in the rebuilt urban
    environment: the United States experience',
    Built Environment, 10, 1, 18-24
Huws, U. (1984) 'New technology homeworkers,
    Employment Gazette, April
Hyman, P. (1980) 'Immigrant women and consumer
    protest: the New York City kosher meat boycott
    of 1902', American Jewish History, 70, Summer,
    91-105
Johnston, R. (1979) Geography and Geographers,
    Edward Arnold, London
Joseph, G. (1983) Women at Work, Philip Allen,
    Oxford
Keller, S. (1968) The Urban Neighbourhood. Random
    House, New York
Knox, P. (1975) Social Well-being: a spatial
    perspective, Oxford University Press, Oxford
Knox, P. (1982) Urban Social Geography, Longman,
    London
Lawrence, E. (1977) 'The working woman's Charter
    campaign', in Mayo, M. (ed.) Women in the
    Community, Routledge and Kegan Paul, London
Lees, R. and Mayo, M. (1984) Community Action for
    Change, Routledge and Kegan Paul, London
Lewis, J. (1984) 'The role of female employment in
    the industrial restructuring and regional
    development of the post-war United Kingdom',
    Antipode, 6,3,47-60
Ley, D. (1977) 'Social geography and the taken-for-
    granted world', Transactions of the Institute
    of British Geographers, New Series, 2,498-512
Ley, D. (1978) 'Social geography and social
    action', in Ley, D. and Samuels, M. (eds.),
    Man's Place: Themes in Geographic Humanism,
    Maaroufa Press, Chicago
Ley, D. (1981) 'Cultural/humanistic geography',
    Progress in Human Geography 5,249-257
Ley, D. (1983) A Social Geography of the City,
    Harper and Row, London
Ley, D. and Samuels, M. (1977) (eds.) Humanistic
    Geography Prospects and Problems, Croom Helm,
    London
McDowell, L. (1983) 'Towards an understanding of
    the gender division of space', Society and
    Space, 1, 1, 59-72

Mackenzie, R. and Rose, D. (1983) 'Industrial change, the domestic economy and home life', in Anderson, J. et al., (eds.) Redundant spaces in cities and regions, Academic Press, London

Massey, D. (1984) Spatial Divisions of Labour, Macmillan, London

Matrix Book Group (1984) Making Space: women in the the man-made environment, Pluto Press, London

Mayo, M. (1977) (ed.) Women in the Community, Routledge and Kegan Paul, London.

Michelson, W. (1970) Man and his Urban Environment: a Sociological Approach, Addison-Wesley, Mass.

Mitter, S. (1986) 'New technology, industrial restructuring and the rise of manufacturing homework', Capital and Class, forthcoming.

Monk, J. and Hanson, S. (1982) 'On not excluding half of the human in human geography', Professional Geographer, 34, 1, 11-23

Morgan, D. (1981) 'Men, masculinity and the process of sociological enquiry', in Roberts, H. (1981) (ed.) Doing Feminist Research, 83-114, Routledge and Kegan Paul, London

Morrill, R. and Wohlenberg, E. (1971) The Geography of Poverty in the United States, McGraw-Hill, New York

Oakley, A (1972) Sex, Gender and Society, Temple Smith, London

Oakley, A. (1974) The Sociology of Housework, Martin Robertson, London

Oakley, A. (1981) Subject Woman, Martin Robertson, London

Pahl, R. (1970a) Whose City?, Longman, London

Pahl, R. (1970b) Patterns of Urban Life, Longman, London

Pahl, R. (1975) Whose City?, 2nd Edition, Penguin, Harmondsworth

Pahl, R. (1984) Divisions of Labour, Basil Blackwell, Oxford

Palm, R. and Pred, A. (1978) 'A time-geographic approach on problems of inequality for women', in Lanegran, D. and Palm, R. (eds) An Invitation to Geography, McGraw-Hill, New York

Phillips, A. and Taylor, B. 'Sex and skill', Feminist Review, 6, Winter, 79-88

Pickup, L. (1984) 'Women's gender-role and its influence on their travel behaviour', Built Environment, 10, 1, 61-68

Pred, A. (1981) Of paths and projects, in Cox, K. and Golledge, R. (eds.). Behavioural Problems in Geography Revisited, Methuen, London

Redclift, N. and Mingione, E. (1984) Beyond Employ-
ment, Basil Blackwell, Oxford
Relph, E. C. (1970) 'An enquiry into the relations
between phenomenology and geography', Canadian
Geographer, 14, 193-201
Relph, E. C. (1977) 'Humanism, phenomenology and
geography', Annals, Association of American
Geographers, 67, 177-179
Rothblatt, D. N., Garr, D. J. and Sprague, J.
(1979) The Suburban Environment and Women,
Praeger, New York
Saunders, P (1979) Urban Politics, Hutchinson,
London
Saunders, P. and Williams, P. (1986) Social
relations, residential segregation and the
home', in Hoggart, K. and Kofman, E. (eds.)
Politics, Geography and Social Stratification,
Croom Helm, London.
Scott, A. (1976) 'Land and land rent : an interpre-
tive review of the French literature',
Progress in Geography, 9, 101-146.
Short, J. R., Fleming, S., and Witt, S. (1986)
Housebuilding, Planning and Community Action,
Routledge and Kegan Paul, London
Signs (1980) 'Women in the American city', Special
Issue, Signs, 5, 3
Smith, D. M. (1973) The Geography of Social Well-
being in the United States, McGraw-Hill, New
York
Smith, D. M. (1974) 'Who gets what where and how: a
welfare focus for human geography', Geography,
59, 289-297
Smith, D. M. (1977) Human Geography : a Welfare
approach, Edward Arnold, London
Taylor, B. (1983) Eve and the New Jerusalem,
Pantheon, New York
Tivers, J. (1978) 'How the other half lives', Area
10, 303-306
Van Vliet, W. (1985) (ed) 'Structured environments
and women's changing roles', Special Issue,
Sociological Focus,18,2.
Wekerle, G. R., Peterson, R., and Morley, D. (1980)
New Space for Women, Westview Press, Boulder,
Colorado.
West, J. (1982) (ed) Work, Women and the Labour
Market, Routledge and Kegan Paul, London
Westwood, S. (1984) All Day Every Day, Pluto,
London
Wilson, E. (1980) Only Halfway to Paradise,
Tavistock, Andover

The Feminist Challenge to Social Geography

Women and Geography Study Group of the I.B.G. (1984) Geography and Gender an introduction to feminist geography, Hutchinson and Explorations in Feminism Collective, London

Zelinsky, W., Monk, J. and Hanson, S. (1982) Women and geography: a review and prospectus, Progress in Human Geography, 6, 3, 317-366

NOTES ON CONTRIBUTORS

Dr F. W. Boal   Department of Geography, Queen's University of Belfast, N. Ireland.

Dr S.R. Bowlby Department of Geography, University of Reading, England.

Mr J. English Department of Applied Social Studies Paisley College of Technology, Scotland.

Dr J. Eyles   Department of Geography and Earth Science, Queen Mary College University of London, England.

Professor D. T. Herbert   Department of Geography University College of Wales, Swansea, Wales.

Professor R. J. Johnston Department of Geography, University of Sheffield, England.

Professor P. L. Knox   Department of Urban Affairs Virginia Polytechnic Institute and State University Blacksburg, Virginia, USA.

Dr L. McDowell   Faculty of Social Science The Open University, Milton Keynes, England.

Ms M. Munro   Centre for Housing Research University of Glasgow, Scotland.

Dr M. Pacione   Department of Geography, University of Strathclyde, Glasgow, Scotland.

Dr A. M. Warnes   Department of Geography, King's College, University of London, England.

324

# INDEX

325

For Product Safety Concerns and Information please contact our EU
representative GPSR@taylorandfrancis.com
Taylor & Francis Verlag GmbH, Kaufingerstraße 24, 80331 München, Germany

www.ingramcontent.com/pod-product-compliance
Lightning Source LLC
Chambersburg PA
CBHW071833270326
41929CB00013B/1975

* 9 7 8 0 4 1 5 6 1 2 3 2 6 *